Family and Succession Law in Pakistan

Family and Succession Law in Pakistan

Muhammad Shahid Malik

This book was originally published as a monograph in the International Encyclopaedia of Laws/Family and Succession Law.

General Editor: Roger Blanpain
Associate General Editor: Michele Colucci
Volume Editor: Walter Pintens

Wolters Kluwer
Law & Business

Published by:
Kluwer Law International
PO Box 316
2400 AH Alphen aan den Rijn
The Netherlands
Website: www.kluwerlaw.com

Sold and distributed in North, Central and South America by:
Aspen Publishers, Inc.
7201 McKinney Circle
Frederick, MD 21704
United States of America
Email: customer.service@aspenpublishers.com

Sold and distributed in all other countries by:
Turpin Distribution Services Ltd.
Stratton Business Park
Pegasus Drive, Biggleswade
Bedfordshire SG18 8TQ
United Kingdom
Email: kluwerlaw@turpin-distribution.com

Printed on acid-free paper.

ISBN 978-90-411-4639-7

This title is available on www.kluwerlawonline.com

Printed and Bound by CPI Group (UK) Ltd, Croydon, CR0 4YY.

The Authors

Born in 1968, Pakistan, Mr Muhammad Shahid Malik is registered Legal Practitioner and Petroleum Sector Lawyer in Pakistan working as Senior Legal Counsel in a foreign Exploration and Production Company named Ocean Pakistan Limited (formerly Orient Petroleum International Inc.). He has done Law Graduation (LL.B.) from University of Punjab, Pakistan, Master Degree in Law (LL.M.) from University of Karachi, Pakistan and Master Degree in Political Science from University of Punjab and attended several local and international training courses in Petroleum Sector. He is also an office bearer of Energy Lawyers Association of Pakistan. He is the author of books titled '*Upstream Petroleum Laws & Regulatory Framework in Pakistan*'; '*Manual of Petroleum Exploration Production Regulatory Regimes Pakistan*'; '*Child Labor & Legislation in Pakistan*' and '*International Encyclopedia for Labor Laws and Industrial Relations Pakistan*'.

He has over 13 years experience in Upstream Oil and Gas sector dealing in Petroleum Sectors laws and provides legal advice on whole range of commercial and governance issues with sensitivity to regulatory compliance. He is also responsible for establishing and implementing legal controls and compliance systems. He has expertise in drafting and finalizing specialized Oil & Gas Contracts which includes PCAs, PSAs, Joint Operating Agreements, GSAs, COSAs, LPG SPAs, MOUs, Assignment Agreements, Novation Agreements, Pricing Agreements, Farmin/ Farmout Agreements, Settlement Agreements and related Supplemental Agreements. In addition, he has also expertise in drafting Seismic Contracts, Drilling Contracts, Construction Facilities Contracts, Service Contracts, Purchase Agreements, Assets Sale & Purchase Agreements, Financial Transaction Agreements, Sale Deeds and Land Lease Agreements. He helps in developing and understanding, risk mitigation strategies for contractual risks which may arise during project implementation phase. He also advises to different departments of the Company on legal and commercial issues.

He has been involved for over ten years in handling, implementation and compliance of employment laws, labour laws and industrial relations laws in the organizations. He handled several disciplinary and grievance cases, collective bargaining agents issues and participated in policy development and trade union negotiations and conducting industrial relations audit of the organization.

Contributor:

Mr Muhammad Ayub Khan Alizai (born 1969 – Bahawalpur, Pakistan) has Graduated from Allama Iqbal Open University, Islamabad and presently studying in MBA – Human Resource Management. He has twenty two years working experience with the top executives in national and multi-national organizations on different supportive positions.

Presently, he is working as Legal Assistant in Ocean Pakistan Limited (formerly Orient Petroleum International Inc. – a multi-national oil & gas exploration and production company) for the last twelve years. He supports the Legal & Commercial Department Team in handling Legal, Joint Venture and Commercial affairs. He has also attended numerous training courses to sharpen different skills.

In addition, Mr Ayub is also proficient in office management latest techniques and tools to support Senior Executives of the Company.

Mr Ayub provided relentless support in writing, gathering of relevant data/laws, reviewing/finalization including typing and formatting this book. Similarly he also supported in finalization of book titled '*International Encyclopedia for Labor Laws and Industrial Relations Pakistan*' published by Wolters Kluwer.

Table of Contents

Table of Contents

List of Abbreviations

CLC	Civil Law Cases
Cr.P.C.	Criminal Procedure Code
FSC	Federal Shariat Court
LHC	Lahore High Court, Lahore
MFLO	Muslim Family Laws Ordinance, 1961
MLD	Monthly Law Digest
PBUH	Peace Be Upon Him
PHC	Peshawar High Court, Khyber Pakhtunkhwa
PKR	Pakistan Rupees
PLC	Pakistan Labour Cases
PLD	Pakistan Legal Decisions
SCMR	Supreme Court Monthly Review
SCP	Supreme Court of Pakistan
SHC	Sindh High Court, Karachi

List of Abbreviations

Preface*

This monograph of Family and Succession Laws in Pakistan includes summary of all major laws relating to contracting and dissolution of marriages, family laws relating to Muslims, Christians, Parsis and Hindu religions, maintenance of wife and child, restitution of conjugal rights, Guardian, Laws of Inheritance, child marriage restraints, Family Courts, Dowry and Bridal Gifts, Guardians and Succession laws. Muhammadan Laws (Islamic Laws) have also been quoted at appropriate places. The important Court decisions have been quoted with reference to relevant Family and Succession Laws to clarify the interpretation done and position taken by the courts in certain cases.

We are thankful to the Almighty Allah who gave us strength, health and ability to complete this endeavour. Our respective families do deserve full acknowledgement for their unconditional support and endurance.

* DISCLAIMER: This monograph is in the nature of general comments only and has been prepared as a suggested guide and may not contain all of the laws, rules and regulations which may be applicable in Pakistan for Family matters. It is not offered as advice on any particular matter and should not be taken as such. The contributing authors expressly disclaim all liability to any person with regard to anything done or omitted to be done, and with respect to the consequences of anything done or omitted to be done wholly or partly in reliance upon the whole or any part of the contents of this monograph. No reader should act or refrain from acting on the basis of any matter contained in this monograph without first obtaining professional advice regarding the particular facts and circumstances at issue. Any and all opinions expressed herein are those of the particular author and are not necessarily those of the editor or publisher of this monograph. Use of this monograph or any portion or variation thereof shall be at the sole discretion and risk of the user parties.

General Introduction

Chapter 1. General Background of the Country

§1. Background

1. The Pakistan is located in South Asia having boundaries with India on its east, Iran on its west, Afghanistan on its northwest and China on its northeast. Pakistan has a total area of 796,095 square kilometres, slightly greater than France and the United Kingdom put together. The main waterway of Pakistan is the Indus River that begins in China, and runs nearly the entire length of Pakistan, flowing through all of Pakistan's Provinces except Balochistan which is fed by the combined waters of three of the five rivers of Punjab, the Chenab, Jhelum and Ravi. The waters of the other two rivers, the Beas and the Sutlej, are largely withdrawn for irrigation in India. Along the Indus and its tributaries are found most of Pakistan's population, its chief agricultural areas, and its major hydroelectric power stations, interconnected by the world's largest system of agricultural canals, join the Indus before it discharges into the Arabian Sea.

2. The northern and western areas of Pakistan are mountainous. Pakistani-administered areas of Kashmir contain some of the highest mountains in the world, including the second tallest, K-2. Northern Pakistan tends to receive more rainfall than the southern parts of the country, and has some areas of preserved moist temperate forest. In the southeast, Pakistan's border with India passes through a flat desert, called the Cholistan or Thal Desert. West-central Balochistan has a high desert plateau, bordered by low mountain ranges. Most of the Punjab, and parts of Sindh, are fertile plains where agriculture is of great importance.

3. Pakistan was created as an outcome of the Indian Independence Act 1947 enforced and made effective on 18 July 1947 which contained provision for the setting up of two independent dominions, to substitute other provisions with certain provisions of the Government of India Act 1935 which apply outside those dominions, and to provide for other matters consequential to or connected with the setting up of those dominions. Pursuant to this Act, two dominions, Pakistan and India, were created from the appointed day, that is, 15 August 1947. Section 6(3) of the Indian Independence Act 1947 gave full powers to the appointed Governor General of each dominion to assent to the existing laws or to make new laws. The Governor General of Pakistan through his order GGP 20 dated 14 August 1947 issued orders titled 'The Pakistan (Adaptation of Existing Pakistan Laws) Order, 1947' whereby various laws in force and effect prior to the creation of Pakistan were adopted, and the country became independent on 14 August 1947 – a day earlier than the appointed date with its official name as Islamic Republic of Pakistan.

4. After independence, Quaid-e-Azam Muhammad Ali Jinnah become first Governor General of Pakistan and appointed Mr Liaquat Ali Khan as first Prime Minister of Pakistan. At the time of independence, Pakistan inherited a lot of difficulties which included riots, refugee problems, administrative system, foreign policy, formulation of constitution, etc. Quaid-e-Azam selected Karachi as the Federal Capital of Pakistan. During the early days, Quaid-e-Azam worked hard to prevail over the deteriorated economic situation in Pakistan. However, he did not remain with Pakistan for a long time and died on 11 September 1948 and was buried in Karachi. Mr Liaquat Ali Khan took steps towards the formulation of the Constitution of Pakistan and passed 'The Objectives Resolution'. Mr Liaquat Ali Khan was unfortunately assassinated on 16 October 1951. The government officially gave Mr Liaquat Ali Khan the title of Shaheed-i-Millat. Pakistan is a State which is founded on the basis of Islamic ideology as it was the demand of the Muslims of subcontinent.

5. Pakistan's Capital Islamabad nestles against the backdrop of the Margalla Hills at the northern end of Pothowar Plateau. It offers a healthy climate, pollution-free atmosphere, plenty of water and lush green area. It is a modern and carefully planned city with wide tree-lined streets, large houses elegant public buildings and well-organized bazaars/markets/shopping centres. The walkways are shaded & safe and separated from the traffic by rows of flame trees, jacaranda and hibiscus. Roses, Jasmine & bougainvillea fill the parks and scenic viewpoints shoe the city to its best advantage.

6. Brief Facts of Pakistan are as under:

Official Name:	Islamic Republic of Pakistan.
Capital:	Islamabad.
Area:	796,095-sq. km.
	Punjab 205,344 sq.km ; Sindh 140,914 sq.km;
	Khyber Pakhtunkhwa 74,521 sq.km;
	Balochistan 347,190 sq.km;
	Federally Administered Tribal Areas 27,220 sq.km; and Islamabad (Capital) 906 sq. km.
Population:	170 million (estimated)
Ethnic Composition:	97% Muslims, 3% others
Per Capita Income:	USD 1000+
Currency:	Pak. Rupee (PKR)

Languages:	Punjabi (44.15%), Pashto (15.42%), Sindhi (14.1%), Saraiki (12.1%), Urdu (7.57%), Balochi (3.57%), Bengali (0.02%)
Archaeological Sites:	Mohenjodaro, Harappa, Taxila, Kot Diji, Mehar Garh, and Takht Bahi
Major Cities:	Islamabad, Karachi, Lahore, Peshawar, Quetta, Rawalpindi, Hyderabad, Faisalabad, Bahawalpur and Multan.

§2. Population

7. The estimated population of Pakistan in 2010 was over 170 million making it the world's sixth most-populous country, behind Brazil and ahead of Russia. In 1951, Pakistan had a population of 34 million. The majority of southern Pakistan's population lives along the Indus River. By population size, Karachi is the largest city of Pakistan. In the northern half, most of the population live in an arc formed by the cities of Lahore, Faisalabad, Rawalpindi, Islamabad, Gujranwala, Sialkot, Gujrat, Jhelum, Sargodha and Sheikhupura.

8. Pakistan is the second-most populous Muslim-majority country and about 97% of the Pakistanis are Muslims.

Population (In Millions) By Province, 2011

	Both	*Male*	*Female*
Pakistan	177.10	91.59	85.51
Punjab	96.55	49.53	47.02
Sindh	42.18	22.20	19.98
Balochistan	9.06	4.83	4.23
Islamabad	1.33	0.71	0.62
Khyber Pakhtunkhwa	23.77	12.11	11.66
FATA	4.21	2.21	2.00

9. The estimated existing population of major cities of Pakistan is given below:

Cities by population (2010 estimate)

Rank	*City*	*Location*	*Population*	*Rank*	*City*	*Location*	*Population*
1	Karachi	Sindh	13,205,339	11	Sargodha	Punjab	600,501
2	Lahore	Punjab	7,129,609	12	Bahawalpur	Punjab	543,929
3	Faisalabad	Punjab	2,880,675	13	Sialkot	Punjab	510,863
4	Rawalpindi	Punjab	1,991,656	14	Sukkur	Sindh	493,438
5	Multan	Punjab	1,606,481	15	Larkana	Sindh	456,544

Cities by population (2010 estimate)

Rank	*City*	*Location*	*Population*	*Rank*	*City*	*Location*	*Population*
6	Hyderabad	Sindh	1,578,367	16	Sheikhupura	Punjab	426,980
7	Gujranwala	Punjab	1,569,090	17	Jhang	Punjab	372,645
8	Peshawar	KP	1,439,205	18	Rahim Yar Khan	Punjab	353,112
9	Quetta	Balochistan	896,090	19	Mardan	KP	352,135
10	Islamabad	Capital Territory	689,249	20	Gujrat	Punjab	336,727

10. The population growth rates of Pakistan are as under:

Years	*Growth Rate*
1951–1961	2.45%
1961–1972	3.66%
1972–1981	3.05%
1981–1998	2.69%
2010	2.05%

11. Official population projections of Pakistan are as under:

Year	**Both Male/Female (in Million)**	**Male (in Million)**	**Female (in Million)**
2030	242.05	124.47	117.58
2029	239.34	123.12	116.22
2028	236.50	121.70	114.80
2027	233.56	120.23	113.33
2026	230.51	118.70	111.81
2025	227.35	117.11	110.24
2024	224.08	115.46	108.62
2023	220.71	113.76	106.95
2022	217.25	112.01	105.24
2021	213.73	110.23	103.50
2020	210.13	108.41	101.72
2019	206.49	106.56	99.93
2018	202.81	104.69	98.12
2017	199.11	102.81	96.30
2016	195.40	100.92	94.48
2015	191.71	99.04	92.67

Year	Both Male/Female (in Million)	Male (in Million)	Female (in Million)
2014	188.02	97.16	90.86
2013	184.35	95.29	89.06
2012	180.71	93.43	87.28
2011	177.10	91.59	85.51

Source: Ministry of Population & Welfare, Government of Pakistan

§3. PEOPLE OF PAKISTAN

12. Predominantly Muslims, the people of Pakistan are culturally homogeneous. Other religious groups include the Christians, Buddhists, Hindus and Parsees. All belong to a composite racial stock although the majority belongs to an Aryan extraction. While Urdu, the national language, is spoken throughout Pakistan, English is extensively used in official and commercial circles, and in the cities. The regional languages are Sindhi in Sindh, Balochi in Balochistan, Punjabi in Punjab and Pushto in the Khyber Pakhtunkhwa Province.

13. Pakistan's official language is English and is used in all government, educational and business entities, and is also understood and spoken at varying levels of competence by many people around Pakistan, especially by the upper classes and people who have gone through higher levels of education. Urdu is the national language and is spoken throughout Pakistan as lingua franca. In addition to Urdu, most Pakistanis speak their regional languages or dialects such as Punjabi, Sindhi, Pashto, Balochi, Saraiki, Shina, Burushaski, Khowar, Wakhi, Hindko, etc.

14. Pakistan has been the cradle of a civilization that dates back more than five millennium. Over the centuries, through successive waves of migrations from the north-west, as well as by internal migrations across the subcontinent, Aryans, Persians, Greeks, Arabs, and Mughals came and settled in this region. However, it was Islam and Islamic traditions that finally took roots and formed the mainspring of Pakistan's cultural heritage.

15. Muslims from the earliest days, built cities, forts, palaces, mosques, madrassas (religious schools), tombs and mausoleums which are marked by simplicity and grandeur, with open spaces and abundance of light in accordance with the Islamic concept of man's direct and open relationship with the Creator. Pakistan inherits immense treasure of culture. There are several government agencies such as Pakistan National Council of Arts, Lok Virsa (Folk Heritage), National Film Development Corporation, Authority for Preservation of Moenjodaro and National Archives of Pakistan, each to perform a given set of functions in this area and in pursuit of preservation and promotion of culture.

16. Pakistan is an Islamic Republic wherein Islam is the State religion. There is also stated in the Preamble of the Constitution that the authority to be exercised by the people of Pakistan within the limits prescribed by Allah Almighty as a sacred trust. Authority and powers shall be exercised through the chosen representatives of the people based on principles of democracy, freedom, equality, tolerance and social justice, but there is no provision in the Constitution making the State as theocracy governed by religious priests.

17. Muslims make up over 97% of the population of Pakistan, of which roughly 80% are Sunni and 20% are Sh'iah. About 1% of the population is Christian with slightly more protestants than Catholics. The Hindus, mostly nomads living in the South account for less than 1%. In Karachi, Lahore, Rawalpindi and Quetta, there are small communities of Buddhists, and there are a tiny group of animist Kalash living in Chitral on the Afghan border.

§4. Land, Heritage and culture

18. Pakistan is situated between latitude 24 and 37 degrees North and longitude 62 and 75 degrees East. The country borders Iran on the West, India on the East, Afghanistan in the North-West, China in the North and the Arabian Sea in the South. The great mountain ranges of the Himalayas, the Karakoram and the Hindukush form Pakistan's northern highlands of North-West Frontier Province and the Northern Area; Punjab Province is a flat, alluvial plain with five major rivers dominating the upper region eventually joining the Indus River flowing south to the Arabian Sea; Sindh is bounded on the east by the Thar Desert and the Rann of Kutch and on the west by the Kirthar range; the Balochistan Plateau is an arid tableland, encircled by dry mountains.

19. The land where the Islamic Republic of Pakistan is situated today had been a seat of world's leading Civilizations from the time immemorial. There is plenty of evidence from the pre-historic and historic period to support this argument, for example, fossil jaws of apes, circa 14 millions years old found from Pothohar. They belong to a species named 'Sivapithecus Pakininsis', said to be the ancestor of Man. A 2 million years old earliest stone hand axe is on display in Islamabad Museum, Islamabad.

20. Pakistan has every reason to be proud of the thousands of years old and rich tradition of its arts and crafts. In the post-independence period, the successive governments have been providing substantial State help and initiative for the upliftment of arts and crafts in the country. A wider recognition of the accomplishments of crafts-people has been facilitated by the activities of the National Crafts Council and promotional plans of organizations such as the Export Promotion Bureau and Small Industries Corporations. Pakistani craftsmen are well reputed in producing quality products in clay, stone, fabrics, carpets, wood, metal, jewellery and leather.

21. Pakistan has four seasons: a cold, dry winter from December through February; a hot, dry spring from March through May; the summer rainy season, or southwest monsoon period, from June through September; and the retreating monsoon period of October and November. The onset and duration of these seasons vary somewhat according to location.

22. The climate in the capital city of Islamabad varies from an average daily low of 2°C in January to an average daily high of 40°C in June. Most of the rainfall occurs in July and August, averaging about 255 millimetres in each of those two months. The remainder of the year has significantly less rain, amounting to about fifty millimetres per month.

23. Pakistan's largest city, Karachi, which is also the country's industrial centre, is more humid than Islamabad but gets less rain. Only July and August average more than twenty-five millimetres of rain in the Karachi area; the remaining months are exceedingly dry. The temperature is also more uniform in Karachi than in Islamabad, ranging from an average daily low of 13°C during winter evenings to an average daily high of 34°C on summer days. Although the summer temperatures do not get as high as those in Punjab, the high humidity causes a great deal of discomfort.

§5. The Economy

24. The economy of Pakistan has been undergoing a stabilization phase since the last three years. The restoration of macroeconomic stability is important and necessary to provide the platform for generating growth, jobs, and improving the quality of life of the people. This period has been marked by the continuing and intensified security challenges the country has confronted since 2001. In addition, the country faced multiple adverse shocks of commodity and oil prices and the fallout of the global financial crisis. During the years 2010–2011, Pakistan faced unprecedented calamity of the great floods. These floods wiped out about 2% points from the growth as well as inflicted a massive damage of USD 10 billion on country's economic structure. Some 20 million people were displaced as more than 50,000 square kilometres area was submerged in water. During the year, oil prices also shot up from USD 70/barrel to USD 125/barrel creating a new threat to the macro framework. Viewed in this background, the growth rate of 2.4% registered during the year 2010–2011 seems reasonable. Although much below its potential, the performance signifies the enormous resilience in the economy as it was tested several times by one crisis after another beginning with the earthquake of 2005.

25. The destruction of major crops, particularly rice and cotton, led to a negative growth of 4% in this sector. The manufacturing sector growth was adversely affected and was negligible due to reduced output in the textiles and petroleum products (affected by submersion of refineries under flood waters and the circular debt problem). Inevitably, the overall quantum of economic activities, captured by services sector was also affected, with a growth of 4.1%, originally targeted at 5.4%. The challenges posed by exogenous shocks affected the pace of the reforms process as the government was forced to make difficult tradeoffs and cater to unexpected demands for flood rehabilitation and the impacts of increasing oil prices. The government, while pursuing a regime of deregulation of pricing of key products was nevertheless forced to intervene in the energy and commodity markets to keep prices from getting completely out of the reach of the public. This burden of subsidies, though significantly reduced from previous years, exerted continuing pressure on the fiscal system, and the adjustment path was affected. In the second half of the year, due to a combination of austerity, resource mobilization measures and bold decisions on pricing the macro-framework was stabilized, and the anticipated damage to the overall fiscal position was avoided.

26. The most significant development during the year was the historic performance of the external sector, which is heading to register a surplus in the current account. First, exports registered a growth of 28% in the first ten months of the year compared to same period last year. Crossing the USD 20 billion mark for the first time, exports are set to exceed USD 24 billion. Second, the remittances have also recorded a strong performance by crossing the double digit mark and are set to reach the historic level of more than USD 11.2 billion. Third, and this is partly attributable to moderated demand for imports the current account shows a Economic Survey 2010–2011 is surplus of nearly USD 748 million. Finally, the combined effect of these positive developments was reflected in the growth of external reserves which also touched a historic height of USD 17.1 billion at the end of April 2011. Pakistan has enjoyed sustained period of exchange rate stability since December 2008. The Real Effective Exchange Rate (REER) depicted unprecedented appreciation of 10% in 2009–2010 and marginally appreciated in the first ten months of the current fiscal year. The SBP is not intervening in the foreign exchange markets, and exchange rate is market determined. The situation regarding inflation remained a key concern for the economy. For most of last fiscal year, inflation was coming down, but the shocks of floods and oil price have reversed the declining trends. It should be noted that with rising commodity and oil prices, inflation has affected all countries both regionally and globally. However, in the second half of the year, the rising inflationary trend has been stemmed and inflation is now hovering around 14%. With fiscal consolidation and abetment of some pressures from international prices, the inflation outlook looks better than in the earlier part of the year.

27. Inflationary pressures inevitably brought pressure on the interest rate, and with much of the credit flowing in the government sector, private credit, despite some growth over the previous year remained weak. With development resources pre-empted by unanticipated expenditures on flood relief and power and petroleum subsidies, fiscal discipline required the government to reduce its public investment to a low level in many years.

28. Accordingly, the overall investment in the year was also below its level in the recent past. The overall monetary survey indicated modest growth in monetary aggregates. The reserves money grew by 17.1% in the period 21 July–May 2010–2011 as against 13.6% growth in the comparable period of last year on the back of strong growth of 73.1% in the NFA of the SBP. The NDA component grew steadily at 11.6% in the period. Broad money expansion by 11.7% in the period 21 July–May 2010–2011 is mainly driven by phenomenal growth 57.3% in the Net Foreign Assets (NFA) which is reflective of the positive developments in the external sector. The NDA of the banking system has expanded by 9.4% in the period. The tight monetary policy stance adopted by SBP is reflected in the rise in the policy rate which registered an increase of 150 bases points since July 2010 in the increments of 50 bases points. The year was the first in the implementation of the NFC Award. The Award represented a radical break from the past as it transferred a larger share of divisible poor revenues to the Provinces. An estimated additional amount of PKR 325 billion will be transferred to the Provinces compared to the last year. Since many of the primary public services are provided by the Provinces, greater availability of resources will facilitate both the improvement in quality as well as scale of such services. The passage of eighteenth Constitutional Amendment has led to the devolution of additional subjects to the Provinces, especially those in the social sectors. It is hoped that undivided responsibility of Provinces in social sectors and availability of enhanced resources will lead to much improvement the quality of social sector indicators that have been lagging behind for some time. Despite many challenges, the overall performance of the economy has been moderately satisfactory. The recent measures announced for fiscal correction should contribute to a faster recovery and resumption of growth. It was felt by some observers, that the budget deficit the key indicator of economic stability will reach unprecedented levels due to the difficult circumstances. However, due to sound economic management and fiscal discipline, the deficit has been contained and is estimated at 5.3% of GDP. To settle the circular debt and get more production out of the existing energy plants, the government has decided to pay additional PKR 120 billion subsidies from previous years. This will add an additional 0.6% to the deficit, bringing it to 5.9%. However, the outlook for the next year looks bright on this account as the year has fully accounted for the subsidies falling due during the year and substantial correction in such burdens is likely to be made in the years ahead.[1]

§6. Constitutional History

29. The history of formulation of the Constitution of Pakistan begins with the Lahore Resolution in 1940. It was here that the idea of Pakistan, a separate homeland for the Muslims of India, was first outlined. It came to be known as the Pakistan Resolution.

30. On 3 June 1947, the British Government accepted in principle the partition of India in order to create two independent dominions of Pakistan and India. The British Parliament passed the Indian Independence Act on 18 July 1947. Accordingly, the new State of Pakistan came into being on 14 August 1947. This new State was formed of East Bengal, a part of Assam (Sylhet), West Punjab, Sindh, Khyber Pakhtunkhwa and Baluchistan Provinces of undivided India. Under section 8 of the

1. Pakistan Economic Survey 2010-2011 (Overview of the Economy).

Indian Independence Act of 1947, the Government of India Act of 1935 became, with certain adaptations, the working Constitution of Pakistan.

31. On 12 March 1949, the Constituent Assembly adopted a resolution moved by Liaquat Ali Khan, the then Prime Minister of Pakistan. It was called the Objectives Resolution. It proclaimed that the future Constitution of Pakistan would not be modelled on European pattern, but on the ideology and democratic faith of Islam. The Objectives Resolution, proclaimed the principles which states that sovereignty belongs to Allah alone, but He has delegated it to the State of Pakistan through its people for being exercised within the limits prescribed by Him as a sacred trust. The State shall exercise its powers and authority through the chosen representatives of the people. The principles of democracy, freedom, equality, tolerance and social justice, as enunciated by Islam, shall be fully observed. Muslims shall be enabled to order their lives in the individual and collective spheres in accordance with the teachings of Islam as set out in the Holy Quran and Sunnah. Adequate provision shall be made for the minorities to freely profess and practice their religions and develop their cultures. Pakistan shall be a federation. Fundamental rights shall be guaranteed. Judiciary shall be independent.

32. The Constitution of the Islamic Republic of Pakistan (1973) is a written Constitution. There is a mechanism provided in the Constitution for interpretation of provisions of Constitution. Judiciary has the mandate to interpret the Constitution. Therefore, the provisions of the Constitution are subject to interpretation by the Superior Courts that is, High Courts and the Supreme Court of Pakistan.

33. The first Constitution came into force on the 23 March 1956. The new Constitution took more than eight years due to inevitable situations. This Constitution based upon the Islamic principles and the structure of the government was federal. The Constitution of the Islamic Republic of Pakistan (1956) was a document which translated the aims and objectives contained in the Resolution into practicable constitutional and political system as well as system of governance. Pakistan was defined as an Islamic Republic wherein the principles of freedom, equality, tolerance and social justice as enunciated by Islam should be fully observed, but unfortunately it proved to be short one and the Constitution was abrogated on 7 October 1958, and Martial Law was proclaimed by Muhammad Ayub Khan. Muhammad Ayub Khan promulgated a new Constitution in 1962. It was fully changed from the soul of the Constitution of 1956. It set up a Presidential form of government and the President possessed greater number of powers. This constitution remained in force till the 25 March 1969 and was abrogated by another military man Mr Yahya Khan after resignation of Muhammad Ayub Khan.

34. The Pakistan first General Elections based on universal adult franchise was held in 1970. However, the results of those elections never translated into formation of the government in the country. The tragedy of the revolt and separation of East Pakistan, now called Bangladesh, sent a wave of despair throughout the remaining Pakistan. The interim Constitution of Pakistan of 1972 was passed and adopted by the National Assembly as a stop-gap constitutional arrangement till framing of formal Constitution for the country.

35. However, during the last quarter of the year 1972, the then Government was able to bring before the National Assembly a draft Constitution which was finalized after accommodating the political views of different political stakeholders of the system. The Constitution Bill was thoroughly discussed and debated in the National Assembly. The Constitution of the Islamic Republic of Pakistan was passed and enacted by the National Assembly of Pakistan on the 10th of April 1973. The formal date of commencement of the Constitution was the 14 August 1973 that is, the 26th birthday of the Pakistan.

36. Till date, there have been nineteen amendments in the 1973 Constitution. Gen Zia-ul-Haq imposed Martial Law on 5 July 1977 and made several amendments. The Constitution of Pakistan was amended to restore its original condition by the Democratic Governments; however, General Pervez Musharaf took over charge of the government in 1999 and thereafter made many changes. In April 2010, once again the democratically elected legislature has unanimously amended the Constitution of Pakistan by passing eighteenth amendment and strike down major changes made by the Army Governments thereby substantially restoring original 1973 Constitution. Lately, nineteenth amendment was assented to by the President on 1 January 2011 mainly relating to the procedure for appointment of judges.

37. Under the Constitution of Pakistan, Fundamental Rights are guaranteed in accordance with the Universal Declaration of Human Rights. Government cannot make any law which is inconsistent or in derogation of these fundamental rights, and such law may be declared as void by the Superior Courts. The Fundamental Rights include security of person, safeguards as to arrest and detention, protection from slavery, forced labour and retrospective punishment, protection against double punishment and self-incrimination. Inviolability of dignity of man, protection of property rights, equality of citizens and preservation of language, its script and separate culture of each segment of population is also guaranteed.

38. Constitution of Pakistan provides freedom of movement anywhere in the country, freedom of assembly, freedom of association, freedom of trade, business or profession, freedom of speech, and freedom to profess religion and manage religious institutions.

§7. Political, Judicial and Administrative System

39. The Constitution of the Islamic Republic of Pakistan provides for a Federal Parliamentary System of government, with President as the Head of State and the popularly elected Prime Minister as Head of Government. The Federal Legislature is the Parliament, composed of the National Assembly and the Senate. The Federal Government of Pakistan includes Head of State, Head of the Government, National

Security Council, National Assembly, Senate, Federal Ministers, Federal Government Ministries, Federal Government Departments and Attorney General. The Provincial Governments of Pakistan includes, Governors, Provincial Chief Ministers and the Ministries and departments under their administrative control including Local Governments.

40. The Constitution of Pakistan, 1973 provides true parliamentary system. Although through several amendments, many army governments tried to change the system of government in the Constitution, but finally through Eighteenth Amendment Act, 2010 dated 20 April 2010, Legislative Assembly of Pakistan has once again restored the original parliamentary system of government in Pakistan. Pakistan is a federation consisting of Federal Government and Provincial Governments. Powers are divided constitutionally between the Government of the Federation and Provinces providing maximum provincial autonomy.

41. The National Assembly of Pakistan is the country's sovereign legislative body. It embodies the will of the people to let themselves be governed under the democratic, multi-party Federal Parliamentary System. The National Assembly makes laws for the Federation in respect of the powers enumerated in the Federal Legislative list. Through its debates, adjournment motion, question hour and Standing Committees, the National Assembly keeps a check over the Executive and ensures that the government functions within the parameters set out in the Constitution and does not violate the Fundamental Rights of citizens. Only the National Assembly, through its Public Accounts Committee, scrutinizes public spending and exercises control of expenditure incurred by the government.

42. The Islamic Republic of Pakistan is a Federal State comprising four Provinces of Balochistan, Khyber Pakhtunkhwa, Punjab and Sindh; Islamabad is the Federal Capital with Federally Administered Tribal Areas (FATA). These federating units offer a lot of diversity and variety in terms of languages, levels of social and economic development, population density and climatic conditions.

43. Article 50 of the Constitution provides that the Parliament of Pakistan shall consist of President and the two Houses known as the National Assembly and the Senate. The National Assembly has an edge over the Senate by legislating exclusively on money matters. With exception to money bills, however, both the Houses work together to carryout the basic work of the Parliament, that is, law making.

44. The Constitution provides for a parliamentary form of Government with a bicameral legislature, comprising of the National Assembly and the Senate. The membership of the Senate, which was originally forty-five, was raised to sixty-three in 1977 and to eighty-seven in 1985. The existing membership of the Senate is hundred which was raised in 2002; twenty-two members are elected from each Province which includes fourteen general, four technocrats/Ulema and four women. For the Federal Capital, two general, one technocrat/Aalim and one woman are elected whereas from Federally Administered Tribal Areas (FATA), eight members are elected. Though seventeen seats have been allocated to women, there is no bar on women to seek elections on the other seats.

45. The Senate is a permanent legislative body which symbolizes a process of continuity in the national affairs. The term of its members is six years. However, one-half of its members retire after every three years. A casual vacancy in the Senate, caused by resignation, death incapacitation, disqualification or removal of a member, is filled through election by the respective electoral college, and the member so elected holds office for the un-expired term of the member whose vacancy he has filled.

46. A person seeking election to the Senate should not be less than 30 years of age and should be registered as a voter in an area or Province from where he seeks election and should meet other qualifications prescribed under Articles 62 and 63 of the Constitution.

47. There are four Provinces of the Federation namely Baluchistan, Khyber Pakhtunkhwa, Punjab and Sindh. Provincial Assembly is the provincial legislature having all necessary powers and subject matters determined in the Constitution. Provincial Assemblies have legislative powers on all those subject matters, which are not enumerated in the Federal Legislative List or relating to such areas, which are not included in the Province. In this way, there is maximum provincial autonomy guaranteed in the Constitution of Pakistan as compared to most of other world federal systems.

48. The President is the Head of State and also the part of the Parliament representing the unity of the Republic. A person being a Muslim of not less than 45 years of age is qualified to be elected as member of the National Assembly eligible for the office of President. President is elected by the members of both Houses and the members of the Provincial Assemblies for a period of five years immediately after taking oath of his office before the Chief Justice of Pakistan. He cannot hold any office of profit in the service of Pakistan or occupy any other position carrying the right to remuneration for the rendering of services. The term of the office is five years or till his successor enters upon his office. However, he may resign by writing under his hand addressed to the Speaker of the National Assembly at any time. President enjoys the power to grant pardon, reprieve and respite and to remit, suspend or commute any sentence passed by any court, tribunal or other authority.

49. The parliamentary system in Pakistan works with a Cabinet of Ministers headed by the Prime Minister to aid and advise the President in the exercise of his functions. Immediately after General Elections and making the oath of office by the members of the National Assembly, the President invites the member of the National Assembly to be the Prime Minister who commands the confidence of the majority of the members of the National Assembly as ascertained in a session of the National Assembly summoned for the purpose. After taking the oath of office of the Prime Minister, he advises the President for appointment of Federal Ministers and Ministers of State who are the members of Parliament to form his Cabinet.

50. The Cabinet headed by the Prime Minister is collectively responsible to the National Assembly in performance of its functions. Prime Minister may also appoint not more than five persons as his advisers on such terms and conditions as he may determine by advising to the President for such appointment.

51. A Governor is the constitutional head of the Provincial Government although the executive authority of the Province is exercised by him while acting on the advice of the Provincial Cabinet or the Chief Minister. The Governor of the Province is appointed by the President after consultation with the Prime Minister, and in political terms he is the representative of the Federation in the Province. No person can be appointed as a Governor if he is not qualified to be elected as a member of the National Assembly and is less than 35 years of age. The Governor has the power to summon the Provincial Assembly to meet at such time and place as he thinks fit and also prorogue the Provincial Assembly from time to time.

52. The Governor may, except when the Provincial Assembly is in session, if satisfied that circumstances exist which render it necessary to take immediate action, make and promulgate an Ordinance as the circumstances may require which is a temporary legislation for a period of three months unless withdrawn or disapproved earlier. The Governor assents all Bills passed by the Provincial Assembly and immediately after such assent they become the Acts of Provincial Assembly. However, the Governor has the power to return a Bill with a message to reconsider or amend it. The Chief Minister is the Chief Executive of the Provincial Government and head the Provincial Cabinet of Ministers which consists of members of the Provincial Assembly appointed on the advice of the Chief Minister. The Chief Minister is the leader of majority party in the Provincial Assembly or enjoys the support of the majority of the members of that Assembly. The Chief Minister is responsible for the executive affairs of the Province and exercises his functions directly or through Cabinet of his Ministers by allocating official business under Rules of Business made by the Governor on the advice of the Chief Minister.

53. The Judiciary is one of the vital organs of the government in a modern political system for administration of justice. The Judiciary in Pakistan is consisting of the Supreme Court of Pakistan, a High Court for each Province & Federal area and such other courts as may be established by law from time to time. In this way, there are two types of courts in Pakistan: Constitutional Courts; and Courts established under or by a law. Constitutional courts are: Supreme Court of Pakistan; High Courts; and Federal Shariat Court.

54. The Supreme Court is the apex Court of the Islamic Republic of Pakistan. It is the Court of ultimate appeal and therefore final arbiter of law and the Constitution. It exercises original, appellate and advisory jurisdiction. Its judgments/decisions are binding on all other courts in the country. All executive and the judicial authorities are bound to act in aid of the Supreme Court.

55. The Constitution of Pakistan, (1973) contains elaborate provisions on the composition, jurisdiction, powers and functions of the Court. The qualifications for, and mode of appointment of judges, their retirement age, grounds and procedure for removal from office and terms and conditions of the service of judges are also specified in the basic document. The Constitution also provides for the independence of Judiciary and its separation from the Executive. Consequently, there prevails in the country, full institutional and decisional judicial independence. The Supreme Court and High Courts also possess a degree of financial autonomy, inasmuch as the concerned Chief Justice is authorized, *inter alia*, to sanction expenditure and to re-appropriate funds within the budgetary allocation without any prior approval or concurrence of the Ministry of Finance. These courts are also empowered to make their own rules of procedure and determine the terms and conditions of service of their staff.

56. Establishing a system of tracheotomy of power, the Constitution assigns the Supreme Court a unique responsibility of maintaining harmony and balance between the three pillars of the State, namely, Legislature, Executive and Judiciary. The idea is to ensure that the state organs perform their respective functions within the stipulated limits and constraints. As a guardian of the Constitution, the Court is required to 'preserve, protect and defend' this document. Seen in this context, the Court plays the role of unifying and integrating the nation, its communities, regions and institutions. Indeed, it occupies a pivotal position in the Constitutional dispensation.

57. The Supreme Court is also a custodian and upholder of citizens' rights, liberties and freedoms. The Court has been given a very significant role of protecting the Fundamental Rights of citizens. For this purpose under Article 184(3), the Supreme Court is empowered to take action, if it considers that a question of public importance with reference to enforcement of any of the Fundamental Rights conferred by the Constitution is involved.

58. The Supreme Court exercises original, appellate and advisory jurisdiction. It possesses exclusive original jurisdiction for settlement of Inter-governmental (federal/provincial) disputes. Under this jurisdiction, the Court pronounces declaratory judgments. The Supreme Court can also exercise original jurisdiction, with respect to the enforcement of fundamental rights, if the case involves a question of public importance. In exercise of its advisory jurisdiction, the Court furnishes its opinion on a question of law of public importance referred to it by the President for consideration. Under its appellate jurisdiction, the Court entertains appeals against orders and decisions of High Courts and other special tribunals and courts. Under the Constitution, the Court is invested with authority to make its rules of practice and procedure. Under the rules, the Chief Justice, as the head of the institution, nominates Judges for hearing of cases and exercising other administrative powers and functions.

59. There are five High Courts working in the country that is, Islamabad High Court, Lahore High Court, High Court of Sindh, High Court of Balochistan and Peshawar High Court. A High Court is consisting of a Chief Justice appointed by the President and other Judges as determined by the President. The Chief Justice makes an oath before the Governor, and thereafter Chief Justice takes oath of other Judges. Retiring age of the Chief Justice and Judges of the High Courts is 62 years unless he resigns or removed earlier. High Courts enjoys original, appellate as well as administrative jurisdiction under different laws. It is also the duty of the High Courts to supervise and control all subordinate courts working within their jurisdictions. They also make rules regulating the practice and procedure of the Court or of any court subordinate to it. Like the Supreme Court of Pakistan, any decision of a High Court is binding on all courts subordinate to it to the extent that it decides a question of law or is based upon or enunciates a principle of law. The Court has exclusive jurisdiction to hear appeals from the decision of criminal courts under any law relating to enforcement of Hudood Law that is, laws pertaining to offences to intoxication, theft, *Zina* (unlawful sexual intercourse) and *Qazf* (false imputation of *Zina*).

60. The Federal Shariat Court is another constitutional court in addition to the Supreme Court of Pakistan and High Courts. It is consisting of not more than eight Muslim Judges including the Chief Justice who is appointed by the President. The principal seat of the Federal Shariat Court is at Islamabad, but it runs circuits at Lahore, Karachi, Peshawar and Quetta. Federal Shariat Court has the power, either of its own motion or on the petition of a citizen of Pakistan or the Federal Government or a Provincial Government, to examine and decide the question whether or not any law or provision of law is repugnant to the Injunctions of Islam, as laid down in the Holy Quran and the Sunnah of the Holy Prophet Muhammad (PBUH). If the Court decides that any law or provision of law is repugnant to the Injunctions of Islam, it shall set out in its decision the reasons for its holding that opinion; and the extent to which such law or provision is so repugnant; and specify the day on which the decision shall take effect provided that no such decision shall be deemed to take effect before the expiration of the period within which an appeal there from may be preferred to the Supreme Court or, where an appeal has been so preferred, before the disposal of such appeal.

61. Courts established under or by laws are of many kinds and in the relevant laws, their composition, powers, jurisdiction and other administrative and procedural matters are prescribed. Following are important courts established under different laws:

- Income Tax Appellate Tribunals;
- Environmental Protection Tribunals;
- Insurance Appellate Tribunals;
- Customs, Excise and Sales Tax Appellate Tribunals;
- Service Tribunals;
- Special Courts (Courts of Narcotics Substances);
- Banking Courts (Recovery of Loans);
- Special Courts (Offences in Banks);
- Special Courts (Customs, Taxation and Anti-Smuggling);
- Special Judges (Central);
- Drug Courts;

- Anti-Terrorism Courts;
- Accountability Courts;
- Labour Courts; and
- Other Courts.

62. In every district of a Province, there is a Court of District Judge which is the principal court of original jurisdiction in civil matters. Courts of General Jurisdiction besides the Court of District Judge, there are courts of Civil Judges. Civil Judges function under the superintendence and control of District Judge, and all matters of civil nature originate in the courts of Judges. The District Judge may, however, withdraw any case from any Civil Judge and try it himself. Appeals against the judgments and decrees passed by the Civil Judges in cases where the value of the suit does not exceed the specified amount lie to the District Judge.

63. In every district, there is a Court of Sessions Judge and Courts of Magistrates. Criminal cases punishable with death and cases arising out of the enforcement of laws relating to Hudood are tried by Sessions Judges. The Court of Sessions Judge is competent to pass any sentence authorized by law. Offences not punishable with death are tried by Magistrates. Among the Magistrates, there are Magistrates of first Class, second Class and third Class. An appeal against the sentence passed by a Sessions Judge lies to the High Court and against the sentence passed by a Magistrate to the Sessions Judge if the term of sentence is up to four years, otherwise to the High Court.

64. To deal with specific types of cases Special Courts and Tribunals are constituted. These are; Special Courts for Trial of Offences in Banks; Special Courts for Recovery of Bank Loans; Special Courts under the Customs Act, Special Traffic Courts; Courts of Special Judges Anti-Corruption; Commercial Courts; Drug Courts; Labour Courts; Insurance Appellate Tribunal; Income Tax Appellate Tribunal and Services Tribunals. Appeals from the Special Courts lie to the High Courts, except in case of Labour Courts and Special Traffic Courts, which have separate forums of appeal. The Tribunals lie to the Supreme Court of Pakistan. Speedy and Inexpensive Justice Steps have been taken to overcome the problems of inordinate delays in dispensing justice and enormous cost involved in litigation – a legacy of the past. The number of High Court Judges, Additional Sessions Judges, Civil Judges and Magistrates has been increased. The Code of Criminal Procedure, 1898, has been amended to grant automatic concession of release on bail to the under-trial prisoners, if the continuous period of their detention exceeds one year in case of offences not punishable with death and two years in case of offences punishable with death. It also made incumbent on the criminal courts to take into consideration the period of detention spent by the accused as an under-trial prisoner while awarding sentence. No fee is payable in criminal cases and for filing any petition before the Federal Shariat Court. Court fee in civil cases up to the value of PKR 25,000 has been abolished.

Chapter 2. Historical Background of Family and Succession Law

§1. Introduction

65. The British left the Muslim Family Laws pertaining to *marriage* and divorce uncodified. The problems that arose were thus bequeathed to the Judiciary to sort out. Evidence of marriage was established through unreliable sources and divorce was allowed in the chaotic manner that characterized the male-dominated Muslim society. In 1955, the Commission on Marriage and Family Laws prepared a Report safeguarding, *inter alia*, the rights of the women.

66. The Commission accepted the principle that Family Laws had to be liberalized in light of modern times, but when it came to making recommendations it inclined to a conservative interpretation. For instance, it did not outlaw divorce pronounced by the husband in violation of the Quranic 'nas'. But it did rule that *nikah (marriage)*, to be of legal value, had to be registered. Its other recommendations are given above. The Report was passionately opposed by the *Ulema* and orthodox Muslims in 1956 for being against Islam. The civilian governments after 1956 avoided legislating on the Report, but General Ayub Khan made selected recommendations of the Report into law through an Ordinance in 1961.

Chapter 3. Sources of Family and Succession Law

§1. Islamic Law

I. Holy Quran

67. According to the belief of the Muslims, the word of God is law and law is the command of God. The words of Holy Quran are laws of God. The supreme source of Islamic Law is the Holy Quran which provides complete code of life. Muslims believe that the Holy Quran was repeatedly revealed from Allah to Muhammad verbally through the angel Jibrīl (Gabriel) over a period of approximately twenty-three years. Muslims hold that the Holy Quran is the verbal divine guidance and moral direction for mankind. Muslims also consider the original Arabic verbal text to be the final revelation of God. The Holy Quran contains about 6000 versus but not more than 200 versus deal with legal principles and if we leave out of account those which concern the State as such, there are about 80 versus, more or less, which deal with the law of personal status. Most of them are concerned with inheritance, marriage, divorce and such like matters.[2]

II. Sunnah / Hadees

68. The principles which were stated in the Holy Quran found their application in the hands of the Holy Prophet Muhammad (PBUH). This gave birth to Hadees of the Holy Prophet Muhammad (PBUH). The Holy Quran and Sunnah form the fundamental roots of Islamic Law. As a source of law, Sunnah or Hadees is as binding as the principles of Holy Quran. The Muslim usage of the term 'Sunnah' refers to the sayings and living habits of Holy Prophet Muhammad (PBUH), the last prophet of Islam. The Sunnah/Hadees of Holy Prophet Muhammad (PBUH) includes his specific words, habits, practices, and silent approvals. It is significant to the spirituality of Islam because it addresses ways of life dealing with friends, family and government.

III. Ijma or consensus of opinion

69. It is equally binding on the people to act on a principle (not contrary to the Holy Quran or Sunnah) which had been established by agreement among highly qualified legal scholars of any generation. This was supported by the Hanafi doctrine that the provisions of law must change with the changing times and the Malikis that new facts require new decisions. Ijma is an Arabic term referring ideally to the consensus of the scholars of Islam.[3]

2. Mulla Principles of Mohamedan Law by M. Hidayatullah.
3. Mulla Principles of Mohamedan Law by M. Hidayatullah.

IV. The Qiyas or analogical deductions

70. This is the last source of Islamic Law. Compared with the other three sources, it is of much lesser significance. It consists in applying some text if the case can be demonstrated to be governed by the reasons of the rule underlying it although the language may not apply. This is reasoning by analogy.[4]

§2. CONSTITUTION

71. The Constitution of Islamic Republic of Pakistan also provides protection to the family. Under Article-35 of the Constitution of Pakistan 1973, the State shall protect the marriage, the family, the mother and child. Under the Constitution of Pakistan, the Federal Government is empowered to make legislation relating to marriage, divorce, infants, minors, adoptions, wills, intestacy and succession.

§3. LEGISLATION

72. The Government of Pakistan enacted several Acts, Rules and Regulations regarding handling of family matters, succession and inheritance matters in Pakistan. Some important and major laws enacted or opted at different times are given below:

Contracting and Dissolution of Muslim Marriages (Statutory Law):

- Azad Jammu and Kashmir Family Courts Act, 1993
- Child Marriage Restraint Act, 1929
- Dissolution of Muslim Marriages Act, 1939
- Dowry and Bridal Gifts (Restriction) Act, 1976
- Dowry and Bridal Gifts (Restriction) Rules, 1976
- Family Court Act, 1964
- Family Courts (Amendment) Act, 1997
- Family Courts (Amendment) Ordinance, 1997
- Family Courts (Amendment) Ordinance, 2002
- Family Courts (Khyber Pakhtunkhwa) (Amendment) Act, 1996
- Family Courts (Sindh Amendment) Act, 1997
- Family Courts (Sindh Amendment) Ordinance, 1997
- Family Courts Ordinance, 1964
- Kazis Act, 1880
- Muslim Family Laws Ordinance, 1961
- Muslim Family Laws Rules, 1961
- Punjab/Sindh/Khyber Pakhtunkhwa/Balochistan Family Courts Act, 1964

4. Mulla Principles of Mohamedan Law by M. Hidayatullah.

- Sindh Muslim Marriages and Divorces Registration Act, 1955
- West Pakistan Family Courts Rules, 1965.

Contracting and Dissolution of Christian, Parsi and Hindu Marriages:

- Births, Deaths and Marriages Registration Act, 1886
- Christian Marriage Act, 1872
- Divorce Act, 1869
- Hindu Marriage Disabilities Removal Act, 1946
- Hindu Married Woman's Right to Separate Residence and Maintenance Act, 1946
- Hindu Widow's Marriages Act, 1856
- Indian (Non-Domiciled Parties) Divorce Rules, 1927
- Parsi Marriage and Divorce Act, 1936.

Anand and Arya Marriages:

- Anand Marriages Act, 1909
- The Arya Marriage Validation Act, 1937.

Marriage Validation and other Acts:

- Majority Act, 1875
- Special Marriage Act, 1872
- The Marriages Validation Act, 1892.

Foreign Marriages:

- The Foreign Marriages Act, 1903.

Offences Relating to Marriages:

- Pakistan Penal Code (XLV of 1860) [sections 493 – 498].

Maintenance of Wife and Child:

- The Claims for Maintenance (Recovery Abroad) Ordinance, 1959
- The Maintenance Orders Enforcement Act, 1921.

Guardian:

- Code of Civil Procedure, 1908
- Guardians and Wards Act, 1890
- Khyber Pakhtunkhwa Court of Wards Regulations, 1904
- Punjab Court of Wards Act, 1903
- Sindh Court of Wards Act, 1905.

Succession Laws:

- Administration of Estates Regulation, 1827
- Court Fees Act, 1870 (Court Fee on Probates, Letters of Administration and Succession Certificates)
- Legal Representatives' Suits Act, 1855
- Sindh Civil Court Rules (Rules under Succession Act)
- Succession Act, 1925.

Law of Inheritance:

- Hindu Disposition of Property Act, 1916
- Hindu Inheritance (Removal of Disabilities) Act, 1928
- Hindu Law of Inheritance (Amendment) Act, 1929
- Hindu Marriage (Disabilities Removal) Act, 1946
- Hindu Women's Rights to Property (Sindh Extension to Agricultural Land) Act, 1943
- Khoja Disposition of Property Act, 1916
- Married Woman's Property Act, 1874
- The Cutchi Memons Act, 1938
- West Pakistan Hindu Women's Rights to Agricultural Land Ordinance, 1959.

Enforcement of Shariat Law:

- Balochistan Civil Disputes (Shariat Application) Rules, 1977
- Khyber Pakhtunkhwa Muslim Personal Law (Shariat) Application Act, 1935
- Muslim Personal Law (Shariat) Application (Amendment) Act, 1964
- Muslim Personal Law (Shariat) Application (Amendment) Ordinance, 1963
- Muslim Personal Law (Shariat) Application (Sindh Amendment) Act, 1950
- Muslim Personal Law (Shariat) Application Act (Punjab Amendment) Ordinance, 1983
- Muslim Personal Law (Shariat) Application Act, 1937
- Muslim Personal Law (Shariat) Application Act, 1962
- Punjab Muslim Personal Law (Shariat) Application (Amendment) Act, 1951
- Punjab Muslim Personal Law (Shariat) Application (Removal of Difficulties) Act, 1975
- West Pakistan Muslim Personal Law (Shariat) Application Act, 1948.

Juvenile Justice System:

- Indian Juvenile Justice (Care and Protection of Children) Act, 2000
- Juvenile Justice Rules, 2001
- Juvenile Justice System Ordinance, 2000
- Khyber Pakhtunkhwa Juvenile Justice System Rules, 2002
- Protection of Breast-Feeding and Child Nutrition Ordinance, 2002
- Punjab Juvenile Justice System Rules, 2002
- Sindh Juvenile Justice System Rules, 2002.

Conciliations:

- Conciliations Courts Ordinance, 1961
- Conciliation Courts Rules, 1962
- Small Claims and Minor Offences Courts Ordinance, 2002.

Marriage Functions Prohibition:

- Marriage Functions (Prohibition of Ostentatious Displays and Wasteful Expenses) Ordinance, 2000
- Punjab Marriage Functions (Prohibition of Ostentatious Displays and Wasteful Expenses) Act, 2003
- The Punjab Marriage Functions (Prohibition of Ostentatious Displays and Wasteful Expenses (Repeal) Act, 2006.

§4. Court Decisions

73. The different decisions made by the courts of Pakistan specially Family Courts, High Courts and Supreme Court of Pakistan, also defined family laws of the country, gave interpretation and set precedents for other lower courts in the family matters.

§5. Customs

74. In the Islamic or Muhammadan laws, there is no space for customs. The Muslims rely on the purports of the Holy Quran, Sunnah or Hadees, Ijma and Qiyas. However, in Christians, Hindu and Parsis, communities customs are followed or obeyed even making decisions by the Courts.

Chapter 4. The Courts Administering Family Law and Succession Law

§1. Arbitration Council

75. Under section 2(a) of the Muslim Family Laws Ordinance, 1961, 'Arbitration Council' means a body consisting of the Chairman and representative of each of the parties to a matter deal with family matters under the said Ordinance, provided that where any party fails to nominate a representative within the prescribed time, the body formed without such representative shall be the Arbitration Council.

76. Pursuant to Rule-3 of the West Pakistan Rules under Muslim Family Laws Ordinance, 1961, the Union Council have the jurisdiction in the following matters:

- In case of an application to contract another marriage, the Union Council of the Union or Town in which the existing wife of the applicant, or where the husband has more wives than one, the wife with whom the applicant was married last, is residing at the time of his making the application.
- In case of a notice of divorce, the Union Council of the Union or Town in which the wife in relation to whom divorce has been pronounced was residing at the time of the pronouncement to divorce.
- In case of an application for maintenance, the Union Council of the Union or Town in which the wife is residing at the time of her making the application, and where application is made by more than one wife, it shall be the Union Council of the Union or Town in which the wife who makes the application first, is residing at the time of her making the application.

77. All proceedings before an Arbitration Council are held in camera unless the Chairman otherwise directs with the consent of all the parties. The Chairman conducts the proceedings of an Arbitration Council as expeditiously as possible (Rules 4 & 5 of the West Pakistan Rules under Muslim Family Laws Ordinance, 1961).

78. All decisions of the Arbitration Council are taken by majority, and where no decision can be so taken, the decision of the Chairman shall be considered the decision of the Arbitration Council.

79. A copy of the decision of the Arbitration Council duly attested by the Chairman, is furnished free of cost to each of the parties to the proceedings. Within seven days of receiving an application of maintenance or divorce notice, the Chairman, by order in writing, calls upon each of the parties to nominate his/her representative, and each such party shall, within seven days of receiving the order, nominate in writing a representative and deliver the nomination to the Chairman or send it to him by registered post.

80. Where a representative nominated by a party is, by reasons of illness or otherwise, unable to attend the meetings of the Arbitration Council, or wilfully absents himself from such meeting, or has lost the confidence of the party, the party, may, with the previous permission in writing of the Chairman, revoke the nomination and make, within such time as the Chairman may allow, a fresh nomination. Where a fresh nomination is made, it shall not be necessary to commence the proceedings before the Arbitration Council de novo, unless the Chairman, for reasons to be recorded in writing, directs otherwise.

81. Where it is made to appear to the Collector whether on the application of a party to the proceedings or on his own information, that the Chairman is interested in favour of a party to any proceedings before the Arbitration Council or is prejudiced against any such party, or that the Chairman is misconducting himself in any such proceedings the Collector may, after giving notice to all the parties to the proceedings, appoint any other member of the Union Council as the Chairman and pending the passing of such orders may stay the proceedings before the Arbitration Council. A Collector passing an order under this rule shall record in writing his reasons for the same.

82. Application for the revision of a decision of an Arbitration Council shall be preferred within thirty days of the decision or of the issue of the certificate, as the case may be. The application shall be in writing, set out the grounds on which the applicant seeks to have the decision or the certificate revised, and bear the signature of the applicant (Rules 16(1)(2) of the West Pakistan Rules under Muslim Family Laws Ordinance, 1961).

83. As soon as may be after the Arbitration Council has given its decision under Rule 6, the record of the proceedings before it in which such decision has been given, shall be forwarded by the Chairman to the office of the Union Council, where it shall be preserved for a period of five years from the date of the decision. No Court shall take cognizance of any offence under the Ordinance or these rules, save on a complaint in writing by the Union Council, stating the facts constituting the offence.

84. SCP (2009 SCMR 1037): Wife having filed suit for maintenance for herself and minor children, against husband prior in time before the Judge, Family Court, petition under section 9(2), Muslim Family Laws Ordinance, 1961 before the Chairman Arbitration Council was not competent, as she had already resorted to the remedy of the exclusive jurisdiction of Family Court.

85. LHC (1989 MLD 3051) Respondent-wife filed application for grant of maintenance before Arbitration Council and during pendency of proceedings, she also filed suit for maintenance before Family Court which was stayed by Family Court pending decision of proceedings before Arbitration Council. Wife had stated during hearing of Constitutional petition that she did not want to prosecute her application before Chairman, Arbitration Council but would like to have dispute decided by Family Court. Constitutional petition filed by husband against remand order passed by Collector having fructified no further proceedings were called for. Family Court was directed to decide the case pending before it within specified time.

86. LHC (2009 YLR 1141) Petitioner husband assailed jurisdiction of appointed officer of Pakistan Mission at United Kingdom to perform functions of Chairman Arbitration Council. Validity: Both the parties being permanent residents of UK, as per Notification No. Section R.O. 1086(K)/61, dated 8 November 1961, function of Chairman Arbitration Council under Muslim Family Laws Ordinance, 1961, were to be performed by an appointed officer of Pakistan Mission abroad. Order passed by authorities with regard to transfer of proceedings to Pakistan Mission abroad was according to law and the same was upheld by High Court. Petitioner failed to point out any illegality or substantial error in the order passed by authorities warranting interference by High Court in exercise of Constitutional jurisdiction. Petition was dismissed in circumstances.

87. LHC (2010 CLC 258) Divorce pronounced thrice in presence of witnesses and communicated to wife at her address and Union Council concerned. Failure of wife to participate in arbitration proceedings initiated by Union Council despite having notice thereof. Application by husband to Union Council for issuance of Divorce Certificate after expiry of requisite period of ninety days. Constitutional petition by wife seeking quashment of proceedings before Union Council. Validity: Petitioner herself had chosen not to attend arbitration proceedings initiated by Union Council. Petitioner had failed to show any lawful reason or justification to quash such proceedings or restrain Union Council from issuing such certificate to husband on expiry of ninety days. High Court dismissed Constitutional petition in circumstances.

§2. Family Courts

88. The Family Courts have been established for the expeditious settlement and disposal of disputes relating to marriage and family affairs and for matters connected therewith through Family Courts Act, 1964. Subject to the provisions of MFLO, and the Conciliation Courts Ordinance, 1961, the Family Courts have exclusive jurisdiction to entertain, hear and adjudicate upon following matters:

- Dissolution of marriage
- Dower
- Maintenance
- Restitution of conjugal rights
- Custody of children and the visitation rights of parents
- Guardianship
- Jactitation of marriage
- Dowry
- Personal property and belonging of a wife.

89. Appeals from the Family Courts lie with the High Court only. Every town and city has court of family judge. In some areas, where it is only Family Court but in most areas Civil Judge Courts have been granted the powers of Family Court Judges.

90. A suit for dissolution of marriage shall finally be disposed of within a period of four months from its institution; provided that where an appeal lies against the dissolution of marriage, such appeal shall be disposed of within four months.

91. A decision given or a decree passed by a Family Court shall be appealable to the High Court, where the Family Court is presided over by a District Judge, an Additional District Judge or a person notified by Government to be of the rank and status of a District Judge or an Additional District Judge, and to the District Court, in any other case.

92. However, no appeal lies from a decree passed by Family Court for dissolution of marriage, except in the case of dissolution for reasons specified in clause (*a*) of item (*viii*) of section 2 of the Dissolution of Muslim Marriages Act, 1939, for dower not exceeding PKR 15,000 and for maintenance of PKR 500 or less per month.

93. A person shall be guilty of contempt of the Family Court if he without lawful excuse offers any insult to the Family Court; or causes an interruption in the work of the Family Court; or refuses to answer any question put by the Family Court, which he is bound to answer; or refuses to take oath to state the truth or to sign any statement made by him in the Family Court; and the Family Court may forthwith try such person for such contempt and sentence him to a fine not exceeding PKR 200. A Family Court does not have the power to issue an injunction to, or stay any proceedings pending before, a Chairman or an Arbitration Council.

94. A Family Court shall not question the validity of any marriage registered in accordance with the provisions of MFLO, nor shall any evidence in regard thereto be admissible before such Court.

95. SCP (2006 PLD 489) Jactitation of marriage. Family Court had exclusive jurisdiction to adjudicate upon the case of jactitation of marriage brought before it even though marriage was registered under MFLO, which Ordinance essentially referred to and dealt with valid marriages solemnized under the Islamic Sharia and not otherwise.

96. LHC (2009 YLR 2341) Suit for dissolution of marriage and recovery of maintenance. Spouses were Muslim holding dual nationality of Pakistan and United Kingdom. Solemnization and registration of marriage of parties in the UK and its subsequent registration in Pakistan. Application by husband for return of plaint to wife as Family Court at Lahore lacked jurisdiction to entertain such suit. Validity: Marriage of Muslim Pakistani spouses irrespective of place of its solemnization would be governed by provisions of Dissolution of Muslim Marriages Act, 1939, Muslim Family Laws Ordinance, 1961 and West Pakistan Family Courts Act, 1964. Husband had not specifically denied wife's assertion in plaint about her residence in Pakistan. Husband in his suit pending against wife in Civil Court had stated that both parties were residing in Pakistan. Application of husband was dismissed in circumstances.

§3. High Courts

97. Appeals can be filed in High Court against the decision of the Family Courts. There is one High Court in each Province, and one in the Federal Capital, Islamabad, including: Lahore High Court, Lahore, Punjab; Sindh High Court, Karachi, Sindh; Peshawar High Court, Peshawar, Khyber Pakhtunkhwa; Balochistan High Court, Quetta, Baluchistan and Islamabad High Court, Islamabad. The High Courts are the Appellate Courts for all family, civil and criminal cases in each respective Province.

§4. Federal Shariat Court

98. The Federal Shariat Court was established by the President's Order No. 1 of 1980 as incorporated in the Constitution of Pakistan, 1973 under Chapter 3A. The Court is a unique institution with no parallel in the entire Muslim world. It is backed by powerful provisions of the Constitution. The preamble to the Constitution explicitly affirms that sovereignty over the entire universe belongs to Almighty Allah alone, and the authority to be exercised by the people of Pakistan within the limits prescribed by Him is a sacred trust. Article 2A lays down that the principles and provisions set out in the Objectives Resolution are a substantive part of the Constitution. Article 227 makes it incumbent that all existing laws shall be brought in conformity with the injunctions of Islam as laid down in the Holy Quran and the Sunnah of the Holy Prophet Muhammad (PBUH), and Chapter 3A which pertains to the functions and organization of Federal Shariat Court, empowers the court and entrusts the court with the responsibility to examine and decide the question whether or not any law or provision of law is repugnant to the injunctions of Islam as laid down in the Holy Quran and the Sunnah of the Holy Prophet Muhammad (PBUH). Law includes any custom or usage having the force of law but does not include the Constitution, Muslim personal law, any law relating to the procedure of any court or tribunal.[5]

99. FSC (2000 PLD 1) Ghulam Asghar versus State: Repugnancy to Injunctions of Islam. Federal Shariat Court has the jurisdiction to examine whether sections 4, 5, 6 & 7 of MFLO are violative of the Injunctions of Islam or not.

5. Website of Federal Shariat Court.

Part I. Persons

Chapter 1. The Status of a Person

§1. Definition of a Person

100. 'Person' can have two meanings, that is, human being and legal Person. 'Person' includes a legal Person which may be a registered firm or a private limited company or any other corporation or body having the status of a legal entity. 'Person' would include not only natural Person, but also a juristic Person. Word 'Person' would not include State, but it referred only to an individual.

§2. Capacity

I. Minors

101. Under the Succession Act, 1925 'minor' means any person subject to the Majority Act, 1875 who has not attained his majority within the meaning of that Act, and any other person who has not completed the age of 18 years; and 'minority' means the status of any such person. Whereas under section 2(d) of the Child Marriage Restraint Act, 1929, 'minor' means person of either six who is under 18 years of age.

II. Child

102. Under the Child Marriage Restraint Act, 1929 section 2(a) 'child' means a person who, if a male, is under 18 years of age, and if a female, is under 16 years of age.

III. Lunacy and Idiocy

103. A lunatic is a commonly used term for a person who is mentally ill, dangerous, foolish, and unpredictable; a condition once called lunacy. The Government of Pakistan promulgated Mental Health Ordinance, 2001 replacing Lunacy Act,

1912 to consolidate and amend the law relating to the treatment and care of mentally disordered persons, to make better provisions for their care, treatment, management of properties and affairs and to provide for matters connected therewith or incidental thereto and to encourage community care of such mentally disordered persons and further to provide for the promotion of mental health and prevention of mental disorder.

104. Under the Mental Health Ordinance, 2001 'mental disorder' means mental illness, including mental impairment, severe personality disorder, severe mental impairment and any other disorder or disability of mind, and 'mentally disordered' shall be construed accordingly and as explained hereunder: (i) 'mental impairment' means a state of arrested or incomplete development of mind (not amounting to severe mental impairment) which includes significant impairment of intelligence and social functioning and is associated with abnormally aggressive or seriously irresponsible conduct on the part of the person concerned, and 'mentally impaired' shall be construed accordingly; (ii) 'severe personality disorder' means a persistent disorder or disability of mind (whether or not including significant impairment of intelligence) which results in abnormally aggressive or seriously irresponsible conduct on the part of the person concerned; (iii) 'severe mental impairment' means a state of arrested or incomplete development of mind which includes severe impairment of intelligence and social functioning and is associated with abnormally aggressive or seriously irresponsible conduct on the part of the person concerned and 'severely mentally impaired' shall be construed accordingly; Explanation: Nothing contained in sub-clauses (i), (ii) and (iii) above shall be construed as implying that a person may be dealt with as suffering from mental disorder or from any other form of such mental disorder defined in this section, by reason only of promiscuity or other immoral conduct, sexual deviancy or dependence on alcohol or drugs.

105. If a person with mental illness owns property and his/her relatives claim that he/she is incapable of taking care of the property, the Court of Protection may order an inquiry to determine whether the person alleged to be mentally ill is competent and capable to handle his/her person, affairs and property. The Court may assign two or more persons as assessors in this inquiry.

106. Under the Mental Health Ordinance, 2001 where it is ascertained that a person is mentally ill and not capable of managing his/her affairs, the Court of Protection may appoint any suitable person as a guardian for his/her care, may direct the person to be admitted for treatment in a mental health care facility and may order for his/her maintenance. The Court may also appoint a suitable person as manager to manage the property.

107. Under the Mental Health Ordinance, 2001 an inventory of all immoveable property will be presented by the manager to Court within three months of the order. Any major transactions by the appointed manager will be made after approval from Court and through a bank authorized by the Court. If the Court believes that the person initially determined to be mentally ill is now recovered and competent and able to manage his/her affairs then the Court, after directing an inquiry for re-assessment of his/her state of mind, may set aside all orders related to appointment of guardian or manager.

108. Under the Mental Health Ordinance, 2001 a person who holds a public office or is a public servant and who is determined to be mentally ill will continue to receive his/her pay or benefits that they are entitled to from the Government even after they cease to work due to their psychiatric condition.

Chapter 2. Registration of Civil Status

§1. Muslim Law

109. Every marriage solemnized under Muslim Family Laws Ordinance, 1961 is required to be registered with the Registrar. For the purpose of registration of marriages, the Union Council shall grant licenses to one or more persons, to be called *Nikah* Registrars (a person who records marriage), but in no case shall more than one *Nikah* Registrar be licensed for any one Ward.

110. The *Nikah* Registrar shall, in the case of a marriage solemnized by him, fill in Form 12, in quadruplicate, in the register, the persons, whose signatures are required in the form, shall then sign, and the *Nikah* Registrar shall then affix his signature and seal thereto, and keep the original intact in the register. The duplicate and triplicate of the *Nikahnama* (marriage document) filed in as aforesaid, shall be supplied to the bride and the bridegroom respectively, on payment of nominal fee each, and the quadruplicate shall be forwarded to the Union Council.

111. If any person required by this rule to sign the register, refuses so to sign, he shall be punishable with simple imprisonment for a term which may extend to one month, or with fine which may extend to PKR 200, or with both.

112. Where a marriage is solemnized in Pakistan by a person other than the *Nikah* Registrar, such person fills Form II, to be had lose on payment of such price as may be determined by the Provincial Government, the persons whose signatures required in the Form, shall then sign, and the person solemnizing the marriage then affix his signature to the Form and ensure delivery, as expeditiously as possible, of the same together with the registration fee to the *Nikah* Registrar of the Ward where the marriage is solemnized. If any person required by this rule to sign the Form refuses so to sign, he shall be punishable with simple imprisonment for a term which may extend to one month, or with fine which may extend to PKR 200, or with both.

113. LHC (2006 YLR 349) Non-registration of *Nikah* although a serious irregularity but same would not derogate from the validity of *Nikah*. Family Court while entertaining the suit of non-registered marriage, was to report the matter to the relevant Union Council. LHC (2001 YLR 644) held that *Nikah* even if not registered under the law remains valid.

114. FSC (1987 MLD 1637) held that Registration of *Nikah*, held, not necessary proof of *Nikah*. *Nikah*, in Muslim Law, could be performed by offer and acceptance in presence of witnesses. Non-registration, only attracted penalty under section 5(4) of Muslim Family Laws Ordinance 1961.

115. LHC (1995 PLD 364) held that violation of procedure in registration of *Nikah* attracts punitive action. Non-production of the *Nikah* Khawan (a person who solemnize marriage) cast a serious doubt on its genuineness.

§2. MINORITIES LAWS

I. Christian Law

116. Christian marriages are considered voluntary union for life between a man and a woman, to the exclusion of all others. Family matters among the Christian community are dealt with by the Christian Marriages Act of 1872 and the Divorce Act of 1869. Under the Christian Marriages Act of 1872, the marriage has to be registered with the Marriage Registrars appointed by the Government in each District.

II. Hindu Law

117. Under the Special Marriage Act, 1872, fourteen days notice of marriage is required before the marriage is solemnized to the Registrar appointed by the Provincial Government. The Registrar immediately enters each notice received by him regarding the marriage in the Marriage Notice Book. The Hindu community in Pakistan does not have any specific codified laws relating to family matters which are instead governed by custom. However, Hindu community can approach country's regular Family Courts since the Family Courts Act of 1964 does not restrict its jurisdiction to Muslims alone. Hindu family matters in Pakistan are primarily governed by custom, and the essentials of a valid custom are that it should be ancient, certain, reasonable and not opposed to public policy, and normally very few family matters among the Hindu community go to courts, and most issues are settled through community forums.

III. Parsi Law

118. Under the Parsi Marriage and Divorce Act, 1936 every marriage contracted shall immediately on the solemnization thereof, be certified by the officiating priest and certificate shall be signed by the said priest, or their fathers or guardians when they shall not have completed the age of 21 years, and two witnesses present at the meeting and the said priest shall thereupon send such certificate together with prescribed fee, to be paid by the husband to the Registrar of the place at which marriage is solemnized. The Registrar on receipt of the certificate and fee enters the certificate in a Register to be kept by him for that purpose and shall be entitled to retain the fee. The Register of marriage can be inspected, and certified extracts can be obtained by paying nominal fee. Every Registrar send copies of the certificates issued and entered into the Register to the Government appointed Registrar General.

§3. Special Marriage Act, 1872

119. To provide a form of marriage for persons who do not profess the Christian, Jewish, Hindu, Muhammadan (Islamic), Parsi, Buddhist, Sikh or Jaina religion, and for persons who profess the Hindu, Buddhist, Sikh or Jaina religion and to legalize, certain marriages the validity of which is doubtful, the Special Marriage Act, 1872 was extended to whole of Pakistan. Under this Act, marriages are celebrated between persons neither of whom professes the Christian or the Jewish, or the Hindu or the Muhammadan (Islamic), or the Parsi or the Buddhist, or the Sikh or the Jaina religion, or between persons each of whom professes one or other of the following religions, that is to say, the Hindu, Buddhist, Sikh or Jaina religion upon the conditions that neither party must, at the time of the marriage, have a husband or wife living; the man must have completed his age of 18 years and the woman her age of 14 years, according to the Gregorian calendar; each party must, if he/she has not completed the age of 21 years, have obtained the consent of his/her father or guardian of the marriage; the parties must not be related to each other in any degree of consanguinity or affinity which would, according to any law to which either of them is subject, render a marriage between them illegal.

Chapter 3. Personality Rights

§1. Minority Rights

120. In order to protect the minorities in Pakistan, their rights have been envisaged under the Constitution of Pakistan, 1973. A full-fledged Ministry of Minorities is working in Pakistan for the betterment and uplift of various religious minorities in Pakistan.

121. Under Article-20 (Chapter-1 Fundamental Rights - Freedom to profess religion and to manage religious institutions) of the Constitution of Pakistan, 1973 subject to law, public order and morality – (a) every citizen have the right to profess, practice and propagate his religion; and (b) every religious denomination and every sect thereof have the right to establish, maintain and manage its religious institutions.

122. Under Article-21 (safeguard against taxation for purposes of any particular religion) of the Constitution of Pakistan, no person can be compelled to pay any special tax the proceeds of which are to be spent on the propagation or maintenance of any religion other than his own.

123. Whereas under Article-22 (safeguards as to educational institutions in respect of religion, etc.) of the Constitution of Pakistan, no person attending any educational institution shall be required to receive religious instruction, or take part in any religious ceremony, or attend religious worship, if such instruction, ceremony or worship relates to a religion other than his own. In respect of any religious institution, there is no discrimination against any community in the granting of exemption or concession in relation to taxation.

124. Under Article 22(3) of the Constitution of Pakistan, subject to law, no religious community or denomination can be prevented from providing religious instruction for pupils of that community or denomination in any educational institution maintained wholly by that community or denomination; and no citizen can be denied admission to any educational institution receiving aid from public revenues on the ground only of race, religion, caste or place of birth. However, nothing in this Article prevents any public authority from making provision for the Advancement of any socially or educationally backward class of citizens.

125. Under Article-25 of the Constitution of Pakistan, all citizens are equal before law and are entitled to equal protection of law. There is no discrimination on the basis of sex alone. However, nothing in this Article prevents the State from making any special provision for the protection of women and children.

126. Under Article-36 of the Constitution of Pakistan, the Government safeguards the legitimate rights and interests of minorities, including their due representation in the Federal and Provincial services.

§2. Minors' Responsibility for Crimes

127. The Government of Pakistan promulgated Juvenile Justice System Ordinance, 2000 to provide protection to children involved in criminal litigation, their rehabilitation in society, re-organization of Juvenile Courts and matters connected therewith and incidental thereto. The Courts have been given powers to evaluate criminal responsibility of a child.

128. Child means a person who has not attained the age of 18 years is child under the Juvenile Justice System Ordinance, 2000. Under section-5 of the Juvenile Justice System Ordinance, 2000 no child is allowed to be charge or tried for an offence together with an adult. However, if a child is charged with the commission of an offence for which under section 239 of the Code, or any other law for the time being in force such child could be tried together with an adult, the Court taking cognizance of the offence shall direct separate trial of the child by the Juvenile Court.

§3. Juvenile rights

129. Under section-3 of the Juvenile Justice System Ordinance, 2000 every child who is accused of the commission of an offence or is a victim of an offence shall have the right of legal assistance at the expense of the State. A legal practitioner appointed by the State for providing legal assistance to a child accused of the commission of an offence, or victim of an offence, shall have at least five years standing at the Bar.

130. Under section-4 of the Juvenile Justice System Ordinance, 2000 the Provincial Governments, in consultation with the Chief Justice of High Court, by notification in the Official Gazette, are required to establish one or more Juvenile Courts for any local within its jurisdiction or confer powers of Juvenile Court to other Session Court of Judicial Magistrate of the First Class. The Juvenile Court have exclusive jurisdiction to try cases in which a child is accused of commission of an offence. All cases pending before a Trial Court in which a child is accused of an offence shall stand transferred to the Juvenile Court having jurisdiction.

131. The Juvenile Courts are obligatory to decide the case within four months on taking cognizance of the offence. A Juvenile Court does not ordinarily take up any other case on a day when the case of a child accused in fixed for evidence on such a day.

132. No person is allowed to be present at any sitting of a Juvenile Court except, Members and officers of the Juvenile Court, Parties to the case before the Juvenile Court, and such other persons who are directly concerned with the proceedings including the police officers. Also, other persons as the Juvenile Court directs to be present and Guardian of the child. At any stage during the course of the trial of a case, the Juvenile Court may, in the interest of such child, decency or morality, direct any person to withdraw from Court for such period as the Court may direct.

133. If at any stage during the course of the trial of a case, the Juvenile Court is satisfied that the attendance of the child is not essential for the purpose of the trial, the Juvenile Court may dispose with the attendance and proceed with the trial of the case in absence of the child.

134. If a child who has been brought before a Juvenile Court and is found to be suffering from serious illness, whether physical or mental, and requires treatment, the Court shall send such child to a hospital or a medical institution where treatment shall be given to the child at the expense of the State. If a question arises as to whether a person before Court is child or not, the Juvenile Court shall record a finding after such inquiry, which shall include a medical report for determination of the age of the child.

135. Under section-8 of the Juvenile Justice System Ordinance, 2000 unless the Juvenile Court specifically authorizes, the Court proceedings are not published in any newspapers, magazine or journal in any form which may disclose the name, address, school or any identification or particulars calculated to lead directly or indirectly to the identification of such child nor shall any picture of the child be published.

136. The Probation Officer assists the Juvenile Court by making a report on the child's character, educational, social and moral background. The report of the Probation Officer submitted to the Juvenile Court shall be treated as confidential. The Juvenile Court may, if so thinks fit, communicate the substance of the report to the child or his guardian and, where anyone of them disputes the contents or views contained therein, the Juvenile Court may give such child or, as the case may be, guardian an opportunity of producing such evidence as may be relevant to the matter stated in the report.

137. Under section-10 of the Juvenile Justice System Ordinance, 2000 if a child is arrested for commission of an offence, the officer in-charge of the police station in which the child is detained shall, as soon as may be, inform the guardian of the child, if he can be found, of such arrest and inform him of the time, date and name of the Juvenile Court before which the child shall be produced and the concerned Probation Officer to enable him to obtain such information about the child and other material circumstances which may be of assistance to the Juvenile Court for making inquiry. If a child accused of non-bailable offence is arrested, he shall, without any delay and in no case later than twenty-four hours from such arrest, be produced before the Juvenile Court.

138. Without prejudice to the provisions of the Criminal Procedure Code of Pakistan, if a child is accused of a bailable offence he shall be released by the Juvenile Court on bail, with or without surety, unless it appears that there are reasonable grounds for believing that the release of the child shall bring him into association with any criminal or expose the child to any danger, in which case, the child shall be placed under the custody of a Probation Officer or a suitable person or institution dealing with the welfare of the children if parents or guardian of the child is not present, but shall not under any circumstances be kept in a police station or jail in such cases.

139. The Juvenile Court, in a case where a child is not granted bail, direct for tracing the guardian of such child and where the guardian of the child is traced out, the Juvenile Court may immediately release the child on bail. Where a child under the age of 15 years is arrested or detained for an offence which is punishable with the imprisonment of less than ten years, he shall be treated as if he was accused of commission of a bailable offence. No child under the age of 15 years can be arrested under any of the laws dealing with the previous detention or under the provisions of Chapter VII of the Code of Criminal Procedure.

140. Notwithstanding anything contained in the Code of Criminal Procedure and except where a Juvenile Court is of the opinion that the delay in the trial of the accused has been occasioned by an act or omission of the accused or any other person acting on his behalf or in exercise of any right or privilege under any law for the time being in force, a child who, for commission of an offence, has been detained, shall be released on bail; if, being accused of an offence punishable with death has been detained for such offence for a continuous period exceeding one year and whose trial for such an offence has not concluded; if, being accused of any offence punishable for improvement for life has been detained for such an offence for a continuous period exceeding six months and whose trial for such offence has not concluded; or who, being accused of any offence not punishable with death, or imprisonment for life, has been detained for such an offence for a continuous period exceeding four months and whose trial for such an offence has not concluded; provided that where a child of the age of 15 years or above is arrested, the court may refuse to grant bail if there are reasonable grounds to believe that such child is involved in an offence which in its option is serious, heinous, gruesome, brutal, sensational in character or shocking to public morality or he is a previous convict of an offence punishable with death or imprisonment for life.

141. Under section-11 of the Juvenile Justice System Ordinance, 2000 if on conclusion of an inquiry or trial, the Juvenile Court finds that a child has committed an offence, then not withstanding anything to the contrary contained in any law for the time being in force, the Juvenile Court may, if it thinks fit; direct the child offender to be released on probation for good conduct and place such a child under the case of guardian or any suitable person executing a bond with or without surety as the court may require, for good behaviour and wellbeing of child for any period not exceeding the period of imprisonment awarded to such child: provided that the child released on probation be produced before the Juvenile Court periodically on such dates and time as it may direct; make an order directing the child offender to be sent to a borstal institution until he attains the age of 18 years or for the period of imprisonment whichever is earlier' reduce the period of imprisonment or probation in the case where the Court is satisfied that further imprisonment or probation shall be unnecessary.

142. Under section-12 of the Juvenile Justice System Ordinance, 2000, notwithstanding anything to the country contained in any low, no child can be awarded punishment of death, or ordered to labour during the time spent in any borstal or such other institution; and handcuffed, put in fetters or given any corporal punishment at any time which is custody; provided that where there is reasonable apprehension of the escape of the child from custody, he may be handcuffed.

143. Under section-13 of the Juvenile Justice System Ordinance, 2000 a child convicted on a trial by a Juvenile Court, or any other person on his behalf, may, within thirty days from the date of such order, prefer an appeal in accordance with the provisions of the Code of Criminal Procedure. The Provisional Government or any person aggrieved by an order or acquittal passed by a Juvenile Court, may within thirty days prefer an appeal against such order in accordance with the provisions of section 417 of the Code of Criminal Procedure.

144. Medical certificate showed that on the day of examination, age of petitioner was found to be 16–17 years and from the certificate it was established, that at the time of commission of offence, petitioner was a child less than 18 years of age. In the present case, petitioner was in custody since November, 2003, whereas it was clearly provided under section 10(7)(a) of Juvenile Justice System Ordinance, 2000, that a child accused of an offence punishable with death becomes entitled to bail if he remained in custody for a continuous period exceeding one year and his trial had not been concluded. Accused, who came within the definition of 'child', was entitled for grant of bail, even if involved in case punishable with death and such concession was subject to limitations contained in the said Ordinance. Bail was granted to accused in circumstances [section 497. Juvenile Justice System Ordinance (XXII of 2000), section 10(7)(a). Penal Code (XLV of 1860), sections 302 & 324/34. Offences Against Property (Enforcement of Hudood) Ordinance (VI of 1979), section 17(2)] SHC (2009 PCrLJ 47).

145. Grant of bail to a child. A child, accused of an offence punishable with death would become entitled to bail under section 10(7) of Juvenile Justice System Ordinance, 2000, if he had remained in custody for a continuous period exceeding one year and his trial had not concluded. In view of the Proviso to sub-section (7) of section 10 of Juvenile Justice System Ordinance, 2000, the Court could refuse to grant bail if reasonable grounds were to believe that such child was involved in an offence which, in the opinion of the Court, was, serious, heinous, gruesome, brutal, sensational in character or shocking to public morality or he was a previous convict of an offence punishable, with death or imprisonment for life. Charge against accused was framed after more than one and half years of his arrest for which delay accused was not responsible. Accused was also not a previous convict. According to Post-mortem examination report, deceased had sustained only one injury caused by a single fire. Accused, in circumstances, had not acted desperately or brutally. In such circumstances, it could not be said that accused was involved in an offence of serious, heinous, gruesome, brutal, sensational in character or shocking to public morality. Accused, in circumstances was entitled to be released on bail [section 497.

Penal Code (XLV of 1860), section 302. Juvenile Justice System Ordinance (XXII of 2000), section 10(7)] SHC (2006 MLD 507).

146. Bail was granted to accused mainly on grounds of delay in lodging FIR and minor age of accused under provisions of Juvenile Justice System Ordinance, 2000. Delay in lodging FIR had been explained, even otherwise delay in lodging FIR in such like cases, was usually ignored. Abundant evidence was on record, showing that at the time of occurrence, accused was more than 16 years. X-Ray report which was more authentic than physical medical examination and school record showed that the accused was more than 18 years of age on the day of occurrence. Case of accused, in circumstances neither was to be governed by proviso to sub-section (1) of section 497, Cr.P.C. nor by definition of 'child ' as given in section 2(b) of Juvenile Justice System Ordinance, 2000. Plea that trial of accused had started, was without any force, in view of facts and circumstances of case. Accused having wrongly been granted bail, same was cancelled and accused was taken into custody and was sent to jail [section 497(5). Offence of *Zina* (Enforcement of Hudood) Ordinance (VII of 1979), sections 6 & 10] PHC (2005 YLR 3196).

147. Age of accused. Accused had pressed his bail application only on the ground of delay in the conclusion of Trial under section 10(7) of Juvenile Justice System Ordinance, 2000, as according to him he was a 'child ' as defined in section 2(b) of Juvenile Justice System Ordinance, 2000 and that despite passage of more than a year, the trial had not concluded and that accused was not responsible for said delay. School Leaving Certificate produced by accused showed that he was of II years at the time of commission of offence and according to Medical Board, accused was between 17 and 18 years. Accused, in circumstances was a 'child' as defined in section 2(b) of Juvenile Justice System Ordinance, 2000 and under section 10(7) of said Ordinance, he being 'child ' was entitled to bail, if he had remained in custody for a continuous period exceeding one year and trial had not concluded. Nothing was on record to show that accused was a previous convict or that delay was occasioned by him. Nothing was also on record to show that offence of accused was serious, heinous, gruesome, brutal, sensational in character or shocking to public morality. Accused was admitted to bail in circumstances [section 497. Penal Code (XLV of 1860), section 302. Juvenile Justice System Ordinance (XXII of 2000), sections 2(b) & 10(7)] SHC (2007 YLR 2079).

148. Accused was of less than 18 years on date of incident. Accused remained in custody for more than four months. Delay in trial was not due to acts of accused. Accused was neither previous convict nor involved in an offence of serious, heinous, gruesome, brutal, sensational in character or shocking to public morality. Punishment for offence committed by accused was not death; thus, such offence could not be said to be serious and heinous. Accused due to abscondence would lose some of his rights, but he being a child would be entitled to concession of bail. Case of accused did not fall within proviso to section 10 of Juvenile Justice System Ordinance, 2000. Accused was granted bail in circumstances {SHC (2006 PCRLJ 1809)}.

149. According to School Certificate and Medical Certificate, accused at the time of incident being under the age of 18 years, was a child within the meaning of section 4(3) of Juvenile Justice System Ordinance, 2000. Juvenile Justice System Ordinance, 2000, being a special law enforced in order to safeguard the rights of children/minors involved in criminal cases, who deserved reasonable concession because of their tender age, its provisions, were to be liberally construed/interpreted in favour of child accused. Once accused had come within the definition of child, he was entitled to grant of bail, even if involved in the case punishable with death. Said concession, however was subject to limitation contained in Cl. (c) of sub-section (7) of section 10 of Juvenile Justice System Ordinance, 2000 and manner in which alleged offence was committed by accused, could not be said to be coming within four corners of the said proviso. No material was on record to show that accused was previously convicted. Accused was in custody since last about one year and record had further shown that after framing of the charge, case was not proceeded, some time due to absence of counsel for accused and some time for other reasons. Overall delay in trial could not be totally attributed to accused in circumstances. Accused, in circumstances was found entitled to concession of bail {SHC (2006 PCRLJ 1648)}.

150. Awarding rigorous imprisonment to a child. Accused had not been named in the FIR, and no identification parade had taken place. No recovery of any Kalashnikov or other arms, identity cards or cash, was made from accused persons. No statement of either of accused persons was recorded under section 161, Cr.P.C. though it was stated that when a Jeep crossed the stolen vehicle, one of accused jumped from the vehicle in question and ran away and was injured by fire shot. No evidence of the persons driving the Jeep or sitting therein had been produced nor was any evidence available as to who fired at accused. One of the prosecution witnesses had stated that no signature of any witness of recovery was obtained, and he also did not remember the time of arrest of accused, and how long he was being questioned. Other prosecution witness who was police officer did not remember as to how long accused had remained in police custody. Cumulative effect of such loopholes, discrepancies and lapses in evidence and procedure necessarily led to benefit of doubt in favour of accused paving way to their acquittal and acceptance of their appeals. Even otherwise accused person being child within the meaning of section 2(b) of Juvenile Justice System Ordinance, 2000, who had not attained the age of 18 years, could not be awarded rigorous imprisonment in flagrant violation of section 12 of Juvenile Justice System Ordinance, 2000. Accepting appeals filed by accused, impugned judgments were set aside with direction to release accused [section 392. Offences against Property (Enforcement of Hudood) Ordinance (VI of 1979), sections 17(3) & 24. Juvenile Justice System Ordinance (XXII of 2000), sections 2(b), 12 & 13] FSC (2007 PCRLJ 497).

Chapter 4. Names

§1. Forename

151. Forename is considered a name to which normally person is called in daily life. As for calling people by their first and second names on the Doomsday, it is correct as reported in *Saheeh al-Bukhari* (an authentic book of Hadith – Holy Prophet Muhammad's PBUH tradition) no matter whether it is a compound or a single name.

152. Giving a good name to a new born child is recommended in Islam. Holy Prophet Muhammad (PBUH) said that the best names are Abdullah and Abdur Rahman as narrated in Sahih Muslim from Ibn Umar, he said that the Holy Prophet Muhammad (PBUH) said*: The names dearest to Allah are Abdullah and Abdur Rahman.*

153. It is narrated Sunan Abu Dawood that the Holy Prophet Muhammad (PBUH) said: 'Call yourselves by the names of the Prophets. The dearest names to Allah are Abdullah and Abdur Rahman, the truest are Harith (the cultivator) and Hammam (always thinking of initiating something) and the worst are Harb (the war) and Murrah (the bitter)'. The Holy Prophet Muhammad (PBUH) himself gave his sons and daughters good names.

154. Among the most favoured names are the names of Prophets, Angels, companions and known pious people. For females, the best names are the names of the wives of the Holy Prophet Muhammad (PBUH), the names of the pious women mentioned in the Holy Quran, the names of the daughters of the Holy Prophet Muhammad (PBUH) and the names of the female companions of the Holy Prophet Muhammad (PBUH) as well as the names of the good, pious Muslim women. It is dislikeable to use names with bad meanings like 'fire' and the similar words.

155. Moreover, Islam forbids names that declare servitude to anyone other than Allah such as 'slave of Jesus. ... '. Islam also forbids names that are similar to the Names of Allah such as Ar Raheem (The most compassionate) or Al Hakeem (The most Wise). But if the definite article 'Al', 'The' is omitted, then such names become permissible. Naming 'Naa'ilah' is allowed; it was the name of the wife of 'Uthmaan ibn Affaan'. If it were a bad name, he would certainly have changed it to a good one.

156. LHC held that it is difficult to enumerate which was an Islamic name and which was un-Islamic. Any name which did not derogate or offend against any of Islamic principles of faith, could be treated and accepted as Islamic name. Muslim names differ from place to place and from country to country. Names which though had no similarity with Arabian names or names used by Muslims of other countries, such names could not be treated as un-Islamic and holders of such names could not be held as non-Muslims (LHC – 1999 CLC 1202).

§2. SURNAME

I. Acquisition of the Surname

157. It is normal practice that name of father of child is given as surname in Pakistan. For females, the surname is normally changed to the name of her husband, which is not allowed according to some Islamic Scholars. However, there is no law in Pakistan which restricts or obligates anybody to opt or leave any surname. It is purely wish of the parents to give the surname or a person opt any surname when he/she is grownup. Normally the father's name is considered as surname.

II. Change of the Surname

158. According to Islamic Scholars, the surname is considered the father's name of child, therefore, change of surname is not allowed. However in Pakistan normally females change their surnames to their husband's names after marriage. However, according to Islamic Scholars change of surname of father to husband is not allowed.

Chapter 5. Nationality

§1. Citizenship

159. The principal legislation is the Pakistan Citizenship Act 1951, as amended by the Pakistan Citizenship (Amendment) Act 1952, the Pakistan Citizenship (Amendment) Act 1972, the Pakistan Citizenship (Amendment) Act 1973, the Pakistan Citizenship (second Amendment) Act 1973 and the Pakistan Citizenship (Amendment) Ordinance 2000 regarding citizenship of Pakistan. According to the Pakistan Laws, any person born in Pakistan after commencement of above Act is considered citizen of Pakistan.

160. Authorities received notice of divorce from husband but having come to know that the wife was British national and the husband had acquired nationality of Zimbabwe, declined to proceed any, further under the provisions of Muslim Family Laws Ordinance, 1961. Nothing to such effect was on record nor had it been urged by the parties that they had ceased to be citizens of Pakistan or if so in what circumstances and through what process. In absence of such express relinquishment of Pakistani citizenship, both the parties would continue to fall within the ambit of section 1(2) of Muslim Family Laws Ordinance, 1961. All the provisions of Muslim Family Laws Ordinance, 1961, were applicable to the parties. Order passed by the authorities was set aside and the case was remanded to them for proceeding on the notice of divorce. Petition was allowed accordingly (LHC 2005 CLC 481).

§2. Acquisition of Citizenship

161. According to the Pakistan Laws any person born in Pakistan after commencement of Pakistan Citizenship Act, 1952 is considered citizen of Pakistan. A person born outside Pakistan before 18 April 2000 can normally only be a citizen of Pakistan by descent if the father was a citizen of Pakistan otherwise than by descent. However, a person born outside Pakistan to a father who, at the time of the birth, was a citizen of Pakistan by descent is also a citizen of Pakistan by descent if: the birth is registered at a Pakistani Consulate or High Commission abroad; or the father was in Pakistan Government service at the time of birth.

162. A person born outside Pakistan on or after 18 April 2000 is a citizen of Pakistan by descent if either parent is a citizen of Pakistan. A citizen of Pakistan who is also (or is about to become) a citizen of another country can make a declaration of renunciation of Pakistani citizenship.

163. Dual nationality is not permitted. A citizen of Pakistan who is, at the same time, a citizen of some other country ceases to be a citizen of Pakistan unless that other citizenship is renounced. However, the Government of Pakistan signed treaty with some countries according to which the nationals of Pakistan need not to surrender their nationality after seeking the nationality of said country.

164. If a Pakistani woman marries a foreigner and acquires his nationality, her Pakistani citizenship is withdrawn but may be restored if the marriage comes to an end, and she renounces her husband's nationality.

165. Minors (i.e., persons under 21 years of age) who qualify for Pakistani citizenship are exempt from the ban on dual nationality if they acquire another citizenship as long as their fathers do not cease to be citizens of Pakistan automatically as a result of acquiring a second citizenship, or due to renunciation of Pakistani citizenship. However, if the father ceases to be a citizen of Pakistan, the minor automatically loses Pakistani citizenship at the same time.

Chapter 6. Domicile and Residence

§1. Domicile

166. The Domicile is a certificate issued by the Government of Pakistan under the Pakistan Citizenship Act, 1952 and Rules made thereunder which confirms the residence of any individual, its nationality, citizenship, place of domicile and date of arrival in the place of domicile. The domicile certificate also provides the names of individual's children, their ages, individual's trade or occupation and marks of identification. The domicile is issued after certain conditions under section-17 of the Pakistan citizenship Act, 1952 are fulfilled by the individual.

§2. Domicile of Origin

167. The Domicile in Pakistan confirms the origin of the individual. The domicile issued under the Citizenship Act, 1952 identifies the person's existing origin which helps the individual in obtaining employment. In the Government sector, number of available job opportunities, are allocated to the residents of each Province of Pakistan. Therefore, the individuals having domicile of their Province applied accordingly. The Succession Act, 1925 (Part-II) provides detail of domicile for succession in Pakistan.

168. Under the Succession Act, 1925 a person can have only one domicile for the purpose of the succession to his moveable property. The domicile of origin of every person of legitimate birth is in the country in which at the time of his birth his father was domiciled; or, if he is a posthumous child, in the country in which his father was domiciled at the time of the fathers death. At the time of the birth of A, his father was domiciled in England. As domicile of origin is in England, whatever may be the country in which he was born. The domicile of origin of an illegitimate child is in the country in which, at the time of his birth, his mother was domiciled. The domicile of origin prevails until a new domicile has been acquired.

169. A man acquires a new domicile by taking up his fixed habitation in a country which is not that of his domicile of origin. A man is not to be deemed to have taken up his fixed habitation in Pakistan merely by reason of his residing therein the civil, military, naval or air force service of Pakistan or in the exercise of any profession or calling. (i) A, whose domicile of origin is in England, proceeds to Pakistan, where he settles as a barrister or a merchant, intending to reside there during the remainder of his life. His domicile is now in Pakistan. (ii) A, whose domicile is in England, goes to Austria, and enters the Austrian service, intending to remain in that service. A has acquired a domicile in Austria. (iii) A, whose domicile of origin is in France, comes to reside in Pakistan under an engagement with the Federal Government for a certain number of years. It is his intention to return to France at the end of that period. He does not acquire a domicile in Pakistan. (iv) A, whose domicile is in England, goes to reside in Pakistan for the purpose of winding up the affairs of a partnership which has been dissolved, and with the intention of returning to England as soon as that purpose is accomplished. He does not by such residence acquire a domicile in Pakistan, however long the residence may last. (v) A, having gone to reside in Pakistan in the circumstances mentioned in the preceding illustration, afterwards alters his intention, and takes up his fixed habitation in Pakistan. A has acquired a domicile in Pakistan. (vi) A, whose domicile is in the French Settlement of Chandernagore, is compelled by political events to take refuge in Peshawar, and resides in Peshawar for many years in the hope of such political changes as may enable him to return with safety to Chandernagore. He does not by such residence acquire a domicile in Pakistan. (vii) A, having come to Peshawar in the circumstances stated in the preceding illustration, continues to reside there after such political changes have occurred as would enable him to return with safety to Chandernagore, and he intends that his residence in Peshawar shall be permanent. A has acquired a domicile in Pakistan.

170. Any person may acquire a domicile in Pakistan, by making and depositing in some office in Pakistan, appointed in this behalf by the Provincial Government, a declaration in writing under his hand of his desire to acquire such domicile; provided that he has been resident in Pakistan for one year immediately preceding the time of his making such declaration.

171. A person who is appointed by the Government of one country to be its ambassador, consul or other representative in another country does not acquire a domicile in the latter country by reason only of residing there in pursuance of his appointment; nor does any other person acquire such domicile by reason only of residing with such first-mentioned person as part of his family, or as a servant.

172. A new domicile continues until the former domicile has been resumed or another has been acquired. The domicile of a minor follows the domicile of the parent from whom he derived his domicile of origin. Exception: The domicile of a minor does not change with that of his parent, if the minor is married, or holds any office or employment in the service of the State, or has set up, with the consent of the parent, in any distinct business.

173. By marriage, a woman acquires the domicile of her husband, if she had not the same domicile before. A wife's domicile during her marriage follows the domicile of her husband. Exception: the wife's domicile no longer follows that of her husband if they are separated by the sentence of a competent Court, or if the husband is undergoing a sentence of transportation. Save as hereinbefore otherwise provided in this Part, a person cannot, during minority, acquire a new domicile. An insane person cannot acquire a new domicile in any other way than by his domicile following the domicile of another person.

174. If a person dies leaving moveable property in Pakistan, in the absence of proof of any domicile elsewhere, succession to the property is regulated by the law of Pakistan.

175. If a person whose domicile is not in Pakistan marries in Pakistan to a person whose domicile is in Pakistan, neither party acquires by the marriage any rights in respect of any property of the other party not comprised in a settlement made previous to the marriage, which he/she would not acquire thereby if both were domiciled in Pakistan at the time of the marriage.

Chapter 7. Mentally Handicapped Persons

§1. Criminal Law

176. Under the Islamic Law, if a person commits sin who is mentally handicapped, he is not held accountable for it. The Holy Prophet Muhammad (PBUH) said: *The pen is lifted (stopped from writing the deeds) from three kinds of people: a sleeping person until he wakes up, a mentally-handicapped or insane person till he can reason, and a child till he reaches the age of puberty.* However, if the sin is related to the right of others such as stealing from someone, then it should be paid back to the rightful person if he is available or to his inheritors, if they are known, if he has died; otherwise, the object should be given as charity.

177. Article-38(d) of the Constitution of Islamic Republic of Pakistan, 1973, stipulates that the State shall provide basic necessities of life, such as food, clothing, housing, education and medical relief, for all such citizens, irrespective of sex, caste, creed or race, as they are permanently or temporarily unable to earn their livelihood on account of infirmity, sickness or unemployment.

§2. Suits by or against Lunatics

178. Under Code of Civil Procedure, 1908 (order XXXII), the procedure for suits by or against minors and persons of unsound mind is provided. Under Order XXXII of the Code of Civil Procedure 1908, Rule-15 the provisions contained in Rules 1~14 are extended to persons adjudged to be of unsound mind and to persons who though not so adjudged are found by the Court in inquiry, by reason of unsoundness of mind or mental infirmity, to be incapable of protecting their interests when suing or being sued. The Rules for suit by or against minors and persons of unsound mind are provided hereinafter.

179. Every suit by a minor shall be instituted in his name by a person who in such suit shall be called the next friend of the minor. Where a suit is instituted by or on behalf of a minor without a next friend, the defendant may apply to have the plaint taken off the file, with costs to us paid by the pleader or other person by whom it was presented.

180. Notice of such application shall be given to such person and the Court after hearing his objections (if any) may make such order in the matter as it thinks fit. Where the defendant is a minor, the Court on being satisfied of the fact of his minority shall appoint a proper person to be guardian for the suit for such minor.

181. An order for the appointment of a guardian for the suit may be obtained upon application in the name and on behalf of the minor or by the plaintiff. Such application shall be supported by an affidavit verifying the fact that the proposed guardian has no interest in the matters in controversy in the suit adverse to that of the minor and that he is a fit person to be so appointed.

182. No order shall be made on any application except upon notice to minor and to any guardian of the minor appointed or declared by an authority competent in that behalf, or, where there is no such guardian upon notice to the father or other natural guardian of the minor, or, where there is no father or other natural guardian, to the person in whose case the minor is, and after hearing any objection which may be urged on behalf of any person served with notice.

183. A person appointed to be guardian for the suit for a minor shall, unless his appointment is terminated by retirement, removal or death, continues as such throughout all proceedings arising out of the suit including proceedings in any Appellate or Revisional Court and any proceedings in the execution of a decree.

184. Any person who is of sound mind and has attained majority may act as next friend of a minor or as his guardian for the suit, provided that the interest of such person is not adverse to that of the minor and that he is not, in the case of a next friend, a defendant or, in the case of a guardian for the suit, a plaintiff.

185. Where a minor has a guardian appointed or declared by competent authority, no person other than such guardian shall act as the next of the minor or be appointed his guardian for the suit unless the Court considers for reasons to be recorded, that it is for the minor's welfare that another person be permitted to act or be appointed, as the case may be. No person shall without his consent be appointed guardian for the suit.

186. Where there is no other person fit and willing to act as guardian for the suit, the Court may appoint any of its officers to be such guardian, and may direct that the costs to be incurred by such officer in the performance of his duties as such guardian shall be borne either by the parties or by any one or more of the parties to the suit, or out of any fund in Court in which the minor is interested, and may give directions for the repayment or allowance of such costs as justice and the circumstances the case may require.

187. Every application to the Court on behalf of a minor, other than an application shall be made by his next friend or by his guardian for the suit. Every order made in a suit or on any application before the Court in or by which a minor is in any way concerned or affected, without such minor being represented by a next friend or guardian for the suit, as the case may be, may be discharged and, where the pleader of the party at whose instance such order was obtained knew, or might reasonably have known, the fact of such minority, with costs to be paid by such pleader.

188. A next friend or guardian for the suit shall not, without the leave of the Court receive any money or other moveable property on behalf of a minor either, (a) by way of compromise before decree or order, or (b) under a decree or order in favour of the minor.

189. Where the next friend or guardian for the suit has not been appointed or declared by competent authority to be guardian of the property of the minor, or, having been so appointed or declared, is under any disability known to the Court to receive the money or other moveable property the Court shall if it grants him leave to receive the property require such security and give such directions as will in its opinion, sufficiently protect the property from waste and ensure its proper application.

190. No next friend or guardian for the suit shall without the leave of the Court expressly recorded in the proceedings enter into any agreement or compromise on behalf of a minor with reference to the suit in which he acts as next friend or guardian. Any such agreement or compromise entered into without the leave of the Court so recorded shall be voidable against all parties other than the minor.

191. Unless otherwise ordered by the Court, a next friend shall not retire without first procuring a fit person to be put in his place and giving security for the costs already incurred. The application for the appointment of a new next friend shall be supported by an affidavit showing the fitness of the person proposed, and also that he has no interest adverse to that of the minor.

192. Where the interest of the next friend of a minor is adverse to that of the minor or where he is so connected with a defendant whose interest is adverse to that of the minor as to make it unlikely that the minor's interest will be properly protected by him, or where he does not do his duty, or, during the pendency of the suit, ceases to reside within Pakistan or for any other sufficient cause application may be made on behalf of the minor or by a defendant for his removal; and the Court, if satisfied of the sufficiency of the cause assigned may order the next friend to be removed accordingly and make such other order as to costs as it thinks fit.

193. Where the next friend is not a guardian appointed or declared by an authority competent in this behalf and an application is made by a guardian so appointed or declared, who desires to be himself appointed in the place of the next friend, the Court shall remove the next friend unless it considers for reasons to be recorded by it that the guardian ought not to be appointed the next friend of the minor and shall thereupon appoint the applicant to be next friend in his place upon such terms as to the costs already incurred in the suit as it thinks fit.

194. On the retirement removal or death of the next friend of a minor, further proceedings shall be stayed until the appointment of a next friend in his place. Where the pleader of such minor omits within a reasonable time to take steps to get a new next friend appointed, any person interested in the minor or in the matter in issue may apply to the Court for the appointment of one, and the Court may appoint such person as it thinks fit.

195. Where the guardian for the suit desires to retire or does not do his duty, or where other sufficient ground is made to appear, the Court may permit such guardian to retire or may remove him, and may make such order as to costs as it thinks fit. Where the guardian for the suit retires, dies or is removed by the Court during the pendency of the suit the Court shall appoint a new guardian in his place.

196. A minor plaintiff or a minor not a party to a suit on whose behalf an application is pending shall, on attaining majority, elect whether he will proceed with the suit or application. Where he elects to proceed with the suit or application made shall apply for an order discharging the next friend and for leave to proceed in his own name. The title of the suit or application shall in such case be corrected so as to read henceforth: 'A. B., late a minor, by C.D., his next friend, but now having attained majority'.

197. Where he elects to abandon the suit or application, he shall if a sole plaintiff or sole applicant, apply for an order to dismiss the suit or application on repayment of the costs incurred by the defendant or apposite-party or which may have been paid by his next friend. Any application under this rule may be made ex parte, but no order discharging a next friend and permitting a minor plaintiff to proceed in his own name shall be made without any notice to the next friend.

198. Where a minor co-plaintiff on attaining majority desires to repudiate the suit, he shall apply to have his name struck out as co-plaintiff; and the Court, if it finds that he is not a necessary party shall dismiss him from the suit on such terms as to costs or otherwise as it thinks fit. Notice of the application shall be served on the next friend on any co-plaintiff and on the defendant. The costs of all parties of such application and of all or any proceedings theretofore had in the suit, shall be paid by such persons as the Court directs. Where the applicant is a necessary party to the suit, the Court may direct him to be made a defendant.

199. A minor on attaining majority may, if a sole plaintiff, apply that a suit instituted in his name by his next friend be dismissed on the ground that it was unreasonable or improper. Notice of the application shall be served on all the parties concerned; and the Court upon being satisfied of such unreasonableness or impropriety, may grant the application and order the next friend to pay the costs of all parties in respect of the application and of anything done in the suit, or make such other order as it thinks fit.

§3. Marriage

200. Marriage in Islam is based on a contract between a man and woman intending to be unified in marriage. Thus, as in any contract in Islam, there are elements which are considered essential to its existence, called 'pillars', as well as the possibility of stipulations of different kinds, legal effects of the contract, etc. Each of these must be understood correctly in order to ensure that the marriage has been performed according to the legal conditions, and that the rightful effects of the marriage are guaranteed to each of the contracting parties. The Pillars of a Marriage Contract according to the majority of Scholars include offer and acceptance from the woman's side and the acceptance from the man; two parties to the contract: the prospective husband and the guardian of the woman; presence of witnesses and dowry. Therefore, any marriage with mentally handicapped person is void under the Pakistani and Islamic Laws.

201. Under Article 2(vi) of the Dissolution of Muslim Marriages Act, 1939 if husband has been insane for a period of two years or is suffering from leprosy or a virulent venereal disease, the woman married under the Islamic Law is entitled to obtain decree for dissolution of her marriage.

Part II. Family Law

Chapter 1. Marriage

§1. The Nature of Marriage

202. Marriage is considered a contract between the husband and wife under the Pakistani laws. SCP declared that it is well-settled that marriage among Muslims is not a sacrament, but is in the nature of a civil contract. Such a contract undoubtedly has spiritual and moral overtones and undertones, but legally, in essence, it remains a contract between the parties which can be subject of dissolution for good cause. In this respect, Islam, the *Din-al-Fitrat*, conforms to the dictates of human nature and does not prescribe the binding together of a man and woman to what has been described as 'holy deadlock'.

203. Marriage in Islam is intended to cater to multiple purposes which include, above all, spiritual tranquility and peace, and cooperation and partnership in fulfilling the divine mandate. According to the Holy Quran, tranquility and peace through a successful union is considered the primary objective of marriage: (Among His signs is that He created for you spouses of your own kind in order that you may repose to them in tranquility and He instilled in your hearts love and affection for one another; verily, in these are signs for those who reflect (on the nature of the reality).) (Ar-Rum 30: 21). In another place, Allah refers to the relationship between males and females in terms of partnership for achieving goodness and fulfilling the divine mandate for their lives. (The believers, males and females, are partners of one another; they shall jointly enjoin all that is good and counsel against all that is evil.) (At-Tawbah 9: 71)

§2. The Capacity to Marry

204. The validity of a marriage under Islamic Law depends primarily on the capacity of the parties to marry each other. The performance of the marriage is according to the form prescribed in the place where the marriage is celebrated or which would impress on the woman by the Customary Law of the Muslims and the status of a wife is matter of secondary consideration.

I. Different Sex

205. Both under the Pakistani and Islamic Laws it is absolute necessary that marriage should be held between male and female. Any other marriage between two males or two females is strictly prohibited in Islam and considered a great sin and punishable under the laws.

II. Consanguinity

206. Under the Islamic Laws, marriage between certain relatives is not allowed and is strictly prohibited. These are the relationships expressly prohibited by the Shari'ah to secure the development and maintenance of a sound family and social structure. It is imperative for the creation of a sound and stable family and social structure to give sanctity to a few relations and to remove all kinds of sexual interaction between these relations. Thus, the stated prohibition secures the existence not only of mothers, fathers, brothers and sisters but also that of aunts and uncles, nieces and nephews, in-laws and foster relationships. All these relations are sanctified by the Qur'an and have, therefore, been declared prohibited for marriage.

207. In the Holy Quran (Sura Al-Nisa) it is stipulated that:

> And marry not women whom your fathers married – except what has been done in the past: it was shameful and odious – an abominable practice indeed. Prohibited to you [for marriage] are your mothers, daughters, sisters, your maternal and paternal aunts, the daughters of your brothers and sisters; your mothers who have suckled you and your sisters through fosterage, the mothers of your wives, your step-daughters raised under you, born of your wives with whom you have la'in – no offence if you have not la'in with their mothers, and the wives of your begotten sons, and two sisters in wedlock at the same time, except for what has already happened. God indeed is Oft-Forgiving, Most Merciful. Also [prohibited are] women already married, except those whom your right hands possess; this is a written obligation upon you from God (4:22-4).

III. Marriageable Age

208. Under the prevailing laws in Pakistan, a male can legally marry at the age of 18 years with a female who has attained the age of 16 years as stipulated under the Child Marriage Restraint Act, 1929. Whoever, being a male above 18 years of age, contracts marriage with female below 16 years of age shall be punishable with simple imprisonment which may extend to one month, or with fine which may extend to PKR 1,000, or with both.

209. Whoever performs, conducts or directs any marriage below the age limit prescribed is punishable with simple imprisonment which may extend to one month, or with fine which may extend to PKR 1,000, or with both, unless he proves that he had reason to believe that the marriage was not a child marriage.

210. Where a minor contracts a child marriage any person having charge of the minor, whether as parent or guardian or in any other capacity, lawful or unlawful, who does any act to promote the marriage or permits it to be solemnized, or negligently fails to prevent it from being solemnized, shall be punishable with simple imprisonment which may extend to one month, or with fine which may extend to PKR 1,000, or with both: Provided that no woman shall be punishable with imprisonment. For this purpose, it shall be presumed, unless and until the contrary is proved, that where a minor has contracted a child marriage, the person having charge of such minor has negligently failed to prevent the marriage from being solemnized.

211. LHC (2006 PCRLJ 1260) held: Quashing of FIR Complainant, who was brother-in-law of alleged abductee, had himself mentioned in FIR the age of alleged abductee as 17 years. Alleged abductee in her affidavit had stated that no body had abducted her; that her age was 19 years; that she entered into a tie of marriage with petitioner/accused out of her own volition. Girl had personally appeared before the Court and supported stance of petitioner/accused. Alleged abductee had stated that her marriage was performed through registered *Nikahnama*, and that since then she was living with her husband/ petitioner/ accused. Under Islamic Law, a girl on attaining age of puberty would be deemed to have attained majority, which in Pakistan was about thirteen years. Alleged abductee, who was major, appeared to be sensible from her appearance. Both spouses were living together for about 11/4 years. In view of respective claims of parties and *Nikahnama* registered with Union Council, it appeared that there had been a lawful marriage union between accused and alleged abductee, and they had not committed any cognizable offence. Law regarding marriage was settled to the effect that where two major Muslims of sound mind solemnized marriage by entering into a contract for procreation and legalization of their children according to Muslim Family Laws Ordinance, 1961, no cognizable offence under Offence of *Zina* (Enforcement of Hudood) Ordinance, 1979 could be made out. Registration of criminal case against petitioner was apparently without commission of cognizable offence and was opted by police concerned, out of sheer misuse of process of law. Both Constitutional petitions were accepted and FIR was quashed [section 11. Constitution of Pakistan (1973), Article 199].

212. LHC (2006 PCRLJ 1277) held: FIR registration of FIR and birth certificate showing girl to be major/sui juris. Affidavit of girl that nobody had abducted her, rather she on her own had left the house of her mother. *Nikahnama* registered with Union Council showing existence of lawful marriage between parties, who were living together. Registration of FIR was without commission of cognizable offence and sheer misuse of process of law.

213. LHC (1994 CLC 1046): Dissolution of Muslim Marriages Act 1939 section 2(vii). Dissolution of marriage. Right of option of puberty exercise of female who was married at the age of 5/6 years, on attaining puberty, exercised her right of option of puberty, repudiated marriage and filed suit for Dissolution of marriage on that ground. Husband had himself stated that age of girl at the time of Rukhsati was below 15 years and that no consummation had taken place after age of 15 years which was, presumptive age of puberty. Suit for Dissolution of marriage was filed by girl well within her right to repudiate her marriage which had taken place during time when she was minor. Court in circumstances had rightly dissolved marriage which was just and fair and could not be interfered with.

214. Every Muslim of sound mind who has attained puberty may enter into a contract of marriage. Puberty is presumed to have been attained on completion of age of 15 years in the absence of evidence. Provision of section 2(vii), Dissolution of Muslim Marriages Act, 1939, does not lay down that female attains puberty at the age of 16 years only; it simply enables a girl to exercise the option of puberty when she attains age of 16 years [Muslim Family Laws Ordinance 1961 section 13. Dissolution of Muslim Marriages Act (VIII of 1939), section 2(vii)]. LHC (1988 CLC 113).

215. Violation of the provisions of Child Marriage Restraint Act, 1929 sections 3 and 6 do not render the Marriage invalid though it makes punishable a marriage made in violation of its provisions (LHC 1988 CLC 113).

IV. Prior Marriage

216. Under MFLO no man, during the subsistence of an existing marriage, is allowed to contract another marriage, nor shall any such marriage contracted without such permission be registered except with the previous permission in writing of the Arbitration Council.

V. Option of Puberty

217. Under the Disolution of Muslaim Marriage Act, 1939 Article 2(viii) a woman married under Muslim Law is entitled to obtain a decree for dissolution of her marriage on the plea that she has been given in marriage by her father or other guardian before she attained the age of 16 years, repudiated the marriage before attaining the age of 18 years.

218. LHC declared that Wife is entitled to Dissolution of her marriage by exercising option of puberty if she could prove that marriage had taken place before she attained age of 16 years; that marriage had not been consummated and that she had repudiated marriage before attaining age of 18 years. Decree of Court was not necessary to invalidate marriage which had been dissolved by wife in exercise of her option of puberty (2000 MLD 1886).

219. LHC held that alleged detenue was present in Court and stated that she had married the respondent and was living with him on her own freewill and consent as his wife, and that she was not in illegal detention. *Nikah* had been duly registered. According to the medical report, the alleged detenue was 15 years old and being sui juris she could marry on her own accord and choice even without permission of Wali/father. Even the child Marriage Restraint Act, 1929, did not invalidate the marriage once it had been performed. Having attained puberty under Islamic Law, the girl could marry. Alleged detenue having not been found in illegal custody, was set at liberty and allowed to accompany her husband (2006 YLR 2936).

220. Legal requirements: (i) performance of marriage during minority with consent of guardian, (ii) non-consummation of marriage and (iii) repudiation between age of 16 and 18 years. Question essentially of fact. Concurrent findings of lower Courts on such points. Cannot be re-examined in second appeal (LHC – 1970 PLD 475).

221. Necessary conditions only two: (i) repudiation before age of 18; and (ii) non-consummation of marriage. Repudiation, though required to be established as fact, can be proved even by conduct of woman. Woman on reaching puberty refusing, despite efforts of husband, to leave parental home. Circumstance furnishes strong corroboration of repudiation. Dissolution of Muslim Marriages Act (VIII of 1939), section 2(vii) (LHC – 1969 PLD 448).

222. Minor girl retains option till age of 18. Right of annulment continues until she expresses her consent or disapprobation in express terms. Mere consummation does not put an end to right consummation, to be effective, must be with wife's consent. Withholding of assent to marriage may be expressed in variety of ways (e.g., remarriage before age of 18 or institution of suit for Dissolution, etc.) Marriage not consummated. Mere institution of suit for Dissolution automatically annuls marriage under Dissolution of Muslim Marriages Act (VIII of 1939), section 2 (vii) (PHC – 1965 PLD 5).

223. The Supreme Court, Azad Kashmir (1962 PLD 7) Minor below 15 years given in marriage before attaining age of 18 provided marriage not consummated. Consummation 'by force' does not disentitle wife to exercise her option of puberty.

224. Nikah of minor girl by her step-brother. Consummation took place. Before attaining puberty marriage repudiated by girl. Marriage held dissolved (LHC – 1952 PLD 548).

225. Dissolution of marriage on ground of '*Khula*' (divorce opted by wife). Trial Court framed issues pertaining to '*Khula*' and option of puberty, but dissolved marriage on basis of '*Khula*' only. High Court also proceeded to uphold judgment and decree of Trial Court without giving any finding on issue pertaining to option of puberty. Marriage on ground of '*Khula*' having been dissolved by Court on the basis of reliable evidence on record, there was no necessity at all under law to have given findings on other issues as marriage could be dissolved on any of the grounds urged by wife. Contention that it was mandatory under law for Court to have decided issue pertaining to option of puberty was repelled. Case having been decided by Courts fairly, justly and in accordance with law on basis of evidence on record and complete justice having been done between the parties, no case whatsoever for interference had been made out in Intra Court Appeal, especially when no violation of law and evidence was apparent from record [Muslim Family Laws Ordinance 1961 (LHC – 1991 MLD 2338).

VI. Failure to consent

226. In accordance with the West Pakistan Rules made under Muslim Family Laws Ordinance, 1961, a form of *Nikahnama* is prescribed under which signatures of bride and bridegroom are compulsory to solemnize the marriage. Under the Muslim Law, it is absolutely necessary that the man or someone on his behalf and the woman or someone on her behalf should agree to the marriage at one meeting and that the agreement should be witnessed by two adult witnesses. In case of a woman who has not attained majority, the consent of marriage can be given by her father, however, the minor can either adopt it or rescind it as he/she chooses after reaching the age of puberty.

227. When a marriage is contracted on behalf of an adult person of either sex, it is an essential condition to its validity that such person should consent thereto, or in other words, marriage contracted without his/her authority or consent is null and void. Any marriage solemnized without the prior consent of the bride or bridegroom or their appointed representatives or Guardian is invalid.

228. LHC held that Guardian is allowed in Islam to marry their daughters after getting their consent. However, thrusting or forcing marriage without one's consent is against the Islamic Laws (1980 PLC 386).

A. Duress

229. If any marriage is solemnized by force, pressure or duress of family, the wife is entitled to obtain divorce ('*Khula*') through judicial process. Under section-2 of the Dissolution of Muslim Marriage Act, 1939 a woman married under Muslim Law shall be entitled to obtain a decree for dissolution of her marriage on many grounds provided therein.

230. According to the Islamic Law, the forced or duress marriage is not allowed. Abu Hurayrah (Razi Allaho Unho) reported that the Holy Prophet Muhammad (PBUH) said: 'A non-virgin woman may not be married without her command, and a virgin may not be married without her permission; and enough permission for her is to remain silent (because of her natural shyness).' [Al-Bukhaari, Muslim & Others]. Thus, the Holy Prophet Muhammad (PBUH) prohibited forcing a virgin in marriage without her permission, whether by her father or anyone else. Furthermore, Aa'ishah Razi Allaho Unha related that she once asked the Holy Prophet Muhammad (PBUH): 'In the case of a young girl whose parents marry her off, should her permission be sought or not?' HE (PBUH) replied: 'Yes, she must give her permission.' She then said: 'But a virgin would be shy, O Messenger of Allah!' HE (PBUH) replied: 'Her silence is [considered as] her permission.' [Al-Bukhaari, Muslim, & Others].

231. The High Court, Azar Kashmir (2003 PLD 34) held that marriage of a girl by itself would not make her live or reside with her husband, if it was a forced marriage and she was compelled to live with him. Marriage was a civil contract between the spouse solemnized according to social and religious rites of the parties with their free and independent consent. Union had to remain free of coercion and duress, not only at time of marriage but throughout life which was both Islamic and common law/principle. If a woman was forced to a marriage or did not feel convenient to live with spouse at the place where husband wanted, but she felt insecure and was threatened to live, it would amount to illegal custody and detention irrespective of validity or otherwise of the marriage.

232. Female accused being major and sui juris had contracted marriage with co-accused without any duress, coercion or compulsion against the wish and to the annoyance of her parents. Inordinate delay of about 1-3/4 months in lodging the FIR was not plausibly explained. Female accused initially had been shown and treated as a prosecution witness, but on her refusal to support the prosecution she was made a co-accused in the case. Sections 494 & 495, P. P. C. were non-cognizable and section 10(1) of the Offence of *Zina* (Enforcement of Hudood) Ordinance, 1979 had been wrongly applied to the circumstances of the case. No offence whatsoever was made out against the accused, and the charge against them was not substantiated. Courts could not be privy to the *ipse dixit* of the persons still believing in the false notions of the pre-Islamic days and could not act in aid of those who were acting contrary to the Injunctions of Holy Qur'an and Sunnah. Where the spouses were puberty and sui juris and their act was not in defiance of the commands ordained by God, they could not be victimized due to family pride. Continuance of proceedings against the accused in the case amounted to abuse of the process of Court in circumstances, and the same were ordered to be quashed accordingly (SHC - 2000 YLR 488).

233. Alleged abductee stated before Investigating Officer that she had not been abducted; had married with her free-will and produced documents in support thereof and requested him not to take any action on FIR. Investigating Officer, however, continued to harass and humiliate her husband. Such facts had not been denied by Investigating Officer. Neither going away of alleged abduatee from house of her father without any duress nor her marriage had been denied or challenged. Held, no offence under sections 10 & 11 of Offence of *Zina* (Enforcement of Hudood) Ordinance, 1979 and under section 452, P.P.C. had been made out. FIR was declared to have been lodged malafidely, frivolous and vexatious and the same was quashed in circumstances (SHC 1999 PCRLJ 638).

B. Insanity

234. According to the majority of Muslim Scholars (and the four Imams are among them), madness or insanity for some time or all times constitutes a genuine defect that gives the choice to a spouse (husband and wife) to revoke the contract of marriage even though such state of madness takes place once a month, and it produces harm in any form, whether it is before or after making the contract of marriage.

235. Under the Dissolution of Muslim Marriages Act, 1939 Article 2(vi) if husband has been insane for a period of two years or is suffering from leprosy or a virulent venereal disease, the woman married under the Muslim Law is entitled to obtain decree for dissolution of her marriage.

VII. Failure to Comply with Necessary Formalities

236. Failure to comply with the necessary formalities to solemnize marriage does not make the marriage void. FSC (2000 PLD 63) Non-registration of *Nikah* Effect. Accused had claimed that age of girl according to her own mother was 16/17 years, and that her *Nikah* with him was proved by three witnesses against whom nothing had been said in cross-examination. Contention of prosecution was that as *Nikah* was not registered and was not found in Register of *Nikah*, and also that thumb impression was also not found to be that of girl, *Nikah* was not proved. Validity: Registration of *Nikah* was not necessarily the proof of *Nikah* as, in Muslim Law *Nikah* could be performed by offer and acceptance in presence of witnesses. Non-registration of *Nikah* would only attract a penalty under section 5(4) of Muslim Family Laws Ordinance, 1961. In absence of any error in *Nikah* of accused with the girl, conviction and sentence awarded to accused by Trial Court were set aside and he was acquitted [Offence of *Zina* (Enforcement of Hudood) Ordinance 1979. Section 10(3). Muslim Family Laws Ordinance (VIII of 1961), section 5].

237. Transfer of immoveable property by husband to wife through *Nikahnama* which had not been registered under Registration Act, 1908. Validity: *Nikah* of parties was in the form prescribed under Muslim Family Laws Ordinance, 1961 and the rules framed thereunder and same was registered with the *Nikah* Registrar in accordance with prescribed mode and thus, *Nikahnama* had a different status than any other unregistered document through which some immoveable property had purportedly been transferred. *Nikahnama* was a public document executed by a Public Officer, certified copy whereof, was sufficient for proof of its contents unless its rebuttal was effected through cogent evidence. Dower deed by which immoveable property was purported to be transferred was, thus, not considered to be compulsorily registrable under Registration Act, 1908, and wife was entitled to claim immoveable property on basis of *Nikahnama* wherein same was incorporated in lieu of dower (PHC – 1996 PLD 64).

238. Suit for recovery of maintenance by wife. Plea raised by husband in written statement dated 14 November 2002 was that he had already divorced plaintiff, thus, she was not entitled to maintenance. Passing of ex parte decree by Family Court due to failure of husband to produce evidence. Photocopy of divorce deed filed before High Court did not show its date of execution except purchasing of its stamp paper on 5 April 2002. Plea of husband was that he had announced divorce orally in presence of witnesses in October, 2001, which was reduced in writing subsequently; and that oral divorce would become effective despite non-issuance of certificate of Divorce. Wife's plea was that alleged divorce deed was a fake/forged document, which was neither produced before Family Court nor sent to Union Council for issuance of certificate of Divorce, and that husband had manoeuvred the same just to avoid payment of decretal amount. Validity: All such facts would show that husband was only gaining time to avoid payment of amount of decree, which had become final. High Court declined to give finding on such factual issue, which husband might raise before Executing Court, if so advised. Impugned judgment and decree did not suffer from any illegality. High Court dismissed Constitutional petition in circumstances (LHC – 2010 YLR 2061).

VIII. Formalities of Marriage

239. Pakistan is an Islamic country and marriages are solemnized under the Islamic Law. MFLO is the basic law which deals with family matters. Every marriage solemnized under Islamic Law is registered. For the purpose of registration of marriages, the Union Council grants licenses to one or more persons, to be called *Nikah* Registrars. If any person to whom a license has been granted contravenes any of the conditions of license, he shall be punishable with simple imprisonment for a term which may extend to one month, or with fine which may extend to PKR 200, or with both (Rules-7 of the West Pakistan Rules under Muslim Family Laws Ordinance, 1961).

240. Any marriage not solemnized by the *Nikah* Registrar, is reported for registration by the person who has solemnized such marriage as stipulated under section-5(1)(2)(3) of MFLO.

241. SCP held (1994 SCMR 1978): License to act as *Nikah* Registrar is granted under the provisions of Rule-7 of the West Pakistan Rules under Muslim Family Laws Ordinance, 1961 as such the license is permanent in nature and can be revoked only for violation of any of the conditions of the license.

242. Petitioner was granted license to act as *Nikah* Registrar and the license was revoked by the Authorities on the complaint that he had shifted his residence. No opportunity of hearing was given to the petitioner to show that he had not shifted his residence. Validity: Where no such opportunity was given to the petitioner to rebut the allegation made against him, he was condemned unheard. Authorities were not competent to pass the order of revocation of license without hearing the petitioner and recording a specific finding to the effect that he had violated any of the conditions of the license. Order passed by the Authorities was without lawful authority and of no legal effect. High Court set aside the order and restored the license in circumstances (2002 CLC 1405 1991 P.Cr.LJ 32).

243. The Union Council provides, on payment of such cost as may be determined by the Provincial Government, supply to every *Nikah* Registrar a bound register of *Nikahnama* forms, and a seal bearing the inscription 'the seal of the *Nikah* Registrar of Ward'.

244. Each register contains fifty leaves consecutively numbered, each leaf having a *Nikahnama*, in the quadruplicate, and the number of leaves shall be certified by the Chairman. The register and the seal remains the property of the Union Council (Rules-8 of the West Pakistan Rules under Muslim Family Laws Ordinance, 1961).

245. For the registration of a marriage registered, the *Nikah* Registrar is paid, by the bridegroom or his representative a registration fee of PKR 2, or when the dower exceeds PKR 2,000, a fee calculated at the rate of one rupee for every thousand or part of thousand rupees of such dower, subject to a maximum fee of PKR 20 (Rules-9 of the West Pakistan Rules under Muslim Family Laws Ordinance, 1961). However, practically the fee is much higher as compared to the prescribed fee, and every *Nikah* Registrar charge the fee according to his will. The *Nikah* Registrar retains 80% fee and remaining 20% deposit with the Union Council.

246. However, where dower consists of property other than money or partly of such property and partly of money, the valuation of the property shall, for purposes of fees, be the valuation as settled between, the parties to the marriage (Rules-9(3) of the West Pakistan Rules under Muslim Family Laws Ordinance, 1961).

247. Nikahnama is document or form on which marriages are solemnized. The *Nikah* Registrars maintain the record of marriage which is to be preserved by Union Councils and provide copies of *Nikahnama* to the Parties on receipt of prescribed fee. Any person, on payment of the prescribed fee, can inspect the marriages record at the office of the Union Council and obtain copy of any entry or record (sections 5 & 6 of the Muslim Family Laws Ordinance, 1961).

248. Specimen of *Nikahnama* (Form-2) as prescribed by Rule-8 and Rule-10 of the Muslim Family Laws Rules, 1961 is appended below:

- *Name of Ward/Moza:______Town/Union:_______Tehsil/Thana:_______ and District:____________ in which the marriage took place.*
- *Name of the bridegroom and his father, with their respective residence and Computerized National Identity Card Number:*
- *Age of bridegroom:*
- *The names of the bride and her father, with their respective residences with Computerized National Identity Card Number:*
- *Whether the bride is a maiden, a widow or a divorce:*

- *5(a).If bride is widow or divorced having children, the number and names of children:*
- *Age of the bride:*
- *Name of Vakil, if any appointed by the bride, father's name and his residence with Computerized National Identity Card Number:*
- *The name of the witnesses to the appointment of the bride's Vakil, with their fathers' names, their residence and their relationship with the bride:*
- *Name of the Vakil, if any, appointed by the bridegroom, his father's name and his residence:*
- *The names of the witnesses to the appointment of the bridegroom's Vakil, with their father's names and their residences :*
- *Names of the witnesses to the marriage, their father's names and their residences:*
- *Date on which the marriage was contracted:*
- *Amount of dower:*
- *How much of the dower is mu'wajjal (prompt) and how much mu'ajjal (deferred):*
- *Whether any portion of the dower was paid at the time of marriage. If so, how much:*
- *Special conditions, if any:*
- *Whether the husband has delegated the power of divorce to the wife, if so, under what conditions?*
- *Whether the husband's right of divorce in any way curtailed?*
- *Whether any document was drawn up at the time of marriage relating to dower, maintenance, etc. If so contents thereof in brief:*
- *Whether the bridegroom has any existing wife, and if so, whether he has secured the permission of the Arbitration Council under the Muslim Family Laws Ordinance, 1961, to contract another marriage:*
  - (a) *Whether the bridegroom's earlier wife died or he is divorced?*
  - (b) *Whether the bridegroom has previous wife or wives; if bridegroom is divorced or his wife died, specify number of children and their names:*
- *Number and date of the communication conveying to the bridegroom the permission of the Arbitration Council to contract another marriage:*
- *Name and address of the person by whom the marriage was solemnized and his father:*
- *Date of registration of marriage :*
- *Registration fee paid:*
- *Signature of the bridegroom or his Vakil*
- *Signature of the witness to the appointment of bridge groom's Vakil with Computerized National Identity Card Numbers:*
- *Signature of the bride :*
- *Signature of the wakil of the bride:*
- *Signature of the witness to be appointment of the wakil of the bride with Computerized National Identity Card Numbers:*
- *Signatures of the witnesses to the marriage with Computerized National Identity Card Numbers:*

- *Signature of the person with Computerized National Identity Card Number who solemnize the marriage:*
- *Signature and seal of the Nikah Registrar with Computerized National Identity Card Number:*
- *Seal*

249. If marriage is solemnized outside Pakistan, by a person who is a citizen of Pakistan, such person shall ensure delivery of *Nikahnama* Form duly filled together with the registration fee, to the Consular Officer of Pakistan in or for the country in which the marriage is solemnized, for onward transmission to the *Nikah*' Registrar of the Ward of which the bride is a permanent resident, and in case the bride is not a citizen of Pakistan, to the *Nikah* Registrar of the Ward of which the bridegroom is such resident (Rule-12(1) of the West Pakistan Rules under Muslim Family Laws Ordinance, 1961).

250. In the case of a marriage solemnized outside Pakistan by a person who is not a citizen of Pakistan, the bridegroom, and where only the bride is such citizen, the bride shall, for purposes of filling in *Nikahnama*, be deemed to be the person who has solemnized the marriage (Rule-12(2) of the West Pakistan Rules under Muslim Family Laws Ordinance, 1961).

251. Anyone who contravenes the marriage registrations laws shall be punishable with simple imprisonment for a term which may extend to three months, or with fine which may extend to PKR 1,000, or with both (section-5(4) of MFLO).

252. Marriage solemnized under Muslim Family Laws Ordinance, 1961, requires its registration but *Nikah* does not become invalid due to its non-registration. If a person does not report marriage to *Nikah* Registrar for the purpose of registration, he may be held liable under section 5 (4) of Muslim Family Laws Ordinance, 1961 (LHC – 2009 MLD 962).

IX. Christian Marriage

253. Family matters among the Christian community in Pakistan are dealt with by the Christian Marriages Act of 1872 and the Divorce Act of 1869. Christian marriage is a voluntary union for life between a man and a woman, to the exclusion of all others. The minimum age for girl should be exceeding 13 years and boy should be over 16 years of age. Either party to be Christian (in practice priests do not solemnize marriages unless both parties are Christian). Free consent of both in public before two witnesses is essential. It is essential to give notice of marriage three consecutive calendar months before marriage and registration of marriage with Registrar. A certificate of marriage is issued. Christian marriage is solemnized in church, or with special permission, at private residence.

254. In Christian community, marriages are prohibited between relatives related by blood by affinity but not clearly defined in the Act. According to the Christian Marriage Act, 1872 (sections 19 & 60), if either of the spouses has not exceeded 18 years of age the certificate of marriage will not be issued unless the consent of the father/guardian/mother has been given. The polygamy is strictly prohibited among Christians.

255. Any person who has received Episcopal ordination provided the marriage is solemnized in accordance with rules, rites, ceremonies, customs of the church of which he is a Minister, any clergy of the Church of Pakistan, any minister of religion holding a license under the Christian Marriages Act, a Marriage Registrar appointed under the Act, any person appointed under the Act to grant certificate of marriage to native Christians can solemnized marriage of Christians.

256. There are strong penalties of fine and imprisonment (in some instances up to ten years) for violation of the provisions in the Christian Marriages Act by the parties and/or the Registrar. Under Part-VII of the Christian Marriage Act, 1872 (sections 66~75) provides the detail of acts which are punishable under the Act which includes false oath, declaration, notice or certificate for procuring marriage; forbidding, by false personation, issue of certificate by Marriage Registrar; solemnizing marriage without due authority; solemnizing marriage out of proper time, or without witnesses; saving of marriages solemnized under special license; solemnizing without notice or within fourteen days after notice marriage with minor; issuing certificate, or marrying without publication of notice; marrying after expiry of notice; solemnizing marriage with minor within fourteen days without authority of Court, or without sending copy of notice; issuing certificate against authorized prohibition; issuing certificate after expiry of notice, or, in case of minor within fourteen days' notice, or against authorized prohibition; persons authorized to solemnize marriage (other than Clergy of Churches of England, Scotland or Rome); issuing certificate or marrying, without publishing notice, or after expiry of certificate; issuing certificate for, or solemnizing marriage with minor; within fourteen days after notice; issuing certificate authorizedly forbidden; solemnizing marriage authorizedly forbidden; unlicensed person granting certificate pretending to be licensed and destroying or falsifying register books.

257. Under section-4 of Part-I of the Christian Marriage Act, 1872, every marriage between persons, one or both of whom is or are a Christian or Christians, shall be solemnized in accordance with the provisions of Christian Marriage Act, 1872; and any such marriage solemnized otherwise than in accordance with Act shall be void.

258. Section-5 of the Christian Marriage Act, 1872 states that the marriage may be solemnized in Pakistan by any person who has received Episcopal ordination, provided that the marriage be solemnized according to the rules, rites, ceremonies and customs of the Church of which he is a minister; or by any Clergyman of the church of Scotland, provided that such marriage be solemnized according to the rules rites, ceremonies customs of the Church of Scotland; or by any Minister of

Religion licensed under this Act of solemnize marriage; or by, or in the presence of a Marriage Registrar appointed under Marriage Act; and by any person licensed under this Act to grant certificates of marriage between Native Christians.

259. The Provincial Government may appoint one or more Christians, either by name or as holding any office for any district subject to its administration, vide section-7 of the Christian Marriage Act, 1872. Where there are more marriage Registrars than one in any district, the Provincial Government shall appoint one of them to be the Senior Marriage Registrar. When there is only one Marriage Registrar in a District, and such Registrar is absent from such District, or, ill, or when his office is temporarily vacant, the Magistrate of the district shall act, as, and be, Marriage Registrar thereof during such absence, illness or temporary vacancy. Section-8 of the Christian Marriage Act, 1872 states that the Central Government may, by notification in the official Gazette appoint any Christian, either by name or as holding any office for the time being, to be a Marriage Registrar in respect of any district or place within any Acceding State.

260. Licensing of persons to grant certificates of marriage between Native Christians is covered under section-9 of the above Act. The Provincial Government or (so far as regards and Acceding State) the Central Government may grant a license to any Christian, either by name or as holding any office for the time being, authorizing him to grant certificate of marriage between Native Christians. Any such license may be revoked by the authority by which it was granted, and every such grant or revocation shall be notified in the Official Gazette.

261. Part-II, section-10 of the Act every marriage under Marriage Act shall be solemnized between the hours of six in the morning and seven in the evening: Provided that nothing in this section shall apply to: (1) a Clergyman of the Church of England solemnizing a marriage under a special license permitting him to do so at any hour other than between six in the morning and seven in the evening, under the hand and seal of the Anglican Bishop of the Commissary; or (2) a Clergyman of the Church of Rome solemnizing a marriage between the hours of seven in the evening and six in the morning, when he has received a general or special license in that behalf from the Roman Catholic Bishop of the Diocese or Vicariate in which such marriage is so solemnized, or from such person as the same Bishop has authorized to grant such license; or (3) a Clergyman of the church of Scotland solemnizing a marriage according to the rule, rites, ceremonies and customs of the Church of Scotland.

262. Under section-11 of the Christian Marriage Act, 1872 no clergyman of the Church of England shall solemnize a marriage in any place other than a church, where worship is generally held according to the forms of the church of England: Unless there is no such Church within five miles distance by the shortest road from such place, or unless he has received a special license authorizing him to do so under the hand and seal of the Anglican Bishop of the Diocese or his Commissary. For such special license, the Registrar of the Diocese may charge such additional fee as the said Bishop from time to time authorizes.

263. Whenever a marriage is intended to be solemnized by a Minister of Religion licensed to solemnize marriage under section 12 of Part-III of the Christian Marriage Act, 1872, one of the persons intending marriage shall give notice in writing according to the form contained in the First Schedule hereto annexed, or the like effect, to the Minister of Religion whom he/she desires to solemnize the marriage, and shall state therein: (a) the name and surname, and the profession or condition, of each of the persons intending marriage; (b) The dwelling-place of each of them; (c) The time during which each has dwelt there; and (d) the Church or private dwelling in which the marriage is to be solemnized: Provided that, if either of such persons has dwelt in the place mentioned in the notice during more than one month, it may be stated therein that he/she has dwelt there one month and upwards.

264. If the persons intending marriage desire it to be solemnized in a particular Church and if the Minister of Religion to whom such notice has been delivered be entitled to officiate therein, he shall cause the notice to be affixed in some conspicuous part of such Church vide section 13 of the Christian Marriage Act, 1872. But if he is not entitled to officiate as a Minister in such church, he shall, at his option, either return the notice to the person who delivered it to him, or deliver it to some other Minister entitled to officiate therein who shall thereupon cause the notice to be affixed as aforesaid.

265. If it be intended that the marriage shall be solemnized in a private dwelling, Minister of Religion, on receiving the notice prescribed in section 15 shall forward it to the Marriage Registrar of the district, who shall affix the same to some conspicuous place in his own office, as provided in section-14 of the Christian Marriage Act, 1872.

266. Under section-15 of the Christian Marriage Act, 1872, when one of the persons intending marriage is a minor, every Minister receiving such notice shall, unless within twenty-four hours after its receipt he returns the same under the provisions of section 13, send by the post or otherwise a copy of such notice to the Marriage Registrar of the district, or, if there be more than one Registrar of such district, to the Senior Marriage Registrar.

267. Section-16 of the Christian Marriage Act, 1872 provides that the Marriage Registrar, as the case may be, on receiving any such notice, shall affix it to some conspicuous place in his own office, and the latter shall further cause a copy of the said notice to be sent to each of the other Marriage Registrar in the same district, who shall likewise publish the same in the manner above directed.

268. The section-17 of the Christian Marriage Act, 1872 states that any Minister of Religion consenting or intending to solemnize any such marriage as aforesaid, shall on being required so to do by or on behalf of the person by whom the notice was given, and upon one of the persons intending marriage making the declaration hereinafter required issue under his hand a certificate of such notice having been given and of declaration having been made. Provided: (1) that no such certificate shall be issued until the expiration of four days after the date of the notice by such

Minister; (2) that no lawful impediment be shown to his satisfaction why such certificate should not issue; and (3) that the issue of certificate has not been forbidden, in manner hereinafter mentioned, by any person authorized.

269. The Declaration before issue of certificate is discussed in section-18 of the Christian Marriage Act, 1872. It is stated that certificate shall not be issued until one of the persons intending marriage has appeared personally before the Minister and made a solemn declaration: (a) that he/she believes that there is not any impediment of kindred or affinity or other lawful hindrance to the said marriage, and when either or both of the parties is or are minor or minors; and (b) that the consent or consents required by law has or have been obtained there is no person resident in Pakistan having authority to give such consent, as the case may be.

270. Consent of father or guardian or mother has been discussed in section-19 of the Christian Marriage Act, 1872. The father, if living, of any minor, or if, the father be dead, the guardian of such minor, and in case there be no such guardian then the mother of such minor, may give consent to the minor's marriage, and such consent is hereby required for the same marriage unless no person authorized to give such consent be resident in Pakistan. Every person whose consent to a marriage is required under section 19 is hereby authorized to prohibit the issue of the certificate by any Minister, at any time before the issue of the same, by notice in writing to such Minister, subscribed by the person so authorized with his/her name and place of abode and position with respect to either of the persons intending marriage by reason of which he/she is so authorized as aforesaid under section-20 of the Christian Marriage Act, 1872.

271. If any such notice be received by such Minster, he shall not issue his certificate and shall not solemnize the said marriage until he has examined into the matter of the said prohibition, and is satisfied that the person prohibiting the marriage has not lawful authority for such prohibition, or until the said notice is withdrawn by the person who gave it vide section-21, of the Christian Marriage Act, 1872.

272. Section-22 of the Christian Marriage Act, 1872 states that when either of the persons intending marriage is a minor, and the Minister is not satisfied that the consent of the person whose consent to such marriage is required by section 19 has been obtained, such Minister shall not issue such certificate until the expiration of fourteen days after the receipt by him of the notice of marriage.

273. Issue of certificate to Native Christians discussed in section 23 of the Christian Marriage Act, 1872. When any Native Christian about to be married takes notice of marriage to a Minister of Religion, or applies for a certificate from such Minister under section 17, such Minister shall, before issuing the certificate ascertain whether such Native Christian is cognizant of the purport and effect of the said notice or certificate, as the case may be, and, if not, shall translate or cause to be translated the notice or certificate to such Native Christian into some language which he understands.

274. The certificate to be issued by such Minister shall be in the form contained in the Second Schedule, or to the like effect vide section 24 regarding Form of Certificate of the Christian Marriage Act, 1872.

275. Under section-25 of the Christian Marriage Act, 1872, after the issue of the certificate by Minister, marriage may be solemnized between the persons therein described according to such form or ceremony as the Minister thinks fit to adopt: Provided that the marriage be solemnized in the presence of at least two witnesses besides the Minister.

276. Whenever a marriage is not solemnized within two months after the date of the certificate issued by such Minister as aforesaid such certificate and all proceedings (if any), thereon shall be void, and no person shall proceed to solemnize the said marriage until new notice has been given and a certificate thereof issued in the manner aforesaid (section-26 of the Christian Marriage Act, 1872).

277. Quarterly returns to Archdeaconry have been discussed in section-29 of the Christian Marriage Act, 1872. Every Clergyman of the Church of England shall send four times in every year return in duplicate, authenticated by his signature, of the entries in the register of marriages solemnized any place where he has any spiritual charge, to the Registrar of the Archdeaconry to which he is subject, or tithing the limits of which such place is situate. Such quarterly returns shall contain all the entries of marriages contained in the said register from the first day of January to the thirty-first day of March, from the first day of April to the thirtieth day of June, from the first day of July to the thirtieth day of September, and from the first day of October to the thirty-first day of December, of each year respectively, and shall be sent by such Clergyman within two weeks from the expiration of each of the quarters above specified. The said Registrar upon receiving the said returns shall send one copy thereof to the Registrar General of Birth Deaths and Marriages.

278. Under section-30 of the Christian Marriage Act, 1872, every marriage solemnized by a Clergyman of the Church of Rome is to be registered by the person and according to the form directed in that behalf by the Roman Catholic Bishop of the Diocese or Vicariate, in which such marriage is solemnized, and such person shall forward quarterly to the Register General of Births, Deaths and Marriages returns of the entries of all marriages registered by him during the three months next preceding.

279. It is stipulated under section-31 of the Christian Marriage Act, 1872 that every Clergymen of the Church of Scotland shall keep a register of marriages, and shall register therein, according to the tabular form set forth in the Third Schedule hereto annexed, every marriage which he solemnizes under this Act, and shall forward quarterly to the Registrar General of Births, Death and Marriages, through the Senior Chaplain of the Church of Scotland, returns, similar to those prescribed in section 29, of all such marriages.

280. Every marriage solemnized by any person who has received episcopal ordination, but who is not a Clergyman of the Church of England, or of the Church of Rome, or by any Minister of Religion licensed under this Act to solemnize marriages, shall, immediately after the solemnization thereof be registered in duplicated by the same (i.e., to say) in a marriage register-book to be kept by him for that purpose, according to the form contained in the Fourth Schedule hereto annexed and also in a certificate attached to be marriage-register-book as a counterfoil, vide section-32 of the Christian Marriage Act, 1872.

281. The entry of such marriage in both the certificate and marriage-register-book shall be signed by the person solemnizing the marriage, and also by the persons married and shall be attested by two credible witnesses, other than the person solemnizing the marriage, present at its solemnization. Every such entry shall be made in order from the beginning to the end of the book, and the number of the certificate shall correspond with that of the entry in the marriage-register-book (section-33 of Christian Marriage Act, 1872).

282. The person solemnizing the marriage shall forthwith separate the certificate from the marriage-register-book and send it, within one month from the time of the solemnization, to the Marriage Registrar of the district in which the marriage was solemnized, or, if there be more Marriage Registrars than one, to the Senior Marriage Registrar, who shall cause such certificate to be copied into a book to be kept by him for that purpose, and shall send all the certificates which he has received during the month, with such number and signature or initials added thereto as are hereinafter required, to the Registrar General of Births, Deaths and Marriages (section-35 of Christian Marriage Act, 1872). Such copies shall be entered in order from the beginning to the end of the said book and shall bear both the number of the certificate as copied and also a number to be entered by the Marriage Registrar indicating the number of the entry of the said copy in the said book, according to the order in which he receives each certificate.

283. The Marriage Registrar shall also add such last-mentioned number of the entry of the copy in the book to the certificate, with his signature or initials, and shall, at the end of every month send the same to the Registrar General of birth Deaths and Marriages. (section-36 of the Christian Marriage Act, 1872)

284. Section-37 of the Christian Marriage Act, 1872 provides that when any marriage between Native Christians is solemnized by any such person, Clergyman or Minister of Religion as is referred to in clause (1) clause (2) or clause (30) of section 5, the person solemnizing the same shall, instead of proceeding in the manner provided by sections 28 to 36, both inclusive, register the marriage in a separate register-book, and shall keep it safely until it is filled, or, if he leaves the district in which he solemnized the marriage before the said book is filled, shall make over the same to the person succeeding to his duties in the said district. Whoever has the control of the book at the time when it is filled, shall send it to the Marriage Registrar of the district, or, if there be more Marriage Registrars than one, to Senior

Marriage Registrar, who shall send it to Registrar General of Birth, Deaths and Marriages, to be kept by him with the records of his office.

285. When a marriage is intended to be solemnized by, or in the presence of, a Marriage Registrar, one, of the parties to such marriage shall give notice in writing, in the form contained in the First Schedule hereto annexed, or to the like effect, to any Marriage Registrar of the District within which the parties have dwelt; or if the parties dwell in different district, shall give the like notice to a Marriage Registrar of each district, and shall state therein the name and surname, and the profession or condition, of each of the parties intending marriage, the dwelling-place of each of them, the time during which each has dwelt therein, and the place at which the marriage is to be solemnized. Provided that, if either party has dwelt in the place stated in the notice for more than one month, it may be stated therein that he/she has dwelt there one month and upwards (section-38 of the Christian Marriage Act, 1872).

286. Every Marriage Registrar shall, on receiving any such notice, cause a copy thereof to be affixed in some conspicuous place in his office. When one of the parties intending marriage is minor, every Marriage Registrar shall, within twenty-four hours after the receipt by him of the notice of such marriage, send, by post or otherwise, a copy of such notice to each of the other Marriage Registrars (if any) in the same district who shall likewise affix the copy in some conspicuous place in his own office (section-39 of the Christian Marriage Act, 1872).

287. The Marriage Registrar shall file all such notices and keep them with the records of his office, and shall also forthwith enter a true copy of all such notices in a book to be furnished to him for that purpose by the Provincial Government and to be called the 'Marriage Notice Book'. And the 'Marriage Notice Book' shall be open at all reasonable times, without fee, to persons desirous of inspecting the same, under section-40 of the Christian Marriage Act, 1872.

288. Section-41 of Christian Marriage Act, 1872 discussed about certificate of notice given and oath made. If the party by whom the notice was given requests the Marriage Registrar to issue the certificate next hereinafter mentioned, and if one of the parties intending marriage has made oath as hereinafter required, the Marriage Register shall issue under his hand a certificate of such notice having been given and of such oath having been made. Proviso provided: (a) that no lawful impediment be shown to his satisfaction why such certificate should not be issued; (b) that the issue of such certificate has not been forbidden in manner hereinafter mentioned, by any person authorized in that behalf by this Act; (c) that four days after the receipt of the notice have expired; and further, (d) that where, by such oath it appears that one of the parties intending marriage is a minor, fourteen days after the entry of such notice have expired.

289. The certificate shall not be issued by any Marriage Registrar, until one of the parties intending marriage appears personally before such Marriage Registrar, and makes oath: (a) that he/she believes that there is not any impediment of kindred or affinity, or other lawful hindrance, to the said Marriage; and (b) that both the parties have, or (where they have dwelt in the district of different Marriage Registrars) that the party making such oath has, had their, his/her usual place of abode within the district of such marriage Registrar, and, where either or each of the parties is a minor; (c) that the consent or consents to such marriage required by law has or have been obtained thereto, or that there is no person resident in Pakistan authorized to give such consent, as the case may be.

290. Consent of father or guardian and protest against issue of certificate has been discussed in section 44 of the Christian Marriage Act, 1872. The provision of section 19 apply to every marriage under this Part, either of the parties to which is a minor; and any person whose consent to such marriage would be required thereunder may enter a protest against the issue of the Marriage Registrar's certificate, by writing, at any time before the issue of such certificate, the word 'forbidden' opposite to the entry of the notice of such intended marriage in the Marriage Notice Book, and by subscribing thereto his/her name and place of abode, and his/her position with respect to either of the parties, by reason of which he/she is so authorized. When such protest has been entered, no certificate shall be issued until the Marriage Registrar has examined into the matter of the protest, and is satisfied that it ought not to obstruct the issue of the certificate for the said marriage, or until the protest be withdrawn by the person who entered it.

291. If any person whose consent is necessary to any marriage under this part is of unsound mind, or if any such person (other than the father) without just cause withholds his consent to the marriage, the parties, intending marriage may apply by petition, to the District Judge, vide section-45 of the Christian Marriage Act, 1872 and the said District Judge may examine the allegations of the petition in a summary way; and, if upon examination such marriage appears proper, such District Judge shall declare the marriage to be a proper marriage. Such declaration shall be as effectual as if the person whose consent was needed had consented to the marriage; and, if he has forbidden the issue of the Marriage Registrar's certificate, such certificate shall be issued and the like proceeding may be had under this Part in relation to the marriage as if the issue of such certificate had not been forbidden.

292. Whenever a Marriage Registrar refuses to issue a certificate under this Part, either of the parties intending marriage may apply by petition to the District Judge. The said District Judge may examine the allegations of the petition in a summary way, and shall decide thereon. The decision of such District Judge shall be final, and the Marriage Registrar to whom the application for the issue of a certificate was originally made shall proceed in accordance therewith (section-46 of the Christian Marriage Act, 1872).

293. Under section-47 of the Christian Marriage Act, 1872, whenever a Marriage Registrar resident in any Acceding State refuses to issue his certificate either of the parties intending marriage may apply by petition to the Central Government, who shall decide thereon. Such decision shall be final, and the

Marriage Registrar to whom the application was originally made shall proceed in accordance therewith.

294. Whenever a Marriage Registrar, acting under the provisions of section 44, is not satisfied that the person forbidding the issue of the certificate is authorized by law so to do the said Marriage Registrar shall apply by petition, to the District Judge. The said petition shall state all the circumstances of the case, and pray for the order and direction of the Court concerning the same and the said District Judge shall examine into the allegations of the petition and the said circumstances of the case: And if, upon such examination, it appears that the person forbidding the issue of such certificate is not authorized by law so to do, such District Judge shall declare that the person forbidding the issue of such certificate is not authorized as aforesaid, and thereupon such certificate shall be issued, and the like proceedings may be had in relation to such marriage as if the issue had not been forbidden. Whenever a Marriage Registrar appointed under section 8 to act within any Acceding State is not satisfied that the person forbidding the issue of the certificate is authorized by law so to do, the said Marriage Registrar shall send a statement of all the circumstances of the case, together with all documents relating thereto to the Central Government. If it appears to the Central Government that the person forbidding the issue of such certificate is not authorized by law so to do, the Central Government shall declare that the person forbidding the issue of such certificate is not authorized as aforesaid, and thereupon such certificate shall be issued, and the like proceedings may be had in relation to such marriage as if the issue of the certificate had not been forbidden (section-48 of the Christian Marriage Act, 1872).

295. Every person entering a protest with the Marriage Registrar, under this Part against the issue of any certificate, on grounds which such Marriage Registrar; under section 44 or the District Judge, under section 45 or 46, declares to be frivolous and such as ought not to obstruct the issue of the certificate, shall be liable for the costs of all proceedings in relation thereto and for damages, to be recovered by suit by the person against whose marriage such protest was entered (section-49 of the Christian Marriage Act, 1872)..

296. After the issue of the certificate of the Marriage Registrar, or, where notice is required to be given under this Act to the Marriage Registrars for different districts, after the issue of the certificates, of the Marriage Registrars for such districts. Marriage may, if there be no lawful impediment to the marriage of the parties described in such certificate or certificates, be solemnized between them, according to such form and ceremony as they think fit to adopt. But every such marriage shall be solemnized in the presence of some Marriage Registrar (to whom shall be delivered such certificate or certificates as aforesaid), and of two or more credible witnesses besides the Marriage Registrar. And in some part of the ceremony each of the parties declare as follows, or to the like effect: 'I do not solemnly declare that I know not of any lawful impediment why I, A.B., may not be joined in matrimony to C.D.' And each of the parties shall say to the other as follows or to the like effect: 'I call upon these persons here present to witness that I, A.B. do take the, C.D., to be my lawful wedded wife [or husband] (section-51 of the Christian Marriage Act,

1872). When Marriage not had within two months after notice, new notice required, vide section-52 of the Christian Marriage Act, 1872.'

297. After the solemnization of any marriage under section-54 of the Christian Marriage Act, 1872, the Marriage Registrar present at such solemnization shall forthwith register the marriage in duplicate that is to say, in a marriage-register-book, according to the form of the Schedule hereto annexed, and also in a certificate attached to the marriage-book as a counterfoil. The entry of such marriage in both the certificate and the marriage-register-book shall be signed by the person by or before whom the marriage has been solemnized, if there be any such person, and by the Marriage Registrar present at such marriage, whether or not it is solemnized by him, and also by the parties married, and attested by two credible witness other than the Marriage Registrar and person solemnizing the marriage. Every such entry shall be made in order from the beginning to the end of the book, and the number of the certificate shall correspond with that of the entry in the marriage-register-book.

298. The marriage shall forthwith separate the certificate from the marriage-register-book and send it, at the end of every month, to the Registrar General of Births, Deaths and Marriages. The Marriage Registrar shall keep safely the said register-book until it is filled, and shall then send it to the Registrar General of Births, Deaths and Marriages, to be kept by him with the records of his office (section-55 of the Christian Marriage Act, 1872).

299. When any Native Christian about to be married gives a notice of marriage, or applies for a certificate from a Marriage Registrar, such Marriage Registrar shall ascertain whether the said Native Christian understands English language, and, if he does not, the Marriage Registrar shall translate, or cause to be translated, such notice or certificate, or both of them as the case may be, to such Native Christian into a language which he understands; or the Marriage Registrar shall otherwise ascertain whether the Native Christian is cognizant of the purport and effect of the said notice and certificate (section-57 of the Christian Marriage Act, 1872).

300. When any Native Christian is married under the provisions of this Part, the person solemnizing the marriage shall ascertain whether such Native Christian understands English language, and if he does not, the person solemnizing the marriage shall, at the time of the solemnization translate, or cause to be translated, to such Native Christian, into a language which he understands, the declarations made at such marriage in accordance with the provision of this Act (section-58 of the Christian Marriage Act, 1872).

301. Part VI, section-60 of the Christian Marriage Act, 1872 states the conditions of marriages of Native Christian which may be certificated. Every marriage between Native Christians applying for a certificate shall without the preliminary notice required under Part III be certified under this Part, if the following conditions to be fulfilled, and not otherwise: (1) the age of the man intending to be married shall exceed 16 years, and the age of the woman intending to be married shall exceed 13 years; (2) neither of the persons intending to be married shall have a wife or husband still living; and (3) in the presence of a person licensed, and of at least two credible witnesses other than such person, each of the parties shall say to the other. 'I call upon these persons here present to witness that I, A.B. in the presence of Almighty God, and in the name of our Lord Jesus Christ, do take thee, C.D., to be my lawful wedded wife [or husband]' or words to the like effect. Provided that no marriage shall be certified under this Part when either of parties intending to be married has not completed his/her 18th year, unless such consent has been given to the intended marriage, or unless it appears that there is no person living authorized to give such consent.

302. When, in respect to any marriage solemnized and the conditions, prescribed in section 60 of the Act have been fulfilled, the person licensed as aforesaid, in whose presence the said declaration has been made, shall, on the application of either of the parties to such marriage, and on the payment of a fee of four annas, grant a certificate of the marriage. The certificate shall be signed by such licensed person, and shall be received in any suit touching the validity of such marriage as conclusive proof of its having been performed (section-61 of the Christian Marriage Act, 1872).

303. Part-VI of the Christian marriage Act, 1872, except so much of sections 62 and 63 as are referred to in section 64, shall not apply to marriages between Roman Catholics. But nothing herein contained shall invalidate any marriage celebrated between Roman Catholics under the provisions of Part invalidate any marriage celebrated between Roman Catholics under the provisions of Part V of Act No. XXV of 1864, previous to the twenty-third day of February, 1865.

304. Whoever, for the purpose of procuring a marriage or license of marriage, intentionally: (a) where an oath or declaration is required by this Act, or by any rule or custom of a Church according to the rites and ceremonies of which a marriage is intended to be solemnized, such Church being the Church of England or of Rome, makes a false oath or declaration, or, (b) where a notice or certificate is required by this Act, signs a false notice or certificate; shall be deemed to have committed the offence punishable under section 193 of the Pakistan Penal Code with imprisonment of either description for a term which may extend to three years and, at the discretion of the Court, with fine (Part-VII section-66 of the Christian Marriage Act, 1872).

305. Under section-67 of the Christian Marriage Act, 1872, whoever forbids the issue, by a Marriage Registrar, of a certificate, by falsely representing himself to be a person whose consent to the marriage is required by law, knowing or believing such representation to be false or not having reason to believe it to be true, shall be deemed guilty of the offence described in section 205 of the Pakistan Penal Code.

306. Solemnizing marriage without due authority has been discussed in section-68 of the Christian Marriage Act, 1872. Whoever, not being authorized by section 5 of the Act to solemnize marriages, solemnizes or professes to be solemnized the absence of a Marriage Registrar of the district in which the ceremony takes place. Marriage between persons one or both of whom is or are a Christian or Christians, shall punished with imprisonment which may extend to ten years, (in lieu of a sentence of imprisonment for seven years or upwards)with transportation for a term of not less than seven years, and not exceeding ten years, and shall also be liable to fine.

307. Whoever knowingly and wilfully solemnizes a marriage between persons one or both of whom is or are a Christian or Christians, at any time other than between the hours of six in the morning and seven in the evening, or in the absence of at least two credible witnesses other than the person solemnizing the marriage, shall be punished with imprisonment for a term which may extend to three years, and shall also be liable to fine, vide section-69 of the Christian Marriage Act, 1872. This section does not apply in marriages solemnized under special licenses granted by the Anglican Bishop of the Diocese or by his Commissary, nor to marriages performed between the hours of seven in the evening and six in the morning by Clergyman of the Church of Rome, when he has received the general or special license in that behalf mentioned in section 10. Nor does this section apply to marriages solemnized by a Clergyman of the Church Scotland according to the rules, rites, ceremonies and customs of the Church of Scotland.

308. Under section-70 of the Christian Marriage Act, 1872, any Minister of Religion licensed to solemnize marriages under this Act, who, without a notice in writing, or, when one of the parties to the marriage is a minor and the required consent of the parents of guardians to such marriage has not been obtained within fourteen days after the receipt by him of notice of such marriage knowingly and wilfully solemnizes a marriage under Part II, shall be punished with imprisonment for a term which may extend to three years, and shall also be liable to fine.

309. Issuing certificate, or marrying without publication of notice; marrying after expiry of notice; solemnizing marriage with minor within fourteen days without authority of Court or without sending copy of notice; issuing certificate against authorized prohibition have been discussed in section-71 of the Christian Marriage Act, 1872. A Marriage Registrar under the Act, who commits any of the following offences: (1) knowingly and wilfully issues any certificate for marriage, or solemnizes any marriage, without publishing the notice of such marriage as directed by this Act; (2) after the expiration of two months after the copy of the notice has been entered as required by section 40 in respect of any marriage, solemnizes such marriage; (3) solemnizes, without any order of a competent Court authorizing him to do so, any marriage, when one of the parties is a minor, before the expiration of fourteen days after the receipt of the notice of such marriage, or without sending, by the post or otherwise, a copy of such marriage, or without sending, by the post or otherwise, a copy of such notice to the Senior Marriage Registrar of the district if there be more Marriage Registrars of the district than one, and if he himself be not the Senior Marriage Registrar; and (4) issue any certificate the issue of which had been prohibited, as in this Act provided, by any person authorized to prohibit the issue thereof shall be punished with imprisonment for a term, which may extend to five years, and shall also be liable to fine.

310. Section-72 of the Christian Marriage Act, 1872 provides about the issuing certificate after expiry of notice, or, in case of minor within fourteen days after notice, or against authorized prohibition. Any Marriage Registrar knowingly and wilfully issuing any certificate for marriage after the expiration of two months after the notice has been entered by him as aforesaid, or knowingly and wilfully issuing, without the order of a competent Court authorizing him to do so, any certificate for marriage, where one of the parties intending marriage is a minor, before the expiration of fourteen days after the entry of such notice, or any certificate the issue of which has been forbidden as aforesaid by any person authorized in his behalf, shall be deemed to have committed an offence under section 166 of the Pakistan Penal Code.

311. Persons authorized to solemnize marriage has been discussed in section-73 of the Christian Marriage Act, 1872. (other than Clergy of Churches of England, Scotland or Rome); issuing certificate or marrying, without publishing notice, or other expiry of certificate; issuing certificate for, or solemnizing marriage with minor within fourteen days after notice; issuing certificate authorizedly forbidden; solemnizing marriage authorizedly forbidden. Whoever, being authorized under this Act to solemnize a marriage, and not being a Clergyman of the Church of England, solemnizing a marriage after due publication of bans, or under a license from the Anglican Bishop of the Diocese or a Surrogate duly authorized in that behalf; or not being a Clergyman of the Church of Scotland, solemnizing a marriage according to the rules, rites, ceremonies and customs of that Church; or, not being a Clergyman of the Church of Rome, solemnizing a marriage according to the rites, rules, ceremonies and customs of that Church; knowingly and wilfully issues any certificate for marriage under this Act, or solemnizes any marriage between such persons as aforesaid, without publishing, or causing to be affixed, the notice of such marriage as directed in Part III of this Act, or after the expiration of two months after the certificate has been issued by him; or knowingly and wilfully issues any certificate for marriage, or solemnizes a marriage between such persons when one of the persons intending marriage is a minor, before the expiration of fourteen days after the receipt of notice of such marriage, or without sending, by the post or otherwise, a copy of such notice to the Marriage Registrar, or, if there be more Marriage Registrars than one, to the Senior Marriage Registrar of the district; or knowingly and wilfully issues any certificate the issue of which has been forbidden under this Act, by any person authorized forbid the issue; or knowingly and wilfully solemnizes any marriage forbidden by any person authorized to forbid the same shall be punished with imprisonment for a term which may extend to four years and shall also be liable to fine.

312. Under section-74 of the Christian Marriage Act, 1872, whoever, not being licensed to grant a certificate of marriage under Part VI of this Act, grants such certificate intending thereby to make it appear that he is licensed, shall be punished with imprisonment for a term which may extend to five years, and shall be liable to fine. Whoever, being licensed to grant certificates of marriage under Part VI of this Act, without just cause refuses, or wilfully neglects or omits, to perform any of the duties imposed upon him by that Part shall be punished with fine which may extend to PKR 100.

313. Section-75 of the Christian Marriage Act, 1872 discussed about destroying or falsifying register books. Whoever, by himself or another wilfully destroys or injures any register-book or the counterfoil certificate thereof, or any part thereof, or any authenticated extract therefrom; or falsely makes or counterfeits any part of such register-book or counterfoil certificates; or wilfully inserts any false entry in any such register-book or counterfoil certificate or authenticated extract, shall be punished with imprisonment for a term which may extend to seven years, and shall also be liable to fine. The prosecution for every offence punishable under this Act shall be commenced within two years after the offence is committed, vide section-76 of the Christian Marriage Act, 1872.

314. What matters need not be proved in respect of marriage in accordance with Part-VIII, Article-77 of the Christian Marriage Act, 1872. Whenever any marriage has been solemnized in accordance with the provision of sections 4 and 5, it shall not be void merely on account of any irregularity in respect of any of the following matters, namely: (1) any statement made in regard to the dwelling of the persons married, or to the consent of any person whose consent to such marriage is required by law; (2) the notice of the marriage; (3) the certificate or translation thereof; (4) the time and place at which the marriage has been solemnized; and (5) the registration of the marriage.

315. Under section-78 of the Christian Marriage Act, 1872, every person charged with the duty of registering any marriage who discovers any error in the form or substance of any such entry, may, within one month next after the discovery of such error, in the presence of the persons married, correct the error, by entry in the margin, without any alteration of the original entry, and shall sign the marginal entry, and add thereto the date of such correction, and such person shall make the like marginal entry in the certificate thereof. And every entry made under this section shall be attested by the witnesses in whose presence it was made. And in case such certificate has been already sent to the Registrar General of Births, Deaths and Marriages, such person shall make and send in like manner a separate certificate of the original erroneous entry, and of the marginal correction therein made.

316. Searches and copies of entries have been discussed in section-79 if the Christian Marriage Act, 1872. Every person solemnizing a marriage under this Act, and hereby required to register the same; and every Marriage Registrar or Registrar General of Births Deaths and Marriages having the custody for the time being of any register of marriages or of any certificate, or duplicate or copies of certificate, under this Act shall on payment of the proper fees, at all reasonable times, allow searches to be made in such register, or for such certificate, or duplicate, or copies, and give a copy under his hand of an entry in the same.

317. Under section-80 of the Christian Marriage Act, 1872, every certified copy, purporting to be signed by the person entrusted under this Act with the custody of any marriage-register or certificate, or duplicate, required to be kept or delivered under this Act, of an entry of a marriage in such register, or of any such certificate or duplicate shall be received as evidence of the marriage purporting to be so entered, or of the facts purporting to be so certified therein, without further proof of such register or certificate or duplicate, or of any entry therein, respectively or of such copy.

318. Certificates of certain marriages for Central Government have been discussed in section-81 of the Christian Marriage Act, 1872. The Register General of Births, Deaths, and Marriages and the officers appointed under section 56 shall, at the end of every quarter in each year, select, from the certificates of marriages forwarded to them, respectively, during such quarter, the certificates of the marriages of which the Government by whom he was appointed may desire that evidence shall be transmitted to England, and shall send the same certificate, signed by them respectively, to the Central Government.

319. Fees are charged under the Christian Act for: (a) receiving and publishing notices of marriages; (b) issuing certificates for marriage by Marriage Registrars, and registering marriages by the same; (c) entering protests against, or prohibitions of, the issue of certificates for marriage by the said Registrars; and (d) searching register-books or certificates, or duplicates of copies thereof, giving copies of entries in the same under sections 63 and 79.

320. Nothing in the Act applies to any marriage performed by any Minister, Consul or Consular Agent between subjects of the State which he represents and according to the laws of such State, vide section-87 of the Christian Marriage Act, 1872. Nothing in the Act shall be deemed to validate any marriage, which the personal law applicable to either of the parties forbids him/her to enter into, vide section-88 of the Christian Marriage Act, 1872.

X. Hindu Marriages

321. The Hindu community in particular do not have any specific codified laws relating to family matters which are instead governed by custom. Members of minority communities also approach the country's regular Family Courts since the Family Courts Act of 1964 does not restrict its jurisdiction to Muslims alone. Hindu family matters in Pakistan are primarily governed by custom, and the essentials of a valid custom are that it should be ancient, certain, reasonable and not opposed to public policy.

322. Very few family matters among the Hindu community go to courts and most issues are settled through community forums. However, the scheduled castes, as opposed to the caste Hindus, do take their cases to the Family Courts. In general, there is no concept of divorce among Hindus, although some file divorce suits in the Family Courts pleading the existence of the custom in their community.

323. According to the Act of 1946, a married Hindu woman can claim separate residence and maintenance on one or more of the grounds which include husband suffering from any loathsome disease not contracted from wife; cruelty by husband and it is not safe for wife to live with husband; desertion or abandonment against her consent; husband has remarried; husband converts to another religion; husband keeps concubine or any other justifiable cause.

324. However, the wife can be denied her claim if she converts to another religion; becomes immoral or fails to comply with decree for restitution of conjugal rights without sufficient cause.

325. A Hindu widow can legally remarry under the Hindu Widow's Marriage Act of 1856. In the event of remarriage, if she is a minor and the previous marriage was not consummated, her father's consent for remarriage is a must; however, if the widow is adult or the previous marriage was consummated, she can consent on her own. On remarriage, a Hindu widow loses her rights over her deceased husband's property. A Hindu widow can be a guardian if this was expressed in the deceased husband's will, or she can approach the court to appoint a guardian if no other male was named as a guardian in the will.

326. The Hindu Widow's Remarriage Act, 1856 is applicable to Hindu community in Pakistan to remove all legal obstacles to the marriage of Hindu Widows. In the preamble, it is stated that whereas it is known that, by the law as administered in the Civil Courts established in the territories in the possession and under the Government of the East India Company, Hindu widows with certain exceptions are held to be, by reason of their having been once married, incapable of contracting a second valid marriage, and the offspring of such widows by any second marriages are held to be illegitimate and incapable of inheriting property; and whereas many Hindus believe that his imputed legal incapacity, although it is in accordance with established custom, is not in accordance with a true interpretation of the precepts of their religion, and desire that the civil law administered by the Courts of Justice shall longer prevent those Hindus who may be so minded from adopting a different custom, in accordance with the dictates of their own conscience; and whereas it is just to relieve all such Hindus from this legal incapacity of which they complain, and the removal or all legal obstacles to marriage of Hindu widows will tend to the promotion of good morals and to the public welfare. It is enacted as follows:

327. Under Article-1 of the Hindu Widow's Remarriage Act, 1856, no marriage contracted between Hindus shall be invalid, and the issue of no such marriage shall be illegitimate, by reason of the woman having been previously married or betrothed to another person who was dead at the time of such marriage, any custom and any interpretation of Hindu Law to the contrary notwithstanding.

328. It is stipulated under Article-2 of the Hindu Widow's Remarriage Act, 1856 all rights and interests which any widow may have in her deceased husband's property by way of maintenance, or by inheritance to her husband or to his lineal successors, or by virtue of any will or testamentary disposition conferring upon her, without express permission to remarry, only a limited interest in such property, with no power of alienating the same, shall upon her remarriage, cease and determine as if she had then died; and the next heirs of her deceased husband, or other persons entitled to the property on her death, shall thereupon succeed to the same.

329. Under Article-3 of the Hindu Widow's Remarriage Act, 1856, it is stated that on the remarriage of a Hindu widow, if neither the widow nor any other person has been expressly constituted by the will or testamentary disposition of the deceased husband the guardian of his children, the father of paternal grandfather or paternal grandmother, of the deceased husband, or any male relative of the deceased husband, may petition the highest Court having original jurisdiction in civil cases in the place where the deceased husband was domiciled at the time of his death for the appointment of some proper person to be guardian of the said children, and thereupon it shall be lawful for the said Court, if it shall think fit, to appoint such guardian, who when appointed shall be entitled to have care and custody of the said children, or of any of them during their minority, in the place of their mother; and in making such appointment the Court shall be guide, so far as may be, by the laws and rules in force touching the guardianship of children who have neither father nor mother: Provided that when the said children have no property of their own sufficient for their support and proper education whilst minors, no such appointment shall be made otherwise than with the consent of the mother unless the proposed guardian shall have given security for the support and proper education of the children whilst minors.

330. It is stipulated nothing in this Act contained shall be construed to render any widow who, at the time of the death of any person leaving any property, is a childless widow, capable of inheriting the whole or any share of such property, if before the passing of this Act, she would have been incapable of inheriting the same by reason of her being a childless widow.

331. Under Article-5 of the Hindu Widow's Remarriage Act, 1856 except as provided in the Act, a widow shall not, by reason of her remarriage forfeit any property or any right to which she would otherwise be entitled; and every widow who has remarried shall have the same rights of inheritance as she would have had such marriage been her first marriage.

332. It is also stated under Article-6 of the Act that whatever words spoken, ceremonies performed or engagements made on the marriage of a Hindu female who has not been previously married, are sufficient to constitute a valid marriage, shall have the same effect if spoken, performed or made on the marriage of a Hindu widow, and no marriage shall be declared invalid on the ground that such words, ceremonies or engagements are inapplicable to the case of a widow.

333. Under Article-7 of the said Act, if the widow remarrying is a minor whose marriage has not been consummated, she shall not remarry without the consent of her father, or if she has no father, of her paternal grandfather, or if she has no such grandfather, of her mother, or, failing all these, of her elder brother, or failing also brothers, of her next male relative.

334. All persons knowingly abetting a marriage made contrary to the provisions of the Hindu Widow's Remarriage Act, 1856 shall be liable to imprisonment for term not exceeding one year or to fine or to both. And all marriages made contrary to the provisions of this section may be declared void by a Court of law: Provided that in any question regarding the validity of marriage made contrary to the provisions of this section, such consent as is aforesaid shall be presumed until the contrary is proved, and that no such marriage shall be declared void after it had been consummated.

335. Under the Act, in the case of a widow who is of full age, or whose marriage has been consummated, her own consent shall be sufficient consent to constitute her remarriage lawful and valid.

336. In order to remove certain disabilities and doubts under the Hindu Law in respect of marriages between Hindus, the Hindu Marriage Disabilities Removal Act, 1946 (Act No. XXVII of 1946) was enacted on 22 November 1946. It is stated under the Act that notwithstanding any text, rule or interpretation of the Hindu Law or any custom or usage, a marriage between Hindus, which is otherwise valid, shall not be invalid by reason only of the fact that the parties thereto belong to the same gotra or gravara, or belong to different sub-divisions of the same caste.

XI. Parsi Marriages

337. The Parsi Marriage and Divorce Act, 1936 regulates the family matters of Parsi community in Pakistan. Under this Act, no marriage shall be valid if (a) the contracting parties are related to each other in any of the degrees of consanguinity or affinity set forth in Schedule-I; or (b) such marriage is not solemnized according to the Parsi form of ceremony called 'Ashirvad' by a priest in the presence of two Parsi witnesses other than such priest; or (c) in the case of any Parsi (whether such Parsi has changed his/her religion or domicile or not) who has not completed the age of 21 years, the consent of his/her father or guardian has not been previously given to such marriage.

338. Under section-4 of the Parsi Marriage and Divorce Act, 1936 no Parsi (whether such Parsi has changed his/her religion or domicile or not) shall contract any marriage under this Act or any other law in the lifetime of his/her wife or husband, whether a Parsi or not, except after his/her lawful divorce from such wife or husband or after his/her marriage with such wife or husband has lawfully been declared null and void or dissolved, and, if the marriage was contracted with such wife or husband under the Parsi Marriage and Divorce Act, 1865 (Rep. by this Act.), or under this Act, except after a divorce, declaration or dissolution as aforesaid under either of the said Acts, XV of 1865. Every marriage contracted contrary to these provisions shall be void. Under section-11 of the Act, any priest knowingly and wilfully solemnizing any marriage contrary to and in violation of this section shall, on conviction thereof, be punished with simple imprisonment for a term which may extend to six months, or with fine which may extend to PKR 200, or with both.

339. It is stipulated under section-5 of the Parsi Marriage and Divorce Act, 1865 that every Parsi who during the lifetime of his/her wife or husband, whether a Parsi or not, contracts a marriage without having been lawfully divorced from such wife or husband, or without his/her marriage with such wife or husband having legally been declared null and void or dissolved, shall be subject to the penalties provided in sections 494 and 495 of the Pakistan Penal Code for the offence of marrying again during the lifetime of a husband or wife.

340. Under section-6, every Parsi marriage contracted shall, immediately on the solemnization thereof, be certified by the officiating priest in the form contained in Schedule II. The certificate shall be signed by the said priest, the contracting parties, or their fathers or guardians when they shall not have completed the age of 21 years, and two witnesses present at the marriage; and the said priest shall thereupon send such certificate together with a fee to be paid by the husband to the Registrar of the place at which such marriage is solemnized. The Registrar on receipt of the certificate and fee shall enter the certificate in a register to be kept by him for that purpose and shall be entitled to retain the fee. The register of marriages can be inspected by making payment of prescribed fee. It is stipulated under section-12 that if any priest neglecting to comply with any of the requisitions affecting him contained in this section shall, on conviction thereof, be punished for every such offence with simple imprisonment for a term which may extend to three months, or with fine which may extend to PKR 100, or with both. Under section-13 every other person required by section-6 to subscribe or attest the said certificate who shall wilfully omit or neglect to do so, shall, on conviction thereof, be punished for every such offence with a fine not exceeding PKR 100. Similarly under section-15 if any Registrar fails to enter the certificate, he shall be punished with simple imprisonment for a term which may extend to one year, or with fine which may extend to PKR 1,000, or with both.

341. Under section-10 of the Parsi Marriage and Divorce Act, 1865, when a Court passes a decree for divorce, nullity or dissolution, the Court shall send a copy of the decree for registration to the Registrar of Marriages within its jurisdiction.

342. It is prescribed under section-14 of the Act, that any person making or signing or attesting any such certificate containing a statement which is false, and which he either knows or believes to be false, shall be punished with simple imprisonment for a term which may extend to three months, or with fine which may extend to PKR 100, or with both; and if the act amounts to forgery as defined in the Pakistan Penal

Code, then such person shall also be liable, on conviction thereof, to the penalties provided in section 466 of the said Code, XLV of 1860.

343. Under section-16 of the above Act, any person secreting, destroying, or dishonestly or fraudulently altering the said register in any part thereof, shall be punished with imprisonment of either description as defined in the Pakistan Penal Code for a term which may extend to two years, or if he be a Registrar, for a term which may extend to five years and shall also be liable to fine which may extend to PKR 500, XLV of 1860. The Districts Courts established under the Act are entitled to hear the suits relating to Parsi community.

344. Under section-38 of the Parsi Marriage and Divorce Act, 1865 no suit shall be brought in any Court to enforce any marriage or any contract connected with or arising out of any marriage, if, at the date of the institution of the suit, the husband shall not have completed the age of 16 years, or the wife shall not have completed the age of 14 years.

345. Under section-39 of the Parsi Marriage and Divorce Act, 1865 in any suit under this Act if the wife shall not have an independent income sufficient for her support and the necessary expenses of the suit, the Court, on the application of the wife, may order the husband to pay her monthly or weekly during the suit such sum not exceeding one-fifth of her husband's net income as the Court, considering the circumstances of the parties, shall think reasonable.

346. As stipulated under section-40 of the Parsi Marriage and Divorce Act, 1865, the court may, if it shall think fit at the time of passing any decree under this Act or subsequently thereto on application made to it for the purpose, order that the husband shall, while the wife remains chaste and unmarried, (a) to the satisfaction of the Court, secure to the wife such gross sum or such monthly or periodical payment of money for a term not exceeding her life as, having regard to her own property, if any, her husband's ability and the conduct of the parties, shall be deemed just, and for that purpose may require a proper instrument to be executed by all necessary parties and suspend the pronouncing of its decree until such instruments shall have been duly executed, or (b) make such monthly payments to the wife for her maintenance end support as the Court may think reasonable.

347. In case any such order shall not be obeyed by her husband, it may be enforced in the manner provided for the execution of decrees and orders under the Code of Civil Procedure, 1908, and further the husband may be sued by any person supplying the wife with necessaries during the time of such disobedience for the price of such necessaries, V of 1908. However, the Court, if satisfied that there is a change in the circumstances of either party at any time, may at the instance of either party vary, modify or rescind such order in such manner as the Court may deem just.

348. Where an order for alimony or maintenance in favour of a wife has been made either under the provisions of the Parsi Marriage and Divorce Act, 1865, or under the provisions of any other Act, the Court, if satisfied that the wife has remarried or has not remained chaste, shall vary or rescind the order.

349. Under section-41 of the Parsi Marriage and Divorce Act, 1865, in all cases in which the Court shall make any decree or order for alimony it may direct the same to be paid either to the wife herself, or to any trustee on her behalf to be approved by the Court, and may impose any terms or restrictions which to the Court may seem expedient, and may from time to time appoint a new trustee, if for any reason it shall appear to the Court expedient so to do.

350. Under section-42 of the Parsi Marriage and Divorce Act, 1865 it is stipulated that in any suit under this Act the Court may make such provisions in the final decree as it may deem just and proper with respect to property presented at or about the time of marriage which may belong jointly to both the husband and wife.

351. Under the Parsi Marriage and Divorce Act, 1865 every suit shall be tried with closed doors should such be the wish of either of the parties. Where in the case of a trial in a Parsi Matrimonial Court not less than five delegates have attended throughout the proceedings, the trial shall not be invalid by reason of the absence during any part thereof of the other delegates.

352. An appeal shall lie to the High Court from (a) the decision of any Court established under the Parsi Marriage and Divorce Act, 1865 on the ground of the decision being contrary to some law or usage having the force of law, or of a substantial error or defect in the procedure or investigation of the case which may have produced error or defect in the decision of the case upon the merits, and on no other ground; and (b) the granting of leave by any such Court: Provided that such appeal shall be instituted within three calendar months after the decision appealed from shall have been pronounced.

353. Under section-48 of the Act, when the time hereby limited for appealing against any decree granting a divorce or annulling or dissolving a marriage shall have expired, and no appeal shall have been presented against such decree, or when any such appeal shall have been dismissed, or when in the result of any appeal a divorce has been granted or a marriage has been declared to be annulled or dissolved, but not sooner, it shall be lawful for the respective parties thereto to marry again, as if the prior marriage had been terminated by death.

354. The section-49 of the Parsi Marriage and Divorce Act, 1865 deals regarding children of the Parties. The Court may from time to time pass such interim orders and make such provisions in the final decree as it may deem just and proper with respect to the custody, maintenance and education of the children under the age of 16 years, the marriage of whose parents is the subject of such suit, and may, after the final decree upon application, by petition for this purpose, make, revoke, suspend or vary from time to time all such orders and provisions with respect to the custody, maintenance and education of such children as might have been made by such final decree or by interim orders in case the suit for obtaining such decree were still pending.

355. Section-50 of the Parsi Marriage and Divorce Act, 1865 provide settlement of wife's property for benefit of children. In any case in which the Court shall pronounce a decree of divorce or judicial separation for adultery of the wife, if it shall be made to appear to the Court that the wife is entitled to any property either in possession or reversion, the Court may order such settlement as it shall think reasonable to be made of any part of such property, not exceeding one-half thereof, for the benefit of the children of the marriage or any of them.

356. Under Schedule-I of the Parsi Marriage and Divorce Act, 1865 a man cannot marry his paternal grand-father's mother; paternal grand-mother's mother; maternal grand-father's mother; maternal grand-mother's mother; paternal grand-mother; paternal grand-father's wife; maternal grand-mother; maternal grand-father's wife; mother or step-mother; father's sister or step-sister; mother's sister or step-sister; sister or step-sister; brother's daughter or step-brother's daughter, or any direct lineal descendant of a brother or step-brother; sister's daughter or step-sister's daughter, or any direct lineal descendant of a sister, or step-sister; daughter or step-daughter, or any direct lineal descendant of either; son's daughter or step-son's daughter, or any direct lineal descendant of a son or step-son; wife of son or step-son, or of any direct lineal descendant of a son or step-son; wife of daughter's son or of step-daughter's son, or of any direct lineal descendant of a daughter or step-daughter; mother of daughter's husband; mother of son's wife; mother of wife's paternal grand-father; mother of wife's paternal grand-mother; mother of wife's maternal grand-father; mother of wife's maternal grand-mother; wife's paternal grand-mother; wife's maternal grand-mother; wife's mother or step-mother; wife's father's sister; wife's mother's sister; father's brother's wife; mother's brother's wife; brother's son's wife and sister's son's wife.

357. Under Schedule-I of the Parsi Marriage and Divorce Act, 1865 a woman is allowed to marry her paternal grand-father's father; paternal grand-mother's father; maternal grand-father's father; maternal grand-mother's father; paternal grand-father; paternal grand-mother's husband; maternal grand-father; maternal grand-mother's husband; father or step-father; father's brother or step-brother; mother's brother or step-brother; brother or step-brother; brother's son or step-brother's son, or any direct lineal descendant of a brother or step-brother; sister's son or step-sister's son, or any direct lineal descendant of a sister or step-sister; son or step-son, or any direct lineal descendant of either; daughter's son or step-daughter's son, or any direct lineal descendant of a daughter or step-daughter; husband of daughter or of step-daughter, or of any direct lineal descendant of a daughter or step-daughter; husband of son's daughter or of step-son's daughter, or of any direct lineal descendant of a son or step-son; father of daughter's husband; father of son's wife; father of husband's paternal grand-father; father of husband's paternal grand-mother; father of husband's maternal grand-father; father of husband's maternal grand-mother; husband's paternal grand-father; husband's maternal grand-father; husband's father or step-father; brother of husband's father; brother of husband's mother; husband's brother's son, or his direct lineal descendant; husband's sister's son, or his direct lineal descendant; brother's daughter's husband; sister's daughter's husband;

§3. DOWER (HAQ MEHR)

358. In old pre-Islamic days, it often happened that the Arabs, after despoiling their wives, turned them out adrift, absolutely helpless and without any means. So it was made an essential condition to the validity of a marriage that the husband should settle on the wife a certain dower, which becomes her exclusive property. However, there is no fix amount or criteria for payment of dower. Under the Holy Quran, it is stated that 'if you separate yourself from wives, send them away with generosity', and it is also stated that 'it is not permitted to you to appropriate the goods you have once given to them (wife)'.

359. Under the Islamic system of jurisprudence, the main object of dower is the protection to the wife against the arbitrary exercise of power of divorce by the husband. In Islamic Law, the husband can divorce his wife at any time he likes without any reason, so the object of dower is to serve as a check upon the capricious exercise by the husband of his power to terminate the marriage at will.

360. Under Islamic Law, specified dower in the *Nikahnama* is usually split into two parts which are payable at different times. The part called 'Prompt Dower' is payable on demand at any time after the contract of marriage. The other part called 'Deferred Dower' is payable after a specified period of time and when no such period is fixed on the death of the husband or dissolution of marriage.

361. Prompt dower is payable immediately on demand. It is not necessary that marriage may have been consummated before demand is made. Wife after *Nikah* becomes entitled to payment of entire amount of prompt dower. She can refuse consummation of marriage without payment of prompt dower. Husband would be liable to pay only half of dower amount in case he divorces wife before consummation of marriage. Consummation would not be relevant factor for demanding amount of dower payable by a husband in case where claim is made in respect of prompt dower during subsistence of marriage. Refusal by husband to pay prompt dower would entitle wife to live separately and be entitled to maintenance.

362. If amount of the dower is not specified or not fixed, the wife is entitled to 'proper dower' even if the marriage was contracted on the express condition that she should not claim any dower. In determining what is 'proper dower' means the amount of dower settled upon other female members of her father's sister. The wife may refuse to live with her husband and admit him to sexual intercourse so long as the prompt dower is paid.

363. Under section-10 of MFLO, where no details about the mode of payment of dower are specified in the *Nikahnama* or the marriage contract, the entire amount of the dower shall be presumed to be payable on demand.

364. PHC (2006 PLD 189): Dower paid and snatched by husband. Dower would remain as dower; neither it would undergo any change nor it would be transformed into a civil liability in case it was snatched or taken back forcibly from wife by husband. Neither Muslim Family Laws Ordinance, 1961 nor provisions of West Pakistan Family Courts Act, 1964 had provided, either impliedly or expressly, that when dower paid was snatched by husband then for its retrieval, wife would have to make recourse to the civil court. Dower paid to wife and snatched by husband would automatically restore his liability to repay the same, and it would remain as a dower due to wife, triable by Family Court alone. Once dower was paid, then it would become the property of wife as her complete domain was established over it. Act of its snatching would amount to the disposal of her property, and Family Court alone would have jurisdiction to take cognizance for the recovery of the same. Appellate Court had committed legal error by refusing to exercise jurisdiction vested in it with regard to dower. Impugned judgment and decree reversing judgment and decree of Family Court with regard to recovery of dower and directing plaintiff to have recourse to Civil Court for its recovery was held to be without lawful authority. Impugned judgment and decree of Appellate Court, was set aside, and it was directed to decide entire case/appeal on merits [section 5 & Schedule. Muslim Family Laws Ordinance (VIII of 1961), section 10].

365. LHC (2008 MLD 1673): Wife sought recovery of PKR 2,000,000 as dower amount. Family Court decreed the suit in favour of wife to the extent of PKR 2,000,000 and in lieu of dower wife was entitled to take 50 tolas of gold ornaments, agricultural land and one-half share in a residential house. Judgment and decree passed by Family Court was maintained by Lower Appellate Court and appeal filed by wife was dismissed. Plea raised by wife was that 50 tolas of gold ornaments, agricultural land and one-half share in a residential house were in addition to dower amount as the same were incorporated in *Nikahnama* through Iqrarnama. Validity: Iqrarnama and its contents had become integral part of *Nikahnama*, and as such the contents/entries in *Nikahnama* were to be read in conjunction with Iqrarnama. Marriage being a contract, the parties to the marriage were at liberty to enter into the terms of their choice. Two Courts below could not interpret the terms on their own when such interpretation specifically stood negated by the contents of *Nikahnama* and Iqrarnama. Both the documents revealed that amount of dower of PKR 20,00,000 was independent in itself, and property and gold ornaments were in addition to the amount of Haqul Mehar. Findings of both the Courts below that gold ornaments and the property were in lieu of amount of Haqul Mehar were totally falsified by evidence on record. Both the Courts below erroneously and illegally held that the wife was not entitled to the property mentioned in *Nikahnama* and Iqrarnama. High Court, in exercise of Constitutional jurisdiction, set aside the findings of both the courts below to the extent of properties mentioned in their judgments. High Court modified the judgments and decrees passed by both the Courts below and included properties and gold ornaments in the decree as envisaged in *Nikahnama* with Iqrarnama. Constitutional petition was allowed accordingly [section 5. Muslim Family Laws Ordinance (VIII of 1961), section 5. Constitution of Pakistan (1973), Article 199].

366. The Shariat Court, Azad Kashmir (1999 YLR 2303) Suit for recovery of dower. Claim of plaintiff wife was that the whole amount of dower was payable to her on demand, whereas defendant husband contended that he had paid full amount of dower and nothing was against him. Burden to prove payment of amount of dower was on defendant, but he failed to discharge that burden through evidence. In absence of anything to the contrary regarding nature of dower fixed at time of *Nikah*, whole dower amount was payable to plaintiff by defendant as he had failed to prove that he had already paid said amount. Trial Court was not justified to dismiss suit for recovery of dower amount [Muslim Family Laws Ordinance 1961 section 10. West Pakistan Family Courts Act (XXXV of 1964), section 5 & Schedule].

367. SCP(2009 SCMR 1458): Leave to appeal was granted by Supreme Court to consider the correct import of 'deferred dower' and whether it could become prompt if and when demanded; whether Family Court could not grant maintenance which instead could be granted by Arbitration Council as mentioned in section 9 of Muslim Family Laws Ordinance, 1961; whether amount of maintenance decree commensurated with status and income of husband; whether restitution of conjugal rights could be allowed subject to condition of separate living of wife with husband abroad; and whether restitution of conjugal rights could be subjected to payment of maintenance [section 5. Muslim Family Laws Ordinance (VIII of 1961), section 9. Constitution of Pakistan (1973), Article 185(3)].

368. LHC (2009 PLD 227): Constitutional petition. Dissolution of marriage by way of '*Khula*'. Restoration to the husband the dower received by the wife. Execution of decree. Held, dower paid at any other time except at the time of marriage cannot be recovered through process of execution on the basis of a decree obtained in terms of section 10(4), West Pakistan Family Courts Act, 1964 granting dissolution of marriage. Principles [section 10(4). Muslim Family Laws Ordinance (VIII of 1961), Form II, Column 15. Constitution of Pakistan (1973), Article 199].

369. SCP (2004 PLD 10): Dower: Factum of gift of property by husband to wife in lieu of dower as recorded in Column No. 13 of *Nikahnama*. Validity: Presumption of truth was attached to *Nikahnama*, which could not be rebutted. Husband after having gifted property to wife in lieu of dower would have no title to dispose of the same [section 5. West Pakistan Rules under Muslim Family Laws Ordinance, 1961, Rr. 8, 10, 11, 12 & Form II, Column 13 *Nikahnama*].

370. PHC(2003 YLR 250): Property given in lieu of dower. Execution of dower deed separately. Validity: If marriage was registered under the provisions of section 5 of Muslim Family Laws Ordinance, 1961, any property transferred to the bride by her father-in-law in lieu of dower would have been mentioned in *Nikahnama* prescribed in form II of West Pakistan Rules under MFLO, and in such case there was no need to execute a dower deed separately. Property mentioned in *Nikahnama* would stand transferred in the name of the bride [Muslim Family Laws Ordinance 1961. Section 5 West Pakistan Rules under MFLO, R. 10, Form II].

371. LHC (2002 MLD 31): Transfer of land by way of dower. Husband of the petitioner at the time of marriage transferred land in name of the petitioner by way of dower. Husband submitted declaration under section 7 of Land Reforms Act, 1977, excluding land transferred to the petitioner but Authority included the said land in his holding and after calculating total produce index units ordered him to surrender excess land in favour of the Government. Validity: Nothing was on record to prove that *Nikahnama* whereby land in question was given/transferred to the petitioner by her husband by way of dower was a fabricated document. Authority considered *Nikahnama* as forged and fabricated one on the ground that columns therein dealing with amount and nature of dower were left blank. Question as to whether leaving blank said columns could lead to an inference that the *Nikahnama* was forged and fabricated, needed consideration, but no opportunity was given to the petitioner to prove that in relevant column of *Nikahnama* it was clearly mentioned that the bridegroom had given said land to his wife/petitioner as dower, and said *Nikahnama* was written long prior to the enforcement of Land Reforms Act, 1977. *Nikahnama* was admissible to prove factum of alienation of property in lieu of dower. Authority which had not seen the matter in its true perspective, had committed material irregularity and illegality while rendering order which had resulted in grave miscarriage of justice. Order passed by the Authority was set aside and case was remanded to be decided afresh on merits [Land Reforms Act, 1977. Section-7 Muslim Family Laws Ordinance (VIII of 1961), section 10, Constitution of Pakistan (1973), Article 199].

372. The Shariat Court, Azad Kashmir (2000 YLR 1857): Dissolution of marriage on ground of '*Khula*'. Repeated attempts for reconciliation made by Court had failed, and wife had openly stated that she would prefer death to live with her husband as his wife. Trial Court concluded that it was not possible for the parties to live together as husband and wife within limits ordained by God and passed decree for divorce subject to return of ornaments or value thereof to the husband as '*Khula*' amount. Wife had herself admitted that she had received ornaments from the husband at the time of *Nikah* as dower. Trial Court, in circumstances, had rightly dissolved marriage directing wife to return ornaments received by her from husband as dower or to pay amount thereof as she had herself gone to Court seeking dissolution of marriage on ground of '*Khula*' [Muslim Family Laws Ordinance 1961. Section 8 West Pakistan Family Courts Act (XXXV of 1964), sections 5, 14 & Schedule].

373. PHC (2000 MLD 1638): Suit for maintenance and dower. Dower and dowery. Distinction. Wife in her suit for maintenance and dower had claimed gold ornaments and a house as dower. Family Court decreed the suit, but Appellate Court in appeal dismissed the claim of wife. Claim of wife qua ornaments and house was specifically mentioned in dower/deed/*Nikahnama*. Wife who admittedly had received gold ornaments at the time of marriage had contended that gold ornaments which were given at the time of *Nikah* were part of dowery but were snatched and kept into possession by the husband. Contention was devoid of force because dowery were those articles which were given to wife by parents at the time of 'Rukhsati' whereas dower was a right of wife which was always paid or to be paid in lieu of marriage by husband. Dower once paid, liability of same would be satisfied. Taking away of dower by husband after marriage could be considered as loan/credit, return of which could only be sought through civil suit. Wife was entitled to payment of dower in shape of house which had been given to her in dower by husband as per dower deed [Muslim Family Laws Ordinance 1961 sections 9 & 10 West Pakistan Family Courts Act (XXXV of 1964), sections 5, Schedule & 14. Constitution of Pakistan (1973), Article 199].

374. LHC (2000 YLR 537): Recovery of deferred dower. Contracting of second marriage without the permission of Arbitration Council. Petitioner/wife filed a suit for recovery and the same was decreed by the Trial Court whereas in appeal the Lower Appellate Court reversed the finding of the Trial Court and dismissed the suit. Validity: Where a man had contracted another marriage without permission of the Arbitration Council such person under the provisions of section 6(5) of Muslim Family Laws Ordinance, 1961 was liable to pay immediately the entire amount of dower whether prompt or deferred due, to the existing wife, and such amount if not so paid would be recoverable as arrears of land revenue. Where it was not pleaded that the subsequent *Nikah* had been contracted with the permission of the Arbitration Council, the husband had become liable to pay the entire amount of dower forthwith. Judgment and decree of the Lower Appellate Court was without lawful authority and the same was set aside [Muslim Family Laws Ordinance 1961. section 6(5). West Pakistan Family Courts Act (XXXV of 1964), section 5 & Schedule Constitution of Pakistan (1973), Article 199].

375. Mandatory for a husband to pay entire amount of dower, whether prompt or deferred in case of entering into contract of second marriage in presence of first wife without her permission. Principles [Muslim Family Laws Ordinance 1961 sections 6(5) & 10] LHC (2000 CLC 1384).

376. Transfer of immoveable property by husband to wife through *Nikahnama* which had not been registered under Registration Act, 1908. Validity: *Nikah* of parties was in the form prescribed under Muslim Family Laws Ordinance, 1961 and the rules framed thereunder and same was registered with the *Nikah* Registrar in accordance with prescribed mode, and thus, *Nikahnama* had a different status than any other unregistered document through which some immoveable property had purportedly been transferred. *Nikahnama* was a public document executed by a Public Officer, certified copy whereof, was sufficient for proof of its contents unless its rebuttal was effected through cogent evidence. Dower deed by which immoveable property was purported to be transferred was, thus, not considered to be compulsorily registerable under Registration Act, 1908, and wife was entitled to claim immoveable property on basis of *Nikahnama* wherein same was incorporated in lieu of dower [Registration Act 1908 section 5. West Pakistan Family Courts Act

(XXXV of 1964), section 5. Registration Act (XVI of 1908), sections 17 & 49. Constitution of Pakistan (1973), Article 199] PHC (1996 PLD 64).

377. LHC (1991 CLC 1620): Defendant female, contended that house sought to be partitioned by plaintiff, had been gifted to her by her deceased husband in lieu of her dower debt. Defendant lady failed to produce any documentary evidence in proof of her claim. Matters like dower debt or its satisfaction through transferring house in favour of lady deserved more pragmatic approach than mere words of mouth before a witness or two and more substantial evidence like transfer deed was expected. Existence of such deed was even affirmed by the lady, but she failed to produce it or prove it by secondary evidence. Finding of Courts below that house was not transferred to lady by way of *hibabilewaz* was unexceptionable in circumstances [Muslim Family Laws Ordinance 1961 section 10].

378. LHC (1989 MLD 989): Recovery of Dower: Husband himself fixed amount of dower at the time of marriage. Marriage was consummated, and a child was born out of the wedlock. Husband, held, neither could resile from his liability to pay dower amount nor disown his responsibility on technicality that since his person and property was under superintendence of Court of Wards, he being under wardship could not fix any dower as consideration for his marriage [Muslim Family Laws Ordinance 1961. section 10].

§4. Dowry and Bridal Gifts

379. Under section 2(b) of the Dowry and Bridal Gifts (Restriction) Act, 1976), 'Dowry' means any property given before, at or after the marriage either directly or indirectly, to the bride by her parents in connection with the marriage, but it does not include property which the bride may inherit under the laws of inheritance and succession applicable to her; whereas under section 2(a) of the Dowry and Bridal Gifts (Restriction) Act, 1976 'Bridal gift' means any property given as a gift before, at or after the marriage, either directly, by the bridegroom or his parents to the bride in connection with the marriage but does not include Mehr.

380. Under section 2(e) of the Dowry and Bridal Gifts (Restriction) Act, 1976, 'Present' means a gift of any property, not being bridal gift or dowry, given before, at or after the marriage, either directly in connection with the marriage, or to the relatives of the bride or bridegroom but does not include 'neundra' and 'salami'. Neither the aggregate value of the dowry and presents given to the bride by her parents nor the aggregate value of the bridal gifts or the presents given to the bridegroom shall exceed PKR 5,000. Explanation: The ceiling of PKR 5,000 specified in this sub-section does not in any way imply that the dowry, bridal gifts and presents of a lesser amount may not be given.

381. No dowry, bridal gifts or presents may be given before or after six months of *Nikah* and if rukhsati takes place sometime after *Nikah*, after six months of such rukhsati. (section-3 of the Dowry and Bridal Gifts (Restriction) Act, 1976).

382. No person gives to either party to the marriage any present, the value of which exceeds PKR 100, provided that the limit of PKR 100 shall not apply to the presents given to the bridegroom by the parents of the bride under sub-section (1) of section 3: Provided further that the President, the Prime Minister, Federal Minister, Chief Minister of State, Adviser, Governor, Speaker, Deputy Speaker, the Chairman or the Deputy Chairman of the Senate, Parliamentary Secretary, Member of the Senate, National Assembly or Provincial Assembly, Government servant or an official serving in any corporation, industry or establishment owned, controlled or managed by Government shall not receive any present in connection with his marriage or the marriage of his son or daughter except from his relations (khandan): Provided further that this restriction shall not apply to a Government servant or official serving in the scale below National Pay Scale 17 not exercising in any manner judicial, revenue or executive authority. (section-4 of the Dowry and Bridal Gifts (Restriction) Act, 1976).

383. All property given as dowry or bridal gifts and all property given to the bride as a present shall vest absolutely in the bride and her interest in property however derived shall hereafter not be restrictive, conditional or limited. (section-5 of the Dowry and Bridal Gifts (Restriction) Act, 1976).

384. The total expenditure on a marriage, excluding the value of dowry, bridal gifts and presents, but including the expenses on mehndi, baarat and valima, incurred by or on behalf of either party to the marriage shall not exceed PKR 2,500. (section-6 of the Dowry and Bridal Gifts (Restriction) Act, 1976).

385. The parents of each party to a marriage, at the time of rukhsati, display all items of dowry, bridal gifts and presents given or received in connection with the marriage so as to be visible to the persons attending the rukhsati. (section-7 of the Dowry and Bridal Gifts (Restriction) Act, 1976).

386. The parents of each party to a marriage shall furnish to the Registrar lists of dowry, bridal gifts and presents given or received in connection with the marriage. The lists shall be furnished in the case of property given or accepted before or at the time of the marriage; and in the case or property given or accepted after the marriage, within fifteen days of its being given or accepted.

387. The lists referred to shall contain details of the property along with the value thereof, and be signed or thumb-marked by the person furnishing them to the Registrar and attested by at least two witnesses.

388. The parents of each party to a marriage shall furnish to the Registrar the details of expenditure incurred on the marriage, duly signed or thumb-marked by them within one week. The Registrar shall forward the lists furnished and the details of expenditure submitted to the Deputy Commissioner within fifteen days of receipt of such list or details of expenditure. (section-8 of the Dowry and Bridal Gifts (Restriction) Act, 1976).

389. Whoever, contravenes, or fails to comply with, any provision of Dowry and Bridal Gifts (Restriction) Act, 1976 shall be punishable with imprisonment of either description for a term which may extend to six months, or with fine which may extend to PKR 10,000, or with both, and the dowry, bridal gifts or presents given or accepted in contravention of the provisions of this Act shall be forfeited to the Federal Government to be utilized for the marriage of poor girls: Provided that if both the parents of a party to the marriage contravene, or fail to comply with, any provision of Act, action shall be taken only against the father: Provided further that if the parent who contravenes, or fails to comply with, any provisions of this Act or the rules made thereunder, is a female, shall be punishable with fine only.

390. An offence punishable under Dowry and Bridal Gifts (Restrictions) Act, 1976 shall be triable only by a Family Court established under the West Pakistan Family Courts Act, 1964 (W.P. Act No. XXXV of 1964). No Family Court takes cognizance of an offence punishable under this Act except upon a complaint in writing made by, or under the authority of the Deputy Commissioner within nine months from the date of *Nikah*, and if rukhsati takes place sometime after *Nikah*, from the date of such rukhsati.

391. While trying an offence punishable under this Act, a Family Court follows the procedure prescribed by the Code of Criminal Procedure, 1898 (Act V of 1898), for the trial of offences by Magistrates. (section-9 of the Dowry and Bridal Gifts (Restriction) Act, 1976).

392. Where marriage was dissolved on various grounds including '*Khula*' then wife would be entitled to recover dower and dowry, but where it was dissolved solely on the ground of '*Khula*' then her offer made for getting marriage dissolved on '*Khula*' would be examined. Wife filed suit for dissolution of marriage on various grounds viz. cruelty, non-payment of maintenance, non-performance of marital obligations, impotency of husband and '*Khula*'. Wife also filed suit for recovery of dowry amount. Family Court decreed the suit for dissolution of marriage on all such grounds holding that wife in lieu of '*Khula*' would not be entitled to claim dower, dowry and maintenance. Husband, in view of such findings, filed in latter suit an application for rejection of the plaint. Wife filed application for clarification of judgment and decree, but it was dismissed by Family Court and its order was maintained by the Appellate Court. High Court accepted Constitutional petition filed by wife and set aside the conditions regarding relinquishment of dower, dowry and maintenance. Contention of husband was that High Court in exercise of Constitutional jurisdiction could not change judgment and decree passed by Family Court, especially when the wife had not challenged same and her petition for clarification had been dismissed by Courts below. 'Held' wife in her deposition recorded before Family Court had forgiven only her claim for remaining amount of dower in lieu of '*Khula*' and had not given up her claim of dowry. Marriage was dissolved on various rounds including '*Khula*'. Where marriage was dissolved on other grounds also, then wife would be entitled to recover amount of dower and dowry, but where it was dissolved solely on ground of '*Khula*' then situation would be different, and it would be examined keeping in view the offer she had made for getting marriage dissolved on '*Khula*'. Findings of High Court were correct and not open to any exception. Supreme Court dismissed the appeal of husband while making it clear that suit filed by wife for recovery of dowry amount would be decided on its own merits (reference West Pakistan Family Court Act 1964. Section 5 & Schedule. Dissolution of Muslim Marriages Act (VIII of 1939), section 2) (SCP – 2002 PLD 273).

393. Bridal Gifts, presents or all the other moveable properties are the belongings of bride and the husband if deprives her of the same, she has the right to recover all these articles even though the same were given in contradiction of provisions of section 3 of the Dowry and Bridal Gifts (Restriction) Act, 1976. Bride can always recover the articles of Dowry and Wari given to her by the bridegroom or the bridegroom side at the time of marriage. Bridal gift given by the husband is the absolute property of the wife, and it could not be snatched away from her (LHC – 2004 PLD 290).

394. Bridal Gift given by husband was absolute property of the wife under the provisions of the Act and could not be snatched away. Violation of such provisions would entail a penalty of fine and imprisonment (LHC – 1991 CLC 1696).

§5. Effects of Marriage

I. General

395. After the marriage some rights and privileges arises which relationship, especially the mutual rights of companionship, aid, and sexual relations.

II. Rights and Duties of Husband

396. There is no specific law in Pakistan which clearly defines the rights and duties of a husband after marriage. However under the Islamic Law, the husband has the right for the following:

- To the sexual obedience and of course the sole enjoyment of his wife, due regard being had to health and decency. This right, being of the essence of the contract, cannot be abrogated.
- As in other system of law, the husband decides the place of conjugal residence. The husband's discretion cannot be abrogated, and a stipulation that the wife shall live in her parents' home and the husband shall only visit her there is void.
- The husband has the right to insist at his discretion that his wife shall either see, be seen by, nor speak to male strangers without his permission. This does not prevent her seeing her children by a previous marriage or her own relatives within prohibited degrees, or her slaves with due regard to his convenience. The husband, however, is not bound to restrict his wife's liberty in this matter, and many in the marriage contract deprive himself partly or wholly of the powers to do so.

– If the husband cannot afford a wet nurse, or if no wet nurse is available, the wife is bound to suckle her own children. That the duty of suckling is not one of the essentials of marriage as is clear from the fact that an agreement by the wife to suckle her own children and thereby relieve the husband from pecuniary liability may be sufficient consideration for a '*Khula*' divorce.
– The wife is bound to general conformity with the husband's wishes, but the management of house is not necessarily part of her duties, as is obvious from the possibility of more than one wife, and cannot be compelled to perform menial duties if unbefitting either her rank or his means.
– Islamic Law recognizes the right of the husband to punish his wife for disobedience by moderate corporal chastisements. However, it is not to be inflicted till other means of correction have failed, and that the blows are to cause no fracture, wound or serious bruise.
– It is undoubted right of the husband that wife shall have no other spouse.
– The husband is solely responsible to maintain his wife, pay her dower, arrange accommodation for her, provide food and cloth and pay pocket money to her for personal usage. In addition, he is also responsible to arrange medical treatment of her wife as and when required and deal with her politely.
– In case there is more than one wife, the husband must divide his time according to regular rotations between his wives.
– A husband is commanded by the law of God to treat his wife with equity, respect her feelings and show kindness and consideration, especially if he has another wife. The Holy Prophet's Muhammad (PBUH) Last Sermon stresses kindness to women.

III. Rights and Duties of Wife

397. After the marriage, it is right of wife that husband pay her dower, arrange accommodation, perform conjugal rights, meet her requirements, deal with her politely and respectable manner, provide medical treatment, provide food and cloth and pay pocket money for her daily use. The husband must provide a suitable matrimonial residence for his wife. If he has more than one wife, he must provide each of them with a separate apartment, according to his means, a separate room with a separate bathroom at least or in case of a wealthy man, a separate suit or house.

398. However, under the customs and court decisions, duties of the wife include having conjugal relations with her husband as per wishes of the husband, conceive baby, take care of husband, children and house, safeguard the property of husband and provide full support to the husband in handling domestic affairs.

399. One of the main duties of the wife is to contribute to the success and happiness of the marriage. She should be attentive to the comfort and wellbeing of her husband and vice-versa. The Quranic Ayah which illustrates this point is: 'Our Lord, grant us wives and offspring who will be the coolness of our eyes and guide us to be models for the righteous'.

400. The wife should be trustworthy and honest. She cannot deceive her husband by deliberately avoiding conceiving. She should not have any sexual intimacy with anyone other than her husband. She should not receive or entertain strange males in the house without his knowledge and consent. She should not accept gifts from other men without his approval. This is meant to avoid jealousy, suspicion and gossip. She should not dispose of his belongings without his permission.

401. A wife should make herself attractive to her husband and be responsive to his advances. The wife should not refuse her husband without reason as this may lead to marital problems and worse still – tempt the man to adultery. The husband, of course, should take into account the wife's health and consideration of circumstances.

402. The wife should be obedient to husband. The purpose of 'obedience' in a relationship is to keep the family unit running as smoothly as possible. Obedience does not mean blind obedience. It is subject to conditions that it is required only if what is asked from the wife is within the permissible categories of action.

403. The Shariat Court, Azad Kashmir (2004 CLC 1168) held that if wife refused to live with her husband without any lawful excuse and deserted her house or otherwise wilfully failed to perform her marital duties, she would have no right to claim maintenance allowance from her husband. If husband in said circumstances would not maintain his wife, it could not be said that there was negligence or failure of husband to provide for maintenance to wife.

IV. Maintenance of Wife

404. The husband is responsible for the wife's maintenance. This right is established by authority of the Holy Quran and Sunnah. It is inconsequential whether the wife is a Muslim, non-Muslim, rich, poor, healthy or sick. A component of his role is to bear the financial responsibility of the family in a generous way so that his wife may be assured security.

405. The wife's maintenance entails her right to lodging, clothing, food and general care, like medication, hospital bills, etc. He must provide for her where he resides himself according to his means. The wife's lodging must be adequate so as to ensure her privacy, comfort and independence.

406. The husband is bound according to all schools to provide for her maintenance irrespective of her private means. Even where she is a rich woman and he is a poor man she is absolutely entitled, if she chooses to be provided at his expense, on a scale suitable to his means, with food, clothing, housing, tailor necessaries, medicine, doctors' and surgeons' fees and bath and also the necessary servants, at least where the wife is of a social position which does not permit her to dispense with these, or in sickness. The wife need not spend a penny of her own money on these objects. Under the Islamic Laws, the arrears of unpaid maintenance are a debt for which the wife can sue and continued inability or failure to pay maintenance is a ground for dissolution of marriage. However in Hanafi Law, inability to pay maintenance is not the ground for dissolution of marriage.

407. Under section-9 of MFLO if any husband fails to maintain his wife adequately, or where there are more wives than one, fails to maintain them equitably, the wife, or all or any of the wives, may in addition to seeking any other legal remedy available apply to the Chairman of Union Council, who shall constitute an Arbitration Council to determine the matter, and the Arbitration Council may issue a certificate specifying the amount which shall be paid as maintenance by the husband. Any amount payable by Husband, not paid in the due time, shall be recoverable as arrears of land revenue. However, a husband or wife may, prefer an application for revision of the certificate, to the Collector and his decision shall be final and shall not be called in question in any Court.

408. Under sections 488–490 of the Criminal Procedure Code of Pakistan, if any person having sufficient means neglects or refuses to maintain his wife or his legitimate or illegitimate child unable to maintain itself, a Magistrate of the first class may, upon proof of such neglect or refusal, order such person to make a monthly allowance for the maintenance of his wife or such child, at such monthly rate, not exceeding PKR 400 in the whole, as the Magistrate thinks fit, and to pay the same to such persons as the Magistrate from time to time direct. If any persons fails without sufficient cause to comply with the orders of the Magistrate, the Magistrate may issue a warrant for levying of fine and sentence for the whole or any part of each month's allowance remaining unpaid after the execution of the warrant, to imprisonment for a term which may extend to one month or until payment if sooner made. However, no wife shall be entitled to receive an allowance from her husband under these sections if she is living in adultery or if without any sufficient reasons, she refused to live with her husband or if they are living separately by mutual consent.

409. Chairman Arbitration Council ordered husband to pay to wife maintenance allowance for a period of ten years and six months. Article 120 of Limitation Act, 1908, providing limitation period of six years from accrual of right to sue, being applicable in respect of claim for past maintenance, decree for maintenance passed by Chairman for a period of ten years and six months prior to institution of application for maintenance, was not warranted by law. Orders passed by Chairman Arbitration Council were set aside being illegal (LHC – 1992 CLC 1926).

410. Controlling Authority set aside order of Arbitration Council according to which past maintenance was granted to wife for a period of eleven years and four months prior to filing of application for grant of past and future maintenance by wife. Controlling Authority after setting aside order of Arbitration Council, granted past maintenance only for three years prior to riling of application for grant of maintenance. High Court found both orders of Authorities below as illegal and found wife entitled to past maintenance for a period of six years prior to filing of application for grant of maintenance as provided under Article 120, Limitation Act, 1908 (LHC – 1993 CLC 2063).

411. Maintenance allowance granted to wife for a period of three years by Arbitration Council reversed by Collector to the period of *Iddat*. Collector had based his finding on the judgment of Family Court whereby children of spouses were granted maintenance allowance from specified date and no past maintenance was allowed to them. Validity: Provisions of section 9, Muslim Family Laws Ordinance 1961, provides maintenance to wife only, on entirely different grounds while Family Court is guided by the law laid down in West Pakistan Family Courts Act, 1964, where wife or the children can invoke their right of maintenance allowance which could not exceed period of six months retrospectively. District Collector had thus, erroneously based his judgment on the basis of decree of Family Court which was granted for maintenance of children of spouses. Judgment passed by District Collector was also devoid of all considerations that husband was bound to maintain his wife who had not demanded divorce and was mother of two children. Order passed by District Collector was completely devoid of reasons and application of mind to the facts, law and circumstances relevant to the case of wife. Order of Collector whereby he had reduced period of maintenance to wife was set aside and that of Arbitration Council which was completely legal and based upon true appraisal of evidence, was restored (LHC – 1995 CLC 914).

412. Two remedies are available to a wife for claiming maintenance: by filing a suit for maintenance against her husband before a Family Court; and by claiming maintenance under section 9, Muslim Family Laws Ordinance, 1961. Muslim Family Laws Ordinance, 1961, is silent so far as past maintenance is concerned; therefore, Court while interpreting the statute must keep in mind the intention of the legislature. Intention of legislature by adding section 9, Muslim Family Laws Ordinance was to grant maintenance allowance to a woman whose husband had failed to maintain her adequately. Such remedy was an expeditious one also available to a wife when there were more wives than one (LHC – 1994 CLC 2403).

413. Application for recovery of maintenance allowance was accepted. Revision against acceptance was allowed. Muslim Family Laws Ordinance, 1961 being silent with regard to past maintenance, the Court, while interpreting the statute, must keep in mind intention of the Legislature. Wife, who did not bother to live with her husband and perform her marital obligations, was not entitled for grant of maintenance allowance. Application of wife, who lived separately and had not performed marital obligations in spite of decree for restitution of conjugal rights in favour of husband, was rightly dismissed by District Officer (Revenue) and thus called for no interference by High Court in Constitutional petition (LHC – 2006 YLR 633).

414. Chairman, Arbitration Council had jurisdiction to decide application of ex-wife for grant of maintenance for period during which marriage subsisted. Findings of Collector that Chairman Arbitration Council could not entertain application for maintenance by a wife who had already been divorced, were not valid. Past maintenance could be awarded by Arbitration Council for a period up to six years and the wife who had been divorced by husband, was also entitled to claim maintenance through application to Chairman, Arbitration Council. Husband, in the present case had not been able to, show that wife was divorced at the time when she filed application for maintenance. Order of Collector to the extent that Arbitration Council had no jurisdiction to award maintenance to wife, was illegal. Chairman, Arbitration Council was competent to, award different quantum of maintenance for different periods [reference Muslim Family Laws Ordinance 1961 section 9] (LHC – 2002 MLD 1716).

415. Petitioner was a British national who had divorced the respondent. Proceedings for recovery of past maintenance and that of the period of *Iddat* were initiated under section 9 of Muslim Family Laws Ordinance, 1961. Both the Courts below granted past maintenance along with period of *Iddat* for ninety days. Grievance of petitioner was that the Courts below had wrongly assumed jurisdiction in the matter as the petitioner was not a Muslim citizen of Pakistan and period of *Iddat* was thirty-nine days which was wrongly fixed as ninety days. Validity: Petitioner did not raise point of jurisdiction in the contents of the revision petition filed below; therefore, he was not permitted to argue the same before High Court in exercise of Constitutional jurisdiction. Judgments of both the Tribunals below to the extent of period of *Iddat* were not in accordance with the dictum laid down by Supreme Court in case titled *Allah Dad v. Mukhtar* reported as 1992 SCMR 1273. High Court modified judgments passed by both the Tribunals below to the extent that instead of granting maintenance of *Iddat* period consisting of ninety days, the same was reduced to thirty-nine days. Petition was disposed of accordingly (LHC – 2002 CLC 1964).

416. Wife of the petitioner/ respondent had approached Chairman, Union Council/respondent with application for maintenance on 9 January 1993. Two notices had been sent to the petitioner by the Chairman, Union Council which had returned undelivered and he had observed in the order sheet that neither of the notices had been received by the petitioner. Petitioner, thereafter was proceeded ex parte and after recording the evidence of the wife of the petitioner, the Chairman, Union Council ordered the petitioner to pay PKR 84,000 as past maintenance for seven years to his wife and minor daughter. Wife of the petitioner had filed the execution petition 6½ years after the order of the Chairman, Union Council while the period of limitation was clearly six years. If first application for execution had been filed within three years, the execution proceedings were patently time-barred. Petitioner had filed a revision petition when he received notice of the execution proceedings and the Deputy Commissioner without taking into consideration contentions of the petitioner that he had been condemned unheard had proceeded to dismiss his revision petition as being time-barred and also dismissed the review petition on merits. Order of the Chairman, Union Council suffered from three legal lacunas; first, Chairman Union Council had not effected service on the petitioner through citation published in some daily of the area where the petitioner resided as the notices had returned unserved and as required under MFLO; second the Chairman had awarded maintenance for seven years to the petitioner while under Article 120 of the Limitation Act, 1908, maximum period for which maintenance could be awarded was six years; and third, application of the wife of the petitioner for execution of decree of Chairman, Union Council had been filed after 6½ years, and therefore, it was time-barred. Orders of the Chairman Union Council and of Deputy

Commissioner were declared to be of no legal effect and were set aside by the High Court (LHC – 2003 YLR 2445).

417. Order granting maintenance to wife simply on statement of wife unsupported by any evidence qua husband's financial status, could not be sustained, especially when statement of wife was absolutely silent as to paying capacity of husband, and wife had not even given any figure as to rate of maintenance allowance. Reference Muslim Family Laws Ordinance, 1961 section 9 (LHC – 1991 CLC 793).

418. Maintenance. Wife specifically claimed maintenance for herself as also for three minor children. Though minors were not impleaded as parties in suit, but it was specifically averred that they were living with plaintiff's wife and that defendant husband was bound to maintain them. In written statement filed by defendant husband, there was no objection that minors should have been impleaded as parties. Both Courts below in circumstances had erred in non-suiting minors. Reference Muslim Family Laws Ordinance 1961, section 9 (LHC – 1991 CLC 784).

419. Application for maintenance has to be filed before Union Council where wife was residing at the time of making her application. Reference Muslim Family Laws Ordinance 1961. Section 9. West Pakistan Rules under MFLO, Rule 3. (LHC – 1989 MLD 905).

420. Wife was turned out by husband from his house after beating her one year before making application for award of maintenance by her. Wife after having been turned out was residing along with her minor son with her parents. Maintenance allowance claimed by wife for one year prior to filing of application in that respect, held, was rightly allowed by Arbitration Council (LHC – 1989 MLD 380).

421. Record showed that father of the husband had undertaken, during the proceedings, that if his son will take any step which may give mental torture or cruel treatment to his wife or the husband will not perform matrimonial relationship, he will pay PKR 400,000 to the wife. Effect. Held, even the equity and natural justice demanded that the wife, who was neglected throughout by her husband and who was divorced by him at his whims and caprice, and she was left alone at the mercy of cruel circumstances in a male dominated society, without any source of income, should be maintained by the divorcing husband who had acted without justification. High Court observed that Legislature, in Pakistan having the supreme power to enact and legislate law, may, if so, deemed fit, look into this aspect of the matrimonial life and make amendment in section 9, Muslim Family Laws Ordinance, 1961 enabling the Chairman, Arbitration. Council to grant maintenance to a destitute divorced wife and may enact separate provisions of law in the same Ordinance (LHC – 2004 CLC 473).

422. When Court had come to the conclusion that wife had developed such aversion for her husband as to justify dissolution of marriage on basis of '*Khula*', then wife was not entitled to either past or future maintenance on dissolution of marriage on basis of '*Khula*' (PHC – 1991 MLD 1732).

V. Maintenance of Children

423. Under the Islamic Law, the maintenance of children is responsibility of the father, even though the custody of children is with mother, of sons until they attain age of puberty and daughters until they are married. In the absence of father, the grandfather of children is responsible to provide maintenance of children. It is the duty of father to spend on children whether their mother is still a wife of the father's children or not until these children reach the age of 15, or until the signs of puberty become apparent on them, as at this age they become able to earn their own daily bread, and they have no excuse. Allah says: 'but the father of the child shall bear the cost of the mother's food and clothing on a reasonable basis' (Al-Baqarah 2:233). As regards his daughters, he should provide for them until they get married. However, if the father is poor and has no money to spend on his children, then the mother should spend on her children if she is able to do so, and she has no right to ask him to compensate her for doing so.

424. To conclude, we should note that if it is determined that fostering of the children is for the father, he can give up fostering them in exchange for not spending on them. A father is responsible to spend on his children on two conditions: (a) While they are needy and cannot earn money. If a child has sufficient money to fulfil his needs or if he is able to earn money then the father is not obliged to spend on him. (b) The father has money exceeding what he spends on himself and his wife. If he does not have any money after fulfilling his necessary expenditures, then he no longer will be responsible to spend on his children. The Holy Prophet Muhammad (PBUH) said: 'Start with your own self and spend on yourself, and if anything is left it should be spent on your family, and if anything is left (after meeting the needs of family) it should be spent on relatives' [Reported by Imam Muslim]. In a narration, the Holy Prophet Muhammad (PBUH) said: 'And begin (spending) on the members of your household' [Reported by Imam Muslim].

425. The Muslim man has to spend on his wife as long as she is his wife and also his children by providing food, shelter and proper education for them until the children become adults and become able to satisfy their own needs by themselves. He should also spend on his poor mother and his poor sisters (although there is a disagreement over spending on sisters) according to his own ability as Allah Says: {Let the rich man spend according to his means, and the man whose resources are restricted, let him spend according to what Allâh has given him ... .}[65:7] He also has the right to save for the future and to invest from his own property. But he is not asked to do the same thing for his mother, sisters and children unless he has some money that belongs to them. In this case, he takes all appropriate steps that increase this money and protect it. The Pakistani Courts have categorically held in different cases that father of children is responsible for the maintenance of his children.

426. Maintenance allowance awarded to minor daughter. Father's suit for restitution of conjugal rights decreed but not put in execution. Wife alongwith minor daughter staying back from father and filing suit for maintenance. Maintenance allowance awarded to minor daughter, affirmed in appeal. Contention that minor daughter was unauthorizedly being kept away from father's custody not tenable in circumstances. Mother was entitled to retain custody of minor girl till she reaches age of puberty, unless mother was deprived of her custody through proceedings before competent forum. Child entitled to separate maintenance till mother was lawfully deprived of minor's custody. Minor could not be made to suffer because of rift between parents. Absolute duty of father to provide maintenance to his minor children regardless of fact where the Stay Order awarding maintenance allowance to child, held, well warranted both on facts and in law and not open to interference. Petition being devoid of merits, dismissed (LHC – 1985 CLC 487).

427. Poverty and weak financial position of father of the minors. Father under such plea could not escape from his liability and would not be allowed to deprive the minors from their legitimate right of maintenance (LHC – 2001 PLD 188).

428. Right of daughter to receive maintenance till her marriage. Father of the minors was Executive Engineer in Pakistan Works Department. Family Court having found minors entitled to the maintenance, fixed the same at the rate of PKR 3000 per child per month. Appeal filed by father was dismissed with the modification that the minor daughter would be entitled to recover the maintenance till her marriage or till her custody was lawfully given to him. Judgment and decree passed by Appellate Court was maintained by High Court in exercise of Constitutional jurisdiction (SCP – 2004 SCMR 1598).

429. Custody of child retained voluntarily or against wishes of father by a person not entitled to custody. Liability of father to maintain such child. Scope. Father not liable to maintain a child separately, if latter keeps away or is kept away by someone not entitled to custody from his house without his consent. Father is bound to maintain an indigent child himself, but not through another, unless so directed by the Qazi or Court. Child already being voluntarily maintained by another does not stand in need of food, cloth or lodging, thus, cannot require father to pay maintenance. Person maintaining child of another voluntarily without reference to his father is not entitled to claim his maintenance from father. Where father is entitled to custody of minor son under personal law, then he cannot be forced to pay maintenance for him, if his wife/ex-wife retains his custody against his wishes. If father establishes that he had all along been anxious and made bona fide demands for custody of minor child, whose legal guardianship under personal law vested in him, then he can well defeat application for grant of maintenance of his child (LHC – 2004 YLR 768).

430. Even if the custody of minor is with mother, father or grandfather is bound to maintain sons, until they attain age of puberty and, daughters until they are married. Father or grandfather not bound to maintain adult sons, unless disabled by infirmity or disease (LHC – 2004 YLR 616).

431. Two courts below having changed the custody of minor from the petitioner/father to respondent/mother, petitioner had impugned said concurrent judgments in the Constitutional petition. Father had an obligation under law to provide maintenance to his minor children. Argument that mother had weak financial position as compared to the father, was misconceived. Father had contracted a second marriage, and he would have to remain out of his house for considerable time in connection with his daily pursuits. Minor could not be left to the surveillance of stepmother who could never be substitute for the real mother. Real mother had inherent right to keep her minor children close to her bosom. Intelligent preference of the minor while considering comparative rights of the real mother vis-a-vis the father, who had already contracted a second marriage, could be legitimately pushed to oblivion and that was what the two courts below had done. Well reasoned findings of facts recorded by the two courts below, could not be interfered within Constitutional petition (LHC – 2009 CLC 1010).

432. Plea raised by petitioner was that his wife was living separately without any justification, and he did not have enough sources to provide interim maintenance fixed by Family Court. Validity: Minors had their independent right to ask maintenance from their father, which right of minors could not be declined merely on the ground that father was not having sources to provide maintenance. Father was legally obliged to provide maintenance. Petitioner asserted that he was a cancer patient whereas he had entered into second marriage. Petitioner, in application, filed under section 25 of Guardians and Wards Act, 1890, for the custody of minors, raised the ground that he had sufficient financial resources to maintain and nourish his son and daughter. Such grounds raised stood belied from petitioner's own version, and his conduct for non-compliance of the orders could entail penal action. Interim maintenance to the tune of PKR 2000 per month per child was justified and was maintained by High Court in exercise of Constitutional jurisdiction. Petition was dismissed in circumstances (LHC – 2009 MLD 724).

VI. Sexual Intercourse

433. Sexual intercourse out of wedlock is prohibited in Pakistan. However, after the marriage some rights and privileges arises relationship, especially the mutual rights of companionship, aid, and sexual relations. The sexual relations are not mandatory immediately after the marriage. Under the Dissolution of Muslim Marriage Act, 1939 wife is entitled to obtain divorce if husband's whereabouts have not been known for a period of four years; or husband has been sentenced to imprisonment for a period of seven years or upwards; or the husband has failed to perform, without reasonable cause, his marital obligations for a period of three years.

434. There are several court decision according to which impotency has been admitted to be ground for the annulment of marriage. However, the right of cancellation by the wife will not be allowed, if the incapacity supervened after the marriage had been consummated or if she had the knowledge of the fact of impotency of the man.

435. According to the four Schools of jurisprudence, the defects for which a spouse is permitted either to preserve the marriage contract or annul it are nine. Some of them are common between men and women and they are as follows: Insanity, Leprosy, and Vitiligo. Two of them are related to men only that is, impotency and having the penis cut off. Four of them are particular to women only which are: a bone inside the vagina which prevents intercourse; having the vagina closed; a gap between the place of intercourse and the place where the urine comes out; Flesh inside the vagina (or a wetness which prevents full enjoyment). If one spouse has one of these defects and the other party knows about it, then the marriage is acceptable if both of them are pleased with the fact. However, if the marriage takes place whereas one of them is unaware that the other partner has one of the above deficiencies, and then he/she comes to know about it, in this case he/she may annul the marriage contract if he/she so wishes.

§6. Polygamy (Second Marriage)

436. The second marriage is not prohibited in Islam, and a Muslim man can marry with four women at one time. However, under the Pakistani Family Laws through MFLO some reforms have been introduced in the law relating to polygamy. Under MFLO before second marriage, the husband must submit an application and pay a prescribed fee to the local union council in order to obtain permission for contracting a polygamous marriage. Thereafter, the Chairman of the Union Council forms an Arbitration Council with representatives of both husband and wife/wives in order to determine the necessity of the proposed marriage. The application must state whether the husband has obtained consent of the existing wife or wives. Contracting a polygamous marriage without prior consent is subject to penalties of fine and or imprisonment, and the husband becomes bound to make immediate payment of dowery to the existing wife or wives. Nonetheless, if the husband has not obtained consent of the existing wife or wives, the subsequent marriage remains valid.

437. Under the MFLO, no man, during the subsistence of an existing marriage, shall except with the previous permission in writing of the Arbitration Council, contract another marriage, nor shall any such marriage contracted without such permission be registered. An application for permission shall be submitted to the Chairman stating reasons for the proposed marriage, and whether the consent of existing wife or wives has been obtained thereto.

438. On receipt of the application, Chairman shall ask the applicant and his existing wife or wives each to nominate a representative, and the Arbitration Council so constituted may, if satisfied that the proposed marriage is necessary and just, grant, subject to such conditions if any, as may be deemed fit, the permission applied for.

439. In deciding the application, the Arbitration Council shall record its reasons for the decision and any party may, prefer an application for revision to the Collector, and his decision shall be final and shall not be called in question in any Court (section 6 of MFLO).

440. In considering whether another proposed marriage is just and necessary during the continuance of an existing marriage the Arbitration Council any, without prejudice to its general powers to consider what is just and necessary, have regard to such circumstances, as the following amongst others: sterility, physical infirmity, physical unfitness for the conjugal relation, wilful avoidance of a decree for restitution of conjugal rights, or insanity on the part of an existing wife (section-14 of the West Pakistan Rules under Muslim Family Laws Ordinance, 1961).

441. An application for permission to contract another marriage during the subsistence of an existing marriage shall be in writing, shall state whether the consent of the existing wife or wives has been obtained thereto, shall contain a brief statement of the grounds on which the new marriage is alleged to be just and necessary, shall bear the signature of the applicant, and shall be accompanied by a fee of PKR 100 (section-15 of the West Pakistan Rules under Muslim Family Laws Ordinance, 1961).

442. Any man who contracts another marriage without the permission of the Arbitration Council shall, pay immediately the entire amount of the dower whether prompt or deferred, due to the existing wife or wives, which amount, if not so paid, shall be recoverable as arrears of land revenue; and on conviction upon complaint be punishable with simple imprisonment which may extend to one year, or with fine which may extend to PKR 5,000, or with both (section 6(5) of MFLO).

443. Arbitration Council of the Union Council concerned had permitted the accused for second marriage, which was the only requirement of law for second marriage. Impugned judgment dismissing the private complaint of the complainant was based on cogent and convincing reasons. Accused after his acquittal by Trial Court had assumed double innocence. Special leave to appeal was refused to the complainant in circumstances, and her petition was dismissed accordingly (LHC – 2010 PCrLJ 950).

444. Accused petitioners had been summoned by the Magistrate to face the trial in the private complaint filed by the respondent under section 6(5)(b) of Muslim Family Laws Ordinance, 1961. Validity: Provisions of section 6(5)(b) of Muslim Family Laws Ordinance, 1961, were meant for the prosecution and punishment of a person who had contracted second marriage without observing the legal formalities as provided in section 6 of the said Ordinance, and the same did not entail any punishment for a person who had abetted or facilitated the commission of the offence. Muslim Family Laws Ordinance, 1961, is a special law and unless the special law itself indicates about the application of certain penal provisions, the same cannot be applied or set into motion. Provisions of section 109, P.P.C., therefore, would not be attracted in the case, and only husband could be prosecuted or punished for the violation of the aforementioned provision. Simply signing of *Nikahnama* being a brother or friend of the bridegroom or to participate in his second marriage would not be an offence within the meaning of section 6 of the Ordinance, as one could be a witness of the *Nikah* between the spouses having taken place in his presence. Accused petitioners could not be saddled for the responsibility of anything wherein they were not a party, and similarly they could not be made responsible for any condition written in the *Nikahnama*. Summoning of the petitioners in the complaint filed under section 6(5)(b) of Muslim Family Laws Ordinance, 1961, was illegal and without jurisdiction. Proceedings pending before the Magistrate qua the petitioners were quashed accordingly (LHC – 2009 PCrLJ 1189).

445. Respondent/complainant wife in her complaint had alleged that applicant/husband had contracted second marriage without her prior permission and consent. Wife had also alleged that husband had not even filed any application to the *Nazim* Union Council for obtaining permission of Arbitration Council. Complaint was returned by the Civil Judge and Judicial Magistrate, with the direction to file same before the Union Council concerned. Appellate Court however, set aside order of the Trial Court and remanded the complaint with the directions to record the statement of wife. Husband who filed application for quashing of the proceedings had contended that provisions of section 6 of Muslim Family Laws Ordinance, 1961 did not contemplate an action on behalf of private person, which could only be initiated on behalf of the Union Council. Validity: As to what had been provided under the law, had to be followed in the same manner, and an aggrieved party could avail normal remedies by approaching the Trial Court. Notwithstanding, it was not the intention of lawmakers that an aggrieved party under section 6(5) of MFLO should approach the court of law for redress, except that Union Council would have the jurisdiction over the subject in the event of Polygamy as said section did not contemplate delegation of authority to the private person for initiating an action on behalf of the Union Council. In the present case, proceedings initiated by the Trial Court in the complaint of wife, were found to be devoid of lawful authority, it would be an exercise in futile to allow the private complaint to linger on which would tantamount to be patent illegality and flagrant abuse of process of law. Bar existed in entertaining a private complaint directly filed by the wife against the husband, which would amount to violation of the principles of justice, and required interference for exercise of power of quashing the proceedings. Impugned order was set aside and proceedings pending before the Trial Court were directed to be quashed (SHC – 2010 MLD 470).

446. Punishment for contracting second marriage without permission from first wife. Accused contracting second marriage during subsistence of existing marriage without permission from first wife was convicted to one year simple imprisonment and a fine of PKR 2,000. Appellate Court reduced sentence of imprisonment to already undergone and fine from two thousand to one thousand. Revision by first wife filed against reduction of sentence. Contention that accused having undergone only four days' simple imprisonment, his sentence should not have been reduced. Case being old one and accused who stood convicted had undergone some period of imprisonment as well, High Court in exercise of revisional jurisdiction in interest of justice refused to award sentence of imprisonment to accused at that stage (LHC – 1989 PCRLJ 749).

447. Petitioner/female accused, through petition under section 561-A, Cr.P.C. had sought quashing of complaint filed by respondent (her previous husband) under section 6(5) of Muslim Family Laws Ordinance, 1961 pending before Special Judicial Magistrate who had issued bailable warrants of arrest of petitioners. Male accused who was married to respondent/complainant, had statedly divorced her through written divorce and thereafter he contracted *Nikah* with female accused which was registered with *Nikah* Registrar. Female accused/petitioner No. 1 had argued that no offence had been committed by her by marrying co-accused/ petitioner No. 3 since according to Shariah every male Muslim was allowed to contract four marriages and that provisions of section 6(5) of Muslim Family Laws Ordinance, 1961 were ultra vires. Reference section 6(S), Criminal Procedure Code (V of 1898), section 561-A. (LHC – 2004 YLR 2242).

448. Suit for specific performance of agreement. Wife had granted permission to the husband to contract a second marriage on the condition that husband will continue to pay PKR 500 per month as maintenance and also transfer one residential room and one shop part of the house, belonging to husband and his father. Parties entered into an agreement incorporating the said conditions. Husband, on the basis of permission from the wife obtained a certificate from the Arbitration Council entitling him to have a second wife and thereafter he entered into second marriage. Husband did not fulfil the promise and instead divorced the first wife. Father of the husband, in divorce proceedings, affirmed that he had transferred the residential room in favour of the first wife of his son and volunteered that whenever she wanted he will execute the sale deed. Such promise was also not fulfilled. Wife filed suit for specific performance of their agreement which was tried and dismissed up to Appellate Court on the ground that the agreement between husband and wife was not enforceable as there was no consideration, and further the same was violative of section 27, Contract Act, 1872. High Court, in revision took the view that grant of permission to marry was a valid consideration for the agreement to transfer the specified property. Validity: Agreement was not without consideration in the facts and circumstances of the case. Provision of section 27, Contract Act, 1872 which otherwise was not attracted to the facts and circumstances of the case, gave way to the provision of section 3, Muslim Family Laws Ordinance, 1961 which provides that the Ordinance shall have overriding effect, notwithstanding the provision of any law to the contrary. Provision of section 6, Muslim Family Laws Ordinance, 1961 which placed a restraint on the right of the husband to enter into an additional marriage during the subsistence of the earlier marriage, except with the permission of the existing wife or in case of her refusal, with the permission of Arbitration Council, section 6 of the Ordinance, therefore, could not be said to be in conflict with the provision of section 27, Contract Act, 1872. Mandate of section 3, Muslim Family Laws Ordinance, 1961 had to prevail in any case. High Court, in circumstances, had rightly interfered in the exercise of revisional jurisdiction conferred by section 115, C. P. C. as the Trial Court, and the Appellate Court had dismissed the suit on the wrong understanding of law that the agreement was without consideration or was violative of section 27 of the Contract Act, 1872 (SCP – 2003 PLD 128).

§7. Re-marriage

449. Under section 7(6) of MFLO if divorce has not been conveyed three times, wife can remarry with the same husband without an intervening marriage with a third person. However, if husband has conveyed divorce three times, a woman cannot remarry with the ex-husband unless and until she has been married to another person and that person divorce the woman.

450. Under the Islamic Laws, a man cannot remarry with his ex-wife after irrevocably divorced, until her ex-wife married to another man and conjugal relations have been developed. The violation of this law leads to the nullity of the marriage. This rule is important to avoid frequent divorces and remarriages and in the interest of the public morality.

451. Law prevailing previous to the enforcement of Muslim Family Laws Ordinance, 1961 had made it obligatory for the couples divorced by any mode of Divorce other than Talaq-e-Ahsan not to remarry each other again, unless wife married another man who died or divorced her after actual consummation, and she married her first husband after period of *Iddat.* Before remarriage parties had to prove that bar to their marriage was removed by intermediate marriage, consummation and dissolution, otherwise their marriage was not considered valid. Mode of Divorce effected under provisions of Muslim Family Laws Ordinance, 1961 being almost that of Talaq-e-Ahsan, the couples could remarry without any intervening marriage except where they had been divorced thrice, and the third divorce had become effective and in that case they could not remarry without an intervening marriage. Plain reading of section 7 of Muslim Family Laws Ordinance, 1961 though had implied that all kinds of Divorces had been made revocable without an intervening marriage and could be that its repugnancy to such extent could validly be agitated on the touchstone of Quranic behest and the traditions of Holy Prophet Muhammad (PBUH), but neither vires of said section 7 had been challenged nor matter raised in case pertained to all kinds of Divorces. Matter, in the present case, pertained, to divorce obtained by wife through Court decree in shape of '*Khula*' (PHC – 2003 PLD 169).

452. Family Court decreed suit filed by wife for dissolution of marriage on ground of '*Khula*' and dissolved marriage between the parties in lieu of dower amount. Husband had challenged the decree in Constitutional petition. During pendency of Constitutional petition, application was filed praying therein to dispose of Constitutional petition in the light of settlement arrived at between the parties. Terms and conditions of said settlement were: that husband had undertaken to maintain wife and to provide her necessities and luxuries according to his status; that wife was ready to join husband as his wife; and that decree for dissolution of marriage by way of '*Khula*' be recalled and parties be allowed to remarry. Dissolution of marriage by way of '*Khula*' was pronounced by Family Court subject to return of dower amount by wife, but said amount of dower neither was returned by wife nor was the same accepted by husband. Pronouncement of '*Khula*' by Family Court, in circumstances, would amount to single divorce and until third divorce would take place, husband would be at liberty to remarry his wife again, and parties could join as husband and wife on solemnization of *Nikah* without intervention of third person (SHC – 2000 MLD 447).

§8. Void and Voidable marriages

I. Impotency

453. A married woman is entitled to obtain a decree for dissolution of her marriage under the Dissolution of Muslim Marriage Act, 1939 if the husband was impotent at the time of the marriage and continues to be so, and Court can declare such marriage void. However under Article 2(ii)(c) of the Dissolution of Muslim Marriage Act, 1939 before passing a decree the Court shall, on application by the husband, make an order requiring the husband to satisfy the Court within a period of one year from the date of such order that he has ceased to be impotent, and if the husband so satisfies the Court within such period no decree shall be passed on the said ground.

454. As for the *Sharee'ah* (Islamic Law) ruling concerning the issue of divorce, there are two possibilities with regard to the husband: The first case is that the husband is obliged to divorce his wife because she is harmed by his impotence, which is most probably the case, unless she accepts it. Sexual intercourse is one of a wife's rights, however she may choose to give it up. The second case is if the wife is not harmed by her husband's impotence. In that case, he is not obliged to divorce her. In fact, it is even more unfavourable for him to do so, because there is no need for it.

455. As for the wife she has two options: either to continue with the marriage or to ask for divorce after the husband has been given a one year respite to seek treatment. *An-Nafraawi* the *Maaliki* scholar stated that a husband should be given a one-year respite if his wife finds him unable to have intercourse with her, whether because of magic or disease. This would also apply to the case where the wife did not know about her husband's impotence at the time of their marriage. However, if she knew this at the time of the marriage, then she has no option here for divorce because she accepted it from the beginning.

456. If husband does not apply under Article 2(ii)(c) of the Dissolution of Muslim Marriage Act, 1939 for one-year period to satisfy the Court regarding his impotency, the dissolution of marriage would become effective after expiration of ninety days of the decision of Court (PHC – 1995 CLC 731).

457. Impotency means that husband is not in a position to perform sexual intercourse. Physical weakness does not reflect on potency. Physical weakness is not provided anywhere in Dissolution of Muslim Marriages Act, 1939 as ground for dissolution or marriage (LHC – 2003 CLC 1954).

458. Plaintiff (wife) in her pleadings as also in evidence had emphatically averred and deposed that her husband suffered from impotency. Such evidence was supported by witnesses who had deposed that husband had admitted before *Panchayat* his disability to perform marital obligations due to his impotency. Such evidence was not controverted by husband. Husband, thus, failed to perform his marital obligations with plaintiff (wife) on account of his impotency (LHC – 1994 MLD 2188).

459. Suit was filed by Hindu wife against her husband on grounds of impotency, imbalance of mind, cruelty, harshness and danger to her life from his hands. Trial Court, after hearing parties, decreed the suit. Judgment of Trial Court, though was not a reasonable and/or a detailed judgment, but when allegations of danger to life, ground of impotency and unsound mind of defendant husband had been raised by plaintiff, then defendant should have volunteered for examination as provided under Order XXXII, Rule-7, CPC whereby he could be referred to for medical examination (SHC – 2004 YLR 1666).

460. Decree for Dissolution of marriage was granted to wife by Family Court on ground of impotency of husband on only evidence furnished by lady doctor to the effect that hymen of the wife being intact, she was a virgin. According to settled medical and scientific phenomenon, fact of hymen being intact was not a conclusive proof of virginity, because hymen in certain cases is so flexible that it is not ruptured and at times was ruptured by incidence of first delivery. Evidence on record indicated that husband and wife had tried to produce their own medical certificates by consulting doctors themselves, but Court had not referred same for examination which had shown touch of personal involvement of Court. Better approach would have been to get the parties medically examined through Court. Application filed by husband under the Dissolution of Muslim Marriages Act, 1939, was also not considered by Family Court before passing decree for Dissolution of marriage on ground of impotency of husband. Family Court had acted without jurisdiction and also had exercised jurisdiction not vested in it as Family Court could not pass decree for Dissolution of marriage on the ground of impotency of husband, unless, on application of husband, he was required to satisfy the Court within one year from the date of such order that he had ceased to be impotent. If husband so satisfies the Court within such period qua the same woman involved, no decree for Dissolution of marriage would be passed on ground of impotency. Judgment of Family Court was set aside, and case was remanded to be decided afresh after complying with provisions of proviso (e) of section 2(v) of Dissolution of Muslim Marriages Act, 1939 (PHC – 1998 MLD 1216).

II. Cruelty

461. The Courts can declare marriage void if husband treats her wife with cruelty, that is to say: habitually assaults her or makes her life miserable by cruelty of conduct even if such conduct does not amount to physical ill-treatment; or associates with women of evil repute or leads an infamous life; or attempts to force her to lead an immoral life; or disposes of her property or prevents her from exercising her legal rights over it; or obstructs her in the observance of her religious profession or practice; or if he has more wives than one, does not treat her equitably in accordance with the injunctions of the Holy Quran, as stipulated under the Dissolution of Muslim Marriage Act, 1939.

462. Cruelty could not be proved by direct evidence, but it was something to be inferred by conduct, behaviour and temperament of husband with wife while living together. Cruelty could be felt by close association with spouse by watching different happenings during wedlock and their habits. Mental torture by husband also would amount to cruelty and want of compatibility, and disharmony of feelings and thoughts could also result into discomfort and hardship to live a harmonious life. Marriage could be dissolved on ground of '*Khula*' despite the fact that grounds given in Dissolution of Muslim Marriages Act, 1939, were not proved (Shariat Court, Azad Kashmir – 1999 YLR 985).

463. Plaintiff in her suit had alleged that behaviour and treatment of defendant husband towards her, had become cruel, and he started beating and abusing her and had resorted to ill and inhuman treatment against her. Wife had alleged that in view of said inhuman and cruel treatment of husband, she had suffered from severe spiritual and mental torture and had developed extreme disliking against the husband with whom she could not live in any case within the limits ordained by Allah. Family Court dismissed suit holding that allegation against husband had not been proved. Wife had contended that when it was made clear before the Family Court that spouses could not live within the limits ordained by Allah, it was obligatory for Family Court to have dissolved the marriage on basis of '*Khula*' even if cruelty or other grounds as alleged by her were not proved. Validity: Wife had throughout maintained that she could not live with the husband against whom she had developed severe hatred and disliking. Said state of affairs itself had made out a case for '*Khula*' even if her pleas of torture, beating, etc. were not proved. Wife was at liberty to take up plea of '*Khula*' before High Court in appeal, even if said plea was not specifically taken before Family Court. Dissolution of marriage on ground of '*Khula*' was a pure question of law and could be raised even before the highest Court of Appeal. Such plea would not require any evidence as it was the statement of plaintiff/wife alone which was the determining factor in case of '*Khula*'. Aversion, disliking, hatred, incompatibility of temperaments, mental, intellectual, social, cultural or ideological disparity or conflict, which had the apprehension of disturbing the family life and happiness, were sufficient grounds for wife to seek '*Khula*'. Wife was empowered to get marriage cancelled on any reason whatsoever, whether husband was at fault or not. Unfettered powers of husband were counter balanced by right of wife to obtain dissolution of marriage through Court subject to condition that if husband was not at fault, she was to compensate him and if he was found at fault, she was not to pay anything. Said right of wife could not be made hostage to husband's pleasure. When relations between the spouses had become so strained that they could not live together in accordance with limits ordained by Allah, Family Court should have dissolved marriage on ground of '*Khula*'. High Court accepting appeal, set aside judgment and decree of Family Court, and decree of dissolution of marriage was passed in favour of wife on '*Khula*' subject to payment of dower amount to the husband (Shariat Court, Azad Kashmir – 2004 CLC 17).

III. Idiocy or Lunacy

464. If husband has been insane for a period of two years or is suffering from leprosy or a virulent venereal disease, the wife has the right to take divorce under the Dissolution of Muslim Marriage Act, 1939 and Courts declare such marriage void.

IV. Consent obtained by Force or Fraud

465. If consent of woman for marriage is obtained by force or fraud, the Court can declared such marriage void. Even under the Dissolution of Muslim Marriage Act, 1939 a woman is entitled to obtain a decree for dissolution of her marriage if she, having been given in marriage by her father or other guardian before she attained the age of 16 years, repudiated the marriage before attaining the age of 18 years, provided that marriage has not been consummated.

466. Lady, in her pleadings categorically contended that she was abducted by the man with the help of his companions and thereafter, without her freewill and accord entered into a marriage contract with her and eventually on the intervention of the respectables of the area she was restored to her parents, and during this period the man started claiming her as his legally wedded wife. Claim of the lady, being in negative form and nature, obviously she could not have been burdened to substantiate the same by producing further evidence that she did not, in the exercise of her own free will and accord, entered into a contract of marriage. Record also showed that the alleged *Nikah* was not performed even in the District where the lady was ordinarily residing rather, hundreds of miles away from her place of ordinary abode. Stated *Nikah* was registered and performed in a mosque, where no relative, friend or any other acquaintance of the bride was present, therefore, in such a situation, the evidence of lady which withstood the test of cross-examination was sufficient to convince that she did not enter into contract of marriage out of her own freewill in exercise of her right of option. Lady, therefore, succeeded in discharging the onus of the issue and thereupon the burden shifted to the man to rebut the same through evidence that *Nikah* between the parties was validly and lawfully performed by the lady in exercise of her free will being the persona majora, who consented for the same and thereby entered into the contract of marriage by performance of *Nikah*. Man, in peculiar facts and circumstances of the case, was obliged to have proved the factum of performance of a valid *Nikah,* and such onus on him could not have been successfully discharged unless the witnesses of *Nikah* and other witnesses in whose presence lady allegedly appointed the cited witness in the *Nikahnama* to act as her Wakil for *Nikah*, was produced, which in the present case was completely wanting. Material evidence in the case having been misread, misconstrued and misapplied by the lower forums that is, Family Court and the Appellate Court, by upholding the marriage as valid one, interference of High Court in exercise of its Constitutional jurisdiction, was very much called for to rectify the manifest error committed by them in the exercise of their jurisdiction (SCP – 2006 PLD 489).

467. Marriage was sought to be dissolved by wife on grounds that, her consent to marriage was obtained by fraud; that there was great difference between ages of parties as husband was nearly 50 years old while she was 26 years old; that she was Post Graduate while her husband was intermediate; that husband was already married and had five children from his first wife and that husband believed in evil spirits. Wife seeking Dissolution of marriage had clearly deposed that it was impossible to live with such a character within limits ordained by God. When a ground was urged for Dissolution of marriage that 'parties could not live as husband and wife within the limits prescribed by God', Court had to judge case that minimum standard could be held intact if the marriage was allowed to stay and not dissolved. If not, then it would be better to bring an end to such an institution. In view of specific allegations levelled by wife against husband, marriage was rightly ordered to be dissolved (SHC – 1998 MLD 1972).

V. Prohibited marriages

468. Under the Islamic Laws marriage between certain relatives is not possible. These are the relationships expressly prohibited by the Shari′ah. The reason for declaring these relations prohibited for marriage is to secure the development and maintenance of a sound family and social structure. It is imperative for the creation of a sound and stable family and social structure to give sanctity to a few relations and to remove all kinds of sexual interaction between these relations. Thus, the stated prohibition secures the existence not only of mothers, fathers, brothers and sisters but also that of aunts and uncles, nieces and nephews, in-laws and foster relationships. All these relations are sanctified by the Holy Qur'an and have, therefore, been declared prohibited for marriage.

469. In the Holy Quran (Sura Al-Nisa) it is stipulated that:

And marry not women whom your fathers married – except what has been done in the past: it was shameful and odious – an abominable practice indeed. Prohibited to you [for marriage] are your mothers, daughters, sisters, your maternal and paternal aunts, the daughters of your brothers and sisters; your mothers who have suckled you and your sisters through fosterage, the mothers of your wives, your stepdaughters raised under you born of your wives with whom you have lain – no offence if you have not lain with their mothers, and the wives of your begotten sons, and two sisters in wedlock at the same time, except for what has already happened.

God indeed is Oft-Forgiving, Most Merciful. Also [prohibited are] women already married, except those whom your right hands possess; this is a written obligation upon you from God. (4:22-4).

470. According to *Surah Al-Nisaa* 4: 23, the relations prohibited for marriage are as follows:

Relations by Birth (or Direct Relations):

- Mothers;
- Daughters;
- Sisters.

Indirect Relations:

- Father's sisters;
- Mother's sisters;
- Sisters' daughters; and
- Brothers' daughters.

Relations by Fosterage:

- Foster Mothers; and
- Sisters on the basis of fosterage.

Relations by Marriage:

- Wives' mothers;
- Wives' daughters, if conjugal relation has been established with the wife;
- Wives of real sons; and
- Wives' sisters, while the wife is still in marriage.

Chapter 2. Divorce

§1. Grounds of Muslim Divorce

471. Any Muslim of sound mind, who has attained puberty, may divorce his wife whenever he desires without assigning any cause. Under the Islamic Law, in Pakistan the contract of marriage may be dissolved: (i) by the husband at his will, without the intervention of a Court; (ii) by mutual consent of the husband and wife, without the intervention of a Court; and (iii) by a judicial decree at the suit of the husband or wife. The wife cannot divorce herself from her husband without his consent, except such right granted under *Nikahnama* (marriage certificate), but she may, in some cases, obtain a divorce by judicial decree. When the divorce proceeds from the husband, it is called *Talak*, when it is affected by mutual consent, it is called '*Khula*' or Mubarat according to the terms of the contract between the parties.

472. According to the four Schools of jurisprudence, the defects for which a spouse is permitted either to preserve the marriage contract or annul it are nine. Some of them are common between men and women like Insanity, Leprosy and Vitiligo. Impotency and having the penis cut off are related to men. Whereas four defects are particular to women only which includes a bone inside the vagina which prevents intercourse; having the vagina closed; a gap between the place of intercourse and the place where the urine comes out; Flesh inside the vagina (or a wetness which prevents full enjoyment). If one spouse has one of these defects and the other party knows about it, then the marriage is acceptable if both of them are pleased with the fact. However, if the marriage takes place whereas one of them is unaware that the other partner has one of the above deficiencies, and then he/she comes to know about it, in this case he/she may annul the marriage contract if he/she so wishes.

I. Divorce by Mutual Consent

473. Both wife and husband have legal and religious rights to dissolve a marriage with mutual consent. A Muslim marriage is a contract and can be dissolved mutually like any other contract at any time. It is automatically dissolved on the death of one of the spouses.

474. If divorce was with mutual consent and on basis of Muba'arat, husband could not retract or withdraw such divorce/*Talaq* nor Chairman Arbitration Council had any authority to adjudicate upon validity of such divorce. Chairman, Arbitration Council was bound to issue a certificate of effectiveness of divorce and had no power to entertain notice of withdrawal of divorce or start proceedings on basis thereof (LHC 2000 MLD 173).

475. If spouses decide to separate with mutual consent and a document in the shape of divorce is prepared and is signed by the husband, divorce becomes final for all intents and purposes, and the husband thereafter cannot withdraw the divorce, and the Chairman, Union Council is bound to register the same under section 8 of Muslim Family Laws Ordinance, 1961 (LHC – 1995 PCRLJ 1247 Islamic Law).

476. Detenue admitting her marriage with petitioner and wishing to go with him. Detenue's previous marriage with one 'B' allegedly subsisting as no Divorce from 'B' effected. Offence of Bigamy and *Zina* allegedly committed. Court on enquiry, finding performance of marriage of detenue with 'B' as Vatta in lieu of which sister of 'B' married to brother of detenue. Later relations between 'B' and detenue becoming strained, and both marriages were decided to be mutually dissolved. Divorce deed executed. 'B' admitting execution of divorce deed. Detenue believing to be divorced under mutual agreement, contracting second marriage with petitioner. Divorce by mutual agreement, held, was in nature of Mubarat and had become irrevocable from date of its execution and provision of revocation in section 7 of Family Laws Ordinance was inapplicable in circumstances (LHC – 1987 CLC 1496).

477. Parties had handed over and taken over articles of dowry, therefore, parties case was not covered by section 7, but under section 8, Muslim Family Laws Ordinance, 1961. No special procedure having been prescribed under section 8 of the Ordinance, provisions of section 7, Muslim Family Laws Ordinance, 1961, have been made applicable, subject, however, to conditions of 'so far as applicable'. Provision of section 7 of the Ordinance deals only with divorce by husband and cases of other forms of divorce recognized by Islam would not be covered by it. Divorce having been effected by parties through mutual agreement, same was 'Talaq Mubaraat' and irrevocable. Divorce deed having been executed between parties of free will and benefits taken thereof, such course would disentitle husband of any relief against issue of divorce certificate in Constitutional jurisdiction (LHC – 1997 CLC 1985).

II. Divorce by Husband

478. A husband has the unilateral right of divorce under the Muhammadan Laws and Muslim Family Laws Ordinance, 1961 which can never be taken away but can be restricted through the *Nikahnama*.

479. Under MFLO, a divorcing husband shall, as soon as possible after divorce has been pronounced, in whatever form, give a notice in writing to the Chairman of the Union Council. The Chairman must then supply a copy of the notice of divorce to the wife. Non-compliance is punishable by imprisonment and/or a fine. Within thirty days of receipt of the notice of divorce, the Chairman must constitute an Arbitration Council in order to take steps to bring about reconciliation between the husband and the wife. If and when such attempts to negotiate reconciliation fail, a divorce that is not revoked in the meantime, either expressly or implicitly, takes effect after the expiry of ninety days from the day on which the notice of repudiation was first delivered to the Chairman. If, however, the wife is pregnant at the time of the pronouncement of divorce, the divorce does not take effect until ninety days have elapsed or the end of the pregnancy, whichever is later.

480. In Islam, a marriage could be dissolved: (i) by the husband at his will without the intervention of a court; (ii) by mutual consent of the husband and wife, without the intervention of a court; and (iii) by a judicial decree in the suit of the husband and wife. Wife could not divorce herself from her husband without his consent, except under a contract, but she could, in some cases, obtain a divorce by judicial decree. Section 7 of Muslim Family Laws Ordinance, 1961, regulates the procedure as to pronouncement of divorce. Under Islamic Law, a Muslim husband enjoys unfettered power to pronounce divorce to his wife; it was also established principle of Islamic Jurisprudence that husband could delegate his power to his wife or to third person by way of contract (2010 YLR 1632).

481. Divorce pronounced thrice in one sitting becomes effective immediately and in such eventuality, the question of its revocation does not arise under MFLO section 7(3) (LHC – 1990 CLC 1683).

482. Divorce pronounced by the husband upon the wife having not been revoked, had become effective after the expiry of ninety days from the date of receipt of notice by the *Nazim*/Chairman, Arbitration Council in view of MFLO sections 7(3) & (5) (LHC – 2004 PLD 316).

483. Restriction on the right of husband to divorce wife. Import, object and scope. Such restriction is not provided under Muslim Family Laws Ordinance, 1961, or Rules framed thereunder, but there is also no provision in the law or rules that such restriction is void. To preserve marriage contract and to safeguard interest of wife against its unjustified termination by husband, if any stipulation is made in *Nikahnama* whereby husband agrees to pay some damages in the event of divorcing wife without just cause, such stipulation is neither against injunctions of Islam nor against public policy. Islam allows husband to divorce his wife without assigning any cause, but it also approves preservation and protection of marriage and does not approve unjustified exercise of the right of divorce by husband as the same leads to innumerable social problems for the divorcee and the children who consequently have an adverse impact on the society as well (LHC – 2004 YLR 482).

484. Provisions of section 7 of Muslim Family Laws Ordinance, 1961 had stipulated three steps to pronounce divorce: first, it had to be verbally pronounced; as mandated by Shariat; second, the same be pronounced in any form whatsoever, which would mean that in any prevalent mode that is, one's own language or in Arabic as some sects prescribed in that behalf; third, verbal pronouncement of divorce had to be reduced into writing and had to be conveyed to the Chairman of Union Council with a copy to the wife. Failure to strictly comply with said procedure would not, invalidate divorce. Necessary requirement or ingredients of divorce was a conscious and wilful pronouncement of divorce with intention to release wife from marriage bond. Failure to follow said procedure could entail or be followed by punishment prescribed under succeeding sub-section (2) of section 7 of Muslim

Family Laws Ordinance, 1961, but validity of divorce or separation of spouses from the marriage bond would not be affected (FSC – 2004 YLR 619).

485. SCP, Azad Kashmir (2004 CLC 984) held that divorce deed was not the requirement of law to be written on a stamp paper under MFLO.

III. Divorce by Wife

486. A wife can also dissolve her marriage unilaterally only if the right of divorce has been unconditionally delegated to her by the husband in the *Nikahnama* under clause-18 at the time of marriage.

487. Under the Islamic Laws, it is believed in principle that divorce is in the hands of the husband; the bond of marriage is in his hands and it is only him who can divorce, and a woman cannot divorce herself unless the husband authorized her to this effect. However, if husband authorizes her to divorce after the marriage contract, then the majority of the Islamic Scholars are of the view that it is valid.

488. Exercising power of Talaq-e-Tafweez. Respondent / wife sent a divorce deed to petitioner / husband on the basis of purported exercise of right of divorce allegedly delegated to her by the husband endorsed in Column No. 18 of *Nikahnama*. Wife also sent copy of divorce deed to the Chairman Arbitration Council along with notice under section 8 of Muslim Family Laws Ordinance, 1961 for constitution of Arbitration Council. Husband had alleged that he never gave any right of divorce to wife nor any such powers were endorsed at the time of *Nikah*. Husband had also alleged that impugned order rendered by Chairman Arbitration Council was against the law and without authority as the 'Sharri Haqooq' as mentioned in column No. 18 of *Nikahnama*, would not mean that he had delegated the right of divorce to wife. Husband had asserted that certificate of effectiveness of divorce was issued by the Council without any lawful authority. Wife had contended that she had rightly exercised the power of Talaq-e-Tafweez given to her by the husband in Column No. 18 of the *Nikahnama*, and that Chairman Arbitration Council had rightly issued certificate of effectiveness of divorce. Validity: Held, it was not a Shairi Right of a wedded woman to get divorce upon herself without specific delegation of such power by the husband. Counsel for respondent / wife had not been able to prove that a woman could divorce upon her as a Sharri Right. Words mentioned in Column No. 18 of *Nikahnama*, did not vest any power in wife to exercise right of Talaq-e-Tafweez. No power was delegated by the husband to wife to exercise right of Talaq-e-Tafweez upon her. If such type of words were allowed to be considered as a right of Talaq-e-Tafweez, it would mean that whatever was incorporated against Column No. 18, would be presumed as a Talaq-e-Tafweez. Husband in the present case had specifically denied that no such power was given to wife at the time of *Nikah*. Divorce deed, in circumstances, was executed without any legal basis by the wife, and the same had no value in the eye of law. Impugned order passed by Chairman Arbitration Council was also not in accordance with law and was liable to be set aside (2010 YLR 1632).

489. Delegated right of divorce given to wife was exercised by her, but no notice was sent to Chairman Arbitration Council. Subsequently husband divorced his wife; sent notice to Chairman Arbitration Council and divorce became effective. Wife filed suit for recovery of dower amount, which was dismissed by Family Court being barred by limitation on the ground that divorce had already been effected when she had exercised her right. Appeal filed by wife was also dismissed by Appellate Court. Plea raised by wife in the Constitutional petition was that divorce did not become effective, after her exercise of such right, as no notice to the Chairman was given by her. Validity: No notice was served in terms of section 7 read with section 8 of Muslim Family Laws Ordinance, 1961, and result was that prescribed period of ninety days never started running so as to make divorce effective at any time after exercise of such right by wife. Divorce pronounced by wife in exercise of her delegated right of divorce never took effect and divorce pronounced by husband did take effect on expiry of ninety days, when notice was delivered to Chairman Arbitration Council. Suit brought by wife was within the period of three years as prescribed in Articles 103 and 104 of Limitation Act, 1908. Judgments and decrees dismissing suit of wife for recovery of dower amount on the sole ground that the claim was barred by time, were declared to be without lawful authority and were set aside. Suit filed by wife for recovery of dower amount against husband was decreed by High Court in exercise of Constitutional jurisdiction. Petition was allowed accordingly (LHC – 2007 CLC 1009).

490. Power to give divorce, though belonged to husband, but he could delegate said power to wife or to third person, either absolutely or conditionally and either for a particular period or permanently. Section 7 of Muslim Family Laws Ordinance, 1961 had specifically provided such divorce which was known as 'Talaq-e-Tafweez'. Person, to whom power was so delegated, could then pronounce same accordingly. Temporary delegation of power was irrevocable, but a permanent delegation could be revoked. Such delegation of option called 'Tafweez' by husband to his wife would confer on her power of divorcing herself. Said 'Tafweez' was of three kinds viz., Ikhtiar, giving her authority to Talak herself; AmrbaYed, leaving the matter in her own hand; and Mashiat, giving her the option to do what she liked. All these factors when analysed would resolve themselves into one, viz., leaving it on her or somebody else's option to do what she/he liked. Wife could not sue to enforce authority alleged to have been given to her, but she would sue after she had given effect to it to make husband liable for dower or to restrain him from seeking conjugal relations. Wife was entitled to exercise her right of 'Tafweez of Talaq', and she was entitled to be separated from her husband (LHC – 2006 YLR 335).

491. One of the conditions of the marriage between parties was that husband had delegated the right to divorce wife and entry to that effect was made in Column No. 18 of *Nikahnama*. Wife in exercise of said right pronounced divorce upon herself for her husband, and a notice was sent to *Nazim* Union Council concerned. *Nazim* had intimated wife that husband being not ready to pronounce divorce, wife could approach the Court as he could not grant '*Khula*', and *Nazim* sent the case to the Family Court. *Nazim* was oblivious of legal position as right of divorce could be lawfully delegated by husband to wife, and that had happened in the present case and notice was sent by wife in compliance with the terms of sections 7 & 8 of Muslim Family Laws Ordinance, 1961. Ninety days prescribed period having expired after receipt of notice issued by wife and reconciliation being not possible between the parties, law as prescribed in sections 7(3) & 8 of Muslim Family Laws Ordinance, 1961 would have its course. *Nazim* would issue requisite document regarding receipt of notice and failure of reconciliation within prescribed time (LHC – 2004 PLD 77).

IV. Divorce through Judicial Process ('*Khula*')

492. The wife has the right to approach the Court for dissolution of marriage through judicial process. Dissolution of marriage which the wife can use are '*Khula*' and judicial divorce (including option of puberty). These both have to be sought through the Family Courts. Judicial '*Khula*' may also be granted without the husband's consent if the wife is willing to forgo her financial rights.

493. Under the Dissolution of Marriage Act, 1939 a married woman is entitled to obtain a decree for dissolution of her marriage on any one or more of the following grounds, namely:

- that the whereabouts of the husband have not been known for a period of four years;
- that the husband has neglected or has failed to provide for her maintenance for a period of two years;
- that the husband has taken an additional wife in contravention of the provisions of MFLO;
- that the husband has been sentenced to imprisonment for a period of seven years or upwards;
- that the husband has failed to perform, without reasonable cause, his marital obligations for a period of three years;
- that the husband was impotent at the time of the marriage and continues to be so;
- that the husband has been insane for a period of two years or is suffering from leprosy or a virulent venereal disease;
- that she, having been given in marriage by her father or other guardian before she attained the age of 16 years, repudiated the marriage before attaining the age of 18 years; provided that marriage has not been consummated;
- that the husband treats her with cruelty, that is to say: habitually assaults her or makes her life miserable by cruelty of conduct even if such conduct does not amount to physical ill-treatment; or associates with women of evil repute or leads an infamous life; or attempts to force her to lead an immoral life; or disposes of her property or prevents her from exercising her legal rights over it; or obstructs her in the observance of her religious profession or practice; or if he has more wives than one, does not treat her equitably in accordance with the Injunctions of the Holy Quran; and
- on any other ground which is recognized as valid for the dissolution of marriage under Muslim Law; provided that: (a) no decree shall be passed on ground until

the sentence has become final; (b) a decree passed on ground shall not take effect for a period of six months from the date of such decree, and if the husband appears either in person or through an authorized agent within that period and satisfies the Court that he is prepared to perform his conjugal duties; the Court shall set aside the said decree; and (c) before passing a decree on ground that the Court shall, on application by the husband, make an order requiring the husband to satisfy the Court within a period of one year from the date of such order that he has ceased to be impotent, and if the husband so satisfies the Court within such period no decree shall be passed on the said ground.

494. The renunciation of Islam by a married Muslim woman or her conversion to a faith other than Islam shall not by itself operate to dissolve her marriage: Provided that after such renunciation, or conversion the woman shall be entitled to obtain a decree for the dissolution of her marriage on any of the grounds mentioned in the Dissolution of Marriage Act, 1939; provided further that the provisions of this section shall not apply to a woman converted to Islam from some other faith who re-embraces her former faith.

495. Decree for dissolution of marriage solemnized under Muslim Family Laws Ordinance, 1961, would not be effective until expiration of ninety days from the day on which copy thereof had been sent to the Chairman and would be rendered of no effect if within the period specified reconciliation, had been effected between the parties in accordance with the provisions of Muslim Family Laws Ordinance, 1961 (SHC – 1991 MLD 403).

496. Dissolution of marriage on ground of '*Khula*'. Marriage on the basis of '*Khula*' could be dissolved and the wife had to return such benefits/considerations agreed upon. Failure on the part of the wife to pay the considerations for the divorce would not invalidate the divorce, though the husband could sue the wife for its recovery, and that it could not be postponed until the execution of the 'Khulanama' (deed of '*Khula*'). Family Court could grant decree for dissolution of marriage on the basis of '*Khula*' when pretrial reconciliation efforts would fail. Court, however, while granting decree for dissolution of marriage on the basis of '*Khula*' would record sound and cogent reasons in support thereof and would also state that after holding trial, if the wife was found liable to pay back the considerations determined by the court which she had received, same were to be returned to the husband. Family Court, however, could not defer the grant of decree on the basis of '*Khula*' for disruption of marriage because the parties were not in agreement on the payment or non-payment of dower, and the decree of '*Khula*' would remain effective from the date on which it was pronounced (PHC – 2009 PLD 92).

497. Suits for dissolution of marriage by wife and for conjugal rights by husband. Constitutional petition by wife. Wife had expressed her hatred by saying that she wanted to spit on her husband. Wife maintained her such aversion and deposed the same on all the occasions including in her plaint, her written statement in the suit for conjugal rights by her husband, in her statement before Family Court, in appeal filed before District Judge and her statement in person in Constitutional petition before the High Court. Held, Courts could otherwise in case of wife's failure to prove the grounds for dissolution of marriage see that she had a right of '*Khula*'. Courts were under a duty of law to pass a judgment on said factum. Failure of Court to do so would tantamount to misapplication of their mind to the Injunctions of Islam in respect of right of '*Khula*' and being not in conformity with law. High Court set aside the order of Family Court and that of Appellate Court having been passed without lawful authority and jurisdiction, accepted the wife's Constitutional petition and decreed the wife's suit for dissolution of marriage on the basis of her right of '*Khula*' and dismissed the suit of husband for restitution of conjugal rights (LHC – 1995 PLD 19).

498. Suit for dissolution of marriage on ground of '*Khula*' filed by wife was dismissed and suit for restitution of conjugal rights filed by husband was decreed. Appellate Court reversed the finding of Trial Court and passed decree of dissolution of marriage on the basis of '*Khula*' in favour of wife. Appellate Court below took into account entire evidence on record and after having appreciated same came to the conclusion that parties could not live together as husband and wife within limits prescribed by God. No justification thus existed for interference with judgment of Court below in exercise of Constitutional jurisdiction (LHC – 1991 CLC 962).

499. Wife, seeking dissolution of marriage insisted on divorce and was not prepared under any circumstances to live with her husband as his wife, and there were no prospects for reconciliation between them as hatred between spouses was deep rooted. Case, held, was fit for grant of '*Khula*' divorce to wife (LHC – 1990 CLC 917).

500. Dissolution of marriage on ground of '*Khula*'. Record showed that parties were at daggers drawn and husband levelled ugly allegations against wife and at one stage matter went before Police. Parties, during the spell of 4/5 months of marriage, had become rivals to each other, and it was beyond their control to live a happy married life. Family Court, thus was justified in dissolving the marriage of parties on the ground of '*Khula*'. Reference Islamic Law, Muslim Family Laws Ordinance 1961 section 8, West Pakistan Family Courts Act (XXXV of 1964, section 7 (SHC – 1990 MLD 1151).

501. Dissolution of marriage on ground of '*Khula*'. Evidence on record showed that relationship between parties had travelled beyond frontiers of mend, and wife seemed to have developed intense irretrievable hatred for husband ruling out even remote possibility of their living together within limits prescribed by God. Dissolution of marriage on ground of '*Khula*' was justified in these circumstances (LHC – 1989 MLD 5007).

502. Dissolution of marriage on ground of '*Khula*'. Where Court after taking into consideration over all circumstances, came to the conclusion that it was not possible for parties to live together as husband and wife and perform their marital obligations within limits prescribed by God, marriage, could be dissolved on basis of '*Khula*'. Parties were not to be forced into a hateful union, if reconciliation had become impossible between them (LHC – 1989 MLD 5005).

503. Wife in plaint as well as in her statement before Court categorically stated that it was no more possible for her to live with her husband. Wife who was not obliged to disclose reasons for her hatred towards husband, by her statement showed her incurable aversion to husband. Trial Court on its assessment of evidence and circumstances appearing in the case, applying its conscious mind, giving sound and cogent reasons came to the conclusion that there was no prospect of harmonious life in future between the parties and dissolved marriage on ground of '*Khula*'. Findings of Court below, held, could not be interfered with particularly when defendant failed to point out any misreading or non-reading of evidence by Trial Court (LHC – 1989 MLD 4518).

504. Dissolution of marriage only ground of '*Khula*'. Where wife had categorically averred in her plaint that she had developed irretrievable hatred against husband, and her aversion had duly been substantiated by evidence, omission on part of Trial Court to specifically frame issue on ground of '*Khula*', held would not invalidate decree for '*Khula*' (LHC – 1989 MLD 3349).

505. Conduct of wife pointer to fact that her marriage with her husband had irretrievably broken down. Wife declining to come to husband's house when her father agreed to send her, relations of wife with husband had become so strained that they could not live within Hadood Ullah, and she was not prepared to live with husband as his wife in any circumstances whatsoever. Courts below taking no notice of her strongly worded averments made in her plaint and before Court. Spouses involved in litigation for two years but bitterness of litigation not softening her feelings towards her husband. To allow marriage to subsist in these circumstances, held, would really be forcing wife to live a life to which she was strongly averse and pushing her in a hateful union with husband. Judgments of Courts below rejecting plea of '*Khula*' set aside and case remanded with direction to consider appeal of wife as pending and dispose of same in light of observations made by High Court (LHC – 1988 MLD 1353).

506. Hatred towards husband. Wife filed suit for dissolution of marriage, but Family Court dismissed the same on the ground that she could not substantiate the alleged hatred and aversion against her husband. Judgment and decree passed by Family Court was maintained by Lower Appellate Court as well as by High Court. Validity: Hatred and aversion could neither be prescribed nor confined within the limited sphere, and no mechanism had been evolved to express 'hatred or aversion' precisely and in a definite manner. Suit for dissolution of marriage was filed by wife on 06 December 2000, which itself was demonstrative of the fact that she did not want to live with her husband, which indicated the degree of hatred and aversion. Wife personally submitted to Supreme Court that the Court might hang her and whatever might be the circumstances, she was not prepared to live with her husband; as such the same was hatred or aversion and nothing else. Judgments and decrees passed by the Courts below were set aside and petition for leave to appeal was converted into appeal. Suit for dissolution of marriage was decreed in favour of the wife. Appeal was allowed (SCP – 2005 PLD 293).

507. Plaintiff wife had clearly stated that she would not live with defendant husband at any cost and would prefer to die because of her hatred towards him. Such statement of plaintiff wife had clearly shown that she had taken plea of '*Khula*' in unequivocal manner. Absence of word '*Khula*' in the plaint was not sufficient to ignore plea of '*Khula*' and even if plaintiff had not taken plea of '*Khula*' in her plaint, Court after satisfying its conscience could dissolve marriage when it reached the conclusion that wife had once for all decided to leave her husband and she was firm to her stand that she would not live any more with him. Woman could not be forced to the hateful union with a man because when spouse could not live together within limits ordained by God, it would always be better to separate them (Shariat Court, Azad Kashmir (1999 YLR 2521).

508. Statements made by plaintiff wife and her witnesses had shown that even after seven years of marital relations parties could not lead a happy life, and even birth of two children could not develop some love and affection between them. Plaintiff wife had categorically deposed before Trial Court that because of defendant husband's attitude and his bad character and habits, she would not live with him at any cost, and that she wanted dissolution of marriage. Parties could not live together and lead a happy life within limits ordained by God. When hatred and disrespect developed between spouses and while wife refused to stay with her husband and expressed view that she did not like her husband, Court had the only option to pass a decree on basis of '*Khula*' (Shariat Court, Azad Kashmir 1999 YLR 1725).

509. Allegations made by wife in her suit against husband were of maltreatment, non-payment of maintenance and of immorality. Plaintiff in her suit had stated that she would prefer death rather than to live with her husband. Attempt to reconcile spouses at different stages in pre-trial and post-trial proceedings had failed. Husband filed case of *Zina* against wife under sections 10, 11, 16 & 19 of Offence of *Zina* (Enforcement of Hudood) Ordinance, 1979, which was contested by her up to Supreme Court and after dismissal of said suit, she filed application against husband under section 14, Offence of Qazf (Enforcement of Hadd) Ordinance, 1979 and many other criminal cases were filed by spouses against each other. Trial Court dismissed suit filed by wife holding that as she remained married to defendant for about thirty years and gave birth to children also, it was possible for spouses to live within Hudood Allah. Validity: Woman who was married thirty years back and give birth to seven children out of whom three were alive and were young, having preference to live separately and sought dissolution of marriage, had shown nothing but a severe hatred against her husband. Had there been any chance to live together wife would have not preferred to seek dissolution, especially when she spent her young life with him as her husband. Happy union was always bilateral. Lady who lived with her husband for about thirty years and then left house of her husband and constantly facing agony of criminal and civil litigation since long and still insisting to dissolve her marriage, could not be said to live within limits ordained by Almighty Allah. Long litigation between parties and series of litigation including allegation of *Zina* against each other, had suggested nothing, but to dissolve marriage by following principle of '*Khula*' as such litigation had wiped out any chance of harmonious life to be led by spouses by observing corresponding rights and liabilities. Shariat Court accepting appeal, set aside judgment and decree of Trial Court and dissolved marriage of spouses on principle of '*Khula*' holding that spouses could not live within limits ordained by Almighty Allah (Shariat Court, Azad Kashmir – 1999 YLR 207).

510. Question of '*Khula*' was to be considered on its own merits. Even if wife was unable to prove grounds available for dissolution of marriage as contained in Dissolution of Muslim Marriages Act, 1939, marriage could be dissolved on '*Khula*'. Wife was entitled to dissolution of marriage on '*Khula*' on restoration of what she had received in consideration of marriage, in case Court apprehended that parties would not observe limits of God (Shariat Court, Azad Kashmir – 1999 MLD 1763).

511. Suit for dissolution of marriage by wife on ground of '*Khula*' was dismissed by Family Court. High Court in its Constitutional jurisdiction after reappraising evidence concluded that Family Court had completely ignored evidence which had clearly established that parties could not live within limits prescribed by God and set aside judgment of Trial Court, dissolved marriage to save parties from violating limits prescribed by God. Contention of husband was that High Court, in exercise of its Constitutional jurisdiction was not competent to substitute its own findings for that recorded by Family Court even if it had come to the conclusion after appraisal of evidence that Trial Court had misread evidence. Validity: Wife having expressly stated before High Court that she had developed hatred against husband and wife stuck to her earlier position even before Supreme Court. Case therefore, was not fit for interference by Supreme Court with judgment of High Court which though suffered from defect as contended by husband (SCP – 1999 SCMR 2631).

512. Dissolution of marriage on several grounds including ground of '*Khula*'. If dissolution of marriage was claimed on number of grounds including '*Khula*', mere fact that wife could not establish her allegations qua other grounds, would not disentitle her to seek independent determination of her right for dissolution of marriage on ground of '*Khula*'. Court could not, on basis of decision on the other issues, decline '*Khula*'. Wife was not required to give objective reasons for seeking dissolution on ground of '*Khula*'. If wife was adamant and all attempts for reconciliation had failed, little choice was left for Court except to grant decree of '*Khula*' for consequences in adopting any other course could be disastrous (LHC 1998 CLC 1929).

513. Wife having developed hatred against husband on account of fact that he compelled her to convert her sect. Held, spouses could not lead their matrimonial life within limits prescribed by Allah. Dissolution of marriage on ground of '*Khula*' not interfered with in exercise of Constitutional jurisdiction (LHC – 1987 MLD 2549).

514. Relations between parties becoming strained within a period of four years of marital life to the extent that they could not live happily together. Wife not only was beaten and thrown out from house of husband on one or two occasions but also character of her husband was bad and insisting on her to lead immoral life. Observations of Appellate Court that such fact could be hardly termed as habitual cruelty or would not be taken into consideration for purpose of '*Khula*', held, were not proper. Case remanded to Appellate Court for disposal after considering plea of '*Khula*' and satisfying its conscience that wife, if forced to live with husband would not be observing limits prescribed by God, and after fixing benefits, if any, to be returned by wife to her husband as consideration of '*Khula*' (LHC – 1987 MLD 2486).

515. Mental torture to wife established. Parties could not live within limits of God as wife had developed internal disliking to husband. Court. held, rightly dissolved marriage on 'principle of '*Khula*' (SHC – 1985 MLD 225).

516. Dissolution of marriage after conversion of religion. If a married non-Muslim woman had embraced Islam, she must inform her husband of said conversion of religion, and the husband could embrace Islam within a period of *Iddat*, and in that case the marriage would continue, but if the husband remained non-Muslim even after expiry of *Iddat* period, the marriage would stand dissolved. Even in that case, the wife had to apply to the Family Court for dissolution of marriage on that ground, and the Court would summon her husband and inform him about the conversion of his wife, and if he did not embrace Islam within *Iddat* period, the Court could declare marriage dissolved. Woman would in that eventuality be entitled to enter into second marriage with a Muslim, and such procedure must be adopted to preclude the possibility of exploitation of religion merely for the purpose of satisfying sexual desire without any regards for one's family responsibility. Observance of *Iddat* period was also compulsory to avoid the possibility of pregnancy and the controversy of paternity of the child. Contention that woman's marriage with her previous non-Muslim husband would dissolve automatically by her embracing Islam, was repelled LHC – 2002 PLD 187).

§2. Procedure of Divorce

517. Under MFLO, complete procedure is provided regarding divorce. Any man who wishes to divorce his wife, after the pronouncement of divorce in any form whatsoever, give the Chairman a notice in writing of his having done so, and shall supply a copy thereof to the wife under section 7(1) of MFLO. If anyone contravenes the divorce procedure and does not give a written notice to the Chairman, he shall be punishable with simple imprisonment for a term which may extend to one year, or with fine which may extend to PKR 5,000, or with both under section 7(2) of MFLO.

518. If the whereabouts of the wife who is to be supplied a copy of the notice of divorce are not known to the husband, or cannot, with due diligence, be ascertained by him, he may, if so permitted by the Chairman, give notice of the divorce to the wife through her father, mother, adult brother or adult sister, or if their whereabouts are not known to the husband or cannot, with due diligence, be ascertained by him, he may, with the permission of the Chairman serve the notice of divorce on her by publication in a newspaper, approved by the Chairman, having circulation in the locality where he last resided with the wife (section 3-A of the West Pakistan Rules under MFLO).

519. Similarly if right to divorce has been delegated to wife under the *Nikahnama* and she wishes to exercise that right, or where any of the parties to a marriage wishes to dissolves the marriage otherwise than by divorce, the procedure of divorce as stated above and defined in MFLO shall apply, *mutatis mutandis*.

520. Petitioner divorced his wife and ninety days period after the pronouncement/sending of notice to the Chairman Arbitration having elapsed, Chairman Arbitration Council, Union Council concerned issued a certificate of effectiveness of Divorce as required under section 7 of MFLO. After more than two years of effectiveness of Divorce, *Naib Nazim* Union Council cancelled certificate of effectiveness of Divorce. Petitioner had challenged cancellation of certificate of effectiveness of Divorce contending that *Naib Nazim* Union Council had no authority to revoke the earlier order of effectiveness of Divorce. On Court Notice, *Nazim* of Union Council concerned appeared in court along with relevant record and appraised the court that *Naib Nazim*, who had cancelled certificate of effectiveness of Divorce, had died and that he did not own the documents allegedly having been issued by deceased *Naib Nazim*. Petition was disposed of with the observation that as no record was available with the Union Council regarding certificate cancelling effectiveness of Divorce, it appeared that it had been manipulated. Even otherwise after a lapse of more than two years, *Naib Nazim* Union Council had no authority to revoke the certificate of Divorce (LHC – 2009 YLR 1879).

521. Period of *Iddat* in absence of resumption of marital ties. When notice of Divorce was served on behalf of husband to the Chairman concerned, and there was no resumption of marital ties within the period of ninety days, the period of *Iddat* would be deemed to have coincided with the said ninety days (LHC – 1990 MLD 243).

522. '*Khula*' Dissolution of marriage under right of '*Khula*' Judge, Family Court coming to conclusion on basis of material on record that spouses could not live together within limits prescribed by Allah. Court, held, justified in dissolving marriage on ground of '*Khula*' on terms and conditions appropriate to facts of case. Husband and wife in litigation, civil, criminal for six years. Wife stating that she was not prepared to live with her husband at any cost, and that no formal Rukhsati had yet taken place. Held, this long drawn out litigation between parties by itself was a circumstance to indicate that relations were severely strained, and that it would be futile to expect that they can live happily together as husband and wife. Finding of Trial Court that case for '*Khula*' was made out, held, called for no interference in exercise of Constitutional jurisdiction Provisional Constitution Order (1 of 1981), Article 9 (SHC – 1984 CLC 3147).

§3. DIFFERENT MODES OF DIVORCE

523. The Muslim jurists differentiate between two kinds of divorce as far as the number is concerned. First, *Rajei* divorce; the revocable divorce, in which a husband has the right to bring his divorced wife back to conjugal life without making any new marriage contract. Taking her back to conjugal life is permissible only before the expiry of the period of *Iddat* (waiting period). Second, the *Bain* divorce; (complete separation). It is of two kinds: First, 'Minor Bain divorce' is a kind of separation. If the husband has made one pronouncement or two pronouncements of divorce, and he did not take his wife back to conjugal life during her *Iddat* (waiting period) and her *Iddat* has expired then it is permissible for him to take her back to conjugal life if he makes a new marriage contract fulfilling all requirements of marriage. Second, 'Major Bain divorce' where if the husband divorces his wife (three) times, then it becomes prohibited for him to take her back or marry her again unless she gets married to another man and has sexual intercourse with that man. If they are then separated by divorce or by the death of the second husband, the first husband can marry her if he wishes through a new marriage contract. Allah Says (interpretation of meaning): {Then, if the other husband divorces her, it is no sin on both of them that they reunite, provided they feel that they can keep the limits ordained by Allâh. These are the limits of Allâh, which He makes plain for the people who have knowledge.}[2: 230]. Under the Muslim Islamic Law Divorce, divorce can be effected in ways as detailed below.

A. Talak Ahsan (Most approved way for Divorce)

524. This consists of a single pronouncement of divorce made during a *Tuhr* (period between menstruations) followed by abstinence from sexual intercourse for a period of *Iddat*. When the marriage has not been consummated, a *Talak* in the *Ahsan* form may be pronounced even if the wife is in her menstruation. Where the wife has passed the age of periods of menstruation, the requirement of declaration during a *Tuhr* is inapplicable; furthermore, this requirement only applies to a oral divorce and not a divorce in writing. A divorce in the *Ahsan* mode becomes irrevocable and complete on the expiration of the period of *Iddat*. Until a *Talak* becomes irrevocable, the husband has the option to revoke it which may be done either expressly, or implied as by resuming sexual intercourse.

525. Effect of enactment of Muslim Family Laws Ordinance, 1961. Legislature had, to a great extent, trammelled and curtailed the arbitrary power of husband to divorce his wife. Muslim Family Laws Ordinance, 1961 had abolished the practice of disapproved form of 'divorce' and mode prescribed in the Ordinance was that of a *'Talaq-e-ahsan'* and by the Ordinance it had been made mandatory that the notice of 'divorce' should be given in writing to the Chairman of Union Council. 'Divorce' would be effected only if efforts of reconciliation would fail. Law prevailing previous to the enforcement of Muslim Family Laws Ordinance, 1961, had made it obligatory for the couples divorced by any mode of 'divorce' other than *'Talaq-e-ahsan'* not to re-marry each other again, unless wife married another man who died or divorced her after actual consummation, and she married her first husband after period of '*Iddat*'. Before re-marriage parties had to prove that bar to their marriage was removed by intermediate marriage, consummation and dissolution; otherwise, their marriage was not considered. Validity: Mode of 'divorce' effected under provisions of Muslim Family Laws Ordinance, 1961 being almost that of *'Talaq-e-ahsan'*, the couples could re-marry without any intervening marriage except where they had been divorced thrice, and the third divorce had become effective, and in that case they could not re-marry without an intervening marriage. Plain reading of section 7 of Muslim Family Laws Ordinance, 1961 though had implied that all kinds of 'divorces' had been made revocable without an intervening marriage and could be that its repugnancy to such extent could validly be agitated on the touchstone of Quranic behest and the traditions of Holy Prophet Muhammad (PBUH), but neither vires of said section-7 had been challenged nor matter raised in case pertained to all kinds of 'divorces'. Matter, in the present case, pertained, to 'divorce' obtained by wife through Court decree in shape of '*Khula*' (PHC – 2003 PLD 169).

B. Talaq Hasan (Approved way for Divorce)

526. This consists of three pronouncements made during successive *Tuhrs*, no intercourse taking place during any of the three *Tuhrs*. The first pronouncement should be made during a *Tuhr*, the second during the next *Tuhr* and the third during the succeeding *Tuhr*. A *Talak* in the Hasan mode becomes irrevocable immediately it is pronounced, irrespective of the *Iddat*.

C. Talaq-ul-bidaat or Talaq-i-badai

527. Under the Islamic Laws, Talaq-ul-bidaat or Talaq-i-badai consists of: (i) three pronouncements made during a single *Tuhr* either in one sentence, for example, 'I divorce you thrice' or in separate sentence for example, 'I divorce you, I divorce you, I divorce you'; or (ii) a single pronouncement made during a *Tuhr* clearly indicating an intention irrevocably to dissolve the marriage for example, 'I divorce you irrevocably'. As the *Talak* becomes irrevocable at once, it is called *Talak-i-bain*, that is, irrevocable *Talak*. According to the majority of the jurists, the divorce holds good, but it is against the spirit of the *Shari'ah*, and, therefore, the man who follows this course in divorce is an offender in the eye of Islamic Law.

528. Muslim Scholars differed in this case. Imams Abu Hanifah, Malik, Shafie, Ahmad and the majority of the Muslim Scholars consider this kind of divorce as divorcing three times. So she cannot be lawful for him unless she marries another person and gets divorce from him after having sexual intercourse with him. Imam Tawoos, some Scholars of Ahle-e-Zahir Sheikh-ul-Islam Ibn Taimiyah and other more contemporary later Scholars consider it as an only one divorce.

529. It is narrated in *Bukhari* and Muslim that during the life of Allah's Apostle. Abdullah Ibn Umar had divorced his wife while she was menstruating. Umar bin al-Khattab asked Allah's apostle about that. Allah's Apostle said, 'Order him (your Son) to take her back and keep her till she is clean and then to wait till she gets her next period and becomes clean again, whereupon, if he wishes to keep her, he can do so, and if he wishes to divorce her he can divorce her before having sexual intercourse with her, and that is the prescribed period which Allah has fixed for the women meant to be divorced'.

530. An-Nasaaee reported in his Sunan on the authority of Mahmood bin Labeed (Radiya Allahu Anhu) that a man divorced his wife three times on a single occasion. The Holy Prophet Muhammad (PBUH) stood up in anger and said, 'Will the Book of Allah be played with while I am still in your midst? (The anger was seen so vividly on him) that a man (among the companions)' said, 'O! Messenger of Allah! Shall I kill him?' This Hadith indicates that any man who divorces his wife this way has committed a sin. As for the rule of this kind of divorces the majority of the scholars are of the view that, the divorce made this way should be implemented, though the divorcing husband incurs a sin. Some scholars are, of the opinion that, divorcing a woman three times with a single word will be counted as one divorce. However majority of the Islamic Scholars believe that such a divorce will be regarded as three.

531. Divorce pronounced by husband to wife thrice. Right of revocation by husband. Withdrawal of notice of divorce by husband from Administrator, Union Council. Validity: Divorce pronounced by husband to wife thrice would become 'bain', and husband would have no right of its revocation as per Injunctions laid down in Holy Qur'an and Sunnah, relating to divorce and its revocation, and to that extent provision of section-7, Muslim Family Laws Ordinance, 1961, would give its way to those Injunctions as enshrined in the Constitution. Contents of Talaqnama in writing clearly indicated that same was irrevocable, and that respondent had no mind to revoke the same. Respondent was wrong in claiming in the alleged application for revoking of divorce that his, wife was also agreeable to have reconciliation with him. Divorce pronounced by respondent being irrevocable, Administrator, Union Council was bound to issue certificate regarding its effectiveness. High Court declared that divorce pronounced by respondent had become effective and irrevocable; respondent could not claim petitioner to be his wife; and Administrator, Union Council was directed to issue certificate confirming effectiveness of divorce (LHC – 1996 MLD 1689).

D. Divorce Under Compulsion

532. Under the Islamic Laws, if the words of divorce used by the husband are 'express', the divorce is valid even if it was pronounced under compulsion or in a state of voluntary intoxication, or to satisfy his father or someone else.

533. However some *fiqas* believe, the divorce of a compelled person is null, that is, not effective. The Holy Prophet Muhammad (PBUH) said: 'There is no divorce during enclosure' [Abu Dawood and al-Syooti graded it as sound]. Enclosure means coercion. The jurists state that any clear harm that could affect the body or wealth of the person, that of his wife, children, or parents if he does not divorce is considered as compulsion on divorce, and a divorce done under such threat is not valid. If wife threatens to kill herself if her husband does not divorce her; in this case the divorce was delivered only to save her life so it is not a valid divorce as long as the husband was sure that she was going to kill herself if he refused divorce, or he believed it strongly.

E. Divorce by Ila (Vow of continence)

534. When a person, who is of sound mind has attained puberty, abstains from sexual intercourse for a period of not less than four months in pursuance of a vow to that effect, he is said to have made *Ila*, and its effect will be that of a single irrevocable divorce.

F. Zihar (Injurious assimilation)

535. *Zihar* is a form of inchoate divorce. If the husband compresses his wife to his mother or any other female within prohibited degrees the wife has a right to refuse herself to him until he has performed penance. In default of expiation by penance the wife has the right to apply for a judicial divorce.

G. 'Khula' (Redemption) and Mubarat (Mutual freeing)

536. A marriage may be dissolved not only by divorce, which is the arbitrary act of the husband, but also by agreement between the husband and wife. Dissolution of marriage by agreement may take the form of '*Khula*' or *Mubarat*. A divorce by '*Khula*' is a divorce with the consent, and at the instance of the wife, in which she gives or agrees to give a consideration of the husband for her release from the marriage tie. In such a case, the terms of the bargain are matters of arrangement between the husband and wife, and the wife may, as the consideration, release her dower and other rights, or make any other agreement for the benefit of the husband. Failure on the part of the wife to pay the consideration for the divorce does not invalidate the divorce through the husband may sue the wife for it.

537. A '*Khula*' divorce is effected by an offer from the wife to compensate the husband if he releases her from her marital rights and acceptance by the husband of the offer. Once the offer is accepted, it operates as a single irrevocable divorce *(Talaq-i-bain)*, and its operation is not postponed until execution of the *Khulanama*.

538. A *Mubarat* divorce like '*Khula*' is a dissolution of marriage by agreement, but there is a difference between the origin of the two. When the aversion is on the side of the wife, and she desires a separation, the transaction is called '*Khula*'. When the aversion is mutual, and both the sides desire a separation, the transaction is called *mubarat*. The offer in a *mubarat* divorce may proceed from the wife, or it may proceed from the husband, but once it is accepted, the dissolution is completed, and it operates as *Talak-i-bain* as in the case of '*Khula*'.

539. Court held that there is a difference between '*Khula*' and mubarat and the main distinction between a '*Khula*' and *mubarat* is that in the former the aversion is on the side of the wife and she desires a separation but in the latter the aversion is mutual and both sides desire separation. Second, in a divorce by '*Khula*' some consideration must be given by the wife to the husband for her release from the marital tie. It is in effect an offer from the wife for her release on payment of compensation. Where a suit filed by the husband for restitution of conjugal rights had been decreed but as against that the wife's suit claiming dissolution of marriage had been dismissed by the Trial Court, it was held that it was the wife who sought severance of the marital tie and not the husband and, therefore, in the circumstances the divorce ultimately agreed upon by the parties was only a *mubarat* and not '*Khula*' (SCP – 1964 PLD 456).

§4. Effects of Divorce

540. After the divorce, if the marriage was consummated, the wife may marry another husband after the completion of her *Iddat*; if the marriage was not consummated, she is free to marry immediately.

541. If the marriage was consummated, the husband had four wives at the date of divorce including the divorced wife; he may marry another wife after completion of the *Iddat* of the divorce wife.

542. If the marriage was consummated, the wife is entitled to immediate payment of the whole of the unpaid dower, both prompt and deferred after the divorce. If the marriage was not consummated and the amount of dower was specified in the contract, she is entitled to half of that amount. If no amount was specified, she is entitled to only three articles of dress. Where a marriage is dissolved upon the apostasy of the wife, she is entitled to the whole of the dower if the consummation of the marriage has taken place.

543. Either party is entitled to inherit from the other until the divorce becomes irrevocable. Immediately the divorce becomes irrevocable, mutual rights of inheritance ceases, except where the divorce was pronounced during the husband's death-illness in which the wife's right to inherit continues until the expiry of her *Iddat*, unless she was repudiated at her own request.

544. Sexual intercourse between the divorced couple is unlawful after the divorce has become irrevocable. The offspring of such an intercourse is illegitimate and cannot be legitimated by acknowledgement.

545. When husband has repudiated his wife by three pronouncements, it is not lawful for him to marry her again until she has married another man and the latter has divorced her or died after actual consummation of the marriage. The presumption of marriage arising from an acknowledgement of legitimacy does not apply to a remarriage between divorced persons unless it is established that the bar to remarriage and subsequent divorce after actual consummation. Even if a remarriage between the divorced persons is proved, the marriage is not valid unless it is established that the bar to remarriage does not raise any presumption as to the fulfilment of the above condition. A marriage presumption as to the fulfilment of the above conditions is irregular, not avoid. In other cases, the divorced parties may remarry as if there had been no divorce either during the *Iddat* or after its completion.

546. Divorce, unless revoked earlier, expressly or otherwise, shall not be effective until the expiration of ninety days from the day on which notice is delivered to the Chairman (section 7(3) of MFLO).

547. If the wife is pregnant at the time divorce is pronounced, divorce shall not be effect until the period of ninety days or the pregnancy, whichever later, ends (section 7(5) of MFLO).

548. Within thirty days of the receipt of divorce notice, the Chairman shall constitute an Arbitration Council for the purpose of bringing about conciliation between the parties, and the Arbitration Council shall take all steps necessary to bring about such reconciliation (section 7(4) of MFLO).

549. Unless divorce has not been conveyed three times, nothing debars a wife to remarry the same husband without an intervening marriage with a third person (section 7(6) of MFLO). However, if husband has conveyed divorce three times, a woman cannot remarry with the ex-husband unless and until she has been married to another person and that person divorce the woman.

§5. *Iddat* (Time limitation for woman to remarry)

550. If a woman is divorced by the husband, the period of *Iddat* is three menstrual periods or where the woman does not menstruate for any reason other than gestation, three lunar months. However if a woman is pregnant, then the *Iddat* lasts until delivery, irrespective of whether the period is shorter or longer that three months.

551. *Iddat* is rendered by the completion of which a new marriage is rendered lawful. It is a period of continuance imposed on a woman on the termination of marriage in the interest of certainty of paternity. In the event of the husband's death, it is mandatory for the woman to wait for four months and ten days to remarry. The marriage with woman before completion of her *Iddat* is considered as irregular, not void by the Courts of Pakistan.

552. Marriage of a woman before completion of her *Iddat*, was irregular and not void. Irregular marriage could have its own consequences under personal law, but same could not be treated as void and could not be regarded as un-Islamic or against the *Shariah* (FSC – 2004 YLR 619).

553. Divorced wife, held, was entitled to payment of maintenance for period of *Iddat* even it was awarded by Union Council after divorce proceedings had been concluded. High Court in Constitutional jurisdiction ordering recovery of maintenance amount of *Iddat* period from ex-husband of petitioner (LHC – 1987 MLD 23).

554. Petitioner, who was a Christian woman, was married to a Christian, and out of said wedlock nine children were born. Later on the lady embraced Islam and only after five days of said conversion she married with a Muslim without observing *Iddat* period. Validity: During *Iddat* period, if any woman entered into *Nikah* that would be against law and also Injunctions of Islam and it would be liable to *Ta'zir*. If a married non-Muslim woman would embrace Islam, she must inform her husband of said conversion and her husband either would embrace Islam within period of *Iddat* in which case marriage would continue, or he would remain a non-Muslim even after expiry of *Iddat* period, in which case marriage would stand dissolved. *Iddat* was compulsory after dissolution of marriage of any character. Within *Iddat* period, *Nikah* would be invalid rather void, and during that period cohabitation would come within definition of *Zina* and would be liable to be punished (LHC – 2005 PLD 126).

555. Plea raised by husband was that suit for maintenance of the plaintiff (wife) was decreed but she was not entitled to maintenance amount after Iddat period and that husband did not avail any of the dowry articles, as he had passed most of his time abroad. Validity: Since the *Iddat* period of the plaintiff had elapsed, therefore, she was not entitled to the maintenance after *Iddat*. Remittance receipts from abroad had established that husband had remitted greater amount than the decretal amount, thus, the plaintiff was not entitled to the recovery of dowry articles. Husband had left for abroad soon after the marriage and did not avail any of the dowry articles which remained in the use of the plaintiff (wife). High Court while partly allowing the Constitutional petition set aside the judgment and decree to the extent of recovery of dowry articles and maintained the judgment and decree for maintenance allowance (LHC – 2009 YLR 190).

§6. Christian Marriage Dissolution

556. Christian marriage dissolution matters are dealt under the Christian Marriages Act of 1872 and the Divorce Act of 1869. Since marriage among Christians is regarded as a holy union, the primary concept of dissolution of marriage is through the death of one of the spouses and divorce during their lifetime is permitted only on very restricted grounds for both husband and wife. There is no concept of unilateral divorce, and the courts have to be approached (although in practice, the Church does also grant dissolution of marriage). Therefore, for dissolution of Marriage either party has to file the Civil Petition before the Civil Judge.

557. The Divorce Act, 1869 (Act No. IV of 1869) deals with the divorce of persons professing the Christian religion, and to confer certain Court jurisdiction in matters matrimonial. Under this Act, Court has the powers to grant relief generally, and to make decrees of dissolution, or of nullity to petitioners or respondents professes the Christian religion; or to make decrees of dissolution of marriage except where the parties to the marriage are domiciled in Pakistan at the time when the petition is presented; or to make decrees of nullity of marriage except where the marriage if solemnized before the 15th day of August, 1947, has been solemnized in India and if solemnized on or after that date has been solemnized in Pakistan and the petitioner is resident in Pakistan at the time of presenting the petition; or to grant any relief under this Act, other than a decree of dissolution of marriage, or of nullity of marriage except where the petitioner resides in Pakistan at the time of presenting the petition.

558. Under the Divorce Act, 1869 'Minor Children' means, in the case of sons of Pakistan fathers, boys who have not completed the age of 16 years, and, in case of daughters of Pakistan fathers, girls who have not completed the age of 13 years; in other cases, it means unmarried children who have not completed the age of 18 years; 'Incestuous adultery' means adultery committed by a husband with a woman with whom, if his wife were dead, he could not lawful contract marriage by reason of her being within the prohibited degrees of consanguinity (whether natural or legal) or affinity; 'Bigamy with adultery' means adultery with the same woman with whom the bigamy was committed; 'Marriage with another woman' means marriage of any person, being married, to any other person, during the life of the former wife, whether the second marriage shall have taken place within Pakistan or elsewhere; 'Desertion' implies an abandonment against the wish of the person charging it; and 'Property' includes, in the case of a wife, any property to which she is entitled for an estate in remainder or reversion, or as a trustee, executrix or administratrix; and the date of the death of the testator or intestate shall be deemed to be the time at which any such wife becomes entitled as executrix or administratrix.

559. Part-III (sections 10~17) of the Divorce Act, 1869 deals with the dissolution of marriage. Under section-10 of the Divorce Act, 1869 any husband can present a petition to the Court of Civil Judge, praying that his marriage may be dissolved on the ground that this wife has, since the solemnization thereof, been guilty of adultery. Every such petition shall state, as distinctly as the nature of the case permits, the facts on which the claim to have such marriage dissolved is founded. Under section-11, upon any such petition presented by a husband, the petitioner shall make the alleged adultere a co-respondent to the said petition, unless he is excused from so doing on one of the following grounds, to be allowed by the Court:

- that the respondent is leading the life of a prostitute, and that the petitioner knows of no person with whom the adultery has been committed;

- that the name of the alleged adulterer is unknown to the petitioner although he has made due efforts of discover it; and
- that the alleged adulterer is dead.

560. Whereas under section-10, any wife can also present a petition to the District Court or to the High Court, praying that her marriage may be dissolved on the ground that, since the solemnization thereof, her husband has exchanged his profession of Christianity for the profession of some other religion, and gone through a form of marriage with another woman; or has been guilty of incestuous adultery; or of bigamy with adultery; or of marriage with another woman with adultery; or of rape, sodomy or bestiality; or of adultery coupled with such cruelty as without adultery would have entitled her to a divorce a *mensa et toro;* or of adultery coupled with desertion, without reasonable excuse, for two years or upwards. Every such petition shall state, as distinctly as the nature of the case permits, the facts on which the claim to have such marriage dissolved is founded.

561. Upon receipt of petition for the dissolution of a marriage, the Court shall satisfy itself, so far as it reasonably cannot only as to the facts alleged, but also whether or not the petitioner has been in any manner accessory to, or conniving at, the going through of the said form of marriage, or the adultery, or has condoned the same, and shall also inquire into any countercharge which may be made against the petitioner.

562. In case the Court, on the evidence in relation to any such petition, is satisfied that the petitioner's case has not been proved, or is not satisfied that the alleged adultery has been committed; or finds that the petitioner has, during the marriage, been accessory to, or conniving at, the going through of the said form of marriage, or the adultery of the other party to the marriage, or has condoned the adultery complained of; or that the petition is presented or prosecuted in collusion which either of the respondent, then and in any of said cases Court shall dismiss the petition.

563. In case the Court is satisfied on the evidence that the case on the petitioner has been proved and does not find that the petitioner has been in any manner accessory to, or conniving at, the going through of the said form of marriage, or the adultery of the other party to the marriage, or has condoned the adultery complained of; or that the petition is presented or prosecuted in collusion with either of the respondents, the Court shall pronounce a decree declaring such marriage to be dissolved: Provided that the Court shall not be bound to pronounce such degree if it finds that the petitioner has, during the marriage, been guilty of adultery; or if the petitioner has, in the opinion of the Court, been guilty of unreasonable delay in presenting or prosecuting such petition; or of cruelty towards the other party to the marriage; or of having deserted or wilfully separated himself/herself from the other party before the adultery complained of, and without reasonable excuse; or of such wilful neglect or misconduct of or towards the other party as has conducted to the adultery. However, no adultery shall be deemed to have been condoned within the meaning of this Act unless where conjugal co-habitation has been resumed or continued.

564. In any suit instituted for dissolution of marriage, if the respondent opposes the relief sought on the ground, in case of such a suit instituted by a husband, of his adultery, cruelty or desertion without reasonable excuse, or, in case of such a suit instituted by a wife, on the ground of her adultery and cruelty, the Court may in such suit give to the respondent, on his/her application, the same relief to which he/she would have been entitled in case he/she had presented a petition seeking such relief, and the respondent shall be competent to give evidence of or relating to such cruelty or desertion.

565. Section-IV of the Divorce Act, 1869 (sections-18~21) deals with the nullity of marriage. Any husband or wife can present a petition to the Court of Civil Judge, praying that his/her marriage may be declared null and void. However, such decree may be made on any of the following grounds:

- that the respondent was impotent at the time of the marriage and at the time of the institution of the suit;
- that the parties are within the prohibited degrees of consanguinity whether natural or legal or affinity;
- that either party was a lunatic or idiot at the time of marriage; and
- that the former husband or wife or either party was living at the time of marriage, and the marriage with such former husband or wife was then in force.

566. However, nothing in this section of the Act effects the jurisdiction of the Court to make decrees of nullity of marriage on the ground that the consent of either party was obtained by force or fraud.

567. Under section-21 of the Act, when a marriage is annulled on the ground that former husband or wife was living, and it is adjudged that the subsequent marriage was contracted in good faith with the full belief of the parties that the former husband or wife was dead, or when a marriage is annulled on the ground of insanity children begotten before the decree is made shall be specified in the decree, and shall be entitled to succeed, in the same manner as legitimate children, to the estate of the parent who at the time of the marriage was competent to contract.

568. Section-IV of the Divorce Act, 1869 (sections 22~25) deals with the judicial separation. It is stated that no decree shall be made for a divorce a *mensa et thoro*, but the husband or wife may obtain a decree of judicial separation, on the ground of adultery, or cruelty, or desertion without reasonable excuse for two years or upwards, and such decree shall have the effect of a divorce a *mensa et thoro,* under the existing law, and such other legal effect. Application for judicial separation on any one of the grounds aforesaid shall be made by either husband or wife by petition to the Court of Civil Judge; and the Court, on being satisfied of the truth of the statements made in such petition and that there is no legal ground why the application should not be granted, may decree judicial separation accordingly.

569. In every case of a judicial separation under the Divorce Act, the wife shall, from the date of the sentence, and whilst the separation continues, be considered as unmarried with respect to property of every description which she may acquire or which may come to or devolve upon her. Such property may be disposed of by her in all respects as an unmarried woman, and on her decease the same shall, in case she dies intestate, go as the same would have gone if her husband has been then dead: Provided that; if any such wife again co-habits with her husband, all such property as she may be entitled to when such co-habitation takes place shall be held to her separate use, subject, however, to any agreement in writing made between herself and her husband whilst separate.

570. In every case of a judicial separation the wife shall, whilst so separated, be considered as an unmarried woman for the purposes of contract, and wrongs and injuries, and suing and being used in any civil proceeding; and her husband shall not be liable in respect of any contract, act or costs entered into, done, omitted or incurred by her during the separation; Provided that whereupon any such judicial separation, alimony has been decreed or ordered to be paid to the wife, and the same is not duly paid by the husband, he shall be liable for necessaries supplied for her use: Provided also that nothing shall prevent the wife from joining, at any time during such separation, in the exercise of any joint power given to herself and husband.

571. Under section-26 of the Divorce Act, any husband or wife, upon the application of whose wife or husband, as the case may be, a decree of judicial separation has been pronounced, may, at any time thereafter, present a petition to the Court by which the decree was pronounced, praying for a reversal of such decree on the ground that it was obtained in his/her absence, and that there was reasonable excuse for the alleged desertion, where desertion was the ground of such decree. The Court may, on being satisfied of the truth of the allegations of such petition, reverse the decree accordingly, but such reversal shall not prejudice or affect the rights or remedies which any other person would have had, in case it had not been decreed, in respect of any debts, contracts or acts of the wife incurred, entered into are done between the times of the sentence of separation and of the reversal thereof.

572. Section-27 of the Divorce Act, 1869 stipulated that any wife to whom section 4 of the Indian Succession Act, 1865 does not apply, may, when deserted by her husband, present a petition to the Court of Civil Judge at any time after such desertion, for an order to protect any property which she may have acquired or may acquire, and property of which she may become possessed after such desertion, against her husband or his creditors, or any person claiming under him. Under section-28, if Court is satisfied of the fact of such desertion, and that the same was without reasonable excuse, and that the wife is maintaining herself by her own industry or property, may make and give to the wife an order protecting her earnings and other property from her husband and all creditors and persons claiming under him. Every such order shall state the time at which the desertion commenced, and shall, as regards all persons dealing with the wife in reliance thereon, be conclusive as to such time.

573. The husband or any creditor of, or person claiming under him, may apply to the Court by which such order was made for the discharge or variation thereof and the Court, if the desertion has ceased, or if for any other reason it thinks fit so to do, may discharge or vary the order accordingly. If the husband, or any creditor of, or person claiming under, the husband seizes or continues to hold any property of the wife after notice any such order, her shall be liable, at the suit of the wife (which she is hereby empowered to bring), to return or deliver to her the specific property, and also to pay her sum equal to double its value So long as any such order of protection remains in force, the wife shall be and be deemed to have been, during such desertion of her, in the like position all respects, with regard to property and contracts and suing and being sued, as she would be under this Act if she obtained a decree of judicial separation (sections 29~31 of the Divorce Act, 1869).

574. Under section-32 of the Divorce Act, 1869, when either the husband or the wife has, either reasonable excuse, withdrawn from the society of the other wife or husband may apply a petition to the High Court or Civil Judge for restitution of conjugal rights, and the Courts, on being satisfied of the truth of the statements made in such petition, and that there is no legal ground why the application should not be granted, may decree restitution of conjugal rights accordingly. However, nothing shall be pleaded in answer to a petition for restitution of conjugal rights which would not be ground for a suit for a judicial separation or for a decree of nullity of marriage.

575. Part-VIII (section-34) of the Divorce Act, 1869, any husband may, either in a petition for dissolution of marriage or for judicial separation, or in a petition to the Court of Civil Judge limited to such object only, claim damages from any person on the ground of his having committed adultery with the wife of such petitioner. Such petition shall be served on the alleged adulterer, and the wife unless the Court dispenses with such service or directs some other service to be substituted. The damages to be recovered on any such petition shall be ascertained by the said Court, although the respondents or either of them may not appear. After the decision has been given, the Court may direct in what manner such damages shall be paid or applied.

576. Section-35 of the Divorce Act, 1869 stipulates that whenever in any petition resented by a husband, the alleged adulterer has been made a co-respondent, and the adultery has been established, the Court may order the co-respondent to pay the whole or any part of the proceedings: Provided that the co-respondent shall not be ordered to pay the petitioner's costs. If the respondent was, at the time of the adultery, living apart from her husband and leading the life of a prostitute, or if the co-respondent had not, at the time of the adultery, reason to believe the respondent to be a married woman.

577. Part-IX (sections 36~38) deals with the alimony. In any suit, whether it be instituted by a husband or a wife, and whether or not she has obtained an order of protection, the wife may present a petition for alimony pending the suit. Such petition shall be served on the husband, and the Court, on being satisfied of the truth of the statements therein contained, may make such order on the husband for payment to the wife of alimony pending the suit as it may deem just: Provided that alimony pending the suit shall in no case exceed one-fifth of the husband's average net income for the three years next preceding the date of the order, and shall continue, in case of a decree for dissolution of marriage or of nullity of marriage, until the decree is made absolute or is confirmed, as the case may be. The Court may, if it thinks fit on any decree declaring a marriage to be dissolved, or on any decree of judicial separation obtained by the wife, order.

578. The Court may make an order on the husband for payment to the wife of such monthly or weekly sums for her maintenance and support as the Court may think reasonable: Provided that if the husband afterwards from any cause becomes unable to make such payments, it shall be lawful for the Court to discharge or modify the order, or temporarily to suspend the same as to the whole or any part of the money so ordered to be paid, again to revive the same order wholly or in part, as the Court seem fit.

579. In all cases in which the Court makes any decree or order for alimony it may direct the same to be paid either to the wife herself, or to any trustee on her behalf to be approved by the Court, and may impose any terms or restriction which the Court seem expedient, and may from time to time appoint a new trustee, if it appears to the Court expedient so to do.

580. Part-X (sections 39~44) of the Divorce Act, 1869 deals with the Settlements. Whenever the Court pronounces a decree of dissolution of marriage or judicial separation for adultery of the wife if it is made to appear to the Court that the wife is entitled to any property, the Court may, if it thinks fit, order such settlement as it thinks reasonable to be made of such property of any part thereof, for the benefit of the husband, or of the children of the marriage, or of both. Any instrument executed pursuant to any order of the Court at the time of or after the pronouncing of a decree of dissolution of marriage or judicial separation shall be deemed valid notwithstanding the existence of the disability of coverture at the time of the execution thereof. The Court may direct that the whole or any part of the damages recovered under section 34 shall be settled for the benefit of the children of the marriage, or as a provision for the maintenance of the wife.

581. The Court after making a decree for dissolution of marriage or a decree of nullity of marriage, may inquire into the existence of ante-nuptial or post-nuptial settlements made on the parties whose marriages is the subject of the decree, and may make such orders, with reference to the application of the whole or a portion of the property settled, whether for the benefit of the husband or the wife, or of the children (if any) of the marriage, or of both children and parents, as the Court seems fit: Provided that the Court shall not make any order for the benefit of the parents or either of them at expense of the children.

582. In any suit for obtaining a judicial separation to Court may, from time to time, before making its decree, make such interim orders, and may make such provision in the decree, as it deems proper with respect to the custody, maintenance and education of the minor children, the marriage of whose parents is the subject of such suit, and may, if it thinks fit, direct proceedings to be taken for placing such children under the protection of the said Court.

583. The Court, after a decree of judicial separation, may upon application (by petition) for this purpose make, from time to time, all such orders and provisions, with respect to the custody, maintenance and education of the minor children, the marriage of whose parents is the subject of the decree, or for placing such children under the protection of the said Court, as might have made by such decree or by interim orders in case the proceedings for obtaining such decree were still pending.

584. In any suit of obtaining a dissolution of marriage or a decree of nullity of marriage, the Court may from time to time, before making its decree make such provision in the decree, as it deems proper with respect to the custody, maintenance and education of the minor children, the marriage of whose parents is the subject of the suit; and may, if it thinks fit, direct proceedings to be taken for placing such children under the protection of the Court.

585. The Court, after a decree for dissolution of marriage or a decree of nullity of marriage, may, upon application by petition for the purpose, make from time to time all such orders and provision, with respect to the custody, maintenance and education of the minor children, the marriage of whose parents was the subject of the decree, or for placing such children under the protection of the Court, as might have been made by such decree or by such interim orders as aforesaid.

586. Section-48 of the Divorce Act, 1869 stipulates that when the husband or wife is a lunatic or idiot, any suit (other than a suit for restitution of conjugal rights) may be brought on his/her behalf by the committee or other person entitled to his/her custody.

587. Under section-49 where the petitioner is a minor, he/she shall sue by his/her next friend to be approved by the Court; and no petition presented by a minor under this Act shall be filed until the next friends has undertaken in writing to be answerable for costs. Such undertaking shall be filed in Court, and the next friend shall thereupon be liable in the same manner and to the same extent as if he/she were a plaintiff in an ordinary suit.

588. Part-XIII (sections 57~59) stipulates provisions relating to re-marriage. After the expiry of six months from the date of decree for the dissolution of a marriage, or, where an appeal has been presented against any such decree, after the dismissal of such appeal or the declaration of the marriage is dissolved as a result of such appeal, but not sooner, it shall be lawful for the parties to the marriage to marry again as if the prior marriage had been dissolved by death. No clergyman in Holy Orders of the Church shall be compelled to solemnize the marriage of any person whose former marriage has been dissolved on the ground of his/her adultery, or shall be liable to any suit, penalty or censure for solemnizing or refusing to solemnize the marriage of any such person. When any minister of any Church or chapel of the said Church refuses to perform such marriage service between any persons who, but for such refusal would be entitled to have same service performed in such Church or chapel, such minister shall permit any other minister in Holy Orders of fee paid Church entitled to officiate within the diocese in which such Church or chapel is situate to perform such marriage service in such Church or chapel.

589. (LHC – 2003 YLR 400) Suit for dissolution of marriage. Both plaintiffs' wives appeared before Court and stated that they would rather prefer to die than to go with husbands. One of the plaintiffs had alleged that her marriage was solemnized during her minority and under undue influence exercised by a 'Peer'. Parties were litigating since 1995 and according to statement of parties they were going through agonizing and painful situation and plaintiff women appearing before Court had refused to go with their husbands. *Effect:* No religion would allow a hateful union which was not based on true consent of parties, especially in Christian Marriages Act, 1872 where marriage was a sacrament and at the time of marriage both parties vow to stand together in sorrow and happiness till death would depart them. Evidence had established beyond doubt that vital role in marriage between spouses who were Christians was performed by one Muslim 'Peer' under whose influence parties were wedded. Trial Court was not justified to dismiss the suit. Appellate Court had rightly decreed the suit of the ladies by setting aside judgment and decree of Trial Court. High Court declined interference in circumstances.

590. (LHC – 1985 CLC 2855) Delegation of right of divorce to wife. Exercise of such right by wife. Notice of Divorce. Non-cognizance by Chairman. Husband being Muslim was governed by his own personal law in matter of divorce. Christian wife exercising her right of divorce delegated to her by Muslim husband had sent notice of Divorce. Refusal of Chairman, Union Council to take cognizance of said notice, held, was illegal and without lawful authority. Case remanded to Chairman for proceeding according to law.

§7. Parsi Marriage Dissolution

591. The Parsi Marriage and Divorce Act, 1936 regulates the divorce matters of Parsi community in Pakistan. The Parsi marriage can be dissolved under section-31 of the Act, if a husband or wife shall have been continually absent from his/her wife or husband for the space of seven years, and shall not have been heard of as being alive within that time by those persons who would have naturally heard of him/her, had he/she been alive, the marriage of such husband or wife may, at the instance of either party thereto, be dissolved.

592. Under section-32 of the Act, any married person may sue for divorce on any one or more of the following grounds, namely (a) that the marriage has not been consummated within one year after its solemnization owing to the wilful refusal of the defendant to consummate it; (b) that the defendant at the time of the marriage was of unsound mind and has been habitually so up to the date of the suit: Provided that divorce shall not be granted on this ground, unless the plaintiff (1) was ignorant of the fact at the time of the marriage, and (2) has filed the suit within three years from the date of the marriage; (c) that the defendant was at the time of marriage pregnant by some person other than the plaintiff: Provided that divorce shall not be granted on this ground, unless (1) the plaintiff was at the time of the marriage ignorant of the fact alleged, (2) the suit has been filed within two years of the date of marriage, and (3) marital intercourse has not taken place after the plaintiff came to know of the fact; (d) that the defendant has since the marriage committed adultery or fornication or bigamy or rape or an un-natural offence: Provided that divorce shall not be granted on this ground if the suit has been filed more than two years after the plaintiff came to know of the fact; (e) that the defendant has since the marriage voluntarily caused grievous hurt to the plaintiff or has infected the plaintiff with venereal disease or, where the defendant is the husband, has compelled the wife to submit herself to prostitution; Provided that divorce shall not be granted on this ground if the suit has been filed more than two years (i) after the infliction of the grievous hurt, or (ii) after the plaintiff came to know of the infection, or (iii) after the last act of compulsory prostitution; (f) that the defendant is undergoing a sentence of imprisonment for seven years or more for an offence as defined in the Pakistan Penal Code, XLV of 1860: Provided that divorce shall not be granted on this ground, unless the defendant has prior to the filing of the suit undergone at least one year's imprisonment out of the said period; (g) that the defendant has deserted the plaintiff for at least three years; (h) that a decree or order for judicial separation has been passed against the defendant, or an order has been passed against the defendant by a Magistrate awarding separate maintenance to the plaintiff, and the parties have not had marital intercourse for three years or more since such decree or order; (i) that the defendant has failed to comply with a decree for restitution of conjugal rights for a year or more; and (j) that the defendant has ceased to be a Parsi: Provided that divorce shall not be granted on this ground if the suit has been filed more than two years after the plaintiff came to know of the fact. Under section-33 of the Act, in every such suit for divorce on the ground of adultery, the plaintiff shall, unless the Court shall otherwise order, make the person with whom the adultery is alleged to have been committed a co-defendant, and in any such suit by the husband the Court may order the adulterer to pay the whole or any part of the costs of the proceedings.

593. Under section-34 of Parsi Marriage and Divorce Act, 1936, any married person may sue for judicial separation on any of the grounds for which such person could have filed a suit for divorce, or on the ground that the defendant has been guilty of such cruelty to him/her or their children, or has used such personal violence, or has behaved in such a way as to render it in the judgment of the Court improper to compel him/her to live with the defendant.

594. If the Court is satisfied that any of the grounds set forth in any suit under sections 30, 31, 32 or 34 of Parsi Marriage and Divorce Act, 1936 whether defended or not, those sections for granting relief exist, that none of the grounds therein set forth for withholding relief exist and that (a) the act or omission set forth in the plaint has not been condoned; (b) the husband and wife are not colluding together; (c) the plaintiff has not connived at or been accessory to the said act or omission; (d) (save where a definite period of limitation is provided by this Act) there has been no unnecessary or improper delay in instituting the suit; and (e) there is no other legal ground why relief should not be granted; then and in such case, but not otherwise, the Court shall decree such relief accordingly.

595. Under section-36 of the Parsi Marriage and Divorce Act, 1936 where a husband shall have deserted or without lawful cause ceased to cohabit with his wife, or where a wife shall have deserted or without lawful cause ceased to cohabit with her husband, the party so deserted or with whom cohabitation shall have so ceased may sue for the restitution of his/her conjugal rights and the Court, if satisfied of the truth of the allegations contained in the plaint, and that there is no just ground why relief should not be granted, may proceed to decree such restitution of conjugal rights accordingly. In any suit under this Act, the defendant may make a counter-claim for any relief he/she may be entitled to under this Act.

596. Under section-30 of the said Act, any case in which consummation of the marriage is from natural causes impossible, such marriage may, at the instance of either party thereto, be declared to be null and void.

Chapter 3. Cohabitation Outside Marriage

597. Under the Pakistani laws and in accordance with the Islamic Laws, in Islam extramarital sex is called *Zina* and considered great sin. In Pakistan, the Offence of *Zina* (Enforcement of Hadood) Ordinance, 1979 was promulgated on 9 February 1979 which stipulates the punishment to male and female who have sexual relations other than marriage as per Islamic Laws.

598. Under the Office of *Zina* (Enforcement of Hadood) Ordinance, 1979 'Adult' means a person who has attained, being a male, the age of 18 years or, being a female, the age of 16 years, or has attained puberty; and 'Muhsan' means a Muslim adult man who is not insane and has had sexual intercourse with a Muslim adult woman who, at the time he had sexual intercourse with her, was married to him and was not insane; or a Muslim adult woman who is not insane and has had sexual intercourse with a Muslim adult man who, at the time she had sexual intercourse with him, was married to him and was not insane; '*Zina*' means a man and a woman are said to commit '*Zina*' if they wilfully have sexual intercourse without being married to each other. Penetration is sufficient to constitute the sexual intercourse necessary to the offence of *Zina*.

599. *Zina* is liable to Hadd if it is committed by a man who is an adult and is not insane with a woman to whom he is not, and does not suspect himself to be married; or it is committed by a woman who is an adult and is not insane with a man to whom she is not, and does not suspect herself to be, married.

600. Whoever is guilty of *Zina* liable to Hadd shall, if he/she is a Muhsan, be stoned to death at a public place; or if he/she is not Muhsan, be punished, at a public place with whipping numbering one hundred stripes.

601. However, no punishment is executed until it has been confirmed by the Court to which an appeal from the order of conviction lies; and if the punishment be of whipping, until it is confirmed and executed, the convict shall be dealt with in the same manner as if sentenced to simple imprisonment.

602. Proof of *Zina* liable to Hadd if the accused makes before a Court of competent jurisdiction a confession of the commission of the offence; or at least four Muslim adult male witnesses, about whom the Court is satisfied, having regard to the requirements of *tazkiyah al-shuhood*, that they are truthful persons and abstain from major sins (kabair), give evidence as eye-witnesses of the act of penetration necessary to the offence; provided that, if the accused is a non-Muslim, the eye-witnesses may be non-Muslims.

603. In a case in which the offence of *Zina* is proved only by the confession of the convict, Hadd, or such part of it as is yet to be enforced, shall not be enforced if the convict retracts his confession before the Hadd or such part is enforced. In a case in which the offence of *Zina* is proved only by testimony, Hadd or such part of it as is yet to be enforced, shall not be enforced if any witness resiles from his testimony before Hadd or such part is enforced, so as to reduce the number of eyewitnesses to less than four.

604. The punishment of stoning to death awarded shall be executed by such of the witnesses who deposed against the convict as may be available shall start stoning him and, while stoning is being carried on, he may be shot dead, whereupon stoning and shooting shall be stopped.

Chapter 4. Filiation

§1. Children Born in Wedlock

605. The doctrine that 'the child of the bed' that is, the paternity of a child born in lawful wedlock in the husband or its mother, it recognized in the Muslim system and such child will necessarily follow the status of the father. A child born in wedlock is presumed to be legitimate by the English Law without any further limitation, but the Muslim Law insists that both birth and conception should take place after marriage. Therefore, a child born, but not begotten, in wedlock is illegitimate under the Muslim Law but legitimate under the English law. Under the Muslim system, a child begotten by *Zina* cannot be legitimate by the subsequent marriage of its parents before its birth and rule of legitimation per subsequent matrimonium is unknown to it. But at the same time, Muslim Law is not averse to raise a presumption in favour of legitimacy, where a child after birth is brought up by man, and he does not repudiate his legitimacy as his offspring, the ordinary rules are in favour of an ordinary presumption of legitimacy, which is not an ordinary presumption of evidence but a strong rule of Muslim Law.

§2. Legitimacy of Child

606. The paternity of child can only be established by marriage between its parents. The marriage may be value, or irregular, but it must not be void. When the paternity of a child is established, its legitimacy is also established.

607. Previous to Islam it seems probable that the customary rules relating to parentage, prevalent in Arabia, were as elastic, and as much a favour of the main in power, as those about marriage and divorce. It must have been source of strength, in those unsettled times, to have sons, real or an adopted, able to bear aromas, and there to seems to have been few, if any, counter balancing duties.

608. A child born after six months from the date of marriage is presumed to be legitimate, unless putative father disclaims the child by li'an. A child born after six months from the date of marriage, but within 280 days of the termination of the marriage is legitimate subject to li'an. A child born in wedlock cannot be bastardized except on clear proof of non-access.

609. Under the Mohamedan Law, where the paternity of a child, that is, his legitimate descent from his father cannot be proved by establishing a marriage between his parents at the time of his conception or birth, the marriage and legitimate descent can be established as a matter of substantive law for purpose of inheritance.

610. Under the Islamic Laws if a child is born six months after the marriage of its parents, or within two years of the dissolution of the marriage, by death or divorce, it is considered to be legitimate child of its father. LHC (2003 PLD 264) held that child who was born within six months of a valid wedlock was a legitimate child under Islamic Law. LHC (2000 YLR 703) held that Courts would be reluctant to stigmatize a child as illegitimate.

611. Court held that legitimate or illegitimate status of a person is established in view of the proof of birth but in a case where such proof is not coming forward then on the rule of acknowledgment by an acknowledger, in respect of status of a person, a conclusive presumption can be drawn that he/she is his/her legitimate child and once such status is confirmed, it cannot be destroyed by any subsequent act of the acknowledger or of anyone claiming through him. Document, produced in the present case, led to the conclusion that the acknowledger had accepted the lady to be one of her legal heirs in his legacy, benefit of which would be drawn by the ladies being his daughter, wife and his mother respectively after his death. Status of the lady as daughter of the acknowledger thus could not be denied in circumstances (SCP – 2005 SCMR 401).

§3. Ex-nupital Children

612. Under the Islamic Law any child born within less than six months after marriage or without marriage is illegitimate. Illegitimate children and foundlings – in a Muslim community – are a part of this community. They have the same rights and obligations as others. There is no discrimination on the basis of illegitimacy. They are not charged for the deeds of their parents. Allah Says (interpretation of meaning): { … No person earns any (sin) except against himself (only), and no bearer of burdens shall bear the burden of another … }. They are entitled to receive all the rights in a Muslim society as others do. The Muslim community and their government are responsible to spend on them, raise them and educate them.

613. The illegitimate child is, like other people, competent person obligated to observe religious duties (if he is sane and adult), and he will be held accountable for his own deeds. If he does righteous deeds, he will be rewarded; otherwise, he will deserve punishment. Allah The Almighty Says (what means): {And no bearer of burdens will bear the burden of another.}[Holy Quran 17:15].

614. However, Imaam Abu Haneefah Rehmatullah Alahe is of the view that if a man commits *Zina* with a woman, and she becomes pregnant from him, then he may marry her in order to conceal her sin and the child will be traced back to him. Also, the jurists differed in opinion about the ruling of marrying a fornicatress before making sure that she is not pregnant; some of them permitted it and some of them forbade it. If the marriage took place before making sure that she is not pregnant while fulfilling the conditions of a correct marriage contract, the most important of which are the consent and presence of the guardian and the presence of two witnesses, then the marriage is valid according to the view of those who consider it to be valid before making sure that she is not pregnant.

I. Name

615. According to the Muslim Scholars illegitimate child – either a boy or a girl – should be given a second name (a virtual father's name) which corresponds to his/her circumstance, like Abdullaah or Abdur-Rahman which means in Arabic the slave of Allah or the slave of the Most Merciful, etc. Such names are attributes (i.e., being a slave of Allah) that apply to all people and are not peculiar to any of them. That is because all people are actually slaves of Allah even if they are disbelievers. This child should not be traced back to a particular family or a given man suggesting that he is his father while in fact he is not.

616. A child born out of an illicit relationship (*Zina* [fornication/adultery]), so he is not traced back to father; he is traced back to his mother according to the preponderant opinion of the Scholars, and this is the view of the majority of the jurists.

II. Maintenance

617. According to Muslim Scholars, an illegitimate child is traced back to his mother, and she is responsible for his care, protection and expenditure. She is not allowed to throw him on the street. If she does so without any religiously accepted reason then she is sinful, whether she is a Muslim or non-Muslim. The sin does not differ whether the woman is a Muslim or non-Muslim. However, sometimes it differs based on other considerations. A Muslim woman might be more of a sinner because she knows the prohibition of throwing her child on the street unattended and endangered.

618. In case the mother of this child disappeared, then it is the Muslim community who should take care of him, and this is a great act of worship by which one gets closer to Allah. He should be raised on faith and good moral conduct. One should not be resentful to him and despise him because he was born as a result of an illegitimate relationship simply because he had nothing to do with the sin of *Zina*. During the caliphate of Umar, a person found a foundling (a small child who may be a son of *Zina*). Umar said: 'Take him with you, you have the right of his 'Wali' (guardianship) and we will spend on him. (In another narration) we will bear the expenses of his feeding'. In a word, the blood relatives from the mother's side, as we mentioned above, are Maharim for illegitimate children, and also all the relatives that become forbidden due to suckling. These children are eligible to have all rights and obligations as others.

III. Guardianship, Custody and Access

619. The mother of the child born out of *Zina* (fornication or adultery) is responsible for his guardianship, and if she is negligent without a valid reason, she is sinful in addition to the sin of *Zina*. There is no doubt that the child who results from adultery or fornication is innocent about what had taken place, and it is not permissible to blame him for this.

620. The child born from adultery or fornication should be traced back to his mother, as she is responsible for nurturing him and spending on him, as he is the outcome of her sin with the man who committed fornication with her. So the mother has to bear the consequence of her sin, but both the fornicators are sinful. However, some jurists are of the view that the child should be attributed to the male fornicator if he marries the woman he committed fornication with, but this is not the most preponderant opinion, because the family lineage is a blessing which the male fornicator does not deserve. It is for this reason that the Holy Prophet Muhammad (PBUH) said: 'The child is to be attributed to the mother [because she is not married] and the male fornicator gets frustration and despair.' [Al-Bukhaari and Muslim].

621. As for the Maharim of illegitimate children (unmarriageable relatives) they are their brothers, sisters, their children from mother side only, and maternal uncles, maternal aunts. Only the relatives of the mother are considered, not of the father because an illegitimate child does not trace back to his father. All the relatives who are forbidden from the mother's side include those forbidden through suckling. Allah Says (interpretation of meaning): { … , your foster mother who gave you suck, your foster milk suckling sisters, … } [4:23]. The Holy Prophet Muhammad (Sallallahu Alaihi wa Sallam) said: 'What is made Haram by reason of blood is made Haram by reason of the relations based on suckling'. [Reported by Imams al-Bukhari and Muslim].

622. Holy Prophet Muhammad (PBUH), said: 'A child is traced to the owner of the bed (i.e., the legitimate husband).' [Al-Bukhaari and Muslim] Since there is no marriage here, so the child is attributed to his mother, who must look after him and support him financially, and she inherits him and he inherits her.

IV. Nationality and Citizenship

623. Since the illegitimate child is traced back to his/her mother, therefore, nationality and citizenship of mother shall be considered the nationality of child even if the child is born in any other country.

V. Inheritance

624. According to the majority of Muslim Scholars, the child of *Zina* (who was born outside wedlock) is traced back to his mother's lineage and to her family. The rules of Mahram apply to him in relation to his relatives from the mother's side only. His/her legal Wali is from the mother's side, and he inherits from that side which is the only one that inherits from him and to which he is legally linked. So, all other rules concerning fatherhood stem directly from the mother's side. Therefore, the child born outside legal wedlock is not traced back to his father, nor does any of them inherit from the other. However, some scholars believe that child can be traced to his father if the latter accepts him as his son. This is the opinion of Is'haq Ibn Rahawahi, Urwa, Sulaiman Ibn Yasar and Abu Hanifa. Imam Abu Hanifa says: 'I do not find any harm that a man who makes *Zina* (adultery and fornication) with a woman and she gets pregnant as a result, that this man protects the honour of this woman by marrying her and the child is his'.

625. There is sound evidence backing the opinion of the majority of scholars which is the judgment reported from the Holy Prophet Muhammad (Sallallahu Alaihi wa Sallam) about the child of *Zina*:

> The Holy Prophet Muhammad (PBUH) decided regarding one who was treated as a member of a family after the death of his father, to whom he was attributed when the heirs said he was one of them, that if he was the child of a slave-woman whom the father owned when he had intercourse with her, he was included among those who sought his inclusion, but received none of the inheritance which was previously divided; he, however, received his portion of the inheritance which had not already been divided; but if the father to whom he was attributed had disowned him, he was not joined to the heirs. If he was a child of a slave-woman whom the father did not possess or of a free woman with whom he had illicit intercourse, he was not joined to the heirs and did not inherit even if the one to whom he was attributed is the one who claimed paternity, since he was a child of fornication whether his mother was free or a slave. [Reported by Imams Ahmad, Abu Dawood, Ibn Majah and al-Darimi].

Chapter 5. Adoption and Foster Care

§1. Adoption

626. According to the Mohamedan Law, there is no legal adoption. It is prohibited for a person to legally adopt a son or a daughter of whom he is not the biological father. If a person adopts a son or daughter, the Sharee'ah will not confer on the adopted person the status or rights of a biological son or daughter. According to the Holy Quran, one cannot become a person's real son merely by virtue of a declaration; Allah Says (what means):

And He [i.e., Allaah] has not made your claimed [i.e., adopted] sons your [true] sons. That is [merely] your saying by your mouths, but Allaah says the truth, and He guides to the [right] way. Call them [i.e., the adopted children] by [the names of] their fathers; it is more just in the sight of Allaah. But if you do not know their fathers, they are your brothers in religion … [Holy Quran 33: 4-5].

627. This shows that the declaration of adoption does not change realities, alter facts, or make a stranger a relative, or an adopted child a son or daughter. A mere verbal expression or figure of speech cannot make the blood of a man run through the veins of the adopted child, produce natural feelings of affection found in normal parent-child relationships, or transfer the genetic characteristics, or physical, mental, or psychological traits.

628. The child is an extension of his father and the bearer of his characteristics. He takes his name and increases his progeny. Likewise, the child in Islam also has the equally inalienable right to legitimacy. The principle of legitimacy holds that every child shall have a father and one father only. This is why Allah has ordained marriage and has forbidden adultery, so that paternity may be established without doubt or ambiguity and that the child may be referred to his father, and the father to his sons and daughters. Hence, adoption cannot be used in Islam to hide the illegitimacy or the paternity of the child.

629. Taking a stranger into the family as one of its members and allowing him to be in privacy with women who are non-mahram (i.e., non marriageable relatives) to him is a deception, for the adopter's wife is not the adopted son's real mother, nor is his daughter the boy's sister, nor is his sister the boy's aunt, since all of them are non-mahram to him and vice-versa for an adopted daughter. The Holy Quran has, thus, declared that only the wives of one's real sons, and not the wives of any sons under one's care, are permanently forbidden in marriage. This is according to the verse (which means): … ' The wives of your sons who are from your [own] loins … ' [Holy Quran 4:23]. Accordingly, it is permissible for a man to marry the divorced wife of any son under his care, since, in actuality; she has been the wife of a 'stranger' who was not related by blood. Also, when the adopted child's lineal identity or paternity is changed, it is quite possible that the adopted child may, unknowingly, enter into incestuous relationships by marrying close relatives of his natural parents; also, his marital chances may, in general, become subject to confusion.

630. Court held that adoption neither defined nor recognized under the Succession Act, 1925. Adoption neither under 'Islamic Law' nor 'Christian Law' creates any kindred relationship between adopted child and adoptive parent. No legal rights or obligations flow from either side, thus, none could be claimed or enforced. Succession to estate of intestate Pakistani is regulated by section 5 of the Succession Act, 1925 (SHC – 2003 PLD 270).

631. LHC held that right of *Hizant* (right of child's custody) of foster mother in respect of an adopted minor. Parties being husband and wife had willingly adopted infant child jointly when they were in marriage. After dissolution of marriage ex-wife in exercise of right of *Hizant* of mother in Islam claimed custody of infant child on the ground that after dissolution of marriage between the parties the man being not real father of the child would have no special or preferential right over female to retain custody of minor child. Validity: Female partner in adoption had accepted duty and responsibility of bringing up the child with motherly love and affection which responsibility could not be discharged by the male. Female being the most essential partner of adoption in light of concept of right of custody of such child in Islam would exclusively be entitled to custody of the female child. Welfare of the child would also demand that minor girl should remain in custody of female partner of adoption. Female partner having enjoyed status of mother of the minor would be entitled to retain her custody in exercise of right of *Hizant* and would not be deprived of such right. High Court directed that custody of minor with female partner was not to be disturbed except in accordance with law (2002 PLD 283).

632. SCP held that adoption does not confer any legal right on adoptee under Muslim Law of any provision of settlement law (1978 SCMR 214). LHC held (2000 YLR 2317) that there is no concept of adoption in Islam.

§2. Adoptees

633. However, adoption of Orphans is allowed in Islam. A man brings home an orphan and wants to raise, educate, and treat him as his own child. In this case, he protects, feeds, clothes, teaches, and loves the child as his own without attributing the child to himself, nor does he give him/her the rights which the Sharee'ah (Islamic Law) reserves for his natural children. This is a meritorious and noteworthy act in Islam, and the man who does it will be rewarded by being admitted to Paradise. Holy Prophet Muhammad (PBUH) once said: 'I and the one who raises an orphan, will be like these two in Paradise (and he pointed his middle and index fingers)'. There are also numerous Quranic verses that support the act of taking care of orphans and enough cannot be said about how pleased Allah is with this noble and charitable act, see: [Holy Quran: 2:220; 4:2; 4:6; 4:10; 4:127; 17:34].

634. A foundling or abandoned child is also regarded as an orphan, and one may apply the term 'wayfarer' to him as well. In this case too, as in that of orphans, the child's lineal identity must be unchanged and parenthood to the natural parents should not be denied. When the parents of such children are unknown, the children must be made brethren in faith; See [Holy Quran: 33:4-5].

635. By adopting someone's child as one's own, the rightful and deserving heirs to the property of a man are deprived of their shares. Hence, Islam has made it Haraam (forbidden) for a father to deprive his natural children of inheritance. Allah has established the distribution of inheritance in order to give each eligible person his/her share. In matters of inheritance, the Holy Quran does not recognize any claim except those based on relationship through blood and marriage. The Holy Quran stipulates (what means): 'And those who believed after [the initial emigration] and emigrated and fought with you – they are of you. But those of [blood] relationship are more entitled [to inheritance] in the decree of Allah. Indeed, Allah is knowing of all things.' [Holy Quran 8:75]. However, if a man is childless and wishes to benefit such a child (orphan or foundling) from his wealth, he may give him whatever he wants during his lifetime.

§3. Foreign Adoption

636. Any foreigner can adopt a baby from Pakistan subject to fulfilment of requisite procedure and Court permission. Some reputable organization like Edhi arrange baby for adoption by the foreigners. However, the foreigners are required to fulfil the requirement of their home country as well. A legal custody of child can be obtained by applying for guardianship of the child in a civil Family Court in Pakistan. Legal custody means the assumption of responsibility for a minor by an adult under the laws of the state and under the order or approval of a court of law or other appropriate government entity. The court also needs to give its permission for the child to be taken abroad, out of its jurisdiction.

637. After obtaining a guardianship decree from the court, Form 'B' (Child Registration Certificate) is obtained from the offices of NADRA and gets a national ID card number issued for the baby on which basis National Identity Card is issued after child attains the age of 18 years. After obtaining B-Form, Pakistan Passport for the child is obtained. Parents who reside overseas can apply for a NICOP (National Identity Card for Overseas Pakistanis) for their child. Without Pakistani Passport, normally Embassies do not issue immigration visa to the child.

Chapter 6. Guardianship and Custody

§1. Introduction

638. Under the Guardian and Wards Act, 1890 'Guardian' means a person having the care of the person of a minor or his property, or of both his person and property; and 'Ward' means a minor for whose person or property, or both, there is a guardian. Whereas 'minor' means a person who, under the provisions of the Majority Act, 1875, is to be deemed not to have attained his Majority.

639. A guardian can only be appointed on receipt of an application from (a) the person desirous of being, or claiming to be, the guardian of the minor; or (b) any relative or friend of the minor; or (c) the Collector of the District or other local area within which the minor ordinarily resides or in which he has property; or (d) the Collector having authority with respect to the class to which the minor belongs.

640. The application for guardianship is made under the provisions of the Guardian and Wards Act 1890) (No. VIII) to the Court having jurisdiction in the place where the minor ordinarily resides. If the application is with respect to the guardianship of the property of the minor, then it may be made either to the Court having jurisdiction in the place where the minor ordinarily resides, or to a court having jurisdiction in a place where the minor has property.

641. A guardian can be a de facto or a de jure one. Legal guardians and those appointed by the court are de jure guardians. A father is the natural guardian of a child under the age of 18 years under the Guardian and Wards Act.

642. As opposed to a de jure guardian, a person, like the mother, brother, uncle, other relations except father and father's father, or an institution like an orphanage, may voluntarily place himself/herself in charge of the person or property of the minor; a mother, however, is the next possible guardian after a father, unless the latter, by his will, has appointed another person as the guardian of the child. She under certain circumstances can appoint a guardian by will. She can do so during the lifetime of her husband if he is incapable of acting, or after his death. A de facto guardian, as opposed to a de jure guardian, is merely a custodian of the person and property of the minor. While appointing a guardian, the character, the capacity and the fitness of the individual is taken into consideration.

643. A charitable society is not a person within the meaning of section 4(2) of the Guardian and Wards Act, 1890 and thus cannot be appointed as the guardian of the person, or property, of the minor. It is due to the fact that anyone having an interest adverse to that of a minor cannot be appointed as a guardian. However, it has been held by courts that a manager of a registered society can be appointed as the guardian of a child. In the latter context, it has also been stated that the meaning of person in the context of being appointed a guardian should not be confined to an individual, despite section 3(39) of the General Clauses Act as would then conflict with Guardian and Wards Act sections 43(4) and 45.

644. Under the Majority Act 1875 (No. IX), minority ceases upon the completion of 18 years, unless a guardian of the person, or property, or both, of the minor has been, or shall be appointed before the minor has attained the age of 18 years, or the property of the minor is under the superintendence of a court of wards, in which case the age of minority is prolonged, until the minor has completed the age of 21 years. Accordingly, notwithstanding Shariah, minority of a child continues until the completion of 18 years. Until then, the court has the power to appoint a guardian for the child and her/his property or both under the provisions of the Guardian and Wards Act. The relevant provision in this respect is section 3 of the Majority Act 1875, which reads as follows:

> Subject as aforesaid, every minor, of whose person or property or both a guardian, other than for a suit within the meaning of Order XXXII of the First Schedule to the Code of Civil Procedure 1908 (No V), has been or shall be appointed or declared by any Court of Justice before the minor has attained the age of 18 years, and every minor of whose property the superintendence has been or shall be assumed by any Court of Wards before the minor has attained that age shall, notwithstanding anything contained in the Succession Act 1925 (No XXXIX) or in any other enactment, be deemed to have attained his majority when he shall have completed his age of 21 years and not before.
>
> Subject as aforesaid, every other person domiciled in Pakistan shall be deemed to have attained his majority when he shall complete his age of 18 years and not before.

645. A court may not be authorized to appoint a guardian if the minor is a married female and whose husband, in the court's opinion, is not unfit to be her guardian; or if the minor's father is living and in the court's opinion, is not unfit to be the minor's guardian; or the minor's property is under the superintendence of a court of wards. A minor is also incompetent to act as a guardian of any other minor, except his own wife or child.

646. Any person, including a relative or friend, interested in becoming a guardian must apply to the court under the provisions of the Guardian and Wards Act for being appointed as a guardian; he is not bound to wait until his legal title or fitness to act as guardian is disputed by another person. The procedure for such an application is stated in section 10 of the Guardian and Wards Act, and no order should be made unless notice of the application is given to persons interested in the minor.

647. During the court proceedings, the court exercises parental jurisdiction over the child. The court is also empowered to give temporary custody and order protection of the person and property of the minor during the maintenance of the case.

648. While appointing a guardian, the court must have regard to the welfare of the minor which covers factors such as the age, sex, and the child's religion, the character and capacity of the proposed guardian and his nearness to the child; the wishes, if any, of the deceased parents, and any existing or previous relations of the proposed guardian with the minor or his/her property; and if the child is old enough to form an intelligent preference, then such preference should also be considered.

649. A guardian is responsible to ensure that the minor is supported, fed, housed, clothed, and educated in a manner suitable to his/her position in life, and to the fortune which he/she is likely to enjoy upon attaining the age of majority. The guardian appointed by the court is entitled to such allowance as the court thinks fit for the minor's care and the effort that he/she goes through while undertaking the duties. The allowance could be paid out of the property of the ward.

§2. Custody of Children

650. The issue of custody is dealt with by the Guardians and Wards Act of 1890, under which it is a well-established principle that the welfare of the child is paramount – that is, the most important thing considered by the Guardian Court when deciding custody.

§3. Adopted Children

651. There is no concept of child adoption in Islam or in Pakistani laws. However, a guardian can be appointed under the Guardian and Wards Act, 1890 to look after the child and property.

652. SHC held that adoption neither defined nor recognized under the Succession Act, 1925. Adoption neither under 'Islamic Law' nor 'Christian Law' creates any kindred relationship between adopted child and adoptive parent. No legal rights or obligations flow from either side, thus, none could be claimed or enforced (2003 PLD 270).

653. Parties being husband and wife had willingly adopted infant child jointly when they were in marriage. After dissolution of marriage ex-wife in exercise of right of *Hizant* of mother in Islam claimed custody of infant child on the ground that after dissolution of marriage between the parties the man being not real father of the child would have no special or preferential right over female to retain custody of minor child. Validity: Female partner in adoption had accepted duty and responsibility of bringing up the child with motherly love and affection which responsibility could not be discharged by the male. Female being the most essential partner of adoption in light of concept of right of custody of such child in Islam would exclusively be entitled to custody of the female child. Welfare of the child would also demand that minor girl should remain in custody of female partner of adoption. Female partner having enjoyed status of mother of the minor would be entitled to retain her custody in exercise of right of *Hizant* and would not be deprived of such right. High Court directed that custody of- minor with female partner was not to be disturbed except in accordance with law (LHC – 2002 PLD 283).

§4. Interim Orders

654. Under the Guardians and Wards Act, 1890 section-12 the Court can direct that the person, if any, having the custody of the minor shall produce him or cause him to be produced at such place and time and before such person as it appoints, and may make such order for the temporary custody and protection of the person or property of the minor as it thinks proper. If the minor is a female who ought not to be compelled to appear in public, the direction for her production shall require her to be produced in accordance with the customs and manners of the country. However, Court is not authorized under this section to place a female minor in the temporary custody of a person claiming to be her guardian on the ground of his being her husband, unless she is already in his custody with the consent of her parents, if any; or any person to whom the temporary custody and protection of the property of a minor is entrusted to dispossess otherwise than by due course of law any person in possession of any of the property.

655. Mother of minor died at the time of her (minor's) birth. Grandmother of the minor girl obtained her custody from her father through habeas petition. During proceedings before Guardian Judge, matter was compromised and as per term of settlement, custody of minor had to be handed over to father on her attaining age of seven years. Father later on contracted second marriage and had an issue from second wife. Deceased mother of minor was a serving lady. Share of minor in the amount left by her mother was deposited by father in his own account, which amount was recovered from him through decree of Court after issuing his warrant of arrest. During pendency of another suit for his appointment as guardian of person and property of minor, father made application for implementation of such compromise seeking custody of minor. Guardian Judge allowed such application and directed grandmother to handover custody of minor to her father. Grandmother remained unsuccessful before Appellate Court and High Court. It was held that paramount consideration in such like cases was welfare of minor. Initially parties had settled the dispute through compromise, but later on due to material change in circumstances, question of welfare of minor had again cropped up in a more serious manner than before. Since birth minor had remained with maternal grandmother and suddenly to ask her to live in different atmosphere would be, if not impossible, at least very difficult for her. Supreme Court allowed the appeal, set side impugned order and permitted the minor to remain with grandmother till petition pending before Guardian Judge was finally decided on merits after recording evidence of the parties.

656. Under section-14 of the Guardian and Wards Act, 1890 if proceedings for the appointment or declaration of a guardian of a minor are taken in more Courts than one, each of those Courts shall, on being apprised of the proceedings in the other Courts, stay the proceedings before itself. If the Courts are both or all subordinate to the same High Court, they shall report the case to the High Court, and the High Court shall determine in which of the Courts the proceedings with respect to the appointment or declaration of a guardian of the minor shall be had. In any other case in which proceedings are stayed under this section, the Courts shall report the case to, and be guided by such orders as they may receive from their respective Provincial Governments.

657. Interim custody granted by Guardian Judge was maintained by Lower Appellate Court. Validity: Normally High Court did not entertain Constitutional petition against interlocutory order. As through order transfer of custody, though interim was likely to take place which was in relation to protection of the person during such intervening period. Making a child a rolling stone by various interim orders was also not appropriate for his personality and well being. Petition was maintainable in circumstances (LHC 2009 CLC 717).

658. Guardian Judge allowed custody of minors to plaintiff in ex parte proceedings. Defendant took away minor children forcibly from the custody of plaintiff who filed an application for restoration of custody of minors and initiation of contempt proceedings. Trial Court ordered restoration of custody of minors to petitioner. Defendant preferred appeal which was allowed and case was remanded. Validity: Constitutional petition having been filed against an interim order which stood merged in the final order passed by a competent court; Constitutional petition had become infructuous and was dismissed (LHC 2010 MLD 790).

659. Respondent/mother filed a guardianship application under sections 7 & 25 of Guardians and Wards Act, 1890, along with application under section 12 of the Act, seeking temporary custody of her minor daughter of tender age. Said application had been accepted directing handing over the custody of minor to the mother. Validity: Minor who was of tender age of 2 years, would definitely need constant care of mother, and there could not be any substitute for a mother as the lap of mother was God's own cradle for a child. Till the matter regarding custody of the minor was decided, the minor was to be given in proper custody keeping in view of her tender age. No infirmity or illegality was found in the impugned orders passed by the courts below, which were founded on the appreciation of material on record. Appellate Court in view of the father's contumacious conduct was perfectly justified in raising adverse inference against him (SHC 2010 MLD 943).

660. Marriage between the petitioner wife and respondent husband still subsisted though the petitioner had been expelled from the house of her husband/ respondent. Minors, who were of tender age, were residing with their father/ respondent. Validity: Mother was a symbol of sacrifice for her children, and there was no substitute for love and affection of the mother. Lap of the mother was a heavenly place, and she had inherent right to keep her children close to her bosom and rear them up under her umbrella. Keeping in view the age of minors which was (5 years male and 2-1/2 years female), their interim custody was directed to be handed over to the petitioner/mother as she could not be deprived of their custody, until and unless decided otherwise by the Guardian Judge concerned on proper showing as to the welfare of the minors (LHC – 2009 YLR 1678).

661. Relationship of wife and husband existed between the parties. Son of the petitioner was 2 years old. Mother was entitled to the custody (*Hizant*) of her male child until he had completed the age of 7 years. Petitioner mother could look after the child in a better way than his father or other relations. Minor was given in the interim custody of the petitioner in circumstances till the final adjudication by the Guardian Judge, if any party approached that forum. Petition was accepted accordingly (LHC – 2006 YLR 2946).

662. Custody of abandoned child: Unclaimed child found within vicinity of a shrine. District Coordination Officer (DCO) handed over custody of child to respondent. Validity: Custody of a destitute and neglected child under provisions of Punjab Destitute and Neglected Children Act, 2004 would be entrusted to a suitable person or he would be admitted to a Child Protection Institution. Such Institution having not been constituted, custody of child would be entrusted to a suitable person under section 28 of Punjab Destitute and a Neglected Children Act, 2004. Respondent's application was prior in time, and there was no other claimant before DCO while handing over to respondent custody of child. Child until his entrustment to respondent had remained in custody of an employee of the shrine. Respondent had developed emotional attachment with child for looking after him for last ten months. Respondent could keep custody of child subject to furnishing bond to the effect that child would be brought up properly, admitted in a school and would not be forced to do any job/work for respondent till attaining age of majority. Respondent as per his undertaking would deposit a sum of PKR 500,000 in the name of child which amount would be incurred on his education. Respondent would submit periodical reports as to welfare of child under section 28(3) of the Act to District/Sessions Judge. High Court disposed of the Constitutional petition in above terms (LHC – 2006 PLD 219).

663. Custody of minor daughter: Contest between father and mother. Entitlement to custody. Second marriage by both father and mother of minor. Father in service of Army as soldier performing full time duty and not permanently stationed at one place but constantly remaining under transfer from one place to another. Paternal grandmother looking after affairs of minor was elderly age and not keeping good health. Mother's second husband was real brother of her stepmother thus was closely related to minor besides being from same brotherhood. Lap of real mother was the best school for a growing child, and no one could look after welfare of minor as compared to woman, who had given birth to child. Minor being of 4 years was living since birth with mother, thus, must have developed deep association/attachment with her. Snatching custody of minor from mother in such a tender age and entrusting to a stepmother though in supervision of paternal grandmother, could not be justified on touchstone of any administration of justice. Mother on account of second marriage might have lost right of *Hizant*, but before to depriving her from supervision of her own blood, welfare of minor would be looked into, which certainly would lie in keeping minor in custody of mother. Welfare of minor would be best served if she lived with mother as compared to father custody of minor was handed over to mother in these circumstances (LHC – 2006 MLD 493).

664. LHC held that High Court had jurisdiction in appropriate cases to issue direction in the nature of habeas corpus under section 491, Criminal Procedure Code and restore custody to the person, from whom the child was forcibly snatched. Petitioner in the present case was not claiming the custody of minor on the basis of her preferential right or on the ground relating to the welfare of minor, but on the score that minor was forcibly snatched and was being kept by respondent illegally. Minor was permanently settled in United Kingdom where he was living with his mother and due to his forcible snatching by respondent, minor was being deprived of proper education and better schooling. People aspire to get their children admitted in institutions in the countries like United Kingdom but in the present case, minor was being kept away from that facility. Minor was epileptic needed constant care and proper treatment which, in present circumstances, was available to minor only in the custody of his mother. Respondent had not so far instituted proceedings under Guardians and Wards Act, 1890. Question of custody of minor, keeping in view welfare of minor could be determined by Guardian Judge. Petition for habeas corpus had been filed on the ground that minor had been snatched forcibly and same was decided on that ground alone. Respondent could claim the custody of minor and Guardian Judge, if approached, could determine the question of custody of minor keeping in view Principles of Islamic Law and welfare of the minor. High Court allowing habeas corpus petition directed that custody of minor be restored to his mother. Reference section 491, Guardians and Wards Act (VIII of 1890), section-7. (LHC – 2006 MLD 136).

§5. Guardians Court

665. Any parent who wants custody and does not presently have custody has to seek custody from the Guardian Court. Under section-25 of the West Pakistan Family Courts Act, 1964 a Family Court is deemed to be a District Court for the purposes of the Guardians and Wards Act, 1890.

666. Court held that Criminal Court or police station are not the competent and proper forums for resolution of any dispute between parents of minor arising out of matrimonial life particularly touching Hizant and custody of minors. No offence whatever including that of kidnapping was made out. Local police unauthorizedly and without any legal or factual justification interfered into a pure family dispute touching custody of minors between their parents. Police official, to whom complainant approached for registration of a case against mother of minors on the charge of kidnapping, was under legal obligation to refer him to Guardian Court for determination of dispute of custody. Local police encroached upon the functions and powers of Guardian Court and such was misconduct which must be deprecated (LHC – 2008 PLD 533).

§6. Restriction on removal of children from Pakistan

667. A guardian appointed by the court with the court's permission, cannot remove the ward from the limits of the court's jurisdiction. The permission could be special or general and could be specified in the court order. Illegal removal of a ward from the court's jurisdiction is punishable with a fine not exceeding PKR 1,000 or a jail term extending to six months.

668. Despite restraining order passed by Court of foreign jurisdiction, father removed the minor to Pakistan. Plea raised by mother was that such custody of minor with father was illegal. Validity: If much sanctity was attached to order passed by Court in Pakistan, then same legal status and sanctity should be conferred and given to orders passed by Court of foreign jurisdiction, when such orders were passed in proper exercise of jurisdiction and especially in the circumstances when delinquent party had surrendered to the jurisdiction of that Court. There were interdictory and residence orders passed by Court of foreign jurisdiction and also an undertaking had been given by father, not to remove the minor from care and control of mother and also jurisdiction of that foreign Court. Bringing the child over to Pakistan and retaining its custody was 'without lawful authority', 'illegal' and 'improper' in circumstances (LHC 2007 PLD 300).

669. Removing custody of minor. Despite restraining order passed by a Court of foreign jurisdiction, father removed the minor to Pakistan. Mother of minor had sought custody of the minor by invoking habeas corpus petition. Plea raised by father was that he being legal and natural guardian of the minor, his custody was not illegal. Validity: Father having himself admitted the jurisdiction of foreign Court and submitted and surrendered thereto and having promised not to remove the child from care and control of mother and Court, was debarred to bring the child to Pakistan. Such was flagrantly illegal, deceitful and dishonest act on the part of father. If a Pakistani Court had passed an order directing not to remove child from custody of a parent by the other and order was violated, such act would fall within the ambit and scope of Article 199 of the Constitution and section 491, Criminal Procedure Code; as such rule was applicable regarding the orders passed by Courts of Pakistan, same rule could be extended to the valid orders of foreign jurisdiction, especially to which jurisdiction the defaulting party (father) had surrendered. High Court in exercise of jurisdiction, under Article 199 of the Constitution and section 491, Criminal Procedure Code, declared that the petition was maintainable in circumstances (LHC 2007 PLD 293).

670. Habeas corpus. Recovery of minor detenue. Due to alleged cruel attitude of respondent, the spouse could not keep their matrimonial fold intact and difference arose between the parties, which constrained the petitioner to settle abroad with her 2 months' son. Parties filed respective suits for custody of minor in the superior Courts abroad. Both suits were decided in favour of the petitioner, and a meeting schedule was prepared according to which, respondent/father had to meet his son for twenty four hours. On third meeting father kidnapped the child and removed him to Pakistan. *Effect:* Respondent/father in violation of order passed by foreign Courts took away the minor to Pakistan without seeking permission from the said Courts. Counsel for respondent contended that judgment passed by foreign courts had no binding force in Pakistan, was repelled, because both the parties had contested that issue before foreign courts and after fulfilling all the legal formalities the foreign courts had handed over the custody of the minor to the petitioner; and respondent having not challenged that order any further, same had attained finality. Removal of the minor in violation of orders passed by the foreign courts, was not only mala fide on the part of respondent, but was also a criminal act for which he was being proceeded there. Even otherwise keeping in view the age of minor, he could be looked after properly by his mother and not the father. Custody of the minor could not be given to father because it would amount to deprive the minor/ detenue from the Nationality of two countries. Previous conduct of respondent/ father had also shown that he could take the child anywhere to escape himself from the courts of law. Proceedings under section 25 of the Guardians and Wards Act, initiated by respondent were based on mala fide. Custody of minor was handed over to the petitioner/mother (LHC – 2008 YLR 2647).

§7. Principles on Guardianship Custody and access awards

671. No matter what customs or personal law rules the parents' community or sect follows regarding custody, any parent who wants custody and does not presently have custody has to seek custody from the Guardian Court. In other words, there is never any automatic transfer of a child's custody to a particular parent. Normally following factors are considered by the Courts when granting custody of children:

- the welfare of the minor is very broadly defined and includes many diverse factors, notably;
- the age, sex and religion of the minor: Courts take into account the personal law of the father. The welfare of younger children is generally regarded as being in the mother's custody;
- the character and capacity of the proposed guardian: Courts usually reject baseless allegations against mothers;
- the wishes, if any, of a deceased parent, for example specified in a will;
- any existing or previous relations of the proposed guardian with the minor's;
- property: Courts do not look on guardians seeking custody just in order to have control over the minor's property. But if, for example, the minor's property is shared with the mother and she is otherwise a suitable guardian, the court will regard the property relationship as an additional factor in the mother's favour;
- the minor's preference if she/he is old enough to form an intelligent preference, usually accepted as about 9 years old;
- whether siblings would be divided: courts prefer to keep children united and award custody of both to either the mother or the father;
- whether either/both parents have remarried and there are step-children: Although the mother's remarriage to someone who is not the children's close blood-relative often means the court will not grant her custody, this rule is not strictly followed. Although the father's remarriage usually denies him custody, sometimes the courts agree to grant him custody especially when the children's step-mother cannot or will not have her own children;

- whether the parents live far apart: Courts sometimes do not give the mother custody because she lives very far away from the father who is the 'natural' guardian. But in 1994, an Uzbek woman living in Uzbekistan was given custody; the judge said modern transport had shortened distances and meant that the father could depart from his home in the morning and return by evening;
- the child's comfort, health, material, intellectual, moral and spiritual welfare: This very broad category includes the adequate and undisturbed education of the child. However, the mere fact that the mother is economically less secure than the father, or that she suffers from ill-health or a disability is not usually reason enough to deny her custody because maintenance is the father's responsibility irrespective of who holds custody; and
- the mental and psychological development of the minor should not be upset by a reversal of the existing status quo: Courts will take into account the likely impact of a change in guardians and the child's reaction to this change.

672. In a decision passed by Guardian Court in respect of custody of minor (consent order or otherwise) may be an order in the best interest and welfare of the minor at that point of time but due to certain future eventuality and subsequent developments the same, may not serve as such. It is for this reason that the Guardian Court has been empowered to modify, set aside or alter an earlier order, and pass an appropriate order at any subsequent stage to safeguard the interest and welfare of the minor. Order passed earlier by Guardian Court with regard to custody of minor cannot operate as a bar of jurisdiction for Guardian Court for all time to come (SHC – 2001 PLD 371).

673. Plaintiff (father) married thrice. Mother an educated lady. *Effect:* Plaintiff (father) had remarried and was living with his third wife. Plaintiff was engaged in the business of poultry, which kept him out of house during most part of the day which would require the children to spend a lot of time with their stepmother. Real mother was an educated lady, had not remarried and could devote her full time and attention towards the children. Welfare of the minors lay if their custody was allowed to remain with their real mother. Displacement of minors from the environment where they were happy, settled and well adjusted might cause physical, and psychological problems, leaving lifelong scars on their personalities. High Court declined interference under Constitutional jurisdiction (LHC – 2010 MLD 1313).

674. Minor son of 8 years age, custody. Contest between mother and father of minor both having remarried. Father of minor employed as school teacher and owning agricultural land. Mother and step father of minor being illiterate and having no permanent source of income as step father was a labourer. Order of Guardian Judge handing over custody of minor to his mother set aside by Appellate Court. Validity: While determining question of custody of a minor, prime consideration would be his welfare. Record showed that father was financially stable, thus, he was in a better position to meet material needs of minor. Father having no child from second wife could keep minor with him in school, supervise his activities and directly take care of his educational, financial, psychological and emotional needs. Present environment at which minor was living and role models which he had were of paramount importance, and this was a stage for laying foundation of his career. Keeping minor in environment of uncertainty and having flaws in his educational foundation and upbringing would affect entire structure of his responsibility and future career. Obligation of father was to provide adequate funds to mother to meet needs of minor, which was likely to be misapplied by her for not having source of income. Depriving minor of opportunity of growing up with support, in company and under direct supervision of his real father would not be in his welfare. All stepmothers were not Cinderella's stepmothers. Possibility of ill-treatment by stepmother in present case was quite remote as minor would spend most part of day and week in school in academic environment under supervision of his father. Record showed that mother could not cater educational needs of minor, who being about 8 years old was still in Class-1. Need of minor for maternal love and affection could be met by providing adequate visitation time to mother. Mother was allowed to meet minor on first Sunday of every month from 11 am to 2 pm, the one week during winter vacations and two weeks during summer vacations. High Court partly accepted Constitutional petition in circumstances (LHC – 2010 MLD 340).

675. Respondent/mother of the minor after the death of her husband continued residing with her in-laws along with minor, but later on she was expelled by the grandmother of the minor retaining the custody of minor. After being turned out of her home, she being mother of the minor filed petition under section 491, Criminal Procedure Code for recovery of the minor, which on the statement of minor that he would prefer living with his paternal grandmother/the petitioner, petition was dismissed. Mother of the minor later on filed petition under section 7 of Guardians and Wards Act, 1890 to appoint her as guardian of person and property of the minor, which again was dismissed on the statement of minor in favour of his paternal grandmother. Appeal filed by the mother of the minor against judgment and decree, however having been accepted, judgment and decree of the Guardian Judge, was set aside with direction to the Guardian Judge, to hand over custody of minor to the mother. Grandmother had impugned said order in Constitutional petition. Minor was brainwashed to the extent that he abhorred his real mother and was making up stories of her having inflicted physical violence on him even in the court, which was abnormal. Petitioner/grandmother of the minor had not adhered to the visitation schedule as determined by the Guardian Court and was teaching the child how to lie and hate. Danger to a child's life was not only physical, but it was also mental. Extent of the mother's sacrifice for her minor son was that despite being a young woman she had not remarried after the death of minor's father; she was educated, holding a job and seemed to be intelligent woman. Initially the minor may not be happy in his mother's custody, but the tie of the umbilical cord was too strong to be severed. Lady was mother of minor and knew the best of her child. No one can take place of real mother. Moreover under Islamic Law, the custody of paternal grandmother was subservient to the custody of the mother. What had to be taken into consideration at each and every stage of litigation involving minors and their custody was the welfare of the minor. Welfare of the minor in the case lay with his real mother. Constitutional petition dismissed (LHC – 2010 MLD 42).

676. Petition for custody of minor son and daughter by mother. Contest between parents of minors, both being Doctors by profession. Private compromise between parties giving custody of minors to father while divorcing their mother. Validity: Court before passing any order would prefer the welfare of minors. Father had not alleged that mother had either remarried or was leading an immoral life or had neglected to take proper care of minors. Father was serving professional doctor and had no female in his house to look after children. Minor so was being looked after by father through a male servant of 14/15 years, while minor daughter was being brought up by his sister residing at another place. Both minors for being of tender age required affection. Mother was a doctor and having sufficient sources. Welfare of minors in circumstances would be in handing over their custody to mother having preferential right of *Hizant*. Private agreement between the parties was neither valid in law nor even enforceable. Application of mother was accepted in circumstances (LHC – 2010 PLD 206).

677. Marriage between the parties was dissolved by way of divorce through written deed. Dissolution of marriage was with mutual consent. Compromise was entered into between the parties with regard to custody of minor on application filed by the petitioner under section 491, Criminal Procedure Code custody of minor was with maternal grandfather of the minor by compromise as well as under the orders of two courts below. Family Court would exercise parental jurisdiction and must consider all aspects relevant to custody of minor; and decide as to what would be in the best interest of the minor. Any previous compromise or any previous order of the court, could not bind hands of the Family Court. Court could recall its previous order, provided sufficient grounds were made that after previous order, what were new and evolving circumstances keeping in view interest of minor. Compromise between the parties, must be looked at by the Family Court, but was not conclusive and binding, as far as Family Court was concerned. Court in appropriate circumstances could pass an order, even setting at nought the compromise. Prime responsibility and obligation of Family Court was welfare of the minor, which was supreme and should not, in any circumstances be lost sight of. In the present case, there were factors which had been considered by the courts below which clearly emerged; first, petitioner mother of minor had no source of income; second, she had remarried and had been blessed with three children after her remarriage; third, her second husband was a stranger as far as minor was concerned; fourth, her second husband had not come in witness box to depose about his income and whether he was willing to shoulder responsibilities of minor; fifth. maternal grandfather was a retired servant and received pension; sixth, the maternal grandfather had his own house, whereas mother and stepfather of minor lived in a rented house; seventh, real father of minor had no objection if child would remain with his maternal grandfather; and eighth, child had been receiving education while living with maternal grandfather. Two courts below, in circumstances, had rightly observed that for welfare of child, he should be under custody of his maternal grandfather with consent of father of the child (SHC – 2010 YLR 513).

678. Application for custody of two minor daughters and one son. Contest between mother and father of minors. Father (a Pakistani born citizen of France) alleged to be in receipt of handicap allowance from French Government. Father's plea was that if children were sent with him, they would get allowance and free education from French Government, but would not get such benefit in Pakistan. Order of Guardian Judge accepting such application of father was set aside by Appellate Court. Validity: Sending children with father to France would deprive mother of meeting her own flesh and blood. Courts, in Pakistan would not be able to enforce an undertaking of father to send children to Pakistan every year to see mother. Father could not be expected to honour such undertaking as he had not respected and complied with court's order for payment of maintenance to children every month. Father in cross-examination had refused to pay maintenance to children in Pakistan. French schools might be better schools, but in Islamic Society of Pakistan, they would have better upbringing as Muslims. Father had neglected children for last three years. Children were being well looked after by mother and were receiving good education. All three children having happy smiling faces had answered court's questions with confidence. Mother was living in a separate portion of her sister's house, where her brother was regularly paying visits and providing necessary protection. Welfare of children would lie in their living with mother in Pakistan. Father would have right to meet children in Pakistan subject to his paying maintenance to them as ordered by Family Court. If children on attaining age of 16 years wanted to visit father in France, then father could take them to France for one month during summer vacations. High Court disposed of Constitutional petition in above terms (SHC – 2010 MLD 544).

679. Custody of minor: Right to life not only included one's own life, but also life, liberty and happiness of one's children. Denying a person right of company of his children was as severe a penalty and curse on him than denying him life altogether. Strongest bond that nature had created was bond between the mother and the child, and it was not restricted only for the period when the child was within the body of the mother, but would continue thereafter. First food of the child, after all, would come from the body of the mother itself, therefore, if a mother was denied her right of company of her child, it would amount to violation of her fundamental right to life. Petition thus, was maintainable both under section 491, Criminal Procedure Code as well as under Article 199(1)(c) of the Constitution. Elder child was already with the mother, for the custody of which application had been filed by his father under the Guardians and Wards Act, 1890. Mother petitioner had right of *Hizant* of her younger child which was only 3 years old. Bringing up of the two children together would be more appropriate. Custody of the minor was, consequently given to the mother. Family Court, however, would finally determine the custody of minors after a proper trial. Constitutional petition was allowed accordingly (SHC – 2010 PLD 119).

680. The Islamabad High Court, Islamabad (2010 YLR 1468) held that no one could take care of minors more than their real mother for being their first institution. Depriving minors of company of their real mother would create deprivation in their lives, which could not be restored back.

681. Application filed by the father of minor for custody of minor having been allowed by the Family Court, mother of minor challenged same in appeal. Validity: Mother was entitled to retain the custody of her minor male child till the age of 7 years and of female child till attaining her puberty. Such right would continue, even if she was divorced, however, if she would contract the second marriage, then, she would lose her right of custody. If husband also would contract the second marriage and live with second wife, then it was incumbent upon the Trial Court to see the convenience and welfare of the minor and keeping in view the question of his welfare, would decide about the custody of the minor. Both husband and wife, in the present case had contracted second marriage; it was, in circumstances obligatory on the part of the Trial/Family Court to look into the matter with reference to Sharia Law along with the question of welfare of the minor. Question was not of a second marriage of mother or otherwise, the main focus for the court was the welfare of the minor. If both claimants of the minor had contracted a second marriage, then the matter of the custody of the minor had to be looked into carefully, keeping in view the welfare of the minor. Father of the minor child was a police employee, who, by virtue of his profession was compelled to remain away from his house. Minor/Female child, if given in the custody of the father, she would ultimately remain at the mercy of her stepmother, who could not be a substitute of real mother having natural love and affection for her female child. Female child would also be happier and familiar with the company and association of her mother. Impugned judgment was set aside and it was ordered that the custody of the minor would remain with the mother (Shariat Court, Azad Kashmir 2009 CLC 230).

682. Mother of minors (an Austrian national), accompanied by her children was arrested at the Airport; on search of luggage, 20 Kilograms and 875 grams heroin was recovered, on which FIR under sections 9(c) & 15, Control of Narcotic Substances Act, 1997 was registered against her and since then she was confined in jail as an under trial prisoner; the minors were also so confined with their mother, especially for the reason that at the time of her remand before the Magistrate she requested that 'I want to keep my children along with myself in judicial lockup, because I am foreigner and has no relation or friend in Pakistan at this time who will take care of my children'. Mother of minors wrote a letter to the Austrian Embassy for sending the minors to Austria so that they could live with her parents (the petitioners). Austrian Embassy could not succeed to get the minors released without the court's order for custody. Maternal grand parents of the minors through their counsel, moved the High Court with reference to Article 199(1)(b)(i) of the Constitution and section 491, Criminal Procedure Code contending that the minors were in an improper and illegal custody , therefore, they should be released and given in the custody of their grandparents and that their mother herself having made a request that the minors be sent to her parents abroad, it was in the welfare of the minors to live with their grandparents and elder brother and to have proper education as the parents of minors were involved in drug trafficking and had blatant track record. Grandparents had obtained a custody order by Austrian Courts for the said minors. Visa of minors for visit to Pakistan had expired. Father of minors whose whereabouts were not known, had moved a superficial custody petition before the Guardian Judge for the minors, and it seemed that the mother and father were in league on the custody issue. Held, it prima facie seemed in the welfare of the minors that they should be sent back to their home country, which, undoubtedly, was a welfare State and capable of taking care of even those children whose parents were not there. High Court observed that there was apprehension that the minors may not be used as a shield or carrier for any sordid business and if it so happened, the life of the minors shall be ruined, therefore, it was in the best interest of the minors that their custody be given to the grandparents as requested, particularly when elder brother of the minors, was there and was old enough to look after them. Deputy Head of Mission, Austrian Embassy, was allowed to take the custody of the minors from the jail authorities and was directed to make arrangements for sending them to Austria to enable the petitioners to take their custody. Constitutional petition was, allowed accordingly (LHC – 2009 PLD 393).

683. Contest between mother and grandfather of minor after death of minor's father. Custody of minor given to mother by Guardian Judge was handed over to grandfather by Appellate Court after remanding case to Guardian Judge for its decision on basis of consent of minor. Validity: Minor only on having attained age of becoming able to decide by exercising an intelligent preference should be allowed to avail same. Mother's right of *Hizant* of a child of 7 years age could not be substituted or equated with any other right. Paramount factor in case of minor girl would be guidance of her mother, which every girl would be required on her attaining age of majority and could not be done by grandfather. Minor was not grown up enough to adjudge her welfare. Remand of case to Guardian Judge for its decision on basis of obtaining consent of minor was not proper. High Court, keeping in view future and welfare of minor modified impugned order and directed Appellate Court to decide custody of minor on sole consideration of her welfare (LHC 2009 YLR 2339).

684. Respondent/father of the minors who had divorced petitioner, filed application for the custody of the minors, one male and one female who were in the custody of the petitioner (mother) since their birth. Guardian Court/Trial Court dismissed application filed by respondent/father. Appellate Court, however, reversed the findings of the Guardian Judge to the extent of the minor boy and gave his custody to respondent father while allowing the custody of the minor girl to remain with the petitioner mother. Respondent father got second marriage and had children in that wedlock too, whereas the petitioner (mother) was still unmarried and had been tending to her minor children who were doing very well in all aspects of their lives. Appellate Court seemed to have considered only the socioeconomic persuasions and no where in the entire judgment and decree any consideration to the welfare of the minor had been given. Appellate Court had overlooked that father of the minor had been negligent father. Minors were compelled to file a suit for recovery of maintenance against the father. Even after the suit was decreed respondent father did not pay the maintenance. Father neither claimed the custody of the minor bothered to offer to maintain them, and it was only after the petitioner (mother) filed a suit for maintenance of the minors that father filed his application for custody of the minors. Respondent father wanted the custody of the minor son for self-aggrandizement, whereas the petitioner mother, who had been looking after the minors since birth, wanted their custody because of her unconditional love for them. Mother was looking after their health, education, wants and needs to the best of abilities. Moreover, separating the minors, who seemed very much attached to each other, would be too harsh a decision for them to sustain. Welfare of both the minors, in circumstances, lay in their custody remaining with the petitioner mother. Impugned judgment/decree of the Appellate Court was set aside and that of the Guardian Court was restored (LHC 2009 YLR 1522).

685. Petitioner had challenged only the schedule of meeting with the minor given by the Appellate Court. Schedule given in the impugned judgment was being complied with by both the parties. Submission of the petitioner, however, was that because of the schedule given in the impugned judgment, education of the minor was being disturbed so a new schedule to meet the child with his father be given. Petitioner had suggested that it was appropriate to allow the father to meet the minor after six weeks. Suggestion was repelled on the ground that it was also part of the education that the minor should meet his father; and even otherwise no ground was urged in the petition or in the argument of the counsel for the petitioner that father should be deprived to meet his son. Appellate Court had given schedule in its judgment keeping in view the welfare of the minor. No reason was at all available to disturb the same or to give new schedule. Constitutional petition was dismissed in circumstances (LHC 2009 YLR 222).

686. Petition filed by petitioner for the custody of his minor son aged 11 years, was decided by the Guardian Judge in favour of the petitioner, with direction to mother of the minor to hand over the custody of the minor boy to the petitioner. Such order was set aside by Appellate Court. Validity: Notwithstanding the personal law of the minor, predominant consideration had always got to be the welfare of the minor. Welfare was not only monetary, but it was also emotional and the emotional welfare of the minor was more important than the monetary aspect; because regardless of fact as to who had the custody of the minor, the father being the natural and legal guardian was bound to maintain minor. Father pays the maintenance to his minor children because it was his bounden duty, from which he could not be absolved under any circumstances. Needs and wants of a minor were taken care of, whereas traumatizing a minor by making him/her go through an emotional upheaval, would debilitate him irreparably and an emotionally debilitated person, could not be a stable individual, and he could not be an asset to the world at large and to the society he belonged to in particular. Petitioner had impugned the judgment and decree of the Appellate Court on the ground that Appellate Court had relied the judgment on the opinion of the minor who was of tender years, and that the minor was too young to form his own opinion as to where his welfare lay. Constant supervision required for an 11 years boy, could not be given to him by father who had to go out and earn a living, regardless of whether he was living in Pakistan or abroad. Handing over the custody of minor to father would be to subject the minor to become a 'Latch key child'. 'Latch key children', was a term given to children whose parents work and they leave the latch key in a hidden place for the children to use when they return home after school and their parents are still at work, in order to let themselves into the house, where they fend for themselves till the parents return home after work. Minor whose custody had been contested, had two other siblings, who were also in mother's custody. To take the minor away from his mother as well as his siblings, would cause further unwarranted emotional agony to the minor boy. Impugned judgment passed by the Appellate Court being well thought of, was upheld, in such circumstances (LHC – 2009 CLC 1143).

687. Applicant/mother of a minor girl had alleged that respondent who had divorced the applicant and had driven her out of his house along with her two daughters, had snatched away one of the daughters aged 14 months from the custody of the applicant, though she had right of *Hizant* till the minor attained majority. Applicant had prayed for restoration of the custody of minor girl to her. Validity: Minor of such a tender age would need constant care of mother, and it was a universal truth that there could not be any substitute for a mother; and that the lap of mother was God's own cradle for child. Custody of minor girl with respondent/father was improper, if not illegal. Application was allowed with the direction that minor girl would be handed over by respondent to the applicant/mother forthwith (SHC – 2009 PLD 325).

688. Both petitioner/father of minor and respondent/mother of minor filed respective applications for custody of minor girl. Guardian Judge dismissed application of respondent/mother and allowed that of petitioner/father, but Appellate Court below on filing appeal, reversed judgment of Guardian Judge. Judgment passed by Appellate Court below confirmed and found respondent/mother of minor entitled to get the custody of minor, holding that minor was about 10 years of age and was not getting education in any school under the custody of petitioner/father; that petitioner/father was spending most of his time away from the house for earning his livelihood, and his mother who was residing with him was aged about 75 years and could not look after the minor girl; that according to Islamic Law, mother was entitled to the custody of her female child until she would obtain puberty; that respondent/mother of minor had not contracted second marriage, and no evidence was available that she was leading an immoral life. Petitioner was directed to hand over the custody of minor to respondent mother. Held, welfare of minor was that minor to remain with her mother and she was entitled to custody of the minor girl in circumstances, Constitutional petitions were dismissed (LHC – 2008 CLC 1317).

689. Matter between the parties with regard to custody of minor children was finally decided by Supreme Court on the basis of a compromise filed by the parties. According to the compromise, custody of minors was handed over to their mother while their father was given a right of visitation. Grievance of father of minors was that mother of minors was not complying with the decision of Supreme Court. Validity: In long legal battle with allegations and counter allegations both father and mother had lost sight of the fact that in ultimate result, the losers were children as their welfare was in the fact that both the parents should have an effective say in upbringing, and children should be attached to both the parents. High Court appointed Deputy Registrar (Judicial) with the task to see implementation of the order in letter and spirit, and either party might approach the official for its implementation. High Court permitted the official so appointed to seek police aid in case the same would be required to get the order implemented. High Court warned the parties concerned that nothing should be done to disobey the order, and all efforts should be employed to implement the same in letter and spirit failing which High Court would adopt effective measures. High Court further directed Deputy Registrar (Judicial) to take such steps to create an environment whereby children would be enabled to meet their parents smoothly. Petition was disposed of accordingly (SHC – 2008 PLD 499).

690. Courts below concurrently gave custody of minor to mother and the father who had divorced her had challenged said concurrent judgments of the courts below in Constitutional petition. Validity: Minor was patient of imperforated disease and had been operated thrice, in such circumstances when minor had attachment with his mother, in case he was given in the custody of his father who was stranger for him, it would deteriorate his health. Father, who had contracted second marriage, when he would leave for his job, child would be at the mercy of step mother. In presence of real mother, who was living in a combined family having sisters and mother, it would not be proper to deprive the child from the natural love and affection of the mother particularly when nothing substantial had come on record to prove that the mother had failed to properly look after her son. Scope of powers of High Court while dealing with the concurrent findings of the two courts below, in exercise of Constitutional jurisdiction, was very limited. Burden of proving that findings recorded by courts below were vitiated by evidence on record or suffered from non-reading of material evidence or there was jurisdictional defect, lay on the petitioner, which the petitioner in the present case had failed to point out. Both courts below had very carefully examined all the aspects of the matter in regard to the welfare of the minor. Concurrent judgments of the courts below could not be interfered with by the High Court in exercise of its Constitutional jurisdiction (SHC – 2008 PLD 132).

691. Application by petitioner/father for custody of minor son under section 25 of Guardians and Wards Act, 1890 was accepted by the Trial Court, but on appeal same was dismissed by Appellate Court. Petitioner had contracted second marriage and mother of minor had also contracted second marriage. Minor, who was aged about 12 years was happily living with his maternal grandfather for the last many years. Appellate Court below interviewed the minor who was not willing to live in the house of his father/petitioner with his stepmother. Minor at the relevant time was student of class-V. Maternal grandfather of minor was looking after minor and was attending to his educational requirements. Petitioner/father who had contracted second marriage had children from his second wife, and it was not safe to remove minor from his present family set up. Welfare of the minor demanded that he should be permitted to continue to live with his maternal grandfather. Appellate Court, in circumstances had rightly accepted appeal against judgment of the Trial Court. Paramount consideration in determining the question of custody of minor was welfare of the minor, and in the present case, welfare of the minor was that he should remain with his maternal grandfather. In absence of any illegality or infirmity in the impugned order of Appellate Court, same could not be interfered with by the High Court in exercise of its Constitutional jurisdiction (LHC – 2007 MLD 1089).

692. In presence of the parents claiming the custody of child, grandfather or other legal guardians, could not be considered for handing over the custody to them under any law including Islamic Law and Guardians and Wards Act, 1890. Rule that welfare of the minor, would be presumed with person who was entitled, to the custody under Islamic Law, was not absolute and matter of custody would always remain subject to the welfare of the minor. Guidelines provided by Islamic Law were not absolute in nature and while appointing a guardian of the person of a minor, her (minor's) choice could not be overlooked. Paramount consideration which had to weigh with the court was welfare of the minor which also included not only her wellbeing, but also had to be determined keeping in view the surroundings in and outside the house where her father or mother lived. Despite disqualification incurred by the mother, she could be handed over the custody of her minor child if welfare of the minor so warranted. Prime consideration for appointment of guardian was the welfare of the minor which must weigh with the court irrespective of the provisions of Personal Law. Conduct of the father or mother must also be considered and choice of minor could not be taken lightly and must be given weight (Supreme Court, Azad Kashmir – 2007 CLC 474).

693. Under section 19 of the Guardian and Wards Act, 1890 Guardian is not appointed by the Court in following cases:

- of a minor who is a married female and whose husband is not, in the opinion of the Court, unfit to be guardian of her person; or
- of a minor whose father is living and is not, in the opinion of the Court unfit to be guardian of the person of the minor; or
- of a minor whose property is under the superintendence of a Court of Wards competent to appoint a guardian of the person of the minor.

§8. Wishes of the Child

694. Under section 17(3) of the Guardian and Wards Act, 1890 (VIII of 1890), if the minor is old enough to form an intelligent preference, the Court may consider that preference and wishes of the child are given considerable weightage. Court is authorized under section 17(3) of Guardians and Wards Act, 1890, to consider an intelligent preference of minor in the matter of custody.

695. Father claimed custody on the ground that minors had attained age of 7 years; and their mother, after contracting marriage, had children from her second husband. Guardian Judge accepted father's petition, but Appellate Court dismissed the same, which judgment was upheld by High Court in Constitutional petition. Minors after staying with father for more than fifteen days at the direction of the High Court, had proclaimed that father was alien for them thereby showing attachment with mother. Minors had been admitted in a standard school, getting education, clothes, food and were enjoying every facility of life in mother's house.

Supreme Court dismissed petition and refused leave to appeal with observations that father might approach proper forum for allowing visiting terms to his children (SCP – 2004 PLD 357).

696. Children's capability of making intelligent preference about which of the parents they choose to live with. Minor's opinion was never obtained by District Judge while deciding question of their custody. Children being present in Court, High Court obtained their opinion and they were intelligent enough to express their opinion as they have been studying in good schools. Minors stated that they would prefer to live with their mother. Petitioner mother would not be disentitled and disqualified to retain custody of minors on the ground that she has contracted second marriage with a person who was not related to minors and is stranger. Courts would preserve to the mother custody of children if interest and welfare of minor so demanded. Impugned order of District Judge whereby he had declared father (respondent) to be the guardian of person and property of minors was set aside. Order of Guardian Judge was modified to the extent that father (respondent) was allowed to see his children once in a month provided their educational programme was not disturbed. Minor children can stay with father once in a month preferably on week ends and also stay for full day on their birthday and for two days on every Eid. (PLJ 2000 Peshawar 175 and PLD 2000 Peshawar 23)

697. Family Court allowed application for custody of minors in favour of mother but Lower Appellate Court, relying upon preference of minors to live with their father, set aside the order passed by Family Court. Validity: Court was authorized under section 17(3) of Guardians and Wards Act, 1890, to consider an intelligent preference of minor in the matter of custody. Lower Appellate Court recorded statements of minors on the date of judgment, when parties had already been in Court for the last two years, and minors had come along with their father. High Court only relied upon statement of the eldest son who was of the age and had grown a beard as well, but statements of remaining two children were not intelligent preference in the matter. Mother of minors had not remarried after divorce and was constantly fighting for custody of her children, while father of minors had contracted marriage and had three children from new wedlock. Daughter and younger son were of tender age and required care which only a mother could provide. High Court in exercise of Constitutional jurisdiction declared judgment passed by Lower Appellate Court to be without lawful authority and set aside the same to the extent of daughter and younger son, who would remain with their mother. Petition was allowed accordingly (LHC – 2009 MLD 33).

698. Welfare of minors. Whether in exercise of Constitutional jurisdiction, interference in findings of facts, can be made by High Court. Principal of law discussed by Honourable Supreme Court in case of *Mst. Mehmooda Begum v. Taj Din* can be invoked, wherein it has been laid down that findings of facts recorded by Tribunal of special jurisdiction in respect of matters, exclusively within its competence, normally is not to be interfered unless, there has been serious mis-reading or mis-appreciation of evidence on part of Tribunal or there had been failure on its part to take into consideration material facts or to apply statutory law or any principle or rule of law. Both courts below have passed impugned judgments without taking into consideration intelligent preference of minors, evidence on record, that petitioner can look after welfare of minors better than respondent No.1, who being male member and of advance age, would not be in a position to look after female minor girls (PLJ1998 Quetta. 137 = 1998 MLD 1697).

I. Performance in Court

699. Under section 17 of the Guardian and Wards Act, 1890 in appointing or declaring the guarding of a minor, the Court shall be guided by what, consistently with the law to which the minor is subject, appears in the circumstances to be for the welfare of the minor.

700. In considering what will be for the welfare of the minor, the Court shall have regard to the age, sex and religion of the minor, the character and capacity of the proposed guardian and his nearness of kin to the minor, the wishes, if any, of a deceased parent, and any existing or previous relations of the proposed guardian with the minor or his property. If the minor is old enough to form an intelligent preference, the court may consider that preference. The Court shall not appoint or declare any person to be a guardian against this will.

701. Custody of minor. Territorial jurisdiction of Family Court. Mother after obtaining custody of a suckling baby at Karachi by filing habeas corpus petition filed case for custody of second child. Family Court at Karachi returned the case for want of jurisdiction as minor by that time was residing with grandmother at Kohat. Appellate Court set aside such order. Validity: Marriage of parties was solemnized at Karachi, where they were still residing. Both children were born at Karachi, where they were available, when habeas corpus petition was filed. Second minor had been shifted to Kohat thereafter. Shifting of minor by father to Kohat in circumstances would not divest Courts at Karachi of its powers to entertain and deal with the matter. Jurisdiction in such circumstances would lie with Family Court at Karachi High Court dismissed Constitutional petition (SHC – 2003 YLR 1625).

II. Preference for Natural parents

702. While appointing or declaring the guardian of a minor or handing over the custody of minor children, paramount consideration would be the welfare of minor. The natural parents of child are always given preference by Courts while handing over the custody of child. The Supreme Court, Azad Kashmir (2002 MLD 1213) held that mother could claim custody of minor son up to seven years as of right. Before attaining age of 7 years, mother could be deprived from custody of male child only if some strong circumstances were brought on record to justify that it would not be in the welfare of minor to keep him in custody of his mother.

703. Principle of preference of either Parents. Whether splitting-up brothers and sisters desirable. Courts below have taken into consideration admitted fact that all three brothers are studying in Lawrence College Ghora Gali, Murree and are studying in College Hostel. They are, therefore, enjoying company of each other which will promote their brotherly feelings intact and elder can look after youngsters. Provision of section 17 of Guardian and Wards Act was followed by both Courts below which are perfectly in accordance with spirit of law. Welfare of minors lay in their remaining in same institution (PLJ 1996 Lahore 577 = 1996 CLC 1603).

704. Whether mother has preferential right of *Hizant*. Mother of minors, having contracted second marriage with person not related to minors within prohibited degrees has lost her right of *Hizant*. Petition dismissed. (PLJ 1998 Lahore 146 = 1998 CLC 846).

705. Application filed by ex-wife of the petitioner, under section 25 of Guardians and Wards Act, 1890 for custody of minors was disposed of by the Guardian Judge/Family Court in view of compromise between the parties, and it was directed that permanent custody of minors would remain with the petitioner who would hand over minors on each Sunday to the ex-wife for visitation. Appeal filed by petitioner against judgment of the Family Court was partly allowed by the Appellate Court below by making some changes in respect of visitation rights of respondent and judgment of Appellate Court below was upheld by High Court. Plea of petitioner was that as ex-wife had contracted a second marriage with a stranger, she had lost her right of *Hizant* or even visitation. Validity: Mother of minors, could not be denied minimum right of access to her minor children nor she be considered like an alien enemy qua them. Appellate Court below adopted a very sensible approach by permitting the mother to meet the minors on the first Sunday of each month. Order passed by the Appellate Court below was upheld by the High Court, being just and fair to which no exception could be taken. Impugned judgment of the High Court, not suffering from any legal infirmity so as to warrant interference by the Supreme Court. Petition was dismissed (SCP – 2008 SCMR 527).

706. Father of minors after divorcing their mother had contracted second marriage. Father, who was a driver of the truck, by virtue of his profession had to remain away from his house, as such the minors if given to his custody, they would ultimately remain at the mercy of their stepmother, who could not be a substitute of real mother having a natural love and affection for her children. Trial Court rejected application filed by father of minors for their' custody on the basis of welfare of the minors. Trial Court, after appreciating evidence, had rightly concluded that as father had contracted second marriage and being a driver of the truck could not look after his minor children himself, they could not be left at the mercy of a stepmother. Father had contended that as mother of minors had also contracted second marriage; that male child being 8 years of age, she had lost the right of custody. Contention of father was repelled because the question was not of the age or of second marriage of mother of the minors, but main focus was on the welfare of the minors. If both claimants for custody of the minors had contracted second marriage, then the matter of custody of the minors had to be decided with more care and caution;

and that was what in the interest of the minors and more importance had to be given to welfare of the minors. Female child, who was 13 months of age, naturally would need the company and association of mother, while male child who was 2-1/2 years of age, would also need the same atmosphere, especially when throughout the period they had been living with their mother. Impugned order rightly passed by the Trial Court could not be interfered with in appeal by the Shariat Court (Shariat Court, Azad Kashmir 2008 YLR 1446).

707. Application for custody of minors having concurrently been dismissed by the Guardian Judge and Appellate Court, petitioner had filed Constitutional petition against said judgments. Both minors were in the custody of the mother of the minors. Male minor who was student of class-2, had a shining academic record. Mother of minors who was serving in a private department, had not gone for second marriage, but was looking after her minor son and daughter. Both minors aged 8-1/2 and 4-1/2 years respectively, who were present in the court, were clad in clean, well stitched clothes. Both were looking bright and happy with their mother. Minors were living with the company of their mother right from pronouncement of divorce to their mother by the petitioner. Decree for maintenance allowance passed against the petitioner was not honoured by him. No substitute was for love and affection bestowed by the mother on her children. Difference of income between father and mother had no overriding consideration. Father was always bound to maintain the minors even if mother was jobless and had no source of her own independent income. Judgment of two courts below could not be interfered with by the High Court in exercise of its Constitutional jurisdiction (LHC – 2008 YLR 127).

708. LHC held that it would be harsh to hand over the custody of the minor son to the father leaving him at the mercy of stepmother in presence of real mother, who otherwise was maintaining her child properly (2008 CLC 1595).

709. LHC held that dual control of minor children by father and mother has been recognized under Islamic Law. Father is a legal and natural guardian of minor, whereas right of *Hizant* (custody of minor) vests in the mother of minor. Mother, under the Sunni law, is entitled to custody of male child until he has completed age of 7 years and of her female child until she has attained puberty. Such right of *Hizant* (custody of minor) of mother continues though she is divorced by the father of minor children (LHC – 2008 PLD 533).

710. Respondent has no woman in his house that can look after children if given to his custody. Respondent claimed that he has a sister in his house that could look after children. Sister of respondent could not be a substitute of mother, and she could not provide love and affection to children which mother can, as lap of mother is God's own cradle for children. Mother was, thus, entitled to custody other minor children (PLJ 2000 Peshawar 175 = PLD 2000 Peshawar 23).

711. Minors remaining in custody of their step-mother after death of their real mother with whom their father contracted second marriage. After death of their father, their paternal uncle applied for their custody which was granted. Petitioner's appeal was dismissed. Constitutional Petition. Welfare of minors. By now it is well settled that while disposing of applications under sections 17 and 25 of Guardian and Wards Act, supreme consideration should be welfare of minors, coupled with their own wishes. Petitioner is undoubtedly step mother of female minors, but they are living with her for last more than eight years, when their real mother expired away. All minors were examined thrice by trial and Appellate Court, who on every occasion, insisted to stay with their step-mother, instead of preferring to live with their real uncle (Respondent). It is noteworthy that in his statement, he has given his age to be of 90 years. Moreover, minors have developed intimacy with petitioner (step mother) and even otherwise, being female minors, it is necessary that they should stay with female instead of male. Findings of Courts below are not based on correct application of law, as well as appreciation of evidence on record (PLJ1998 Quetta 137 = 1998 MLD 1697).

III. Economic Factors

712. While giving the custody of child, the Court also considers the economic factors of the Guardian for the welfare of the child. If the financial position of the Guardian is not sound, he/she may not be able to provide good food, health and education to the child.

713. Trial Court had declared mother of minors to be the guardian of their person and property. District Judge, however, declared minor's father to be the guardian of person and property of minors and directed that custody of minors be handed over to him. Validity: Petitioner (mother) had annexed detailed list of cases which had been registered against respondent and in which he has been convicted also. No rebuttal was placed on record from respondent's side that he was not involved, convicted and as not under trial in cases detailed in the list. Respondent did not mention in Court his income or his source of income. Neither any document regarding ownership of property was produced nor any other document showing that he had been deriving any income from said property was produced nor any proof that he was working anywhere was produced before Court. Petitioner, however, has placed on record certified copies of certificates from various educational institutions that she had been serving in those schools as a teacher and that at present she was teaching Fauji Foundation School. Petitioner had also placed on record certificate of tuition fee of minor children being paid by petitioner as also certificate showing balance of specified amount in her account in Habib Bank Ltd. In addition to salary, she has been giving tuition to students and earning hand some amount. Minor children have been admitted in best available schools, they are getting proper education and being looked after properly. Respondent in his statement before Court had admitted that petitioner was graduate and has been serving in Fauji Foundation School and that children were also studying in that school. Welfare of children being of fundamental importance, preference should be given to their welfare. Respondent although is natural guardian of minors yet his right was subordinate to welfare of minors. Evidence on record would suggest that minors were being well-educated and looked after by petitioner mother who had been supporting them since their birth while respondent had not spent a penny on them. Nothing on record was brought to indicate that petitioner was a woman of bad character. On the contrary she was graduate and teacher in a school of good standard and leading respectable life, welfare of minors, therefore, lies with petitioner (mother) and she was, thus, entitled to their custody (PLJ 2000 Peshawar 175 = PLD 200 Q Peshawar 23).

714. Court and Appellate Court having given the custody of minors to the mother, father of minors had challenged said concurrent judgments in Constitutional petition. Validity: Prime consideration for determination of custody of minors being their welfare, the court had to consider the same before handing over their custody to their mother or father. For the purpose of consideration of the welfare of the minors, evidence available on record was to be considered by the court. Father of the minors was residing in a rented house in a joint family system; he was running electric shop used to remain outside the house in connection with his work, and his parents were not surviving, and he was residing with his two married brothers, which had shown that at his house no one was available to look after the minors properly as they could be looked after and maintained by real mother of the minors. Said evidence on record had shown that welfare of the minors lay with their mother who being natural guardian, could maintain her minors with love and affection in comparison to the others. Maintenance of the minors was the bounden and primary duty of the father of the minors till the age of his majority in the case of his son and till the marriage in case of daughter. Non-availability of funds or paucity of the mother to maintain her minor children, in circumstances could not be treated as disqualification of mother to refuse her the custody of her children. Consent of minors to reside with father, was of not much significance while determining the facts of their welfare. Consent of minor was only to be considered, if the minor was old enough to form his preference, but in the present case age of minor girl was not more than 10 years, whereas minor boy was not more than 8 years. Both were not old enough so as to give any preference to their consent. Mere assumption and presumption that education of minors would be disturbed, custody of minors could not be refused to their mother. Judgments passed by the courts below did not suffer from any illegality so as to declare them as ultra vires the Constitution. Constitutional petition was dismissed, in such circumstances (SHC – 2008 CLC 654).

§9. Cessation of Guardianship

715. In different court cases, the Court removed the guardian appointed or declared by it, or even a guardian appointed by will, on the application of any interested person or on its own motion, for the following reasons:

- for abuse of trust;
- for continued failure to perform the duties of his trust;
- for incapacity to perform the duties of his trust;
- for ill-treatment, or neglect to take proper care of the ward;
- for contumacious disregard of any of the Guardians and Wards Act’s provisions or of any of the court orders;

- for conviction of an offence implying a defect of character;
- for having an interest adverse to the faithful performance of his duties;
- for ceasing to reside within the local limits of the court's jurisdiction; and
- for bankruptcy or insolvency in the case of a guardian of property.

716. A guardian may also apply to the court for discharging him/her from the responsibility of being a guardian. A person also ceases to be a guardian in the case of his/her death, removal, or discharge; upon the ward ceasing to be a minor; upon the female ward's marriage whose husband is not unfit to be her guardian; or upon the court itself assuming superintendence of the minor.

Part III. Matrimonial Property Law

Chapter 1. Matrimonial Property

§1. Introduction

717. The husband and wife are entitled to each other's property in case of death. According to Islamic Laws, the husband's share is one-half of the property of the deceased wife if she has no children, but in case of children it is one-fourth. The wife is entitled to one-fourth if the husband dies childless; otherwise it is one-eighth.

§2. Property Regime during Marriage and Cohabitation

718. Under PART-III (Marriage) of the Succession Act, 1925 no person shall, by marriage, acquire any interest in the property of the person whom he/she marries or becomes incapable of doing any act in respect of his/her own property which he/she could have done if unmarried. However, this (a) shall not apply to any marriage contracted before the first day of January, 1866; (b) shall not apply, and shall be deemed never to have applied, to any marriage one or both of the parties to which professed at the time of the marriage the Hindu, Muslim, Buddhist, Sikh or Jaina religion.

719. Under section-21 of the Succession Act, 1925 if a person whose domicile is not in Pakistan marries in Pakistan a person whose domicile is in Pakistan neither party acquires by the marriage any right in respect of any property of the other party not comprised in a settlement made previous to the marriage, which he/she would not be acquired thereby if by where domiciled in Pakistan at the time of the marriage.

720. Under section-22 of the Succession Act, 1925 the property of a minor may be settled in contemplation of marriage, provided the settlement is made by the minor with the approbation of the minors father, or, if the father is dead or absent from Pakistan, with the approbation of the High Court.

721. However, this shall not apply to any will made or intestacy occurring before the first day of January, 1866, or to intestate or testamentary succession to the property of any Hindu, Muslim, Buddhist, Sikh or Jaina.

§3. ADJUDICATION OF PROPERTY DISPUTES

722. Share of predeceased son. Plaintiff being the only daughter of predeceased son, claimed her share in property of her grandfather, under the provisions of section 4 of Muslim Family Laws Ordinance, 1961. All the Courts below concurrently granted the share of predeceased son to the plaintiff. Validity: Plaintiff being the only daughter of the predeceased son would inherit one-half share from the property of her father while the remaining share of father of plaintiff (predeceased son) would go to other collateral. Supreme Court reduced the share of the plaintiff to the extent of one-half of the share of the father of the plaintiff and declined to interfere with the concurrent findings of facts by the Courts below. Petition for leave to appeal was converted into appeal and the same was allowed accordingly (SCP – 2003 SCMR 1664).

723. Inheritance. Suit for declaration. Trial Court decreed the suit holding that plaintiffs being children of predeceased sons/daughters of original owner of suit-land were entitled to inherit their shares alongwith other children of deceased owner. Appellate Court set aside judgment and decree of the Trial Court and dismissed the suit on the ground that section 4 of Muslim Family Laws Ordinance, 1961 had been declared against Injunctions of Islam by FSC. Validity: Relevant mutation of the property in dispute was sanctioned long before the judgment of Federal Shariat Court, wherein section 4 of Muslim 'Family Laws Ordinance, 1961 was declared against the Injunctions of Islam. Said case of FSC had no effect on the present case in circumstances. Appellate Court having committed material irregularity by misinterpreting section 4 of Muslim Family Laws Ordinance, 1961, judgment and decree passed by it, were set aside and that of Trial Court decreeing suit filed by plaintiff, was restored (LHC – 2003 MLD 933).

Part IV. Succession Law

Chapter 1. Intestate Succession

§1. The Open of the Succession

724. Under the Succession Act, 1925, succession to the immoveable property in Pakistan of a person deceased shall be regulated by the law of Pakistan, wherever such person may have had his domicile at the time of his death. Succession to the moveable property of a person deceased is regulated by the law of the country in which such person had his domicile at the time of his death. (i) A, having his domicile in Pakistan dies in France, leaving moveable property in France, moveable property in England, and property, both moveable and immoveable, in Pakistan. The succession to the whole is regulated by the law of Pakistan. (ii) A, an Englishman, having his domicile in France, dies in Pakistan, and leaves property, both moveable and immoveable, in Pakistan. The succession to the moveable property is regulated by the rules which govern, in France, the succession to the moveable property of an Englishman dying domiciled in France, and the succession to the immoveable property is regulated by the law of Pakistan.

§2. Death

725. The Succession Act, 1925 and Islamic Laws in Pakistan provide the rules and regulations for distribution of immoveable and moveable property after the death of an individual. The will of an individual is a primary document for succession after the death of an individual. All assets are distributed in accordance with the Islamic Laws by the Muslims.

§3. The Heir and Other Beneficiaries

726. The Succession Act, 1925 Part-V deals with the intestate succession. This Part shall not apply to any intestacy occurring before the first day of January 1866, or to the property of any Hindu Muslim, Buddhist, Sikh or Jaina. (2) Save as provided in sub-section (1) or by any other law for the time being in force, the provisions of this Part shall constitute the law of Pakistan in all cases of intestacy.

727. A person is deemed to die intestate in respect of all property of which he has not made a testamentary disposition which is capable of taking effect. Illustrations: (i) A has left no will. He has died intestate in respect of the whole of his property. (ii) A has left a will, whereby he has appointed B his executor; but the will contains no other provisions. A has died intestate in respect of the distribution of his property. (iii) A has bequeathed his whole property for an illegal purpose. A has died intestate in respect of the distribution of his property. (iv) A has bequeathed PKR 1,000 to B and PKR 1,000 to the eldest son of C, and has made no other bequest; and has died leaving the sum of PKR 2,000 and no other property. C died before A without having ever had a son. A has died intestate in respect of the distribution of PKR 1,000.

728. The property of an intestate devolves upon the wife or husband, or upon those who are of the kindred of the deceased, in the order and according to the rules hereinafter contained in this Chapter. Explanation: A widow is not entitled to the provision hereby made for her if, by a valid contract made before her marriage; she has been excluded from her distributive share of her husband's estate.

729. Where the intestate has left a widow (a) if he has also left any lineal descendants, one-third of his property shall belong to his widow, and the remaining two-thirds shall go to his lineal descendants, according to the rules hereinafter contained; (b) save as provided by section 33A, if he has left no lineal descendant, but has left persons who are of kindred to him, one-half of his property shall belong to his widow, and the other half shall go to those who are of kindred to him, in the order and according to the rules hereinafter contained (c) if he has left none who are of kindred to him the whole of his property shall belong to his widow.

730. Where the intestate has left a widow but no lineal descendants and the net value of his property does not exceed PKR 5,000, the whole of his property shall belong to the widow.

731. Where the net value of the property exceeds the sum of PKR 5,000, the widow shall be entitled to PKR 5,000 thereof and shall have a charge upon the whole of such property for such sum of PKR 5,000, with interest thereon from the date of the death of the intestate at 4% per annum until payment. The provision for the widow made by this section shall be in addition and without prejudice to her interest and share in the residue of the estate of such intestate remaining after payment of the said sum of PKR 5,000, with interest as aforesaid, and such residue shall be distributed in accordance with the provisions of section 33 as if it were the whole of such intestates property.

732. The net value of the property shall be ascertained by deducting from the gross value thereof all debts, and all funeral and administration expenses of the intestate, and all other lawful liabilities and charges to which the property shall be subject. (5) This section shall not apply (a) to the property of (i) any Pakistan Christian, (ii) any child or grandchild of any male person who is or was at the time of his death a Pakistan Christian, or (iii) any person professing the Hindu, Buddhist,

Sikh or Jaina religion the succession to whose property is, under section 24 of the Special Marriage Act, 1872, regulated by the provisions of this Act; (b) unless the deceased dies intestate in respect of all his property.

733. Where the intestate has left no widow, his property shall go to his lineal descendants or to those who are of kindred to him, not being lineal descendants, according to the rules hereinafter contained; and, if he has left none who are of kindred to him, it shall go to the Government.

734. A husband surviving his wife has the same rights in respect of her property, if she dies intestate, as a widow has in respect of her husband's property, if he dies intestate.

735. Where the intestate has left surviving him a child or children, but no more remote lineal descendant through a deceased child, the property shall belong to his surviving child, if there is only one, or shall be equally divided among all his surviving children.

736. Where the intestate has not left surviving him any child, but has left a grandchild or grandchildren and no more remote descendant through a deceased grandchild, the property shall belong to his surviving grandchild if there is only one, or shall be equally divided among all his surviving grandchildren. Illustrations (i) A has three children, and no more, John, Mary, and Henry. They all die before the father, John leaving two children, Mary three, and Henry four. Afterwards A dies intestate, leaving those nine grandchildren and no descendant of any deceased grandchild. Each of his grandchildren will have one-ninth. (ii) But if Henry has died, leaving no child, then the whole is equally divided between the intestates five grandchildren, the children of John and Mary.

737. In like manner the property shall go to the surviving lineal descendants who are nearest in degree to the intestate, where they are all in the degree of great-grandchildren to him, or are all in a more remote degree.

738. If the intestate has left lineal descendants who do not all stand in the same degree of kindred to him, and the persons through whom the more remote are descended from him are dead, the property shall be divided into such a number of equal shares as may correspond with the number of the lineal descendants of the intestate who either stood in the nearest degree of kindred to him at his decease, or, having been of the like degree of kindred to him, died before him, leaving lineal descendants who survived him.

739. One of such shares shall be allotted to each of the lineal descendants who stood in the nearest degree of kindred to the intestate at his decease; and one of such shares shall be allotted in respect of each of such deceased lineal descendants; and the share allotted in respect of each of such deceased lineal descendants shall belong to his surviving child or children or more remote lineal descendants, as the case may be; such surviving child or children or more remote lineal descendants always taking the share which his or their parent or parents would have been entitled to respectively if such parent or parents had survived the intestate. Illustrations: (i) A had three children, John, Mary and Henry. John died, leaving four children, and Mary died, leaving one, and Henry alone survived the father. On the death of A, intestate, one-third is allotted to Henry, one-third to John's four children and the remaining one-third to Mary's one child. (ii) A left no child, but left eight grandchildren, and two children of a deceased grandchild. The property is divided into nine parts, one of which is allotted to each grandchild, and the remaining one-ninth is equally divided between the two great-grandchildren. (iii) A has three children, John, Mary and Henry; John dies leaving four children, and one of John's children dies leaving two children. Mary dies leaving one child. A afterwards dies intestate. One-third of his property is allotted to Henry, one-third to Mary's child, and one-third is divided into four parts, one of which is allotted to each of John's three surviving children, and the remaining part is equally divided between John's two great-children. (iv) A has two children, and no more; John and Mary. John dies before his father, leaving his wife pregnant. Then A dies leaving Mary surviving him, and in due time a child of John is born. A's property is, to be equally divided between Mary and the posthumous child.

740. Where an intestate has left no lineal descendants, the rules for the distribution of his property (after deducting the widows share, if he has left a widow) shall be those contained in sections 42 to 48. If the intestates father is living, he shall succeed to the property.

741. If the intestates father is dead, but the intestates mother is living and there are also brothers or sisters of the intestate living, and there is no child living of a any deceased brother or sister, the mother and each living brother or sister shall succeed to the property in equal shares. A dies intestate survived by his mother and two brothers of the full blood, John and Henry, and a sister Mary, who is the daughter of his mother but not of his father. The mother takes one-fourth, each brother takes one-fourth and Mary, the sister of half blood, takes one-fourth. Illustration: A dies intestate survived by his mother and two brothers of the full blood, John and Henry, and a sister Mary, who is the daughter of his mother but not of his father. The mother takes one-fourth, each brother takes one-fourth and Mary, the sister of half blood, takes one-fourth.

742. If the intestates father is dead, but the intestates mother is living, and if any brother or sister and the child or children of any brother or sister who may have died in the intestates life time are also living then the mother and each living brother or sister, and the living child or children of each deceased brother or sister, shall be entitled to the property in equal shares, such children (if more than one) taking in equal shares only the shares which their respective parents would have taken if living at the intestates death. Illustration: A, the intestate, leaves his mother, his brothers John and Henry, and also one child of a deceased sister, Mary, and two children of George, a deceased brother of the half blood who was the son of his father but not of his mother. The mother takes one-fifth, John and Henry each takes one-fifth, the child of Mary takes one-fifth, and the two children of George divides the remaining one-fifth equally between them.

743. If the intestates father is dead, but the intestates mother is living, and the brothers and sisters are all dead, but all or any of them have left children who survived the intestate, the mother and the child or children of each deceased brother or sister shall be entitled to the property in equal share, such children (if more than one) taking in equal shares only the shares which their respective parents would have taken if living at the intestates death. Illustration: A, the intestate, leaves no brother or sister, but leaves his mother and one child of a deceased sister, Mary, and two children of a deceased brother, George. The mother takes one-third, the child of Mary takes one-third, and the children of George divide the remaining one-third equally between them.

744. If the intestates father is dead, but the intestates mother is living, and there is neither brother, nor sister, nor child of any brother or sister (the intestate), the property shall belong to the mother.

745. Where the intestate has left neither lineal descendant, nor father, nor mother, the property shall be divided equally between his brothers and the child or children of such of them as may have died before him, such children (if more than one) taking in equal shares only the shares which their respective parents would have taken if living at the intestates death.

746. Where the intestate has left neither lineal descendant, nor parent, nor brother, nor sister, his property shall be divided equally among those of his relatives who are in the nearest degree of kindred to him. Illustrations: (i) A, the intestate, has left a grandfather, and a grandmother and no other relative standing in the same or a nearer degree of kindred to him. They, being in the second degree, will be entitled to the property in equal shares exclusive of any uncle or aunt of the intestate, uncles and aunts being only in the third degree. (ii) A, the intestate, has left a great-grandfather, or a great-grandmother, and uncles and aunts, and no other relative standing in the same or a nearer degree of kindred to him. All of these being in the third degree will take equal shares. (iii) A, the intestate, left a great-grandfather, an uncle and a nephew, but no relative standing in a nearer degree of kindred to him. All of these being in the third degree will take equal shares. (iv) Ten children of one brother or sister of the intestate, and one child of another brother or sister of the intestate, constitute the class of relatives of the nearest degree of kindred to him. They will each take one-eleventh of the property.

747. Where a distributive share in the property of a person who has died intestate is claimed by a child, or any descendant of a child, of such person, no money or other property which the intestate may, during his life, have paid, given or settled to, or for, the advancement of, the child by whom or by whose descendant the claim is made shall be taken into account in estimating such distributive share. Nothing in this Chapter shall apply to Parsis.

§4. Islamic Law of Inheritance and Succession

748. The Muslims are divided into two major sects, namely, the Sunnis and the Shias. The majority of the Muslims in Pakistan are Sunni. The Sunnis are divided into four sub-sects, namely, Hanfis, the Malikis, the Shafeis and the Hanbalis.

I. Sunni Laws

749. Under the Islamic Law Sunni sect following the following law of inheritance:

1. **Father:** Father gets 1/6 when there is child or child of a son besides other heirs; or when there is no child or child of a son, but there are husband, mother and son's daughter. Father gets 1/3 when there is no child or child of son, or son's daughter, but there are husband and mother; hen there is no child or child of a son or sons daughter but there are husband and maternal true grand-mother; when there is no son, but there are more than one daughter; when there is no son, no daughter or son's son, but there is son's daughter or son's son's daughter.

750. Father gets one-half when there is no child or child of a son or son's daughter, but there is husband; then there is no son but there is a daughter; then there is no child or child of a son or son's son's daughter, but there are wife and mother; when there is child of a son or son's daughter, but there are wife and maternal true grand-mother.

751. Father would get two-third when there is no child or child of a son, or son's son's daughter, but there is mother or, maternal true grand-mother. He will get two-fourth when there is no child or child, of a son or son's daughter, but there is widow. He will get five-sixth when there is no-son, no daughter, no son's son, no son's daughter, no husband, no wife, but there are mother and more than one brother or sister. He gets the whole when there is no son, no daughter, no son's son, no son's daughter, no husband, no wife, no mother, no maternal true grand-mother, no son, or no son's daughter.

752. In the presence of father, the following sharers do not inherit at all, and their presence does not affect the above-mentioned shares of the father. Such shares are uterine brother, uterine sister, full sister, consanguine sister, true grand-father. Moreover, residuaries of Classes Ill and IV do not inherit in the presence of the father.

753. True grand-father does not inherit where the father is alive. If the father is dead, the true grand-father takes the position of father and inherits like the father.

754. **Mother:** The mother gets one-sixth, when there is a child or child of a son, or when there are two or more brothers or sisters, or even one brother and one sister, whether full, consanguine or uterine. She gets one-third, when there is no child or child of a son, and not more than one brother or sister if any. She gets one-fourth, when there are also wife and father plus one-third as above. She gets one-sixth, when there are also husband and father plus one-third as above.

755. **Maternal true grand-mother**: She gets one-sixth, when, is no mother, father no nearer true grand-mother; either parental or maternal, and no near true grand-mother, either paternal or maternal.

756. **Paternal true grand-mother:** She gets one-sixth, when there is no mother, father no nearer true grand-mother, either paternal or maternal, and no intermediate true grand-father.

757. **Husband:** He gets one-fourth, when there is child or child of a son. He gets one-half, when there is no child or a son.

758. **Wife:** She gets one-eighth, when there is child or child of a son. If the number of wives is more than one, they jointly get four-eighth. When no child and the wife is one or more, she or they get one-fourth.

759. **Daughter:** She gets one-half, when one and no son. When the number is more than one, they get two-third, provided there is no son. If there is son, she becomes residuary with the son, and takes one-half share than that of the son. In caner words the son takes a double portion. For instance if twenty-three remains after ducting the sharers of the shares, a son will get nine and daughter will get two-ninth. If sharers are three sons and two daughters, each son will get one-sixth and each daughter will get one-twelfth.

760. **Son's Daughter:** Son's daughter. She inherits only where there is no son, no daughter, or no son's son. She will get one-half if only one, and it more than one they will get two-third jointly. She or they will get one-sixth, if there is only one daughter, and there is no son or son's son. If there is son's son and no heirs as mentioned above she will inherit with him as residuary and her share will be like a daughter. If there is no equal son's son, but there is a lower son's son, she takes as a residuary with him, provided she cannot inherit as a sharer. In either case, each son son's son takes double the shares of each son's daughter. When the son's daughter becomes a residuary with a lower son's son, and there are son's daughter equal in degree with the lower son's son she shares equally with them as if they were all of the same grade.

761. **Son's son's daughter:** If one she will get one-half, provided there is no (1) son (2) daughter (3) son's son (4) son's daughter, or (5) son's son. If more than two they will get two-third jointly. Whether one or inure will get one-sixth, when there is only one daughter or son's daughter, provided there is no son, no son's son, nor son's son's son. If there is son's sons, she will inherit with them as residuary and her share will be like a sons s daughter.

762. **Uterine brother/sister:** When one, will get one-sixth, provided there is 'no child, no child of a son, no father, no true grand-father. When more than one, they will get one-third jointly. If there is uterine sister also the uterine brother will get half of his share that is instead one-sixth, he will get one-twelfth. In other words uterine brother and uterine sister inherit equally. The same share as given under uterine brother. Both inherit jointly.

763. **Full sister:** When only one and no (1) child (2) child of son (3) father (4) true grand-father or (5) full brother, she will get one-half, but if the number of sisters exceeds one, they get two-third jointly. In the circumstances given above, but when there is also brother, she does not inherit as barer. However, she will then inherit as residuary with the full brother. But the brother will take a double portion. In default of full brother, son, son's son, son's daughter, daughter, father and true grand-father, the full sister takes the residue if any, if there by (1) a daughter or daughters or to (2) a son's daughter or daughters or even if there he (3) one daughter and son's daughter or daughters.

764. **Consanguine brother:** He does not inherit as a sharer. He inherits as residuary with the Consanguine sister. He gets double portion. He gets share only, when there is no (1) son (2) son's in (3) daughter (4) son's daughter (5) father (6) true grand-father (7) full brother, (8) full sister.

765. **Consanguine sister:** When only one, she will get one-half, provided there is no (1) child to other. When more than one, they will get three jointly sharing equally. Whether one or more will get one-sixth, provided there is only one full sister and she succeeds sharer, provided further she is not otherwise excluded from inheritance. With the consanguine brother she inherits as a residuary. But the consanguine brother taking a double portion. She also inherits as residuary, if there be no heirs as mentioned under consanguine brother.

766. **Son:** The son is not a sharer. He inherits with the daughter as residuary. The son will get a double portion. Supposing two-third remains after allotting shares of the shares and there is one son and one daughter. The son will get four-ninth, and the daughter will get two-ninth. But if there are two sons and three daughters, then in such case each son will get 4/21, while each daughter will get 2/21. The son and daughter belong to Class-I of residuaries, and the son or the daughter and son together exclude all other residuaries and get the whole residue. Daughter alone inherits as sharer only.

767. **Son's son:** He does not inherit as sharer. He inherits as residuary, provided there is no son or no son's son nearer is degree. If there is son's daughter also, he inherits as residuary with the son's daughter. The son's son will get a double portion.

768. **Full brother:**Full brother does not inherit as sharer. He can however, inherit as residuary, if there is no residuary of classes I and II. He gets a double portion with the full sister.

769. **Full brother's son:** He inherits as residuary, if there be no heirs as already mentioned above. In their absence he gets the residue. Consanguine brother's son: In absence of heirs as already mentioned above, he gets the residue.

770. **Full brother's son's son:** In absence of heirs mentioned above, he gets the residue. Consanguine brother's son's son. In absence of heirs mentioned above, he gets the residue.

771. Then come remoter male descendants of full brother's son's son and consanguine brother's son's son, that is, the son of hill brother's son's son then the son of consanguine brother's son's son, then the son's son of full brother's son, then the son's son, of consanguine brother's son's son and so on in like order.

772. **Full paternal uncle:** In absence of above heirs, he will get, the residue, if any. Consanguine paternal uncle. In absence of above heirs, he will get the residue, if any. Full paternal uncle's son. In absence of above heirs, he will get the residue, if any. Consanguine paternal uncle's son. In absence of above heirs, he will get the residue, if any. Full paternal uncle's son's son. In absence of above heirs, he will get the residure, if any. Consanguine paternal uncle's son's son. In absence of above heirs, he will get the residue, if any.

773. Note: Then come remoter male descendants of full paternal uncle's son's son and consanguine paternal uncle's son's son, in the order and manner of descendants of full brother's son's son given above.

774. Then come the male descendants of more remote true grand-fathers in the order and manner as the deceased's paternal uncles and their sons and son's sons.

775. **Distant kindred:** If there be no sharers or residuaries, the inheritance is divided among Distant Kindred. If the only sharer be a husband or wife, and there be no relation belonging to the class of residuaries, the husband or wife will take his or her full share and the remainder of the estate will be divided among Distant Kindred.

776. The Distant Kindred are divided in four classes, Class-I succeeds in priority to Class-II, Class-II succeeds in priority to Class-III and Class-III succeeds in priority to Class-IV.

777. The order of succession in the first class is to be determined by applying the following two rules:

- The nearer in degree excludes the more remote. For instance daughter's son is preferred to a son's daughter's daughter; and

- Among claimants in the same degree of relationship, the children of sharers and residuaries are preferred to those of Distant Kindred. For instance, a son's daughter' son succeeds in preference to a daughter's daughter's son.

778. The following is the order of succession among Distant Kindred of the first class: (1) daughter's children; (2) son's daughter's children; (3) daughter's grand children; (4) son's son's daughter's children; (5) daughter's great grand-children and son's daughters' grand-children; (6) other descendants of the deceased in like order. Of the above groups, each in turn must be exhausted before any member of the next group can succeed.

779. After ascertaining, which of the descendants of the deceased are entitled to succeed, the next step is to distribute the estate among them. The distribution in this case is governed by the rules, which are as follows:

- If the intermediate ancestors do not differ in their sexes, the estate is to be divided among the claimants per capita according to the rule of the double share of the male.
- If the intermediate ancestors differ in their sexes, the estate is to be distributed according to the following rules:
  (a) The simplest case is where there are only two claimants, the one claiming through one line of ancestors, and the other, claiming through another line. In such a case, the rule is to stop at the first line of descendant in which the sexes of the intermediate ancestors differ and to assign to the male ancestor a portion double that of the female ancestor. The share of the male ancestor will descend to the claimant who claims through him, and the share of the female ancestor will descend to the claimant who claims through her, irrespective of the sexes of the claimants.
  (b) The next case is where there are three or more claimants, each claiming through a different line of ancestors. Here again the rule is to stop at the first line in which the sexes of the intermediate ancestors differ, and assign to each male ancestor a portion double that of each female ancestor. But in this case, the individual share of each ancestor does not descend to his/her descendants as in the preceding case, but the collective share of all the male ancestors is to be divided among all the descendants claiming through them, and the collective share of all the female ancestors is to be divided among their descendants, according to the rule as between claimants in the same group of a double portion the male.
  (c) The last case is where there are two or more claimants claiming through, the same intermediate ancestor. In such a case, there is this further rule to be applied, namely, to count for each such ancestor, if male, as many males as there are claimants claiming through him, and if females as there are claimants claiming through her, irrespective of the sexes of the claimants.

780. If there be no Distant Kindred of first class, the whole state will devolve upon the mother's father as being the nearest relation among Distant Kindred of the second class.

781. If there no mother's father's the estate will devolve upon such of the false ancestors in the third degree as are connected with the deceased through shares, namely, the father's mother's father and the mother's mother's father and of these two, the former, as belonging to the paternal side, will take two-third, and the latter, as belong to the material side, will take one-third.

782. If there be none of those, the estate will devolve upon the remaining false ancestors in the third degree, namely the mother's father's father and the mother's father's mother. And as these two belong to the same (maternal) side, and as, the sexes also of the intermediate ancestor are the same, the former, being a male, will take two-third and the latter, being a female, will take one-third according to rule that the nearer in degree excludes the more remote.

783. If there be no Distant Kindred of the first or second class, the estate devolves upon Distant Kindred of the third class. This comprises such of the descendants of brothers and sisters as are neither shares nor residuaries. The order in succession in this class is to be determined by applying the following three rules on order:

- The nearer in degree excludes the more remote;
- Among claimants in the same degree of relationship, the children or residuaries are preferred to these of Distant Kindred; and
- Among claimants in the same degree of relationship, and not excluded by reason of rule (2), above, the descendants of full brothers exclude those of consanguine brothers and sisters. But the descendants of full sisters do not exclude the descendants of consanguine brothers or sisters, and the latter take the residue, if there be any, after allotting sharers to the descendant of full sisters and of uterine brothers and sisters. The descendants of uterine brothers and sisters are not excluded by descendants either of full or consanguine brothers or sisters but they inherit with them. The above rules lead to the following order of succession among Distant Kindred of the third class. Of the below groups, each in turn must be exhausted before any member of the next group can succeed:
- Full brother's daughters, full sister's children and children of uterine brothers and sisters;
- Full sister's children, children of uterine brothers and sisters, consanguine brother's daughters and consanguine sister's children, the consanguine group taking the residue, if any;
- Consanguine brother's daughters, consanguine sister's children, and children of uterine brothers and sisters;
- Full brothers' sons' daughters (children of residuaries);
- Consanguine brothers' sons' daughters (children of residuaries);
- Full brothers' daughters' children, full sister's grand-children, and grand-children of uterine brothers and sisters;
- Full sister's grand-children, grand-children of uterine brothers and sisters, consanguine brother's daughter's children and consanguine sister's grand-children the consanguine group taking the residue if any;

- Consanguine brother's daughters' children, consanguine sisters' grand-children, and grand-children of uterine brothers and sisters; and
- Remoter descendants of brothers and sisters in like order.

784. After ascertaining which of the descendants of brothers and sisters are entitled to succeed, the next step is to distribute the estate among them, and this is to be done by applying the following rules in order.

785. Rule-1: First, divided the estate among the Roots, that is to say, among the brothers and sisters (as if they were living) and in doing so, treat each brother who has two or more claimants descended from him as so many brothers and each sister who has two or more claimants descended from her as so many sisters. If there is a residue left after assigning their shares to the Roots, but there are no residuaries among the Roots (i.e., neither a full nor consanguine brother), apply the doctrine of return as described in section 5. The hypothetical claimants being brothers and sisters, no case of increase is possible at all.

786. Rule-2: After determining the hypothetical shares of the Roots, the next step is to assign its share to the uterine group. If there be only one claimant in that group, assign one-sixth to him, that being the hypothetical share of his parents. But if there be two more claimants in that group, whether descended from a single uterine brother, or a single uterine sister, or two or more uterine brothers or sisters, assign one-third to them, that being the hypothetical share of their parent or parents, and divide it equally among them without distinction of sex.

787. Rule-3: Lastly, divided the hypothetical shares of the full and consanguine brothers and sisters among their respective descendants as among Distant Kindred of the first case.

788. If there are no Distant Kindred of the first, second or third class, the estate will devolve upon distend kindred of the fourth class in the other given below:

- paternal and maternal uncles and aunts of the deceased, other than his full and consanguine paternal uncles who are residuaries;
- the descendants of all the paternal and maternal uncles and aunts of the deceased, other than sons of his full and consanguine paternal uncles (they being residuaries), the nearer excluding the more remote;
- paternal and maternal uncles and aunts of the parents, other than the full and consanguine paternal uncles of the father who are residuaries;
- the descendants of all the paternal and maternal uncles and aunts of the parents, their sons, of the full and consanguine paternal uncles of the father (they being residuaries), the nearer excluding the more remote;
- paternal and maternal uncles and aunts of the grand-parents, other than the full and consanguine paternal uncles of the father's father who are residuaries;

- the descendants of all the paternal and maternal uncles and aunts of the grandparents, other than the sons of the full and consanguine paternal uncles of the father's father (they being residuaries), the nearer excluding the more remote;
- remoter uncles and aunts and their descendants in like manner and order; and
- of the above groups each in turn must be exhausted before any member of the next group can succeed.

789. To distribute the estate among uncles and aunts of the deceased, proceed as follows:

- First, assign two-third to the paternal side, that is, to paternal uncles and aunts, even if there be only one such, and one-third to the maternal side, that is, to maternal uncles and aunts, even in there be only one such;
- Next, divide the portion assigned to the paternal side, that is, two-third of the estate, among:
  - Full paternal aunts in equal shares: failing them, among;
  - Consanguine paternal aunts in equal shares: and failing them, among; and
  - Uterine paternal uncles and aunts, according to the rule of the double share to the male.
- Lastly divide the portion assigned to the maternal side, that is, one-third of the estate, among:
  - Full maternal uncles and aunts, failing them, among;
  - Consanguine maternal uncles and aunts, and failing them, among; and
  - Uterine maternal uncles and aunts, according to the rule, in each case, of the double share, to the male.

790. If there be no uncle or aunt on the paternal side, the maternal side will take the whole. Similarly, if there be no uncle or aunt on the maternal side, the paternal side will take the whole.

791. **Descendants of uncles and aunts:** If there are no uncles or aunts of the deceased, the estate will devolve upon the descendents of uncles and aunts, other than sons howsoever of full paternal uncles and consanguine paternal uncles who are residuaries. To distribute the estate among these relations, proceed as follows:

- First, assign two-third to the paternal side, that is, to descendants of paternal uncles and aunts, even if there be only one such, and one-third to the maternal side that is, to descendants of maternal uncles and aunts, even if there be only one such;
- Next, divide the portion assigned to the paternal side, that is, two-third of the estate, among:
  - Full paternal aunt's children, failing them, among;
  - Full paternal aunt's children, failing them, among;
  - Consanguine paternal uncle's daughters, failing them, among;
  - Consanguine paternal aunt's children, and failing them, among; and

  - Children to uterine paternal uncles and aunts, the division among the members of each of the five groups above to be made as among Distant Kindred of the first class.
- Lastly, divide the portion assigned to the maternal side, that is, one-third of the estate among:
  - Children of full maternal uncles and aunts, failing them, among;
  - Children of consanguine maternal uncles and aunts, failing them, among; and
- Children of uterine maternal uncles and aunts, the division among the members of each of the three groups above to be made among Distant Kindred of the first class.
- If there be no children of paternal uncles and aunts, the children of maternal uncles and aunts will take the whole. Similarly, if there be no children of maternal uncle and aunts, the children of paternal uncles and aunts will take the whole.
- If there be no children either of paternal uncles and aunts or maternal uncles and aunts, the estate will be divided among their grand-children on the same principles. Failing grand-children, it will be divided among remoter descendants, the nearer decree excluding the more remote.

792. **Other Distant Kindred of the fourth class**: If there are no descendants of uncles and aunts, the estate will devolve upon other Distant Kindred of the fourth class in the order of succession given on pages above the distribution among higher uncle and aunts being governed by the principles stated above and that among their descendants by those stated above.

793. In absence of Distant Kindred inheritance devolves on Successor by Contract, 'and in his absence on' 'Acknowledged Kindred' and in his absence on 'Universal Legatee' and in absence of all, the property escheats to the State.

TABLE OF SHARES – SUNNI LAW

(1)	(2)		(3)	(4)
Shares	Normal Share		Conditions under which the normal share is inherited	This columns sets out:- (A)Shares of Sharers Nos. 3, 4, 5, 8 and 12 as varied by special circumstances; (B)Conditions under which Shares Nos. 1, 2, 7, 8, 11 and 12 succeed as Residuaries.
	of one	of two or more collectively (b)		
1. FATHER	1/6	–	When there is a child or child of a son h.l.s.	[When there is no child or child of a son h.l.s, the father inherits as a residuary: see Tab. of Res., No.3.]
2. TRUE GRANDFATHER [sec. 62 cl. (a)].	1/6	–	When there is a child or child of a son h.l.s. and no father or nearer true grandfather.	[When there is no child or child of a son h.l.s., the Tr. G.F. inherits as a residuary, provided there is no father or nearer Tr. G.F.: see Tab. of Res., No.4].
3. HUSBAND	1/4	–	When there is a child or child of a son h.l.s.	1/2 when no child or child of a son h.l.s.
4. WIFE (c)	1/8	1/8	When there is a child or child of a son h.l.s.	1/4 when no child or child of a son h.l.s.
5. MOTHER	1/6	–	(a)When there is a child or child of a son h.l.s., or (b)When there are two or more brothers or sisters, or even one brother and one sister, whether full consanguine or uterine.	1/3 when no child or child of a son h.l.s., and not more than one brother or sister (if any); but if there is also a wife or husband and the father, then only 1/3 of what remains after deducting the wife's or husband's share.

6. TRUE GRANDMOTHER [sec. 62, cl. (c)].	1/6	1/6	A.Maternal – when no mother, and no nearer true grandmother either paternal or maternal. B.Paternal – when no mother, no father, no nearer true grandmother either paternal or maternal, and no intermediate true grandfather.	
7. DAUGHTER	1/2	2/3	When no son.	[When the son she becomes a residuary: sec Tab. of Res., No.1.]
8. SON'S DAUGHTER h.l.s. [sec. 62, cl. (f)].	1/2	2/3	When no (1) son, (2), daughter, (3) higher sons son, (4) higher son's daughter, or (5) equal son's son (d).	When there is only one daughter, or higher son's daughter but no (1) son, (2) higher son's son, or (3) equal son's son, the daughter will take ½ and the son's daughter h.l.s. (whether one or more) will take 1/6, i.e., 2/3—1/2] [With an equal son's son she becomes a residuary: see Tab. of Res., No.2].
e.g. (i) Son's Daughter	1/2	2/3	When no (1) son, (2), daughter, or (3) son's son.	When there is only one daughter, the son's daughter (whether one or more) will take 1/6, if there be no son or son's son. [With the son's son she becomes a residuary: see Tab of Res. No.2].

(ii) Son's Son's Daughter	1/2	2/3	When no (1) son, (2), daughter, (3) son's son, (4) son's daughter, or (5) son's son's son.	When there is only one daughter or son's daughter, the son's son's daughter (whether one or more) will take 1/6, if there be no (1) son (2) son's son or (3) son's son's son. [With the son's son's son she become: residuary: see Tab of Res. No.2].
9. UTERINE BROTHER	1/6	1/3	When no (1) child, (2) child of a son h.l.s., (3) father or (4) true grandfather.	
10. or SISTER				
11. FULL SISTER	1/2	2/3	When no (1) child, (2) child of a son h.l.s., (3) father (4) true grandfather, or (5) full brother.	[When the full brother she becomes a residuary: see Tab. of Res. No.5.]
12. CONSANGUINE SISTER	1/2	2/3	When no (1) child, (2) child of a son h.l.s., (3) father (4) true grandfather, (5) full brother, (6) full sister, or (7) consanguine brother.	But if there is only one full sister and she succeeds as a sharer, the consanguine sister (whether one or more) will take 1/6, provided she is not otherwise excluded from inheritance. [With the consanguine brother she becomes a residuary: see Tab. of Res., No.7.]

(a) The collective share is always divided equally among those to whom it is allotted.
(b) A Mahomedan can have as many as four wives at a time.
(c) If there be a son's son and a son's son's daughter, the former is a higher son's son in relation to the latter. If there be a son's son and a son's daughter the former is a lower son's son in relation to the latter. And if there be a son's son and son's daughter or a son's son's daughter, the former is in equal son's son in relation to the latter, both being equally removed from the deceased.

B. Shia Laws

794. The Shias divide heirs to two groups namely, (1) heirs by consanguinity, that is, blood relations, and (2) heirs by marriage, that is, husband and wife. Heirs by consanguinity are divided into three classes, and each class is sub-divided into two sections. These classes are respectively composed as follows:

1. (i) Parents;
   (ii) Children and other lineal descendants h.l.s.

2. (i) Grand-parents h.h.s. (true as well as false);
   (iii) Brothers and sisters and their descendants h.l.s.

3. (i) Paternal, and
   (ii) maternal, uncles and aunts, of the deceased, and of his parents and grandparents h.h.s., and their descendants h.l.s.

795. Of these three classes of heirs, the first excludes the second from inheritance, second excludes the third. But the heirs of the two sections of each class succeed together, the nearer degree in each section excluding the more remote in that section.

796. **Husband and wife:** The husband or wife is never excluded from succession, but inherits together with the nearest heirs by consanguinity, the husband taking one-fourth or one-half, and the wife taking one-eighth or one-fourth under the conditions mentioned in the table of sharers.

797. **Table of Sharer Shia Law:** For the purpose of determining the shares of heirs; the Shias divide heirs into two classes, namely, shares and residuaries. There is no separate class of heirs corresponding to the 'Distant Kindred' of Sunni Law.

798. The Sharers are nine in number. The table of shares gives the list of shares together with the shares assigned to them is Shia Law. The descendants h.l.s. of Sharers are also Sharers.

799. **Residuaries:** All heirs other than Sharers and Residuaries. The descendants h.l.s. of Residuaries are also Residuaries.

800. **Distribution of property:** If the deceased left only one heir, the whole property would devolve upon that heir, except in case of a wife. If the only heir be a wife, the older view is that she is entitled to not more than her Quranic share (one-fourth) and the residue (three-fourths) escheats to the Government.

801. If the deceased left two or more heirs, the first step in the distribution of the estate is to assign his/her share to the husband or wife. The next step is to ascertain which of the surviving relations are entitled to succeed, and this is to be done with the help of the rules laid down *infra*. The estate (minus the share of the husband or wife, if any) is then to be divided among those entitled to success according to the rules of distribution applicable to the class to which they belong.

802. **Representation:** The principle of representation has more than one meaning. It may be applied for the purpose of deciding:

(a) what persons are entitled to inherits, or
(b) the quantum of the share given to person on the footing that he is entitled to inherit

803. Where for purpose (a) the rule of exclusion applies that is, the nearer in degree excludes the more remote it is true both of Sunnis and Shias that the principle of representation is not recognized qualifying the rule of exclusion. Thus if A dies leaving him surviving a son and grand-sons by a predeceased son, the grand-sons exclude from inheritance by their uncle. They do not take in their father's stead though he would have been an heir had he survived his father. But if both sons predeceased the propositus who died leaving the grand-sons by one son and two by the other, then all the grand-sons are heirs. In that case, is the principle of representation to be applied for purpose (b), that is for ascertaining the share of each grand-sons? This is a further and different question. If the principle is applied, the grand-sons of one branch will have to divide into three what the grand-sons of the other branch divide in half.

804. For the limited purpose of calculating the share of each heir, as distinct from the purpose of ascertaining the heirs, the Shia Law accepts the principle of representation as a cardinal principle throughout. According to that principle, the descendants of a deceased son, if they are heirs, take the portion which he is living would have taken and in that sense represent the son. In the same limited sense, the descendants of a deceased daughter represent the daughter; if they inherit, they take the portion which the daughter if living would have taken. The principle is applicable in the same way to the descendants of a deceased brother, sister or aunt.

805. The principle of representation is not confined in its operation to descendant, only. It applies in the ascending as well as in the descending line. Thus great grand-parents take the portion which the grand-parents, if living, would have taken:

and the father's uncles and aunts take the portion which the deceased's uncles and aunts if living would have taken.

TABLE OF SHARERS – SHIA LAW:

Sl. No.	*Shares*	*Normal Share*		*Condition under which the share is inherited*	*Share as varied by special circumstances*
		of one	*of two of more collec-tively*		
1.	Husband	1/4	–	When there is a lineal descendant.	1/2 when no such descendant.
2.	Wife	1/8	1/8	When there is a lineal descendant.	1/4 when no such descendant.
3.	Father	1/6	–	When there is a lineal descendant.	[If there be no lineal descendant, father inherits as a residuary.]
4.	Mother	1/6	–	When there is a lineal descendant: or When there are two or more full or consanguine brothers. Or one such brother and two such sisters. Or four such sisters, with the father.	1/3 in other cases.
5.	Daughter	1/2	2/3	When no son –	[With the son she takes as a residuary.]
6.	Uterine Brother	1/6	1/3	When no parent. or lineal descendant. [see section 88]	
7.	or sister				
8.	Full sister	1/2	2/3	When no parent, or lineal descendant, or full brother, or father's father [see sections 88, 101.]	[The full sister takes as a residuary with the full brother and also with the father's father: see section 101.]

Sl. No.	*Shares*	*Normal Share*		*Condition under which the share is inherited*	*Share as varied by special circumstances*
		of one	*of two of more collectively*		
9.	Consanguine sister	1/2	2/3	When no parent or lineal descendant, or full brother, or sister, or consanguine brother, or father's father [see sections 99, 101.]	[The consanguine sister takes as a residuary with the consanguine brother and also with the father's father: see section 101.]

Note – The descendants h.l.s. of sharers are also sharers.

806. **Stirpital succession:** Succession among descendants in each of three classes of heirs is per stripes and not per capita.

807. **Succession among descendants:** The descendants of a person who, if living, would have taken as Sharers, succeed as Sharers. The descendants of a person who, if living, would have taken as a Residuaries.

808. **Distribution among Heirs of the First Class:** Rules of succession among heirs of the first class. The persons who are entitled to succeed to the estate of a deceased Shia Muslim are the heirs of the first class alongwith the husband or wife, if any. The first class of heirs comprises parents, children, grand-children, and remoter lineal descendants of the deceased. The parents inherit together with children named, failing children, with grand-children, and, failing grand-children, with remoter lineal descendants of the deceased, the nearer excluding the more remote [section 88]. Succession in this class is governed by the following rules:

(1) **Father:** The father takes one-sixth as a Sharer if there is a lineal descendant; as a Residuary, it there be no lineal descendant [see Tab. of Sh. No. 3].
(2) **Mother:** The mother is always a Sharer, and her share is one-sixth or one-third [see Tab. of Sh. No.4].
(3) **Son:** The son always takes as a Residuary.
(4) **Daughter:** The daughter inherits as a Sharer, unless there is a son in which case she takes as a Residuary with him according to the rules of the double share to the male [see Tab. of Sh. No. 5].
(5) **Grand-children:** On failure of children, the grand-children stand in the place of their respective parents, and they inherit according to the principle of representation described in sections 93, 94 and 95, that is to say:

(i) The children of each son take the portion which their father, if living, would have taken as a Residuary, and divide it among them according to the rule of the double share to the male.
(ii) the children of each daughter take the portion which their mother, if living would have taken either as a Sharer or as a Residuary and divide it among them also according to the double share to the male.

(6) **Remoter lineal descendants:** Succession among remoter lineal descendants is governed by the same principle of representation, that is to say, great-grandchildren take the portion which their respective parents, if living, would have taken, and divide it among them according to the rule of the double share to the male, and great great-grandchildren take the protection which their respective parents, if living, would have taken, and divide it among them also according to the same rule.

809. **Distribution among Heirs of the Second Class:** Rules of succession among heirs of the second class. If there are no heirs of the first class, the estate (minus the share of the husband or wife, if any) devolves upon the heirs of the second class. The second class of heirs comprises grand-parents h.h.s. and brothers and sisters and their descendants h.l.s. (section 88). The rules of succession among the heirs of their class are different accordingly as the surviving relations are:

(1) grand-parents h.h.s. without brothers or sisters or their descendants;
(2) brothers and sisters or their descendant, without grand-parents or remoter ancestors;
(3) grand-parents h.h.s. with brothers and sisters or their descendants.

810. **Grand-parent h.h.s., without brothers of sisters of their descendants:** If there are no brothers of sisters, or descendants of brothers of sisters, the estate (minus the share of the husband or wife, if any) is to be distributed among grand-parents according to the following rules:

(1) if the deceased left all his four grand-parents surviving, the paternal grand-parents take two-thirds, and divide it between them according to the rule of the double share to the male, and the maternal grand-parents take one-third, and divide it equality between them;
(2) if there is only one grand-parent on the paternal side, he/she takes the entire two-third. Similarly, if there is only one grand-parent on the maternal side, he/she takes the entire one-third; and
(3) if there are no grand-parents the property will devolve according to the same rules upon remoter ancestors of the deceased, the nearer excluding the more remote.

811. **Brothers and sisters, without any ancestor:** If the deceased left no ancestors, but brothers, of various kind, the estate (minus the share of the husband or wife, if any) will be distributed among them according to the same rules as those in Hanafi Law.

812. **Descendants of brothers and sisters, without any ancestor:** If there are no brothers of sisters of any kind, and no ancestors, but there are children of brothers and of sisters, the estate (minus the share of the husband or wife, if any) will devolve upon them according to the principle of representation described in sections 93, 94, 95, that is to say:

(1) the children of each full or consanguine brother will take the portion which their father, if living, would have taken as a Residuary, and they will divide it among them according to the rule of the double share to the male; and the children of each full or consanguine sister will take the portion which their mother, if living, would have taken either as a Sharer or as a Residuary, and they will divide it among them accordingly also to the rule of the double share to the male;
(2) the children of each uterine brother will take the portion which their father, if living, would have taken as a Sharer, and they will divide it equally among them and so will the children of each uterine sister; and
(3) if there are no children of brothers or sisters, the estate will, devolve upon the grand-children of brothers and sisters according to the principle of representation, that is to say the grand-children of full or consanguine brothers and sisters take the portion which their respective parents, if living, would have taken and divide it among them according to the rule of the double, share in male, he and the grand-children of uterine brothers and sisters take the portion which their respective parents, if living, would have taken, and divide it equally among them without distinction of sex.

813. **Grand-parents and remoter ancestor with brothers and sisters of their descendants:** If the deceased left grand-parents, and also brother or sisters, the estate (minus the share of the husband or wife, if any) is to be distributed among grand-parents and brothers and sisters, according to the following rules:

(a) a paternal grand-father counts as a full or consanguine brother, and a paternal grand-mother counts as a full or consanguine sister; and
(b) a maternal grand-father counts as a uterine brother and a maternal grand mother counts as a uterine sister.

814. On failure of grand-parents, the remoter ancestors of the deceased stand in the place of the grand-parents through whom they are respectively connected with the deceased. On failure of brothers or sisters, their descendants stand in the place of their respective parents.

815. **Distribution among Heirs of the Third class:** Order of succession among heirs of the third class. If there are no heirs of the first or second class, the estate (minus the share of the husband or wife, if any) devolves upon the heirs of the class in the order given below:

- paternal and maternal uncles and aunts of the deceased;
- their descendants h.l.s. nearer in degree excluding the more remote;
- paternal and maternal uncles and aunts of the parents;
- their descendants h.l.s. the nearer in degree excluding the more remote;
- paternal and maternal uncles and aunts of the grand-parents;
- their descendants h.l.s., the nearer in degree excluding the more remote;
- remoter uncles and aunts and their descendants in like order; and
- of the above groups each in turn must be exhausted before any member of the next group can succeed.

816. Exception: If the only claimants be the son of a full paternal uncle and consanguine paternal uncle, the former, though he belongs to group (2), excludes the latter who is nearer though he belongs to group (1).

817. Uncles and Aunts: To distribute the estate among uncles and aunts proceed as follows:

(1) First, assign two-third of the estate to the paternal side, that is, to paternal uncles and aunts, even if there be only one such, and one-third to the maternal side, that is, to maternal uncles and aunts, even if there be only one such.
(2) Next, divide the portion assigned to the paternal side (i.e., two-third of the estate) among the paternal uncles and aunts exactly as if they were brothers and sisters of the deceased, that is to say:

   (i) assign to uterine paternal uncles and aunts:
      (a) if there be two or more of them, one-third to be equally divided among them; and
      (b) if there be only one of them, one-sixth.
   (ii) divide the remainder among full paternal uncles and aunts according to the rule of the double share to the male, and, failing them, among consanguine paternal uncles and aunts according to same rule.

(3) Lastly, divide the portion assigned to the maternal side, among the maternal uncles and aunts as follows:

   (i) assign to uterine maternal uncles and aunts:
      (a) if there be two or more of them, one-third to be equally divided among them; and
      (b) if there be only one of them, one-sixth.
   (ii) divide the remainder equally among full maternal uncles and aunts, and, failing them among consanguine maternal uncles and aunts.

(4) If there be no uncle or aunt on the maternal side paternal side takes the whole. Similarly if there be no uncle or aunt on the paternal side, the maternal side takes the whole.

818. **Descendants of uncles and aunts.** If there are no uncles or aunts of any kind, children of deceased uncles and aunts take the portion of their respective parents according to the principle of representation described in sections 80, 81 and 82, the children of each full or consanguine paternal uncle or aunt dividing their parents share among them according to the rule of the double share to the male, and the children of each of the remaining uncles, and aunts, that is, of uterine paternal uncles and of maternal uncles and aunts, whether full, consanguine or uterine, dividing their parents share equally among them.

819. If there are no children of uncles or aunts, the grand-children of uncles and aunts take the portion of their respective parents according to the same principle.

820. **Other heirs of the third class:** If there are no descendants of uncles or aunts, the estate will devolve upon the other heirs of the third class in the order of succession the distribution among higher uncles and aunts being governed by the principles and that among their descendants being governed by the principles, the 'Return' and the 'Increase.'

821. Doctrine of 'Return': If there is a residue left after satisfying the claims of Sharers, but there are no Residuaries in the class to which the sharers belong the residue reverts, subject to the three exceptions noted in sections 107, 108 and 109, to the Sharers in the proportion of their respective shares.

822. Husband and wife and 'Return': Neither the husband nor the wife is entitled to the Return if there is any other heir. If the deceased left a husband but no other heir, the surplus will pass to the husband by Return. If the deceased left a, wife, but no other heir, the older view was that the wife will take her share of one-fourth, and the surplus will escheat to the Crown; in other words that the surplus never reverts to a wife.

823. Mother when excluded from 'Return': If the deceased left a mother, a father, and one daughter, and also:

(a) two or more full or consanguine brothers, or
(b) one such brother and two such sisters, or
(c) four such sisters,

the brothers and sisters, though they themselves excluded from inheritance as being heirs of the second class, prevent the mother from participating in the Return, and the surplus reverts to the father and the daughter in the proportion of their respective shares. This is the only case in which the mother is excluded from the Return.

824. **Uterine brothers and sisters when excluded from 'Return':** If there are uterine brothers or sisters, and also full sisters, the uterine brothers, and sisters are not entitled to participate in the Return, and the residue goes entirely to the full sisters. This rule does not apply to consanguine sisters. Consanguine sisters and uterine brothers and sisters divide the Return in proportion to their shares.

825. **Doctrine of 'Increase':** The Sunni doctrine of increase is not recognized in the Shia Law. According to the Shia Law, if the sum total of the sharers exceeds unity, the fraction in excess of the unity is deducted invariably from the share of:

(a) the daughter or daughters; or
(b) full or consanguine sister or sisters.

826. **Escheat:** On failure of all natural heirs, the estate of a deceased Shia Islamic escheats to the Government.

827. **Miscellaneous:** Eldest son: The eldest son, if of sound mind is, exclusively entitled to the wearing apparel of the father, and to his Koran, sword and ring, provided the deceased has left property besides those articles. Childless widow: A childless widow takes no share in her husband's lands, but she is entitled to her one-fourth share in the value of trees and buildings standing thereon, as well as in his moveable property including debts due to him though they may be secured by a usufructuary mortgage or otherwise. Illegitimate child: An illegitimate child does not inherit at all, not even from his mother or her relations, nor do they inherit from him.

828. Inheritance. Shia Law. Paternal and maternal uncles and aunts of deceased and their descendants. Order of succession. Maternal uncles and aunts living at the time of death of propositus would be entitled to inherit estate of deceased as against descendants of paternal uncles and aunts. Paternal uncles and aunts would get two-third share of estate, but in their absence, maternal uncles and aunts would take the whole of estate of deceased. In absence of any uncle or aunt on both paternal and maternal sides, children of deceased uncles and aunts could inherit proportionate share of his/their predecessor (LHC – YLR 227).

829. Islamic Law. Inheritance. Shia law. Issueless widow of a deceased who belonged to Fiqah Jafaria was excluded from the estate of the deceased. Validity: Mutation of inheritance suffering front no legal or jurisdictional defects, Court declined interference (LHC – 2000 YLR 2580).

830. Islamic Law Inheritance. Shia sect. Original owner of house in question admittedly being Shia by faith, plaintiff being his sister, was his sole heir (he having died issueless). Ownership of house in question, would automatically vest in plaintiff sister by way of inheritance (LHC – 1993 CLC 2152).

831. Islamic Law Inheritance. Deceased Muslim dying issueless. Question of sect of deceased. Determination. Initial presumption is in favour of Hanafi Fiqa. Plaintiffs though averred in plaint that deceased was a Sunni by faith, yet did not produce an iota of evidence in rebuttal to defendant's evidence that deceased's father was Shia by faith. Initial presumption is that the Muslim population of the sub-continent belongs principally to Hanafi School. Muslim male or female is presumed to have the faith of his/her father and can renounce the faith when he/she acquired the age of puberty. Deceased Muslim having died at the tender age would be presumed to have the faith of his father who had been proved on record to be a

Shia. Deceased Muslim would thus be deemed to be a Shia by faith (LHC – 1989 CLC 1712).

832. Islamic Law Inheritance (Shia Law). Childless widow of an 'Asna Asharia' Muslim could not inherit any portion of the lands left behind by him (SCP – 1972 PLD 346).

833. Inheritance. Sunny or Shia faith, of deceased. Proof. Witnesses alleged that deceased was Shia; her funeral rites were conducted in accordance with Shia faith; she had attended Majalis and made contribution to a Shia organization. Validity: Witnesses had not disclosed their source, basis and reason for deceased having Shia faith. Witnesses had not disclosed particulars of modalities of alleged burial and funeral rights of deceased. Neither ladies having given last bath and coffin to deceased nor Imam leading Janaza prayer of deceased had been produced in evidence. No witness had been produced to prove as to whether deceased had ever offered prayers, if so, then under which Fiqah and faith (LHC – 2005 YLR 233)

834. Widow and brother. Plea of brother was that he to the exclusion of childless widow was entitled to inherit whole land left by deceased belonging to Shia Sect. Proof. Burden to prove such plea was lying on brother. Widow was still receiving family pension of deceased as supported by an entry made in Pension Book. Mutation of land sanctioned in accordance with Sunni Personal Law had not been challenged by brother in Revenue hierarchy. Widow had applied for partition of land and notice had been issued to brother. Brother had not produced any convincing evidence that deceased belonged to Fiqa Jafria. Brother and his witness in their statements in Court had shown ignorance about the manner in which funeral ceremonies of deceased had been conducted (SCP – 2004 SCMR 1783).

835. Islamic Law Inheritance. Deceased survived with one daughter, children of predeceased daughter and a sister. Petitioners claimed inheritance in the estate of the deceased on the basis of their being collaterals of deceased. Validity: Deceased was whether 'Shia' or 'Sunni', the petitioners could in either case, have no right to inherit any share in the estate left by the deceased. Findings of the two Courts below and that of the High Court were upheld. No fault could be found with the judgment of the High Court, as the same proceeded on correct application of the relevant principles of law to the facts and circumstances of the case. Supreme Court declined to interfere with order of the High Court. Leave to appeal was refused in circumstances (SCP – 2000 SCMR 672).

III. Case Laws Inheritance and Succession

836. Inheritance. Plaintiff claimed that his father was son of real brother of female who was widow of person who died issueless in India; that said female was limited owner of property in question and that after her death property in-question had to be reverted to him and not to female who was sister of his grandfather, who died issueless. Suit was dismissed by Trial Court, but decreed in appeal. Validity:

No evidence was available on record to prove that said female died issueless as limited owner. Mutation of her inheritance of property devolving upon her from her husband, had not been produced on record. Whether she received disputed property as full owner or limited owner, had not been proved. Plaintiff, in circumstances had failed to prove that said female was limited owner, and that father of plaintiff was her real brother. Suit filed by plaintiff otherwise was hopelessly barred by time. Revision filed by defendants was allowed and judgment of Appellate Court was set aside and that of Trial Court was restored. (LHC – 2005 CLC 419).

837. Amount of Benevolent Fund and Group Insurance would devolve upon the heirs, of the deceased being his 'Tarka'. Mother of the deceased, who was nominee, would not be entitled exclusively to claim such amounts except to the extent of her share as per Shariat with other legal heirs of the deceased (SCP – 2005 SCMR 512).

838. Inheritance. Estoppel. Under Islamic Law of Inheritance as soon as owner dies succession to his property opens. Due share of inheritance vests in the heirs. Any entry in mutation contrary to law did not operate as estoppels (LHC – 2005 MLD 1).

839. Inheritance. Hanfi Law. Share of sister of issueless deceased brother. Concurrent findings of fact by the Courts below. Owner of suit property died issueless leaving behind one sister and two sons of predeceased brother. Trial Court declared that under Hanfi Law, sister was entitled to one-half the share of land owned by issueless deceased brother. Judgment and decree passed by Trial Court was maintained by Appellate Court. Validity: Table of shares as given in Hanfi Law prescribed one-half share for sister of issueless deceased. Both the Courts below had rightly decided the suit and appeal in favour of plaintiffs. Defendants failed to point out any legal infirmity in the conclusion recorded in the judgments and decrees passed by the Courts below. High Court declined to interfere in the well-reasoned judgments and decrees of Trial Court and Appellate Court concurrently adjudicating the question of law and facts involved in the controversy (LHC – 2005 MLD 280).

840. Distant Kindred. Distant Kindred inherit only when there are no sharers or residuaries. If a sharer or residuary exists, the Distant Kindred are completely ousted from the inheritance. Principles (SCP – 2004 PLD 768).

841. Limitation would not apply to enforcement of right of inheritance in estate of deceased predecessor (LHC – 2004 PLD 1).

842. Custom, applicability of land in dispute was not devolved upon original owner from his ancestors, but same was his self-acquired property. Original owner died in 1942 leaving behind one son and two daughters; but mutation of inheritance was got sanctioned by the only son of deceased in his name without disclosing existence of two 'daughters of deceased as his legal heirs. Mutation in favour of son of deceased was challenged by two daughters of deceased 'claiming their inheritance rights in disputed land in accordance with Islamic Law of inheritance. Son of deceased had asserted that in the Mauza concerned custom was prevalent under which daughters of deceased were not entitled to get any inheritance from their father (LHC – 2004 CLC 1665).

843. Deceased not owning property at time of death, but only his claim, according to which allotment was to be made was pending. Such claim would go to entire family on death of deceased before allotment (SCP – 2004 SCMR 94).

844. Share of daughters in absence of son. Declaration of title. Co-sharers. Limitation. Dispute was with regard to sanction of inheritance whereby whole property of deceased owner was transferred in the name of two daughters. Plea raised by the plaintiffs was that in absence of son, the whole property could not be inherited by the daughters and sale of land by the daughters in excess of their share was void. Validity: In absence of son, two daughters, under Islamic Law could not inherit whole property, and both of them could inherit two-third share in the land devolved on them. Remaining one-third share had devolved on the collaterals of the deceased owner, and they had become joint owners along with two daughters. Suit was not barred to the extent of declaration that the sale of land made by the, daughters in excess of two-third share was not valid and thus ineffective against one-third share of the collaterals. Suit filed by the plaintiffs was partly decreed, and the plaintiffs and the other collaterals of the deceased owner were declared as entitled to inherit one-third of the suit-land. Sale made in excess of two-third of the share was invalid and ineffective against the rights of collaterals. Appeal was allowed by the Supreme Court accordingly (SCP – 2004 SCMR 432).

845. Opening of succession. Inheritance under Muslim Personal Law takes place automatically, and each legal heir is entitled to get his respective share irrespective of any claim or demand therefore (SCP – 2004 SCMR 1391).

846. Existence of custom depriving females from inheritance at time of opening of succession. Proof. Once such custom was not proved, then property would devolve in accordance with normal principles of Islamic inheritance (SCP – 2004 SCMR 1524).

847. Sect. Proof. Sunni or Shia sect of deceased. Deceased left a childless Inheritance. Hanfi Law. Original owner of the property died leaving behind only one daughter and two daughters of his deceased brother. Inheritance mutation was sanctioned in favour of only daughter of deceased wherein one-half share out of estate of deceased was granted to her as Sharer and remaining one half was granted to her on return of the residue in absence of any residuaries. Daughters of deceased brother of original owner, claimed residue one-half after satisfaction of the share of daughter of original owner as the sharer. Validity: In the present case, there being no residuaries, only daughter of deceased owner was held entitled by the Board of Revenue to one-half as sharer and residue one-half on the right of reverter or 'Return'. Only daughter of deceased owner under Hanfi Law of Inheritance was entitled to inherit from the estate of her deceased father one-half share as the sharer and the remaining one-half share as the residue in absence of residuary (LHC – 2004 MLD 1136).

848. Court, in the cases which involved inheritance inter se among legal heirs, should make efforts to ensure that no legal heir was denied his legal share in the estate of deceased on a technical ground (PHC – 2004 YLR 340).

849. Islamic Law Inheritance. Opening of. Inheritance of Muslim deceased opens at the time of death of Muslim owner of the property (LHC – 2003 PLD 186).

850. Islamic Law Inheritance. Gift. Contest between brother and sister. Brother claiming entire property to the exclusion of his sister on the basis of gift made by his mother. Proof. Mother ordinarily is much more concerned about welfare of her daughter and is not expected to deprive her daughter of her share in inheritance without exceptionally strong reasons. Exceptionally strong reason must exist to satisfy judicial conscience that daughter had rightly been disinherited by mother (LHC – 2003 CLC 485).

851. Plaintiff's plea was that she, as sole widow of deceased, was entitled to inherit one-fourth share in his estate as he had died issueless, and he after divorcing his first wife had contracted second marriage with her. Defendant (legal heirs of first wife) claimed that she survived deceased as his wedded wife. Defendants in written statement admitted plaintiff as second wife of deceased, but denied that deceased had earlier divorced his first wife. Suit was decreed by Trial Court and was upheld by Appellate Court. Validity: None of defendant's witnesses had categorically denied suggestion that deceased had married plaintiff after divorcing his first wife. Courts below after reviewing entire evidence on record had come to concurrent conclusion that first wife had been divorced by deceased before contracting marriage with plaintiff. Conclusion drawn by Courts below that plaintiff was only surviving widow of deceased and thus, was entitled to her Muslim Law share of one-fourth in his estate, was neither fanciful nor arbitrary. Courts below were justified in reaching such conclusion on basis of facts such as admitted residence of plaintiff with deceased prior to his death; performance of Hajj by deceased and plaintiff together, and the fact that the other wife had died in house of her parents instead of in the house of deceased. No misreading or non-reading of evidence on record or any material irregularity in exercise of jurisdiction was indicated. High Court dismissed revision petition in circumstances (LHC – 2003 CLC 849).

852. Original owner of property in dispute died unmarried and his mother after death of her husband/father of deceased owner, married with brother of her deceased husband/uncle of the original owner. Mutation of inheritance was attested in favour of the mother, real sister and five uterine brothers and sisters of deceased original owner. Mother of deceased owner was thus entitled to one-sixth share, his real sister was entitled to one-half share while his uterine brothers and sisters were collectively entitled to one-third as sharers. Entire estate of deceased owner, in circumstances, was devolved on mother, real sister and uterine brothers and sisters of deceased as sharers. Since nothing was left after satisfying claim of sharers, residuaries would not be entitled to inherit estate of deceased (LHC - 2003 CLC 897).

853. Devolution of property would take place through inheritance immediately without any other intervention irrespective of the fact whether mutation of inheritance was recorded or not or was incorrectly recorded. Wrong mutation would confer no right in property as Revenue Record was maintained only for the purposes of ensuring realization of land revenue. No question of limitation in inheritance suits. Co-heirs-co-sharer who was in possession, would be deemed to hold possession on behalf of other co-sharers. Persons in possession of land being in constructive possession on behalf of other co-sharers, mere omission by them to pay their share of produce would not constitute their ouster (LHC – 2003 CLC 1593).

854. Islamic Law Inheritance. Relationship of husband and daughter with deceased woman. Proof. Last male owner was survived by his mother and sister. Petitioners as collateral of last male owner claimed to be exclusive owner of suit land. Respondents claimed to be entitled to one-half share in suit land being husband and daughter of the deceased sister of last male owner. Trial Court declared petitioners to be entitled to one-half share in suit land, while remaining half would vest in respondents as husband and daughter of deceased sister of last male owner. Appellate Court in appeal by petitioners accepted their claim to be exclusive owners of suit land. High Court in revision set aside such findings of Appellate Court. Contention of petitioners was that respondents had not proved their such relationship with deceased sister of last male owner, thus, her half share would revert back to petitioners as collateral of last male owner. Validity: Copy of judgment of Family Court placed on record showed that deceased sister of last male owner while appearing as defence-witness in a suit for restitution of conjugal rights filed against her by another person had stated that she was married to respondent husband and that respondent-daughter was born as a result of such wedlock, and that she was never married to plaintiff in that suit. Such statement was supported by another witness, who stated that she had been living with respondent-husband for the last thirty-two years. Such other person while appearing as witness in a suit filed against him by deceased sister of last male owner claiming damages for defamation had stated on oath that respondent-daughter was born as result of her wedlock with respondent-husband. Findings of Appellate Court were based on gross misreading of such overwhelming evidence and same were perverse, which had rightly been reversed by High Court in exercise of its jurisdiction under section 115, C.P.C. Impugned judgment was based on proper appreciation of evidence and material available on record, wherein no misreading or non-reading of evidence or misconstruction of facts and law was found. Supreme Court dismissed the petition for leave to appeal in circumstances. Constitution of Pakistan (1973), Article 185(3). Civil Procedure Code (V of 1908), section 115 (SCP – 2003 SCMR 125).

855. Islamic Law Inheritance. Upon opening of inheritance, rights and interests in the estate of deceased, automatically would devolve upon the heirs of deceased. Denial of right of one heir by others would not mean that if such heir was legitimately entitled to his share in inheritance, he would be deprived of same upon denial or incorporation of illegal mutation of inheritance. Sanctioning of mutation of inheritance would not deprive the person of the title because inheritance mutation was not a document of title and would not settle question of ownership between the parties (LHC – 2003 MLD 399).

856. Islamic Law Inheritance. Daughter of predeceased son of original owner was only entitled to her Quranic share from estate of her deceased father. Other successors-in-interest of original owner would get their shares according to principles of inheritance (LHC – 2003 MLD 484).

857. Children of predeceased son, right of. Such children would be excluded from succession in presence of their uncles and aunts (i.e., sons and daughters of deceased). Illustration (SHC – 2003 YLR 1250).

858. Islamic Law Inheritance. In absence of residuaries, entire property left by the owner would revert to real sister of owner on account of principle of return, if owner died issueless (Supreme Court Azad Kashmir – 2003 YLR 389).

859. Sections 42 & 54. Islamic Law. Inheritance. Suit for declaration and permanent injunction. Original owner of suit property who had two sons and two daughters having died, property left by him was to be inherited by his sons and daughters as his legal heirs. No proof was available that suit property was partitioned between legal heirs of deceased. Plaintiffs who were legal heirs of one of daughters of deceased owner of suit property, had claimed themselves to be exclusive owners of suit property. Plaintiffs could not produce any title deed in proof of their claim, but had placed on record a copy of assessment for year 1951–1952 according to which suit property was in name of their mother who was one of daughters of deceased owner of said property. Suit was resisted by legal heirs of one of sons of deceased owner contending that suit property being ancestral property owned by their grandfather, could not be solely claimed by plaintiffs. Suit was dismissed by Trial Court on ground that plaintiff could not produce any title document in favour of their deceased mother, but Appellate Court reversed finding of Trial Court and accepted claim of plaintiffs on basis of assessment for year 1951–1952. Admitted position between parties being that predecessor-in-interest was owner of property in dispute, none of parties could claim exclusive ownership of property. Assessment for year 1951–1952 relied upon by plaintiffs, was not title deed. Judgment and decree passed by Appellate Court below were modified declaring that parents were joint owners of suit property and parties could seek their remedy for partition of suit property in accordance with law (LHC – 2002 YLR 2398).

860. Inheritance Opening. When a person demises, his succession opens at the same moment and according to the Sharia, all the persons who are entitled to inherit his estate, immediately and automatically become co-sharers of the estate left by the deceased (LHC – 2002 YLR 3247).

861. Occupancy tenant died leaving behind four sons and two daughters, but mutation in respect of property comprising in occupancy tenancy left by deceased was attested in favour of four sons of deceased and names of his daughters of deceased were omitted. Legal heirs of deceased daughters had filed suit to the effect that their deceased mothers being daughters of deceased occupancy tenant were entitled to inherit property comprising in occupancy tenancy of the deceased. Omission of names of daughters of deceased was without any legal or moral justification when at the relevant time rule of inheritance was Islamic Law. Even if mothers of plaintiffs were not in possession of suit property, sons of deceased who happened to be sharers, would be deemed to be in possession on their behalf as well. Heir in possession of property of his predecessor, had to be considered to be in constructive possession of property on behalf of other heirs in spite of his exclusive possession. Possession of brothers in circumstances would be taken to be possession of their sisters as well. Dispute being among legal heirs of deceased same could be taken to Civil Court without having recourse to any other proceedings. Trial Court, in circumstances, had rightly decreed the suit, and Appellate Court was not justified to set aside judgment and decree of Trial Court. High Court set aside judgment and decree passed by Appellate Court and restored those of Trial Court (PHC – 2002 YLR 608).

862. Mutation qua legacy of deceased initially was attested in names of petitioners who claimed to be sisters of deceased and respondents who were widows of deceased. Subsequently on basis of 'Fatwa', names of other two respondents were also added in mutation of inheritance as residuaries. Petitioners questioned mutation alleging that respondents other than two respondents being not related to deceased, had no concern with legacy of deceased. Courts below without framing issue and recording evidence on such salient feature of the case merely on scanty record on the issue involved, accepted respondents said two other respondents in capacity of residuaries and gave the respondents inheritance of deceased. Judgments and decrees of Courts below being open to exception, were set aside by High Court and remanded case to decide the same after framing fresh issue and allowing parties to lead their evidence on freshly framed issues (PHC – 2002 YLR 3849).

863. Deceased having died issueless was survived by progeny of his two brothers. Question of inheritance was to be resolved by keeping in view the position/ status of the progeny of such two brothers that is, as residuaries being at equal distances from the deceased, and they will inherit not as representing their respective fathers as a group but equally being placed in scenario for the purposes of inheritance to the estate of the deceased (SCP – 2000 SCMR 1574).

864. Islamic Law Inheritance. Release deed in favour of defendant. Effect. Partition suit was decreed by Trial Court. Appellate Court upheld the findings of the Trial Court and appeal was dismissed. Validity: Release deed relied upon by defendant did not stand in the way of the plaintiff to inherit his legal share in the property left by his predecessor-in-interest, as he was undisputedly son of the deceased. Both the Courts below had concurrently held the plaintiff entitled to his share in the property. Where the defendant failed to point out any illegality, irregularity, misreading of the evidence or non-reading of material evidence or any jurisdictional error in coming to the concurrent findings of fact, judgments and decrees of both the Courts below did not require any interference by the High Court in revision (PHC – 2000 MLD 1868).

865. Islamic Law Gift. Death-bed gift and acknowledgment. Alienation of property. Only restraint imposed by Muslim Laws upon a Muslim relates to will and gifts on death-bed (LHC – 2000 YLR 242).

866. Requirement of mutation. Necessity. When a Muslim owner dies, his estate passes on to the legal heirs in accordance with the Quranic Injunctions. No mutation or any other act of the State or individual is required for acquisition of the proprietary rights by inheritance (LHC – 2000 YLR 621).

867. Devolution of estate of a Muslim deceased. Scope. Estate of the last male owner comes to vest in his heirs, the moment he breaths his last. Under the Islamic jurisprudence no State or individual intervention is required or is necessary for such devolution upon the heirs of the deceased defined in the Holy Quran in accordance with the shares allocated to them (LHC – 2000 YLR 633).

868. Appellants asserted that respondent was not daughter of the deceased and had been wrongly included in the legal heirs of the deceased. Validity: Evidence led by parties preponderantly showed that respondent, although daughter of the widow yet was not daughter of the deceased. Judgment and decree passed by Court, in favour of the respondent were set aside (LHC – 2000 YLR 1496).

869. Petitioners had claimed that after death of the lady who was a limited owner and refugee right holder of land in dispute their deceased father was entitled to inherent said land as collateral on basis of pedigree-table, and he filed suit in this behalf. Respondents who later on had also filed suit, had claimed that deceased lady was not limited owner, and plaintiffs were not collateral of deceased lady and, thus, respondents were entitled to inherent land in dispute. Both suits were consolidated, and suit filed by predecessor-in-interest of petitioners was dismissed up to High Court, whereas suit filed by respondents was decreed. Leave to appeal to Supreme Court was granted to consider as to whether decrees in suit were passed in accordance with law and evidence on record. Constitution of Pakistan (1973), Article 185(3) (SCP – 1999 SCMR 1318).

870. Limitation. No principle of limitation could be used to defeat visible right of inheritance (LHC – 1999 MLD 1140).

871. Sect of deceased person. Reliance was placed on the death certificate of the deceased to prove the sect of the deceased. Validity: Person who reported the death of the deceased appeared as a 'witness' in the Trial Court and denied the assertion that the deceased was Shia by sect. Presumption was that every Muslim citizen was a Sunni sinless otherwise proved (LHC – 1999 YLR 2692).

872. No one is to be excluded from succeeding to the estate on the basis of technicalities (SHC – 1999 YLR 2078).

873. Specific Relief Act (I of 1877), section 42. Constitution of Pakistan (1973), Article 185(3). Inheritance. Adverse possession. Limitation. Last male owner having died in 1936, his inheritance mutation was attested in 1937, whereby his daughters and widow were deprived of their share of inheritance while his nephews got his whole property claiming that their tribe was governed by custom whereby females were excluded from inheritance. Trial Court dismissed plaintiff's claim while Appellate Court and High Court decreed their suit on the ground that tribe of plaintiffs was governed by Islamic Law and not by custom, and that two daughters and widow were entitled to succeed to their respective shares of inheritance. Validity: Land in question, admittedly, belonged to predecessor-in-interest of plaintiffs who died sometime in 1935–1936, and his inheritance mutation was attested in 1937 wherefrom plaintiffs were excluded from inheritance whose relationship with deceased male owner was not denied. Main question, however, for determination was that of limitation and adverse possession for more than twelve years. Leave to appeal was, thus, granted to determine legal question relating to limitation and adverse possession (SCP – 1998 PLD 1512).

874. Constitution of Pakistan (1973), Article 185(3). Inheritance of last Muslim male owner. Trial Court found collateral to be entitled to two-third share of property left by deceased who had died issueless while mother of deceased was entitled to one-third share of property left by deceased. Plaintiff's share was, thus, calculated to be 2 Marlas and he being in possession of same to the extent of 2 Marlas, his suit was dismissed. First Appellate Court concurred with finding of Trial Court. High Court in second appeal on basis of evidence on record worked out share of plaintiff to be 4 Marlas instead of 2 Marlas as found by Courts below. Validity: Judgment of High Court was assailed on the ground that while hearing second appeal, it could not interfere with concurrent findings of fact recorded by two Courts below; that in absence of any misreading of evidence by two Courts below, mere fact that on reappraisal of evidence another view was possible, concurrent finding of fact could not be disturbed in second appeal by High Court. Contention raised would require examination. Leave to appeal to Supreme Court was granted to examine the contention raised (SCP – 1998 SCMR 733).

875. Co-heirs. Co-sharer claiming title through adverse possession. Presumption relating to possession of joint property. Defendant being co-heirs claimed to have matured their title through adverse possession. Validity: Parties to suit being co-heirs/co-sharers, possession of one co-sharer/co-heir was presumed to be possession of others. Male co-heir could not allege adverse possession against female co-heir (PHC – 1998 MLD 1857).

876. Issueless widow. Full brothers sons. Entitlement to inherit widows share on her death. Widow had inherited estate left by her husband as sharer to the extent of one-fourth whereas remaining three-fourth share had gone to legal descendants of deceased male landowner. Respondents who were sons of her brothers on widow's death, were entitled to inherit estate left by the widow as being full brothers sons. Courts below had committed no error in law while declining claims of appellants that is, descendants of male landowner. Azad Jammu and Kashmir Interim Constitution Act (VIII of 1974), section 42 (Supreme Court, Azad Kashmir – 1998 MLD 411).

877. Islamic Law Inheritance. Duty of Court. In cases which involve inheritance inter se among the legal heirs, Court should make efforts to ensure that no legal heir is denied of his legal share in the estate of the deceased concerned on a technical ground. Such an approach will also be in consonance with the Injunctions of Islam (SCP – 1997 SCMR 281).

878. Distant Kindred. In presence of residuaries, Distant Kindred was not entitled to inheritance. Inheritance. Distant Kindred could not have inherited land in question in presence of residuaries. Where land was mutated in favour of Distant Kindred while residuaries were denied such portion of land in question and Distant Kindred had sold such land in favour of vendees, no title had passed to alleged vendees. Alleged vendor (Distant Kindred) having got no title in property, could pass no title to vendees, thus vendees could not claim better title than vendor herself had got. Provisions of section 41, Transfer of Property Act, 1882, would have no application to facts and circumstances of case, for it was not a case of defect in title of vendor but was a case where she had no title at all. Judgments and decrees of Courts below being correct, no interference was warranted. Transfer of Property Act (IV of 1882), section 41 (LHC – 1997 CLC 48).

879. Articles 64 & 114(g). Islamic Law. Inheritance. Withholding the best evidence. Effect. Defendant not producing those witnesses who were presumed to have knowledge of relationship of plaintiff with deceased land owner. Where any party withholds best evidence, presumption would be that if such evidence had been produced, it would have gone against that party. Two Courts below, on material available on record had concurrently found that plaintiff was the real sister of deceased. There being no other heirs of such deceased, she was entitled to inherit legal estate of deceased to the extent of two-third of his estate. Concurrent findings of two Courts below on basis of evidence on record on relationship of parties being correct, no interference with such finding was called for. Judgment and decree of First Appellate Court, although holding plaintiff to be sister of deceased land owner, yet deprived her of inheritance on grounds extraneous to legal proposition (LHC – 1997 MLD 67).

880. Islamic Law Inheritance. Person committing homicide is excluded from inheriting the property of the victim (BHC – 1997 PCRLJ 247).

881. Islamic Law Inheritance. Exclusion of legal heir (daughter) from inheritance. Quality of evidence required. Held, to exclude a legal heir from inheritance, strong and convincing evidence was required to discharge the burden. Plaintiff in order to succeed, must prove his case and stand on his own legs rather to take advantage of weakness of the case of adversary and must have special knowledge about the defendant's relationship with the deceased (Supreme Court, Azad Kashmir – 1997 CLC 1768).

882. Islamic Law Inheritance. Share of daughters sold by brothers without their consent. Effect. Land devolved on two daughters of deceased landowner was alienated by their brothers. Two Courts below decreed plaintiffs' (daughters') suit. High Court remanding case for fresh decision. Validity: Leave to appeal was granted to consider the contention that defendants had not denied factum of plaintiff and one of the defendants being daughters of deceased land owner; that property in question to the extent of one-third share devolved on daughters could not have been alienated by brothers in favour of vendees without their (daughters') consent; and whether observations of High Court to the effect that vendees of land in question, appeared to be bona fide purchasers without notice was untenable and contrary to evidence on record. Constitution of Pakistan (1973), Article 185(3) (SCP – 1996 SCMR 1213).

883. Islamic Law Constitution of Pakistan (1973), Article 185(3). Dispute relating to inheritance. Parties' common ancestor had two wives. Deceased land-owner and respondents were from one wife of common ancestor while petitioners were born from the other wife. Respondents being real brothers of deceased were thus, entitled to his inheritance to the exclusion of their step-brothers. Both parties being in joint possession of land in question, mere wrong entry in Revenue Record would not deprive respondents from ownership in respect of land left by deceased, their real brother. High Court had effectively and correctly dealt with question of inheritance. Leave to appeal was refused in circumstances (SCP – 1996 SCMR 1964).

884. Islamic Law Inheritance. Sale of land by one heir before attestation of mutation of inheritance. Validity: Inheritance under Islamic Law opens immediately on the death of last owner. Attestation of mutation and entries in other official record were mere formalities. Heir of deceased (vendor) thus became owner as son of deceased immediately after the death of his father; therefore, date of attestation of mutation was immaterial for sale of land to be effective. Judgments of Trial Court and that of Appellate Court decreeing plaintiff's suit to the extent of their shares and setting aside sale on behalf of the male heir (son) was modified to the extent that plaintiffs' decree to the extent of their shares was maintained while sale over and above of defendants' share was set aside while to the extent of defendant's share was maintained in circumstances (LHC – 1996 CLC 1403).

885. Islamic Law. Inheritance. Plaintiff (daughter) seeking entitlement to 7/104th share in accordance with Shariah in cash amount deposited by her father (deceased) in different Banks. During lifetime of deceased when he was allegedly on death bed some amount was stated to have been withdrawn illegally and fraudulently by one of defendants in the name of deceased. Plaintiff also claiming her share from that amount. Trial Court decreed plaintiff's suit in respect of amount which stood deposited at the time of death of deceased but ignored her claim to that amount which had been withdrawn during lifetime of deceased by one of defendants on behalf of their deceased father. Plaintiff filed appeal against that claim which was rejected. Defendant filed appeal against order of execution whereby decree was to be executed against him alone. Plaintiff could not claim her share in those payments or funds exhausted during lifetime of deceased, for her suit was for her share in the heritage that is, moveable property left by deceased; plaintiff was only entitled to her 7/104th share in the assets of deceased after his death. Plaintiff had produced no evidence that deceased was not in a position to understand what he was doing, or that he was pressurized by defendant to sign specific cheques. Trial Court had, thus, rightly refused to grant decree to plaintiff for the amount already drawn by her father before his death. Decree in favour of plaintiff was although against all defendants yet it could be executed against any one of judgment-debtors. Record showed that defendant against whom decree in question, was being executed had received the amount of legacy more than his due share in the estate left by his deceased father. Executing Court had thus, rightly rejected, such defendant's objection application that decree be executed against all defendants (PHC – 1996 CLC 1512).

886. Islamic Law. Inheritance. Where personal actions have matured into a decree, they become part of the estate of the deceased and can be inherited. Maxim '*actio personalis moritur cum persona*'. Exception. [Maxim] (LHC – 1995 PLD 381).

887. Islamic Law. Inheritance. Exclusion. Heir of deceased who was disobedient and involved in criminal litigation could not be deprived of legal right of inheritance on that account (LHC – 1995 MLD 1841).

888. Islamic Law. Constitution of Pakistan (1973), Article 185(3). Estate of deceased male owner opening up for succession after the death of his widow who was holding it as a limited owner. Sister of deceased and his collateral alone coming forward to claim inheritance. No other person claiming to be the heir of deceased coming forward to claim inheritance over the period of years when litigation was going on nor coming forward thereafter. Except heirs of deceased and those of widow (to the extent of her share), no one including donee whose gift was declared to be invalid was entitled to inherit the estate of deceased. Judgment of High Court to that extent was valid. Leave was refused in circumstances (SCP – 1994 SCMR 2044).

889. Islamic Law. Inheritance. Entitlement to property in question, as an heir of deceased. Leave to appeal was granted to consider, whether from the evidence on record, purported grandmother (maternal) of respondent was proved to be the sister of deceased land owner and respondent her grandson that is, 'Nawasa' and was thus entitled to inherit and if so, to what extent, from the estate of deceased land owner. Constitution of Pakistan (1973), Article 185 (3) (SCP – 1994 SCMR 2292).

890. Islamic Law. Inheritance. Property of deceased full owner held by his wife as limited owner, would revert to full owner after death of limited owner and would devolve upon heirs of full owner (LHC – 1994 CLC 976).

891. Islamic Law. Inheritance. Appellants who were legal heirs of deceased daughter of original owner of land in dispute had claimed that said daughter of original owner died after death of original owner whereas claim of respondents was that she died much earlier than the death of original owner, and thus heirs of pre-deceased daughter could not inherit property of original owner under Islamic Law. Courts below on basis of evidence on record had concluded that daughter had died much earlier to death of original owner. Concurrent findings of fact of Courts below based on evidence on record and not suffering from any illegality such as misreading or non-reading or misconstruction of any material piece of evidence, could not be interfered with (LHC – 1994 CLC 1964).

892. Islamic Law. Inheritance. Inter se relationship of parties to propositus. Proof. Onus to prove relationship set up in plaint lay upon plaintiffs who claimed to succeed to land in question, on the ground that they were descendants of a common ancestor. No member of the family or person having special means of knowledge on the subject appeared to prove plaintiffs' link with the common ancestor. Pedigree-table produced in Court did not link plaintiffs' ancestor with the common ancestor. Oral evidence produced on that behalf did not inspire confidence. In default of connecting link in the pedigree-table, mention of plaintiffs ancestors in parallel boxes in the same line was not a presumptive proof of their common parentage with that of propositus. Plaintiffs thus, failed to prove that they were a nearer collateral of propositus for inheriting the land left by him to the exclusion of defendants. Qanun-e-Shahadat (10 of 1984), Article 64 (LHC – 1994 MLD 1383).

893. Inheritance. Death of deceased employee during course of his employment. Social insurance death compensation amount awarded to defendants of deceased by employer whether to be treated as 'Tarka' of deceased so as to devolve upon his legal heirs. Social insurance death compensation was a type of group insurance and a sort of Benevolent Fund or grant from employer, which was not realizable in the lifetime, thus, it could not be treated as 'Tarka' of deceased and would not devolve upon the legal heirs of deceased but would go to dependents of deceased as compensation. Widow and children of deceased would be entitled to such amount but not the other heirs of deceased. Deceased having nominated his father to recover debt, such nomination was simply due to the fact that deceased keeping in view local culture and traditions had nominated his father to recover debt. Father of deceased was although not entitled to inherit anything out of compensation amount, yet, keeping in view his nomination by deceased, he was allowed his 'Sharai share' out of the said amount. Share given to mother of deceased was, however, directed to be refunded for depositing the same in Trial Court which had to be disbursed among the widow and children of deceased according to their 'Sharai shares' (PHC – 1994 PLD 1).

894. Islamic Law. Inheritance. Heir loses the right to inherit, if found guilty of having murdered the person who was the source of inheritance (SCP – 1993 SCMR 1073).

895. Islamic Law. Inheritance. Debts and liabilities of deceased. Heirs of deceased would be liable to pay all the debts and liabilities of their deceased predecessor to the extent of share of the debt proportionate to their share of the estate inherited by them. One of the heirs of deceased defendant (appellant) was though, not personally liable for payment of decretal amount, but he was bound to pay the proportionate share of the same to the extent of the estate inherited by him from the deceased judgment-debtor (SCP – 1993 SCMR 1185).

896. Inheritance. Principles. As soon as a Muslim owner dies, succession of estate left by him immediately opens and title passes to the heirs without any intervention by State functionaries or clergy. Theory of representation of estate by intermediary is unknown to Islamic Law of Inheritance. Inheritance. Limitation. No principle of limitation can be used to defeat the visible right of inheritance. (LHC – 1993 PLD 575).

897. Islamic Law. Inheritance. Widow of deceased son would not inherit his due share. Remainder would revert to collaterals. Inheritance. Evidence on record was insufficient for a final determination of all the true heirs to the deceased land owner and their actual shares in the estate left by him. Case was remanded to the limited extent for determining true heirs and their actual shares in the property left by the deceased (LHC – 1993 CLC 133).

898. Islamic Law. Inheritance. Co-sharer. Adverse possession. Rights of female. Plaintiff, being daughter of deceased landowner whose inheritance was in question, on death of her father, would inherit automatically alongwith other heirs and would become a co-sharer. Other co-sharers could not claim title by adverse possession against plaintiff. Even otherwise, there was no evidence about claim of adverse possession by defendants co-sharers as being open, continuous and hostile to the knowledge of plaintiff. Defendants co-sharers, thus, could not deny title of plaintiff as co-sharer. Bar of limitation would not apply in such case. [Adverse possession] (LHC – 1993 CLC 228).

899. Islamic Law. Inheritance. Dispute relating to inheritance of deceased who was the real brother of plaintiffs. Defendants claiming share in inheritance, were stepbrothers and sisters of deceased. Inheritance of deceased would, thus, devolve on plaintiffs alone being his direct heirs; defendants being step-brothers and sisters could not inherit property in question, in presence of real brothers of deceased (LHC – 1993 CLC 2539).

900. Islamic Law. Inheritance. Co-heirs. Bar of limitation would not stand amongst co-heirs and their successors. Suit fled by a co-heir inheriting under Islamic Law, would not be barred by limitation. Limitation Act (IX of 1908), section 3. [Co-sharer] (LHC – 1993 MLD 1207).

901. Islamic Law. Gift. Essentials. Declaration of gift by the donor; acceptance of subject-matter of gift by the donee expressly or impliedly; and handing over possession by donor to donee of the subject-matter of gift are the essential ingredients of a gift. Where any of the three ingredients was lacking, gift would not be deemed to have been proved (SHC – 1993 MLD 1542).

901.1. Inheritance. Heirs under Hanafi School. Classification of sharers; residuaries, and Distant Kindred, and mode of their inheritance to the property left by a deceased. Sharers are those heirs who have been named in the Holy Qur'an and have been assigned specific shares. Residuaries are all those persons for whom there are no specified shares and who take the residue after sharers have been satisfied, or they take the whole estate if there was no sharer. Distant Kindred is only entitled to succeed when there is no sharer or residuary (PHC – 1993 PLD 117).

902. Islamic Law. Constitution of Pakistan (1973), Article 185(3). Inheritance. Entitlement of heirs. Predecessor of parties having died and rule of inheritance being Muslim Personal Law, special forums and High Court had rightly concluded that Islamic Law of Inheritance would govern parties regarding inheritance of their predecessor. No legal infirmity in the order of High Court was found. Leave was refused in circumstances (SCP – 1992 SCMR 1741).

903. Inheritance. Plaintiff's exclusion from inheritance on charge of murder of propositus. Trial Court, consequent upon acquittal of plaintiff by High Court, of charge of murder, found him entitled to his share of inheritance. Trial Court's finding was upheld in appeal. Validity: Independent of judgment of acquittal by High Court, by which plaintiff was exonerated of charge of murder, there was neither any convincing nor sufficient evidence to support such charge against him. Plaintiff's acquittal on consideration of evidence led in support of charge of murder, was an acquittal on merits and not due to technical defects. Acquittal being judicial discharge from accusation washed away the charge and completely exonerated plaintiff of the taint. Plaintiff, thus, could not be deemed to be guilty of homicide and debarred from inheriting property owned and left by his mother. Decisions of Courts below granting plaintiff his share of inheritance were maintained (LHC – 1992 CLC 92).

904. Inheritance. Heirs of deceased Muslim. Shares in inheritance. Plaintiffs 1 and 2 were sons and plaintiffs 3 and 4 were daughters while defendant was 'the widow of deceased'. Shares of parties would be that each son's share would be to the extent of 29 paisa, while each daughter would inherit to the extent of 14.5 paisa. Defendant wife's share would be 13 paisa in the property left by deceased (SHC – 1992 PLD 234).

905. Islamic Law. Inheritance. Entitlement to inherit as co-sharer. Question of inheritance of a house built on encroached land. Plaintiff's and defendants' predecessor having built house on an encroached land, died. Plaintiff claimed her share in house in question. Plaintiff and defendants could not claim a better title in house in question, by inheritance than the deceased himself had over the land, which was nil. Parties being in possession of land would be deemed to be in unauthorized possession. Superstructure built on land which deceased had raised from his own resources, even that could not be inherited by his heirs because, it had no separate entity from land over which it stood. Such superstructure being integral part of land, same could not be inherited by heirs of deceased (SHC – 1992 CLC 1898).

906. Islamic Law. Inheritance. Co-sharer. Rights of females. Islamic Law affords special protection to Muslim females. Relinquishment deed from inheritance executed by a female while she was living under roof of her father, brother, husband or any other male relative had no value whatsoever, and she could not be deprived of her property on basis of such relinquishment deed. Relinquishment deed in question, was, however, executed in such circumstances that it tended to violate protection afforded by Islam to females (SHC – 1992 MLD 1598).

907. Islamic Law. Inheritance. Inherent powers of Courts to do complete justice between the parties. Exercise of female heir of deceased land-owners was cited as a pro forma defendant in suit. Plaintiffs suit filed under section 42, Specific Relief Act, 1877 would not present any insurmountable difficulty in granting relief to such female heir who was pro forma defendant before the Court to which she was found to be entitled. Court under its inherent power to do complete justice between parties could exercise such power by undoing an un-Islamic mode of devolution of inheritance whereby a female heir had been deprived of her valuable right of inheritance. Supreme Court could exercise such power under Supreme Court Rules, 1980, OXXXIII, Rule 5. High Court also had similar powers. Trial Court had inherent powers like the present one on the analogy of provisions contained in O.XLI (SCP – 1991 PLD 218).

908. Inheritance. Constitution of Pakistan (1973), Article 185(3). Leave to appeal was granted on contention that there was a difference of opinion amongst the Muslim Jurists and Aima on the question whether the heirs of the murderer would also be excluded from inheritance and that this was a case of first impression as far as Supreme Court was concerned (SCP – 1991 PLD 724).

909. Islamic Law. Inheritance. Last male owner having died issueless, land left by him was mutated in favour of his wife with regard to her limited estate in that land, and she before her death gifted away a portion of that land to petitioners who were her brothers. Petitioners contended that last male owner having died issueless, his widow was entitled to one-fourth share and not one-eighth as awarded by Courts below. Ever if it was accepted that last male owner had two sons who died subsequently as contented by respondents, in that case besides inheriting one-eighth share, widow was also entitled to inherit one-sixth share as mother of two deceased sons of last male owner. Then, aspect of case having not been examined by all three Courts below, contention raised by petitioners required further examination. Leave to appeal was granted (SCP – 1991 SCMR 1335).

910. Articles 30 & 133. Islamic Law. Inheritance. Appellant in previous suit, as a defendant had taken a definite plea that he was heir of deceased and had led evidence in support of such plea. In present suit, he had produced evidence to the effect that he was the son of deceased and entitled to her property. No attempt was made in cross-examination to show that he had made a wrong statement. One of the co-heirs/respondent had admitted that appellant was his brother. Such admission by one of the respondents could be examined in two different contexts; one, that insofar as his own share in inheritance was concerned respondent could not prevent sharing the same with appellant; and second, that as a witness he had deposed in favour of appellant stating that he was the son of deceased, which statement not only was against his own interest but also against the interest of other respondent that is, his real sister. Respondent's statement was thus, a strong piece of evidence in favour of appellant. Appellant as a son of deceased was a co-heir of respondents and thus, entitled to inherit his share in property in question (SCP – 1991 SCMR 1381).

911. Islamic Law. Inheritance. Constitution of Pakistan (1973), Article 185(3). Respondent's father having died, mutation of inheritance was sanctioned in favour of his widow and two daughters. On death of widow, mutation was sanctioned in favour of her two daughters and two brothers of deceased bind owner. Petitioners as brothers of deceased land owner, challenged earlier mutation of inheritance which was dismissed by Collector. Collector, however, on review set aside earlier order but Additional Commissioner in appeal set aside review order passed by Collector. Petitioner's revision petition before Board of Revenue failed. On review application, however, Board of Revenue directed that said mutation be reviewed for Sehat, keeping the allotment intact. Respondents' Constitutional petition succeeded wherein order passed in review by Board of Revenue was declared to be without lawful authority and of no legal effect. Leave to appeal. Board of Revenue, having dismissed petitioners' revision on merit had no jurisdiction or justification to re-open the matter on review. Continuous dragging of respondent females in litigation smacked of ill-will. Courts could not be used to give vent to unhealthy emotions. Out of the entire land owned by deceased land owner, petitioners had got their share. Leave refused (SCP – 1991 SCMR 1745).

912. Islamic Law. Constitution of Pakistan (1973), Article 185(3). Inheritance. Relationship with deceased landowner. Petitioner lady was deprived of inheritance of deceased on the ground that she was not his real sister. Petitioner's claim to be the real sister of deceased failed upto the High Court. Leave to appeal. Petitioner had produced copies of entries from Death Register and Birth Register of her predecessors to prove that she was real sister of deceased. Contentions raised by petitioner required examination. Leave to appeal was granted in circumstances (SCP – 1991 SCMR 1839).

913. Islamic Law. Constitution of Pakistan (1973), Article 185(3). Inheritance. Plaintiffs/petitioners' suit was decreed, and a finding was recorded that deceased was a Shia. Such finding was, however, reversed in appeal and revision, wherein deceased was treated to be a Sunni, and his property was divided according to law of inheritance applicable to that sect. Findings of fact rendered against plaintiffs/ petitioners by the two higher Courts, notwithstanding acceptance of their plea by Trial Court, were unexceptionable. No infirmity, legal or of principle, having been discovered, nor there being any misreading or non-reading of evidence, no justification was found for interference. Leave to appeal was refused in circumstances (SCP – 1991 SCMR 2049).

914. Islamic Law. Civil Procedure Code (V of 1908), section-96. Constitution of Pakistan (1973), Article 185(3). Inheritance. Parties having co-heirs, second appeal was disposed of by High Court by an agreed order whereby parties agreed that instead of passing a decree for possession in favour of plaintiffs, shares of parties be declared and be given effect to by the revenue authorities in revenue record, and that same would be the end of litigation in the family. Parties' predecessor having died in 1944, had made a will presumably under custom in 1926, giving half property to his son from his one wife and other half to his other wife. Latter disposition was, however, conditional that on death of his wife, her half would go to his daughters, from her womb excepting the one who would marry outside the family. Plaintiff's side, on death of their father (son of deceased predecessor) having already obtained half of the property which had been bequeathed to their father sued defendants viz., daughters of predecessor for possession of property. Trial Court decreed the suit and defendants' appeal was dismissed. Parties, however, compromised in High Court. Although there was no serious dispute with regard to the specification of shares if property was treated as that of parties common predecessor, and mode of devolution was treated as under Islamic Law of inheritance yet defendants complained that compromise had been applied only to the property which went to the wife of predecessor and regarding which plaintiff's side had filed a suit, while understanding between them was that such compromise would apply to the entire property of deceased predecessor by ignoring the devolution through the Will of 1926, because same would not have stood the test of Islamic Law of Wills. Court while examining the preliminary objection that compromise between parties having been effected through High Court's judgment was a consent decree and same could not be challenged in appeal, came to conclusion that inherent features of High Court's judgment in question, strongly corroborate and support the position taken by defendants that entire property left by predecessor of parties was to be treated and dealt with in accordance with the devolution determined in the judgment of High Court. Compromise was a final settlement of all disputes between the parties which had arisen and which could arise. Such finding was not only supported by the use of the sentence in the impugned judgment that settlement between parties was in accordance with 'Islamic Law of Inheritance' and that same 'would be the end of litigation in the family', but also from the fact that persons and parties who had not appealed before High Court also obtained benefit. Appeal was allowed with direction that the defects if any in the decree passed as a result of judgment of High Court under appeal would be removed and corrected with a further declaration that revenue authorities would give effect to the shares determined in the judgment in question in the revenue record, and the parties would take the entire property left by predecessor of parties whether it had gone initially to his son or to his wife (SCP – 1991 SCMR 2051).

915. Inheritance. Muslim male owner died without leaving male issue. Deceased's wife and three daughters got their share respectively as one-eighth and two-third. Remainder 5/24th share was claimed by two rival residuaries. Trial Court found plaintiff to be a descendant in the fifth degree in the male line of descent from common ancestor. Court in appeal reversed the finding of the Trial Court and found that the defendant was a nearer residuary. Held, plaintiff and defendant both being descendants of a common ancestor, defendant was found to be a remoter residuary as compared to plaintiff. Plaintiff was thus, entitled to take the residue to the extent of 5/24th share of estate left by deceased (LHC – 1991 PLD 330).

916. Trial Court had correctly found plaintiff to be entitled to the residue of 5/24th share left by deceased. Appellate Court's finding that defendant was a nearer residuary was erroneous. Trial Court's judgment and decree was restored while that of Appellate Court was set aside (LHC – 1991 PLD 330).

917. Islamic Law. Inheritance. Deceased was survived by one daughter, two widows and one sister. Parties being Sunni, daughter and widows of deceased were his legal heirs while his sister was a residuary. In presence of sister, paternal cousins of deceased were excluded from inheritance as being residuaries of remoter degree qua sister of deceased (LHC – 1991 MLD 1681).

918. Islamic Law. Inheritance. Deceased had left alive two brothers and one sister. Plaintiff (brother) was entitled to two-fifth share out of property of deceased while two-fifth share would go to other brother who was in India and not a party in suit and one-fifth would be inherited by the sister (SHC – 1991 CLC 1580).

919. Inheritance. Co-sharer. Rights of females. Brother cannot legally claim 'adverse possession' against his sister and much less 'ouster'. [Co-sharer] (SCP – 1990 PLD 1).

920. Islamic Law. Constitution of Pakistan (1973), Article 185(3). Inheritance. Leave to appeal granted to consider whether daughter of last male owner was entitled to have her share in his self-acquired property where the parties were governed by Law of Shariat and not by Custom (SCP – 1990 SCMR 305).

920.1. Islamic Law. Inheritance. Courts below had found that divorce of lady was not proved as original document of divorce had not been produced before Trial Court. Only marginal witnesses could not be believed in absence of divorce deed. Lady was thus rightly held to be a widow and as such was entitled to the inheritance of her husband as co-sharer (SCP – 1990 SCMR 629).

921. Islamic Law. Inheritance. Person, entitled to inheritance, becomes a vested holder of due rights the moment succession opens (SHC – 1990 MLD 164).

922. Constitution of Pakistan (1973), Article 185(3). Inheritance. Will. Leave to appeal arising out of inheritance suit was granted to examine the question that even if the Will made in favour of plaintiff/respondent by deceased was proved as alleged what would be its effect vis-a-vis rights of petitioners/defendants and their predecessor-in-interest to inherit property of deceased (SCP – 1989 SCMR 755).

923. Inheritance. Mere fact that the owner of the property is living in Dar-ul-Harab while heirs are living in Dar-ul-Islam does not have the effect of depriving the heirs from inheriting the property of their predecessor-in-interest if both the parties are believers. Such heirs are not prevented from inheriting the property (SCP – 1989 SCMR 828).

924. Constitution of Pakistan (1973), Article 185(3). Inheritance. Petitioner's claim to be the daughter of deceased and her entitlement to inheritance on that score decided against her by all the Courts below. Leave to appeal was granted to examine, *inter alia*, whether the paternity of petitioner had been correctly decided. Effect of Supreme Court decision in Shahnawaz's case reported as PLD 1976 SC 767, as also other questions arising in the petition also required examination (SCP – 1989 SCMR 1220).

925. Inheritance. Relinquishment. Proof. Daughter of deceased Muslim claiming her share from property of deceased. Deceased owned agricultural land in several villages. Excepting one village, said daughter's share in inheritance had been mutated. Daughter's share of inheritance having not been mutated with regard to suit land; she brought a suit to establish her entitlement. Deceased's, other heirs pleaded relinquishment of her share on part of daughter. Suit dismissed by Trial Court but decreed by First Appellate Court. Record showed that daughter had not relinquished her share of inheritance at any stage. Omission of her name from the pedigree-table entered in impugned mutation either designedly or accidentally had led to her exclusion in the distribution of the estate and such omission had been tried to be twisted by other co-heirs into urging a case of relinquishment by her of the share of inheritance which had neither been pleaded specifically nor proved satisfactorily (LHC – 1989 PLD 372).

926. Islamic Law. Inheritance, opening of Inheritance, under Islamic Law opens immediately on death of ancestor. Sanction of mutation was only an executive step to give effect to law of inheritance. Person becomes owner in the estate immediately on death of his father (LHC – 1989 CLC 795).

927. Islamic Law. Inheritance. Presumption. Initial presumption is that every Muslim in Pakistan is Sunni unless otherwise proved (LHC – 1989 CLC 1591).

928. Islamic Law. Civil Procedure Code (V of 1908), section 115. Inheritance. Two brothers dying issueless. Plaintiff and defendant both claiming to be the brothers of deceased persons claiming share in property left by them. Defendant conceding before Appellate Court that defendant was born from different mother but same father, thus he was consanguine brother of the deceased while plaintiff was full brother of deceased. Title thus stood determined by the finding of fact justified on the record reached in appeal below on the basis of binding admission that the defendant was born of a lady other than the plaintiff's mother and the two deceased. No justifiable reason for that aspect of the dispute being re-opened to be considered again at revisional stage (LHC – 1989 CLC 2140).

929. Inheritance. Child in womb. Right to inherit. Foetus, viz. the child in womb is an heir alongwith other heirs, provided such child was present in the womb of the mother at the time of death of his ancestor and was born alive within six months from his death. Such child if born after a period of more than six months would not be entitled to inherit. Period of six months is the minimum period of gestation (SHC – 1989 PLD 85).

930. Islamic Law. Inheritance. Plaintiffs and defendants' shares in inheritance specified by Court and decree in accordance with such specified shares granted (SHC – 1989 CLC 1274).

931. Islamic Law. Inheritance. Residuary. Petitioner a cousin-brother of deceased from paternal side praying for grant of Letters of Administration in respect of property left behind by deceased. Petitioner's sisters whether residuaries and entitled to inherit property of their deceased cousin. Female residuaries are only four in number of whom two are descendants of deceased viz. the daughter and son's daughter howsoever and the other two are descendants of deceased's father viz., full sister and consanguine sister. No other female can inherit as a residuary. Petitioner thus alone was entitled to inherit the property left by deceased, and his two sisters would be excluded from inheritance (SHC – 1989 MLD 1316).

932. Islamic Law. Inheritance. Initial presumption where parties were Muslims. Custom as a rule of inheritance. Mode of proof. Muslims in Azad Jammu and Kashmir were governed vis-a-vis inheritance by personal law. Rule was, however, subject to exception of Custom. Where a particular tribe or family was governed by Custom vis-a-vis inheritance of estate, it could prove Custom to the exclusion of personal law. Where exception of Custom was alleged, same had to be proved by very cogent and convincing evidence. Initial presumption would always be in favour of personal law. [Presumption] (Supreme Court, Azad Kashmir – 1989 CLC 407).

933. Islamic Law. Faith. Faith of a person at time of death was determinative of mode of inheritance to his estate (LHC – 1989 MLD 1013).

934. Inheritance. Shares of collateral and daughter. Re-calculation. Collateral challenging share of respondent-daughter of deceased in estate left by deceased. Respondent inheriting one-half share out of share of her sisters who died issueless and one-eighth share belonging to her mother. Supreme Court after recalculation of share of respondent coming to conclusion that total of her share would come to same extent which had been decreed in her favour. No interference being called for, leave to appeal refused (SCP – 1988 SCMR 1).

935. Inheritance. Deceased at time of her death was living in India while plaintiff as heir of deceased was living in Pakistan. Impediment to succession on account of deceased living in Darul-Harab not applicable to plaintiff. At the time of death of deceased, Pakistan was not at war with India. Place of residence of deceased, therefore, could not be treated as Darul-Harab. Held, even if deceased had been living in

Darul-Harab her heirs living in Pakistan could not have been deprived of her inheritance because both parties were believers. Impediments to successions were applicable only to non-believers (LHC – 1988 PLD 588).

936. Islamic Law. Inheritance. Collateral, proof of. Prepositus dying issueless and his entire land mutated by revenue authorities in name of his widow by applying Doctrine 14 Return. Persons claiming one-fourth of share in property on basis of being collaterals and leading oral as well as documentary evidence in this regard. Documentary evidence consisting of copies of Shajra Nasab and Jamabandi. Shajra Nasab rendering no assistance to determine the claim while Jamabandi merely indicating that prepositus was a co-sharer in a Khata jointly with claimant. Shares of various co-owners in Khata being different, merely because prepositus was a co-sharer in same Khata with claimants, held, would not necessarily imply that he was their collateral (LHC – 1988 MLD 786).

937. Islamic Law. Inheritance. Entitlement to inheritance. Right to inherit as daughters of propositus, proof of. Cause of action for petitioners, arose on demise of propositus, to prove themselves to be his daughters. Concurrent findings of Courts below on such point of fact that respondents were daughters of deceased would remain decisive (LHC – 1988 MLD 1015).

938. Islamic Law. Inheritance. Where a person had received his due share as 'sharer' from property left by deceased that person, held, could not claim as 'residuary' also from that property (LHC – 1988 MLD 1403).

939. Islamic Law. Inheritance. Properties of deceased for distribution amongst legal heirs. Functions of nominee appointed by deceased. Nominee would be entitled to recover properties of deceased for distribution amongst legal heirs who were entitled to inherit the same (SHC – 1988 CLC 1765).

940. Islamic Law. Inheritance. Claim of one of the heirs in respect of property left by deceased was disputed by other heirs on the ground that deceased had settled question of inheritance during his lifetime. Such settlement is binding on heirs only if they agreed to the same after death of their predecessor as inheritance would open in favour of heirs only on death of predecessor (SHC – 1988 CLC 2195).

941. Constitution of Pakistan (1973), 185(3). Inheritance. Leave to appeal, grant of. Progeny of murder, whether to inherit property of his victim. Case of first impression. Leave to appeal granted to consider *inter alia* that petitioner having ultimately been found guilty only of culpable homicide not amounting to murder, whether rule of Islamic Law pressed in service against petitioner/his progeny would be attracted (SCP – 1987 SCMR 976).

942. Hanafi Law. Inheritance. Heirs connected with deceased divided into three classes: Sharers, agnates and uterine relations. Agnates are called residuaries and uterine relations Distant Kindred. When neither 'sharer' nor 'agnate' present only then is the estate divided among uterine relations. Distant Kindred related to deceased through intervention of female cannot inherit in presence of agnate (SCP – 1987 SCMR 1560).

943. Islamic Law. Inheritance. Land of original owner taken over by his widow as limited owner, held, would devolve upon heirs of such original owner in accordance with Muslim Laws after death of widow. Where any person entitled to inherit such land died prior to death of widow, heirs of such person at time of death of widow, would inherit his share according to Islamic Law. (LHC – 1987 CLC 579).

944. Islamic Law. Inheritance. After giving away Dhawi-al-Furud (sharer) their fixed share, remainder estate, if any, is inherited by Asbah, residuary (SHC – 1987 CLC 138).

945. Section 42. Qanun-e-Shahadat Order (10 of 1984), Article 118 Islamic Law. Inheritance. Daughter's claim to one-half share of estate of deceased decreed by Trial Court and finding thereof upheld by Appellate Court. Son's claim to entire estate in lieu of sale-deed executed during lifetime of deceased rejected by Courts below. Finding arrived at by Courts below that sale-deed was fictitious borne out by evidence on record. During lifetime of deceased, defendant son was neither in possession of land on basis of impugned sale nor any entry in support of such sale-deed appeared in revenue record. Inheritance mutation entered at the instance of defendant wherein all the heirs were shown entitled to inheritance of deceased had no mention of sale and thus would falsify claim of defendant based on such sale-deed. Purchase of stamp paper and execution thereof at a place far away from ordinary place of residence whereat such documents were usually purchased and executed, held, would make the deed of sale as fictitious and doubtful (PHC – 1987 PLD 65).

946. Article 185(3) Islamic Law. Inheritance. Parties allowed shares in accordance with law applicable to evacuee land under laws of. Rehabilitation and Settlement. Petitioner admitting that there would be no defect in distribution of inheritance. Otherwise too, he was unable to satisfy that principles of Muslim law relied upon by him had in any way been contravened. Leave to appeal refused. (SCP – 1986 SCMR 1369).

947. Islamic Law. Inheritance. Will in favour of minor daughter. Effect. Will by testator in favour of his minor daughter assented to, after death of testator by heirs, would entitle such minor daughter to one-third share of estate. Out of remaining property widow would get one-eighth share while two daughters would get two-third. Remaining share, held, would go to residuary (LHC – 1986 MLD 1829).

948. Inheritance. Doctrine of inheritance not governed by rule of necessity (SHC – 1986 PLD 269).

949. Islamic Law. Inheritance. Four sons and seven daughters left by deceased. Each son, held, would get twice the share of each daughter of property left by deceased Muslim (SHC – 1986 MLD 163).

950. Inheritance. Sunni Law. Residuaries. Inheritance devolves from descendants of true grand-father how highs ever on full paternal uncle, then on full paternal uncle's son and thereafter on full paternal uncle's son's son. Plea that remoteness or closeness of relationship of residuaries with last male holder of property is of no consequence, repelled (SCP – 1985 SCMR 947).

951. Hiba-bil-Ewaz distinguishable from a simple gift. Conditions to make 'Hiba-bil-Ewaz' valid. West Pakistan Land Reforms Regulation, 1959 (MLR 64), para 25(4), proviso (SCP – 1985 SCMR 1131).

952. Article 98. West Pakistan Muslim Personal Law (Shariat Application) Act (V of 1962), section 2. Civil Procedure Code (V of 1908), section 9. Islamic Law. Inheritance. Question as to who amongst parties entitled to inherit property in dispute and to which extent, held, basically a question of title which could only be decided by civil Courts. [Islamic Law. Jurisdiction] (LHC – 1985 CLC 89).

953. Sections 35 & 112. Legitimacy, proof of. Entries pertaining to birth and death of deceased in register of birth and death admittedly showing him as son of N. Such entries made long before dispute arose between parties. Entries indicating that at time of birth and death of deceased as well as at time of death of deceased's mother, deceased was known, accepted and entered in official papers as son of N. Deceased, held, proved to have been born during subsistence of marriage of his mother with N and taken to be legitimate son of N in circumstances (LHC – 1985 CLC 2737).

954. Article 185(3). Leave to appeal granted to consider whether respondent's ouster for more than ten years prior to the institution of suit had been established in facts and circumstances of case (SCP – 1984 SCMR 1444).

955. Inheritance. Lady fully establishing her marriage with deceased, who executed divorce deed but since notice of divorce deed not becoming effective during his lifetime lady, held, became his widow on death and thus entitled to inherit his estate. Mutation under which such lady deprived from succession, held further, void and lady being a co-sharer would be deemed to be in possession through other co-sharers to extent of her share in property in dispute (LHC – 1984 CLC 869).

956. Islamic Law. Inheritance. Heirs holding share in land in excess of their due inheritance. Decree of appellate Court could be modified to extent what heirs rightfully inherited (LHC – 1984 MLD 272).

957. Section 100. Islamic Law. Second Appeal. Inheritance. Land. Documentary evidence not connecting appellants with lineage so as to make his claim inheritable whereas no dispute appearing with regard to lineage reaching respondents. Appellants indicated to have improved upon their case by introducing a name in pedigree so as to make their case consistent with documentary evidence, and person through whom appellants agitating their claim appeared in picture from back door. Lineage of appellant's father not finding uninterrupted support from documentary evidence and appellant standing excluded from inheriting suit land which developed upon respondents as Distance Kindred. Appeal dismissed (SHC – 1984 CLC 2544).

958. Inheritance. Uterine brother or sister is entitled to one-sixth and not one-half of share. Inheritance. Uterine brother. A uterine brother of M dying in 1947, while M dying in 1948. A, held, would not get anything from share of M. (SCP – 1983 SCMR 824).

959. Inheritance. Nearer in degree excludes more remote. Deceased brother of petitioners dying issueless. Petitioners, held, have no locus standi for substitution for original pre-emptor in presence of their father. Civil Procedure Code (V of 1908), O. XXII, r. 3.. [Pre-emption] (LHC – 1982 CLC 2001).

960. Inheritance. F deceased leaving behind widow and two daughters Widow marrying another man M and after death leaving behind two more daughters from second husband M. Entitlement of four daughters to shares in land left by widow out of share inherited by her from deceased husband F. worked out (Supreme Court, Azad Kashmir – 1982 CLC 1709).

961. Inheritance. Deceased leaving wife and a sister. Death occurring on 14 August 1950 hence inheritance to be governed by Shariat Law and not by custom. Courts below failing to determine actual share of sister of deceased and also not caring to see that deceased had also a wife and that share of widow had to be excluded from consideration while allowing portion of property to sister and cousin. Held: After subtracting one-fourth of property as widow's share remaining property to be apportioned between sister and cousin of deceased and thence parties through them to have their due share according to law of inheritance (Supreme Court, Azad Kashmir – 1981 CLC 766).

962. Inheritance. Objection that without amending plaint share of plaintiff could not be determined though specious, held, has no force. Parties being aware of substance of controversy and contesting matter on merits. Too late to raise hyper-technical objection of procedure. Share in inheritance to be determined in accordance with law. Applicable (LHC – 1980 CLC 937).

963. Section 47 read with Ordinance XXI, Rule 58 and Islamic Law, rule of inheritance. Discharge of debts of deceased out of deceased's estate before distributing same among themselves. Religious duty of legal heirs of Muslim deceased. Court of law to lean towards enforcement of such religious duty. Estate of Muslim deceased represented by one or more legal heirs, decree passed in any such suit, held, cannot be defeated on ground of non-joinder of some other legal heirs, particularly in event of such other legal heirs having knowledge of pendency of suit. [Islamic Law] (SHC – 1980 CLC 1794).

964. Inheritance. Muslim law. Rule of day in liberated territory of Jammu & Kashmir and governs parties in respect of disposal of property without drawing any distinction between self acquired and ancestral property (Supreme Court, Azad Kashmir – 1980 CLC 2209).

965. Inheritance. Heir apparent under Muslim Law possesses mere possibility to inherit. Heir apparent can inherit nothing, if predecessor disposes of property (LHC – 1979 CLC 699).

966. Islamic Law. Inheritance. Marazul Maut. Divorce. Person under fear of death divorcing his wife. Such woman, held, not deprived of inheritance if person dies within period of *Iddat*. Marazul Maut a question of fact (LHC – 1976 PLD 119).

967. Divorce. Inheritance. Husband paralytic and on his death-bed. Woman entitled to inheritance from his estate if he dies prior to expiration of her period of *Iddat* (SCP – 1974 PLD 22).

968. Inheritance. Custom. Property wrongly mutated in name of a female as limited owner but such person remaining in possession as limited owner for more than twelve years. Such person, held, perfected her title to property as limited owner by prescription and to be treated as limited owner. Limited interest having come to an end. Property to be distributed according to Islamic Law and not custom (PHC – 1974 PLD 7).

969. Consanguine sisters. Heirs under Islamic Law and thus interested in property subject-matter of inheritance (SCP – 1972 SCMR 477).

970. Islamic Law. Conversion to Islam Hindu having wife and children embracing Islam and marrying a Muslim lady. Muslim wife and children by her inherit, on his death, entire property to exclusion of Hindu wife and children (LHC – 1971 PLD 1020).

971. Islamic Law. Inheritance. Will. Provident fund of employee. Forms part of un-disposed of estate of subscriber on his death. Nomination of person to receive Provident Fund. Not equivalent to a will, gift or trust in favour of nominee. Muslim deceased survived by widow, sons and daughter. Brother of deceased as his nominee cannot claim fund as having been bequeathed to him by 'will' a fortiori when such fund non-existent at time of nomination. Provident Funds Act (XIX of 1925), sections 4 & 5 (SHC – 1968 PLD 523).

972. Islamic Law. Inheritance. Residuaries. Female children of grandfather, how-high-soever, are not included in category of residuaries in their own right. The female children of the grand-father how-high-soever are not included in the category of 'residuaries in their own right' (LHC – 1967 PLD 1214).

973. Islamic Law. Last full owner dying issueless in 1932 and inheritance devolving on his mother (widow) as limited owner. Widow remarrying and succession re-opening in 1955. Shares to be determined after considering all persons who were entitled to inheritance in 1932, according to Shariat Law. West Punjab Muslim Personal Law (Shariat) Application Act (IX of 1948). (West Pakistan Board of Revenue – 1965 PLD 12).

974. Islamic Law. Inheritance. Murderer or his progeny cannot be allowed to benefit by crime of murder. Principles of justice, equity and good conscience (LHC – 1964 PLD 451). Ascertainment of shares of co-heirs is not tantamount to partition of estate. Shares can be separated only by an actual partition (Dhaka High Court – 1958 PLD 68). Estate of deceased Muslim devolves on his heirs at the moment of his death (Supreme Court, Azad Kashmir – 1958 PLD 19).

975. Succession. 'Nomination' and 'gift'. Distinction. Unless a nomination could amount to a valid gift inter vivos, same could not pass title to nominee in respect of immoveable property. Making of a nomination could not give right to nominator at his choice to change Law of Succession, which otherwise would be applicable in case of his death. Nomination could not operate as a valid gift under Islamic Law as gift in order to confer title on donee must be accompanied by delivery of possession of property gifted (SCP – 2004 SCMR 1219).

976. Succession: Heir becomes owner of Sharai share, the moment the person dies from whom he inherits (LHC – 2004 YLR 2438).

977. Succession. Gift. Making nomination in respect of property. Validity: Nomination, unless amounted to a valid gift inter vivos, cannot pass title in property to nominee nor can give right to nominator to change Law of Succession, which would be applicable in case of his death. Nomination cannot operate as a valid gift under Islamic Law as gift, in order to confer title on donee, must be accompanied by delivery of possession of the property gifted. Nomination does not stop succession of estate of deceased to his legal heirs as per succession law applicable to him (SHC – 2003 CLC 1521).

978. Succession. Gift. Will. Nomination by member of a Cooperative Society. Such nomination does not operate as a gift or will, thus cannot deprive other heirs, who may be entitled thereto under law of succession. Nominee is merely a trustee of allottee, and he cannot become owner of property after demise of original allottee. Nominee remains accountable to legal heirs of original allottee for all benefits derived out of such property. As nomination does not confer any title in favour of nominee, mutation and transfer of title on basis of nomination would not be legal. Nominee by virtue of nomination simpliciter is not seized or possessed of any right, title or interest in property (SHC – 2003 MLD 1095).

979. Section 3. Civil Procedure Code (V of 1908). Islamic Law. Succession. Estate of deceased Muslim. Mode of distribution. Rule of decision of deceased Muslim's estate would be according to Muslim Personal Law, as if that law had been applicable at the time of such death. Impliedly, even before promulgation of Khyber Pakhtunkhwa Province Muslim Personal Law (Shariat) Application Act,

1935, succession to estate of deceased Muslim had to be regulated according to personal law, and Courts had to decide disputes between legal heirs of deceased regarding their share in relevant estate in accordance with Muslim Personal Law. Courts below having decreed plaintiff's suit in accordance with Injunctions of Islam as enunciated in Khyber Pakhtunkhwa Province Muslim Personal Law (Shariat) Application Act, 1935, such decision neither suffered from any misreading of evidence nor was based on surmises or conjectures; therefore, no exception, thereto, could be taken in revisional jurisdiction of High Court. [Islamic Law. Succession] (PHC – 1999 MLD 249).

980. Islamic Law. Constitution of Pakistan (1973), Article 185(3). Succession. Deceased land owner's property was divided between his widow to the extent of one-fourth and his brother to the extent of three-fourth. Petitioner's predecessor was excluded being the consanguine brother. Petitioner on the death of his father brought a suit claiming that his father was the real brother of deceased and thus was entitled to three-eighth of the land in question. Trial Court dismissed suit but First Appellate Court decreed the suit. High Court in second appeal set aside decision of First Appellate Court and restored that of Trial Court. Leave to appeal. Two documents having been referred to in judgments of Courts below having been withheld by the petitioners, petition for leave to appeal was not properly documented, and same had to be dismissed on that ground alone. Leave to appeal was refused in circumstances (SCP – 1991 SCMR 309).

981. Islamic Law. Succession. Civil Procedure Code (V of 1908), section 11. Constitution of Pakistan (1973), Article 185(3). Leave to appeal was granted to consider whether previous judgment could operate as res judicata and as to whether, under Islamic Law, Appellant's predecessor could be treated as brother of deceased and son of 'R' (SCP – 1991 SCMR 1196).

982. Succession. Administration of the estate of a deceased person. Locus standi of each heir. Estate of a deceased person vests in predetermined proportions in the legal heirs. All such heirs, on opening of succession, become tenants-in-common in such estate. All the heirs have equal rights and none of them has precedence over the other (SHC – 1989 PLD 350).

983. Islamic Law. Succession. Custom. Devolution of estate of a Muslim residing in Jammu and Kashmir before 1947. Prior to 1947, Muslims residing in State of Jammu and Kashmir, held, were governed by personal law. Party to such succession, however, could plead and prove special custom prevailing in the family (Supreme Court, Azad Kashmir – 1988 PLD 1).

984. Sections 7 to 11. Islamic Law. Talaq. Special Oath. Connotation. Special oath relates to offer by one party to be bound by such oath made by other party or by any witness in proceedings. Court is, however, not bound to take notice of such offer. Discretionary with Court to ask the other party or witness that if such offer was accepted and special oath was administered, statement made thereon, would be conclusive proof of matter stated in it. To propose and take special oath though permissible, yet oath administered under section 8, Oaths Act, 1873, held, could not be repugnant to justice or decency and should not a fact third party. Taking oath on Talaq to ones wife, and that too without fault on her part was not an approved action in Islam to which parties belonged. Oath proposed and accepted by parties on divorce to wife for decision of civil suit was in contravention of section 8 of Oaths Act, 1873 and could neither be proposed nor taken because of being opposed to rule of decency and also affecting the third party (LHC – 1987 CLC 1602).

985. Not necessary that a Muslim must either be a Sunni, or, a Shia and it may well be that he is free from all sectarian feelings, sentiments and faith (SHC – 1985 PLD 365).

986. Section 59. Alienation. Custom (Punjab). Islamic Law. Succession. Alienation of occupancy rights. Held, could also be challenged by Muslim law heirs. [Custom (Punjab). Islamic Law] (SCP – 1982 SCMR 956). Property devolves on all heirs as tenants in common (SCP – 1980 SCMR 873).

987. Succession. Interpretation by Courts. Contention that since deceased disowned her affiliation to any particular sect of Islam and claimed to be a simple Muslim she had to be governed by Islamic Law interpreted by Courts on basis of Holy Qur'an (Sura Nissa referred) free from jurisprudential theories of two sects. Held: Legal relevance of question whether deceased belonged to Shia or Sunni sect arising by virtue of operation of provisions of West Pakistan Muslim Personal Law (Shariat) Application Act, 1962 and each sect having to be governed according to law applicable to such sect as already prevalent and applied; and Shariat Act not allowing interpretation by Courts by process of reasoning in their own light, contention fallacious Acceptance of contention tantamount, to creation of a new system of personal law applicable to cases of Muslims not belonging to any sect. New theories cannot be propounded independent of rival theories of great antiquity and authority propounded by two sects of Shias and Sunnis (SHC – 1977 PLD 320).

988. Succession. Widow succeeding to estate-of her deceased husband as limited owner and later transferring property to her daughter M (petitioner) by way of gift. Widow's share of one-eighth on her death, held, devolved upon all her heirs including daughter (SCP – 1976 SCMR 382).

989. Islamic Law. Succession. Distinction between immoveables and moveables. Islamic Law as administered in Pakistan does not accept any such distinction. Principle of scission not recognized by Islamic Law in matters of succession (SHC – 1968 PLD 480). Distant Kindred cannot succeed in presence of sharer (LHC – 1960 PLD 261).

990. Islamic Law. Succession. Punjab Rehabilitation Re-settlement Scheme, Part II, paragraph 46. Grandson whose father has pre-deceased his own father.

Inherits grandfather only in cases of allotment simpliciter and not where grandfather has filed his claim or allotment is on quasi-permanent basis. Genesis of rule (LHC - 1960 PLD 265).

§5. Parsi Intestates

991. Under the Succession Act, 1925 Chapter-III provides the special rules for Parsi intestates. For the purpose of intestate succession among Parsis: (a) there is no distinction between those who were actually born in the lifetime of a person deceased and those who at the date of his death were only conceived in the womb, but who have been subsequently born alive; (b) a lineal descendant of an intestate who has died in the lifetime of the intestate without leaving a widow or widower or any lineal descendant or a widow of any lineal descendant shall not be taken into account in determining the manner in which the property of which the intestate has died intestate shall be divided; and (c) where a widow of any relative of an intestate has married again in the lifetime of the intestate, she shall not be entitled to receive any share of the property of which the intestate has died intestate, and she shall be deemed not to be existing at the intestates death.

992. The property of which a male Parsi dies intestate shall be divided: (a) where he dies leaving a widow and children, among the widow and children, so that the share of each son and of the widow shall be double the share of each daughter; or (b) where he dies leaving children but no widow, among the children, so that the share of each son shall be double the share of each daughter. Where a male Parsi dies leaving one or both parents in addition to children or a widow and children, the property of which he dies intestate shall be divided so that the father shall receive a share equal to half the share of a son, and the mother shall receive a share equal to half the share of a daughter.

993. The property of which a female Parsi dies intestate shall be divided: (a) where she dies leaving a widower and children among the widower and children so that the widower and each child receive equal shares; or (b) where she dies leaving children but no widower, among the children in equal shares.

994. In all cases where a Parsi dies leaving any lineal descendant, if any child of such intestate has died in the lifetime of the intestate, (the division of the share of the property of which the intestate has died intestate which such child would have taken if living at the intestates death shall be in accordance with the following rules, namely: (a) If such deceased child was a son, his widow and children shall take shares in accordance with the provisions of this Chapter as if he had died immediately after the intestates death : Provided that where such deceased son has left a widow or a widow of lineal descendant but no lineal descendent, the residue of his share after such distribution has been made shall be divided in accordance with the provisions of this Chapter as property of which the intestate has died intestate, and in making the division of such residue the said deceased son of the intestate shall not be taken into account. (b) If such deceased child was a daughter, her share shall be divided equally among her children. (c) If any child of such deceased child has also died during the lifetime of the intestate, the share which he/she would have taken if living at the intestates death shall be divided in like manner in accordance with clause (a) or clause (b) as the case may be. (d) Where a remoter lineal descendant of the intestate has died during the lifetime of the intestate, the provisions of clause (c) shall apply mutates mutants to the division of any share to which he/she would have been entitled if living at the intestates death by reason of the predeceased of all the intestates lineal descendants directly between him/her and the intestate.

995. Where a Parsi dies without leaving any lineal descendant but leaving a widow or widower or a widow of a lineal descendant, the property of which the intestate dies intestate shall be divided in accordance with the following rules, namely:

(a) if the intestate leaves a widow or widower but no widow of a lineal descendant, the widow or widower shall take half the said property;
(b) if the intestate leaves a widow or widower and also a widow of any lineal descendant, his widow or her widower shall receive one-third of the said property, and the widow of any lineal descendant shall receive another one-third, or if there is more than one such widow, the last mentioned one-third shall be divided equally among them;
(c) if the intestate leaves no widow or widower but one widow of a lineal descendant, she shall receive one-third of the said property or, if the intestate leaves no widow or widower but more than one widow of a lineal descendant, two-thirds of the said property shall be divided among such widows in equal shares;
(d) the residue after the division specified in clause (a), (b) or (c) has been made shall be distributed among the relatives of the intestate in the order specified in Part I of Schedule II. The next-of-kin standing first in Part I of the Schedule shall be preferred to those standing second, the second to the third, and so on in succession, provided that the property shall be so distributed that each male shall take double the share of each female standing in the same degree of propinquity; and
(e) if there are no relatives entitled to the residue under cause (d), the whole of the residue shall be distributed in proportion to the share specified among the persons entitled to receive shares under this section.

996. When a Parsi dies leaving neither lineal descendants nor a widow or widower nor a widow of any lineal descendant, his/her next-of-kin, in the order set forth in Part-II of Schedule II, shall be entitled to succeed to the whole of the property of which he/she dies interstate. The next-of-kin standing first in Part-II of that Schedule shall be preferred to those standing second, the second to the third, and so on in **succession**, provided that the property shall be so distributed that each male shall take double the share of each female standing in the same degree of propinquity.

997. Where there is no relative entitled to succeed under the other provisions, of Chapter-III of the Succession Act, 1925, to the property of which a Parsi has died intestate, the said property shall be divided equally among those of the intestates relatives who are in the nearest degree of kindred to him.

Chapter 2. Testamentary Succession

§1. Introduction

998. Under the Islamic Law of Muslims, any Muslim of sound mind and not a minor can dispose of his property by will. However a Muslim cannot by will dispose of more than a third of the surplus of his estate after payment of 'underal' expenses and debts. Bequests in excess of the legal third cannot take effect, unless the heirs consent thereto after the death of the testator.

§2. Capacity to make a Will

999. The Succession Act, 1925 (Part VI) deals with the wills and codicils made by any Hindu, Buddhist, Sikh or Jaina. Every person of sound mind not being a minor may dispose of his property by will. Explanation-1. A married woman may dispose by will of any property which she could alienate by her own act during her life. Explanation-2. Persons who are deaf or dumb or blind are not thereby incapacitated for making a will if they are able to know what they do by it. Explanation-3. A person who is ordinarily insane may make a will during an interval in which he is of sound mind. Explanation-4. No person can make a will while he is in such a state of mind, whether arising from intoxication or from illness or from any other cause that he does not know what he is doing. Illustrations: (i) A can perceive what is going on in his immediate neighbourhood, and can answer familiar questions, but has not a competent understanding as to the nature of his property, or the persons who are of kindred to him, or in whose favour it would be proper that he should make his will. A cannot make a valid will. (ii) A executes an instrument purporting to be his will, but he docs not understand the nature of the instrument, nor the effect of its provisions. This instrument is not a valid will. (iii) A, being very feeble and debilitated, but capable of exercising a judgment as to the proper mode of disposing of his property, makes a will. This is a valid will. A father, whatever his age may be, may by will appoint a guardian or guardians for his child during minority.

§3. Different types of Will

1000. **Unprivileged Wills:** Every testator, not being a soldier employed in an expedition or engaged in actual warfare, not an airman so employed or engaged, or a mariner at sea, shall execute his will according to the following rules: (a) The testator shall sign or shall affix his mark to the will, or it shall be signed by some other person in his presence and by his direction. (b) The signature or mark of the testator, or the signature of the person signing for him, shall be so placed that it shall appear that it was intended thereby to give effect to the writing as a will. (c) The will shall be attested by two or more witnesses, each of whom has seen the testator sign or affix his mark to the will or has seen some other person sign the will, in the presence and by the direction of the testator, or has received from the testator a personal acknowledgment of his signature or mark, or of the signature of such other person; and each of the witnesses shall sign the will in the presence of the testator, but it shall not be necessary that more than one witness be present at the same time, and no particular form of attestation shall be necessary. If a testator, in a will or codicil duly attested, refers to any other document than actually written as expressing any part of his intentions, such document shall be deemed to form a part of the will or codicil in which it is referred to of privileged wills.

1001. **Privileged wills:** Any soldier being employed in an expedition or engaged in actual warfare, or an airman so employed or engaged or any mariner being at sea, may, if he has completed the age of 18 years, dispose of his property by a will made in the manner provided in section 66. Such wills are called Privileged wills. Illustrations: (i) A, a medical officer attached to a regiment, is actually employed in an expedition. He is a soldier actually employed in an expedition, and can make a privileged will. (ii) A is at sea in a merchant-ship, of which he is the purser. He is a mariner, and, being at sea, can make a privileged will. (iii) A, a soldier serving in the field against insurgents, is a soldier engaged in actual warfare, and as such can make a privileged will. (iv) A, a mariner of a ship, in the course of a voyage, is temporarily on shore while he is lying in harbour. He is, for the purposes of this section, a mariner at sea, and can make a privileged will. (v) A, an admiral who commands a naval force, but who lives on shore, and only occasionally goes on board his ship, is not considered as at sea, and cannot make a privileged will. (vi) A, a mariner serving on a military expedition, but not being at sea, is considered as a soldier, and can make a privileged will.

1002. Privileged wills may be in writing, or may be made by word of mouth. The will may be written wholly by the testator, with his own hand. In such case, it need not be signed or attested. It may be written wholly or in part by another person, and signed by the testator. In such case, it need not be attested. If the instrument purporting to be a will is written wholly or in part by another person and is not signed by the testator, it shall be deemed to be his will, if it is shown that it was written by the testators directions or that he recognized it as his will. If it appears on the face of the instrument that the execution of it in the manner intended by the testator was not completed, the instrument shall not, by reason of that circumstance, be invalid, provided that his non-execution of it can be reasonably ascribed to some cause other than the abandonment of the testamentary intentions expressed in the instrument. If the soldier, airman or mariner has written instructions for the preparation of his will, but has died before it could be prepared and executed, such instructions shall be considered to constitute his will. If the soldier, airman or mariner has, in the presence of two witnesses, given verbal instructions for the preparation of his will, and they have been reduced into writing in his lifetime, but he has died before the instrument could be prepared and executed, such instructions shall be considered to constitute his will, although they may not have been reduced into writing in his presence, nor read over to him. The soldier, airman or mariner may make a will by word of mouth by declaring his intentions before two witnesses present at the same time. A will made by word of mouth shall he null at the expiration of one month after the testator, being still alive, has ceased to be entitled to make a privileged will.

1003. A will shall not be deemed to be insufficiently attested by reason of any benefit thereby given either by way of bequest or by way of appointment to any person attesting it, or to his/her wife or husband; but the bequest or appointment shall be void so far as concerns the person so attesting, or the wife or husband of such person, or any person claiming under either of them. Explanation: A legatee under a will does not lose his legacy by attesting a codicil which confirms the will.

1004. No person, by reason of interest in, or of his being an executor of, a will, shall be disqualified as a witness to prove the execution of the will or to prove the validity or invalidity thereof.

1005. No obliteration, interlineations or other alteration made in any unprivileged will after the execution thereof shall have any effect, except so far as the words or meaning of the will have been thereby rendered illegible or undiscernibly, unless such alteration has been executed in like manner as hereinbefore is required for the execution of the will: Provided that the will, as so altered, shall be deemed to be duly executed if the signature of the testator and the subscription of the witnesses is made in the margin or on some other part of the will opposite or near to such alteration, or at the foot or end of or opposite to a memorandum referring to such alteration, and written at the end or some other part of the will.

1006. The payment and apportionment of annuities has been prescribed under sections 338-340 of the Succession Act, 1925. Where an annuity is given by a will and no time is fixed for its commencement, it shall commence from the testators death, and the first payment shall be made at the expiration of a year next after that event.

1007. Where there is a direction that the annuity shall be paid quarterly or monthly, the first payment shall be due at the end of the first quarter or first month, as the case may be, after the testators death; and shall, if the executor or administrator thinks fit, be paid when due, but the executor or administrator shall not be bound to pay it till the end of the year.

1008. Where there is a direction that the first payment of an annuity shall be made within one month or any other division of time from the death of the testator, or on a day certain, the successive payments are to be made on the anniversary of the earliest day on which the will authorizes the first payment to be made. If the annuitant dies in the interval between the times of payment, an apportioned share of the annuity shall be paid to his representative.

§4. Revocation of Will

1009. Every will can be revoked by the marriage of the maker, except a will made in exercise of a power of appointment, when the property over which the power of appointment is exercised would not, in default of such appointment, pass to his/her executor or administrator, or to the person entitled in case of intestacy.

Explanation: Where a man is invested with power to determine the disposition of property of which he is not the owner, he is said to have power to appoint such property.

1010. No unprivileged will or codicil, nor any part thereof, shall be revoked otherwise than by marriage, or by another will or codicil, or by some writing declaring an intention to revoke the same and executed in the manner in which an unprivileged will is hereinbefore required to be executed, or by the burning, tearing or otherwise destroying the same by the testator or by some person in his presence and by his direction with the intention of revoking the same. Illustrations: (i) A has made an unprivileged will. Afterwards, A makes another unprivileged will which purports to revoke the first. This is a revocation. (ii) A has made an unprivileged will. Afterwards, A, being entitled to make a privileged will, makes a privileged will, which purports to revoke his unprivileged will. This is a revocation.

1011. A privileged will or codicil may be revoked by the testator by an unprivileged will or codicil, or by any act expressing an intention to revoke it and accompanied by such formalities as would be sufficient to give validity to a privileged will, or by the burning, tearing or otherwise destroying the same by the testator, or by some person in his presence and by his direction, with the intention of revoking the same. Explanation: In order to the revocation of a privileged will or codicil by an act accompanied by such formalities as would be sufficient to give validity to a privileged will, it is not necessary that the testator should at the time of doing that act be in a situation which entitles him to make a privileged will.

1012. No unprivileged will or codicil, nor any part thereof, which has been revoked in any manner, shall be revived otherwise than by the re-execution thereof, or by a codicil executed in manner hereinbefore required, and showing an intention to revive the same. When any will or codicil, which has been partly revoked and afterwards wholly revoked, is revived, such revival shall not extend to so much thereof as has been revoked before the revocation of the whole thereof, unless an intention to the contrary is shown by the will or codicil.

§5. Void Will

1013. A will or any part of a will, the making of which has been caused by fraud or coercion, or by such importunity that takes away the free agency of the testator, is void. Illustrations: (i) A, falsely and knowingly represents to the testator that the testator's only child is dead, or that he has done some undutiful act and thereby induces the testator to make a will in his A's favour; such will has been obtained by fraud, and is invalid. (ii) A, by fraud and deception, prevails upon the testator to bequeath a legacy to him. The bequest is void. (iii) A, being a prisoner by lawful authority, makes his will. The will is not invalid by reason of the imprisonment. (iv) A threatens to shoot B, or to burn his house or to cause him to be arrested on a criminal charge, unless he makes a bequest in favour of C. B, in consequence, makes a bequest in favour of C. The bequest is void, the making of it having been caused by coercion. (v) A, being of sufficient intellect, if undisturbed by the influence of others, to make a will yet being so much under the control of B that he is not a free agent, makes a will, dictated by B. It appears that he would not have executed the will but for fear of B. The will is invalid. (vi) A, being in so feeble a state of health as to be unable to resist importunity, is pressed by B to make a will of a certain purport and does so merely to purchase peace and in submission to B. The will is invalid. (vii) A being in such a state of health as to be capable of exercising his own judgment and volition, B uses urgent intercession and persuasion with him to induce him to make a will of a certain purport. A, in consequence of the intercession and persuasion, but in the free exercise of his judgment and volition, makes his will in the manner recommended by B. The will is not rendered invalid by the intercession and persuasion of B. (viii) A, with a view to obtaining a legacy from B, pays him attention and flatters him and thereby produces in him a capricious partiality to A. B, in consequence of such attention and flattery, makes his will, by which he leaves a legacy to A. The bequest is not rendered invalid by the attention and flattery of A. A will is liable to be revoked or altered by the maker of it at any time when he is competent to dispose of his property by will.

§6. Provisions and Interpretation of Will

1014. The Succession Act, 1925 (Chapter VI) deals with the preparation of wills. It is not necessary that any technical words or terms of art be used in a will, but only that the wording be such that the intentions of the testator can be known therefrom.

1015. For the purpose of determining questions as to what person or what property is denoted by any words used in a will, a Court shall inquire into every material fact relating to the persons who claim to be interested under such will, the property which is claimed as the subject of disposition, the circumstances of the testator and of his family, and into every fact a knowledge of which may conduce to the right application of the words which the testator has used. Illustrations: (i) A, by his will, bequeaths PKR 1,000 to his eldest son or to his youngest grandchild, or to his cousin, Mary. A Court may make inquiry in order to ascertain to what person the description in the will applies. (ii) A, by his will, leaves to B 'my estate called Black Acre'. It may be necessary to take evidence in order to ascertain what is the subject-matter of the bequest; that is to say, what estate of the testators is called Black Acre. (iii) A, by his will, leaves to B 'the estate which purchased of C'. It may be necessary to take evidence in order to ascertain what estate the testator purchased of C.

1016. Where the words used in a will to designate or describe a legatee or a class of legatees sufficiently shows what is meant, an error in the name or description shall not prevent the legacy from taking effect. A mistake in the name of a legatee may be corrected by a description of him, and a mistake in the description of a legatee may be corrected by the name. Illustrations: (i) A bequeaths a legacy 'to Thomas, the second son of my brother John'. The testator has an only brother named

John, who has no son named Thomas, but has a second son whose name is William. William will have the legacy. (ii) A bequeaths a legacy 'to Thomas, the second son of my brother John'. The testator has an only brother, named John, whose first son is named Thomas, and whose second son is named William. Thomas will have the legacy. (iii) The testator bequeaths his property 'to A and B, the legitimate children of C'. C has no legitimate child, but has two illegitimate children, A and B. The bequest to A and B takes effect, although they are illegitimate. (iv) The testator gives his residuary estate to be divided among 'my seven children and, proceeding to enumerate them, mentions six names only. This omission will not prevent the seventh child from taking a share with the others.' (v) The testator, having six grandchildren, makes a bequest to 'my six grand children' and, proceeding to mention them by their Christian names, mentions one twice over omitting another altogether. The one whose name is not mentioned will take a share with the others. (vi) The testator bequeaths 'PKR 1,000 to each of the three children of A'. At the date of the will, A has four children. Each of these four children will, if he survives the testator, receive a legacy of PKR 1,000.

1017. Where any word material to the full expression of the meaning has been omitted, it may be supplied by the context. Illustration: The testator gives a legacy of 'PKR 500' to his daughter A and a legacy of 'PKR 500' to his daughter B. A will take a legacy of PKR 500.

1018. If the thing which the testator intended to bequeath can be sufficiently identified from the description of it given in the will but some parts of the description do not apply, such parts of the description shall be rejected as erroneous, and the bequest shall take effect. Illustration (i) A bequeaths to B 'my marsh-lands lying in L and in the occupation of X'. The testator had marsh-lands lying in L but had no marsh-lands in the occupation of X. 'The words in the occupation of X' shall be rejected as erroneous, and the marsh-lands of the testator lying in L will pass by the bequest. (ii) The testator bequeaths to A 'my zamindari of Rampur'. He had an estate at Rampur, but it was a Talaq and not a zamindari. The Talaq passes by this bequest.

1019. If a will mentions several circumstances as descriptive of the thing which the testator intends to bequeath, and there is any property of his in respect of which all those circumstances exist, the bequest shall be considered as limited to such property, and it shall not be lawful to reject any part of the description as erroneous, because the testator had other property to which such part of the description does not apply. Explanation: In judging whether a case falls within the meaning of this section, any words which would be liable to rejection under section 78 shall be deemed to have been struck out of the will. Illustrations: (i) A bequeaths to B 'my marsh-lands lying in L and in the occupation of X'. The testator had marsh-lands lying in L, some of which were in the occupation of X, and some not in the occupation of X. The bequest will be considered as limited to such of the testators marsh-lands lying in L as were in the occupation of X. (ii) A bequeaths to B 'my marsh-lands lying in L and in the occupation of X, comprising 1,000 "bighas" of lands'. The testator had marah-lands lying in L some of which were in the occupation of X and some not in the occupation of X. The measurement is wholly in applicable to the marsh-lands of either class, or to the whole taken together. The measurement will be considered as struck out of the will, and such of the testators marsh-lands lying in L as were in the occupation of X shall alone pass by the bequest.

1020. Where the words of a will are unambiguous, but it is found by extrinsic evidence that they admit of applications, one only of which can have been intended by the testator, extrinsic evidence may be taken to show which of these applications was intended. Illustrations: (i) A man, having two cousins of the name of Mary, bequeaths a sum of money to 'my cousin Mary'. It appears that there are two persons, each answering the description in the will. That description, therefore, admits of two applications, only one of which can have been intended by the testator. Evidence is admissible to show which of the two applications was intended. (ii) A, by his will, leaves to B 'my estate called Sultanpur Kliurd'. It turns out that he had two estates called Sultanpur Kliurd. Evidence is admissible to show which estate was intended.

1021. Where there is an ambiguity or deficiency on the face of a will, no extrinsic evidence as to the intentions of the testator shall be admitted. Illustrations: (i) A man has an aunt, Caroline, and a cousin, Mary, and has no aunt of the name of Mary. By his will he bequeaths PKR 1,000 to 'my aunt. Caroline' and PKR 1,000 to 'my cousin, Mary' and afterwards bequeaths PKR 2,000 to 'my before-mentioned aunt, Mary'. There is no person to whom the description given in the will can apply, and evidence is not admissible to show who was meant by 'my before-mentioned aunt, Mary'. The bequest is therefore void for uncertainty. (ii) A bequeaths PKR 1,000 to leaving a blank for the name of the legatee. Evidence is not admissible to show what name the testator intended to insert. (iii) A bequeath to B rupees, or 'my estate of'. Evidence is not admissible to show what sum or what estate the testator Intended to insert.

1022. The meaning of any clause in a will is to be collected from the entire instrument, and all its parts are to be construed with reference to each other. Illustration: (i) The testator gives to B a specific fund or property at the death of A, and by a subsequent clause gives the whole of his property to A. The effect of the several clauses taken together is to vest the specific fund or property in A for life, and after his decease in B; it appearing from the bequest to B that the testator meant to use in a restricted sense the words in which he describes what he gives to A. (ii) Where a testator having an estate, one part of which is called Black Acre, bequeaths the whole of his estate to A, and in another part of his will bequeaths Black Acre to B, the latter bequest is to be read as an exception out of the first as if he had said 'I give Black Acre to B, and all the rest of any estate to A'.

1023. General words may be understood in a restricted sense where it may be collected from the will that the testator meant to use them in a restricted sense; and words may be understood in a wider sense than that which they usually bear, where it may be collected from the other words of the will that the testator meant to use them in such wider sense. Illustrations: (i) A testator gives to A 'my farm in the occupation of B', and to C 'all my marshland in L'. Part of the farm in the occupation of B consists of marsh-lands in L, and the testator also has other marsh-lands in L. The general words, 'all my marsh-lands in L', are restricted by the gift to A. A takes the whole of the farm in the occupation of B, including that portion of the farm which consists of marsh-lands in L. (ii) The testator (a sailor on ship-board) bequeathed to his mother his gold ring, buttons and chest of clothes and to his friend, A (a shipmate), his red box, clasp-knife and all things not before bequeathed. The testators share in a house does not pass to A under this bequest. (iii) A, by his will, bequeathed to B all his household furniture, plate, linen, china, books, pictures and all other goods of whatever kind; and afterwards bequeathed to B a specked part of his property. Under the first bequest, B is entitled only to such articles of the testators as are of the same nature with the articles therein enumerated.

1024. Where a clause is susceptible of two meanings according to one of which it has some effect, and according to the other of which it can have none, the former shall be preferred. No part of a will shall be rejected as destitute of meaning if it is possible to put a reasonable construction upon it. If the same words occur in different parts of the same will, they shall be taken to have been used everywhere in the same sense, unless a contrary intention appears.

1025. The intention of the testator shall not be set aside because it cannot take effect to the full extent, but effect is to be given to it as far as possible. Illustration: The testator by a will made on his death-bed bequeathed all his property to CD for life and after his decease to a certain hospital. The intention of the testator cannot take effect to its full extent, because the gift to the hospital is void, but it will take effect so far as regards the gift to CD.

1026. Where two clauses or gifts in a will are irreconcilable, so that they cannot possibly stand together, the last shall prevail. Illustration: (i) The testator by the first clause of his will leaves his estate of Gujrat 'to A', and by the last clause of his will leaves it 'to B and not to A'. B will have it. (ii) If a man at the commencement, of his will gives his house to A, and at the close of it directs that his house shall be sold and the proceeds invested for the benefit of B, the latter disposition will prevail.

1027. A will or bequest not expressive of any definite intention is void for uncertainty. Illustration: If a testator says 'I bequeath goods to A', or 'I bequeath to A', or 'I leave to A all the goods mentioned in the Schedule' and no Schedule is found, or 'I bequeath money, wheat, oil', or the like, without saying how much, this is void.

1028. The description contained in a will of property, the subject of gift, shall, unless a contrary intention appears by the will, be deemed to refer to and comprise the property answering that description at the death of the testator.

1029. Unless a contrary intention appears by the will, a bequest of the testator shall be construed to include any property which he may have power to appoint by will to any object he may think proper, and shall, operate as an execution of such power; and a bequest of property described in a general manner shall be construed to include any property to which such description may extend, which he may have power to appoint by will to any object he may think proper, and shall operate as an execution of such power.

1030. Where property is bequeathed to or for the benefit of certain objects as a specified person may appoint or for the benefit of certain objects in such proportions as a specified person may appoint, and the will does not provide for the event of no appointment being made; if the power given by the will is not exercised, the property belongs to all the objects of the power in equal shares. Illustration: A, by his will, bequeaths a fund to his wife, for her life, and directs that at her death it shall be divided among his children in such proportions as she shall appoint. The widow dies without having made any appointment. The fund will be divided equally among the children.

1031. Where a bequest is made to the 'heirs' or 'right heirs' or 'relations' or 'nearest relations' or 'family' or 'kindred' or 'nearest of kin' or 'next-of-kin' of a particular person without any qualifying terms, and the class so designation forms the direct and independent object of the bequest, the property bequeathed shall be distributed as if it had belonged to such person, and he had died intestate in respect of it, leaving assets for the payment of his debts independently of such property. Illustration: (i) A leaves his property 'In my own nearest relations'. The property goes to those who would be entitled to it if A had died intestate, leaving assets for the payment of his debts independently of such property (ii) A bequeaths PKR 10,000 'to B for his life, and, after the death of B, to my own right heirs'. The legacy after B's death belongs to those who would be entitled to it if it had formed part of A's un-bequeathed property. (iii) A leaves his property to B; but if B dies before him, to B's next-of-kin; B dies before A; the property devolves as if it had belonged to B, and he had died intestate, leaving assets for the payment of his debts independently of such property. (iv) A leaves PKR 10,000 'to B for his life, and after his decease to the hairs of C'. The legacy goes as if it had belonged to C, and he had died intestate, leaving assets for the payment of his debts independently of the legacy.

1032. Where a bequest is made to the 'representatives' or 'legal representatives' or 'personal representatives' or 'executors or administrators' of a particular person, and the class so designated forms the direct and independent object of the bequest, the property bequeathed shall be distributed as if it had belonged to such person and he had died intestate in respect of it. Illustration: A bequest is made to the 'legal representatives' of A. A has died intestate and insolvent. B is his administrator. B is entitled to receive the legacy, and will apply it in the first place to the discharge of such part of A's debts as may remain unpaid: if there be any surplus, B will pay it to those persons who at A's death would have been entitled to receive any property of A's which might remain after payment of his debts, or to the representatives of such persons.

1033. Where property is bequeathed to any person, he is entitled to the whole interest of the testator therein, unless it appears from the will that only a restricted interest was intended for him.

1034. Where property is bequeathed to a person with a bequest in the alternative to another person or to a class of persons, then, if a contrary intention does not appear by the will, the legatee first named shall be entitled to the legacy if he is alive at the time when it takes effect; but if he is then dead, the person or class of persons named in the second branch of the alternative shall take the legacy. Illustrations: (i) A bequest is made to A or to B. A survives the testator. B takes nothing. (ii) A bequest is made to A or to B. A dies after the date of the will, and before the testator. The legacy goes to B. (iii) A bequest is made to A or to B. A is dead at the date of the will. The legacy goes to B. (iv) Property is bequeathed to A or his heirs. A survives the testator. A takes the property absolutely. (v) Property is bequeathed to A or his nearest of kin. A dies in the lifetime of the testator. Upon the death of the testator, the bequest to A's nearest of kin takes effect. (vi) Property is bequeathed to A for life, and after his death to B or his heirs. A and B survive the testator. B dies in A's lifetime. Upon A's death the bequest to the heirs of B takes effect. (vii) Property is bequeathed to A for life, and after his death to B or his heir; B dies in the testators lifetime. A survives the testator. Upon A's death, the bequest to the heirs of B takes effect.

1035. Where property is bequeathed to a person, and words are added which describe a class of persons but do not denote them as direct objects of a distinct and independent gift, such person is entitled to the whole interest of the testator therein, unless a contrary intention appears by the will. Illustration (i) A bequest is made to A and his children, to A and his children by his present wife, to A and his heirs, to A and the heirs of his body, to A and the heirs male of his body, to A and the heirs female of his body, to A and his issue, to A and his family, to A and his descendants, to A and his representatives, to A and his personal representatives, to A, his executors and administrators. In each of these cases, A takes the whole interest which the testator had in the property. (ii) A bequest is made to A and his brothers. A and his brothers are jointly entitled to the legacy. (iii) A bequest is made to A for life and after his death to his issue. At the death of A, the property belongs in equal shares to all persons who then answer the description of issue of A.

1036. Where a bequest is made to a class of persons under a general description only, no one to whom the words of the description are not in their ordinary sense applicable shall take the legacy. In a will (a) the word 'children' applies only to lineal descendants in the first degree of the person whose 'children are spoken of'; (b) the word 'grandchildren' applies only to lineal descendants in the second degree of the person whose 'grandchildren' are spoken of; (c) the words 'nephews' and 'nieces' apply only to children of brothers or sisters; (d) the words 'cousins', or 'first cousins', or 'cousins-german', apply only to children of brothers or of sisters of the father or mother of the person whose 'cousins', or 'first cousins', or 'cousins-german', are spoken of; (e) the words 'First cousins once removed' apply only to children of cousins-german, or to cousins-german of a parent of the person whose 'first cousins once removed' are spoken of; (f) the words 'second cousins' apply only to grandchildren of brothers or of sisters of the grandfather or grandmother of the person whose 'second cousins' are spoken of; (g) the words 'issue' and 'descendants' apply to all lineal descendants whatever of the parson whose 'issue' or 'descendants' are spoken of; (h) words expressive of collateral relationship apply alike to relatives of full and of half blood; and (i) all words expressive of relationship apply to a child in the womb who is afterwards born alive.

1037. In the absence of any intimation to the contrary in a will, the word 'child', the word 'son', the word 'daughter', or any word which expresses relationship, is to be understood as denoting only a legitimate relative, or, where there is no such legitimate relative, a person who has acquired, at the date of the will, the reputation of being such relative. Illustration: (i) A having three children, B, C and D, of whom B and C are legitimate and D is illegitimate, leaves his property to be equally divided among 'my children'. The property belongs to B, and C in equal shares, to the exclusion of D. (ii) A, having a niece of illegitimate birth, who has acquired the reputation of being his niece, and having no legitimate niece bequeaths a sum of money to his niece. The illegitimate niece is entitled to the legacy. (iii) A, having in his will enumerated his children, and named as one of them B, who is illegitimate, leaves a legacy to 'my said children'. B will take a share in the legacy alongwith the legitimate children. (iv) A leaves a legacy to 'the children of B'. B is dead and has left none but illegitimate children. All those who had at the dale of the will acquired the reputation of being the children of B are objects of the gift. (v) A bequeaths a legacy to 'the children of E'. B never had any legitimate child. C and D had, at the date of the will, acquired the reputation of being children of B. After the date of the will and before the death of the testator, E and F were born, and acquired the reputation of being children of B. Only C and D are objects of the bequest. (vi) A makes a bequest in favour of his child by a certain woman, not his wife, B had acquired at the date of the will the reputation of being the child of A by the woman designated. B takes the legacy. (vii) A makes a bequest in favour of his child to be born of a woman who never becomes his wife. The bequest is void. (viii) A makes a bequest in favour of the child of which a certain woman, not married to him, is pregnant. The bequest is void.

§7. CONSANGUINITY

1038. The Succession Act, 1924, sections 23~28 (Part IV) deals with the consanguinity. Succession to moveable and immoveable property of any intestate in Pakistan is governed under the laws in Pakistan in terms of section 5 of the Succession Act, 1925. Property in case of Christian succession devolves upon surviving spouses or upon those who are kindred in ascending or descending order to the intestate (PLD 2003 Kar. 270).

1039. Kindred or consanguinity in the connection or relation of persons descended from the same stock or common ancestor. Property in case of Christian succession devolves upon surviving spouses or upon those who are kindred in ascending or descending order to the intestate (PLD 2003 Kar. 270).

1040. Lineal consanguinity is that which subsists between two persons, one of whom is descended in a direct line from the other, as between a man and his father, grandfather and great-grandfather, and so upwards in the direct ascending line; so between a man and his son, grandson, great-grandson and so downwards in the direct descending line. Every generation constitutes a degree, either a sending or descending. A persons father is related to him in the first degree, and so likewise is his son; his grandfather and grandson in the second degree; his great-grandfather and great-grandson in the third degree, and so on.

1041. Collateral consanguinity is that which subsists between two persons who are descended from the same stock or ancestor, but neither of whom is descended in a direct line from the other. For the purpose of ascertaining in what degree of kindred any collateral relative stands to a person deceased, it is necessary to reckon upwards from the person deceased to the common stock and then downwards to the collateral relative, a degree being allowed for each person, both ascending and descending.

1042. For the purpose of succession, there is no distinction (a) between those who are related to a person deceased through his father, and those who are related to him through his mother; or (b) between those who are related to a person deceased by the full blood, and those who are related to him by the half blood; or (c) between those who were actually born in the lifetime of a person deceased and those who at the date of his death were only conceived in the womb, but who have been subsequently born alive. Degrees of kindred are computed in the manner set forth in the table of kindred set out in Schedule I of the Succession Act, 1925.

1043. Illustrations: (i) The person whose relatives are to be reckoned, and his cousin-german, or first cousin, are, related in the fourth degree; there being one degree of ascent to the father and another to the common ancestor, the grandfather; and from him one of descent to the uncle, and another to the cousin-german, making in all four degrees. (ii) A grandson of the brother and a son of the uncle, that is, a great nephew and a cousin-german, are in equal degree being each four degrees removed. (iii) A grandson of a cousin-german is in the same degree as the grandson of a great-uncle, for they are both in the sixth degree of kindred.

1044. Under section 138 of the Succession Act, 1925 if a fund is bequeathed absolutely to or for the benefit of any person, but the will contains a direction that it shall be applied or enjoyed in a particular manner, the legatee shall be entitled to receive the fund as if the will had contained no such direction. Illustration: A sum of money is bequeathed towards purchasing a country residence for A, or to purchase an annuity for A, or to place A in any business. A chooses to receive the legacy in money. He is entitled to do so.

1045. Where a testator absolutely bequeaths a fund, so as to sever it from his own estate but directs that the mode of enjoyment of it by the legatee shall be restricted so as to secure a specified benefit for the legatee; if that benefit cannot be obtained for the legatee, the fund belongs to him as if the will had contained no such direction. Illustrations: (i) A bequeaths the residue of his property divided equally among his daughters, and directs that the shares of the daughters shall be settled upon themselves respectively for life and be paid to their children after their death. All the daughters die unmarried. The representatives of each daughter are entitled to her share of the residue. (ii) A directs his trustees to raise a sum of money for his daughter, and he then directs that they shall invest the fund and pay the income arising from it to her during her life, and divide the principal among her children after her death. The daughter dies without having ever had a child. Her representatives are entitled to the fund.

1046. Where a testator does not absolutely bequeath a fund, so as to sever it from his own estate, but gives it for certain purposes, and part of those purposes cannot be fulfilled, the fund, or so much of it as has not been exhausted upon the objects contemplated by the will; remains a part of the estate of the testator. Illustrations: (i) A directs that his trustees shall invest a sum of money in a particular way, and shall pay the interest to his son for life, and at his death shall divide the principal among his children. The son dies without having ever had a child. The fund, after the son's death, belongs to the estate of the testator. (a) A bequeaths the residue of his estate, to be divided equally among his daughters, with a direction that they are to have the interest only during their lives, and that at their decease the fund shall go to their children. The daughters have no children. The fund belongs to the estate of the testator.

1047. If a legacy is bequeathed to a person who is named an executor of the will, he shall not take the legacy, unless he proves the will or otherwise manifests an intention to act as executor. Illustration: A legacy is given to A, who is named an executor. A orders the funeral according to the directions contained in the will, and dies a few days after the testator, without having proved the will. A has manifested an intention to act as executor.

1048. Under the Succession Act, 1925 (sections 180~190), where a person, by his will, professes to dispose of something which he has no right to dispose of, the person to whom the thing belongs shall elect either to confirm such disposition or to dissent from it, and, in the latter case, he shall give up any benefits which may have been provided for him by the will.

1049. An interest relinquished in the circumstances stated in section 180 shall devolve as if it had not been disposed of by the will in favour of the legatee, subject, nevertheless, to the charge of making good to the disappointed legatee the amount or value of the gift attempted to be given to him by the will.

1050. The provisions of sections 180 and 181 apply whether the testator does or does not believe that which he professes to dispose of by his will to be his own.

Illustrations: (i) The farm of Sultanpur was the property of C. A bequeathed it to B, giving a legacy of PKR 1,000 to C. C has elected to retain his farm of Sultanpur, which is worth PKR 800. C forfeits his legacy of PKR 1,000, of which PKR 800 goes to B, and the remaining PKR 200 falls into the residuary bequest, or devolves according to the rules of intestate succession, as the case may be. (ii) A bequeaths an estate to B in case B's elder brother (who is married and has children) shall leave no issue living at his death. A also bequeaths to C a jewel, which belongs to B. B must elect to give up the jewel or to lose the estate. (iii) A bequeaths to B PKR 1,000, and to C an estate which will under a settlement, belong to B is his elder brother (who is married and has children) shall leave no issue living at his death. B must elect to give up the estate or to lose the legacy. (iv) A, a person of the age of 18, domiciled in Pakistan but owning real property in England, to which C is heir at law, bequeaths a legacy to C and, subject thereto, devises and bequeaths to B 'all my property whatsoever and wheresoever', and dies under 21. The real property in England does not pass by the will. C may claim his legacy without giving up the real property in England.

1051. A bequest for a persons benefit is, for the purpose of election, the same thing as a bequest made to himself. Illustration: The farm of Sultanpur Khurd being the property of B, A bequeathed it to C: and bequeathed another farm called Sultanpur Buzurg to his own executors with a direction that it should be sold and the proceeds applied in payment of B's debts. B must elect whether he will abide by the will, or keep his farm of Sultanpur Khurd in opposition to it.

1052. A person taking no benefit directly under a will, but deriving a benefit under it indirectly, is not put to his election. Illustration: The lands of Sultanpur are settled upon C for life, and after his death upon D, his only child. A bequeaths the lands of Sultanpur to B, and PKR 1,000 to C. C dies intestate shortly after the testator, and without having made any election. D takes out administration to C, and as administrator; elects on behalf of C's estate to take under the will. In that capacity, he receives the legacy of PKR 1,000 and accounts to B for the rents of the lands of Sultanpur which accrued after the death of the testator and before the death of C. In his individual character, he retains the lands of Sultanpur in opposition to the will.

1053. A person who in his individual capacity takes a benefit under a will may, in another character, elect to take in opposition to the will. Illustration: The estate of Sultanpur is settled upon A for life, and after his death, upon B. A leaves the estate of Sultanpur to D, and PKR 2,000 to B, and PKR 1,000 to C, who is B's only child. B dies intestate, shortly after the testator, without having made an election. C takes out administration to B, and as administrator elects to keep the estate of Sultanpur in opposition to the will, and to relinquish the legacy of PKR 2,000. C may do this, and yet claim his legacy of PKR 1,000 under the will.

1054. Notwithstanding anything contained in sections 180 to 185, where a particular gift is expressed in the will to be in lieu of something belonging to the legatee which is also in terms disposed of by the will, then, if the legatee claims that thing, he must relinquish the particular gift, but he is not bound to relinquish any other benefit given to him by the will. Illustration: Under A's marriage-settlement his wife is entitled, if she survives him, to the enjoyment of the estate of Sultanpur during her life. A by his will bequeaths to his wife an annuity of PKR 200 during her life, in lieu of her interest in the estate of Sultanpur, which estate he bequeaths to his son. He also gives his wife a legacy of PKR 1,000. The widow elects to take what she is entitled to under the settlement. She is bound to relinquish the annuity but not the legacy of PKR 1,000.

1055. Acceptance of a benefit given by a will constitutes an election by the legatee to take under the will, if he had knowledge of his right to elect and of those circumstances which would influence the judgment of a reasonable man in making an election, or if he waives inquiry into the circumstances. Illustrations: (i) A is owner of an estate called Sultanpur Khurd, and has a life interest in another estate called Sultanpur Buzurg to which upon his death his son B will be absolutely entitled. The will of A gives the estate of Sultanpur Khurd to B, and the estate of Sultanpur Buzurg to C. B, in ignorance of his own right to the estate of Sultanpur Buzurg, allows C to take possession of it, and enters into possession of the estate of Sultanpur Khurd. B has not con-finned the bequest of Sultanpur Buzurg to C. (ii) B, the eldest son of A, is the possessor of an estate called Sultanpur. A bequeaths Sultanpur to C, and to B the residue of A's property. B having been informed by A's executors that the residue will amount to PKR 5,000, allows C to take possession of Sultanpur. He afterwards discovers that the residue does not amount to more than PKR 500. B has not confirmed the bequest of the estate of Sultanpur to C.

1056. Such knowledge or waiver of inquiry shall, in the absence of evidence to the contrary, be presumed if the legatee has enjoyed for two years the benefit provided for him by the will without doing any act to express dissent.

Such knowledge or waiver of inquiry may be inferred from any act of the legatee which renders it impossible to place the persons interested in the subject-matter of the bequest in the same condition as if such act had not been done. Illustration: A bequeaths to B an estate to which C is entitled, and to C a coal mine. C takes possession of the mine and exhausts it. He has thereby confirmed the bequest of the estate to B.

1057. If the legatee does not, within one year after the death of the testator, signify to the testators representatives his intention to confirm or to dissent from the will, the representatives shall, upon the expiration of that period, require him to make his election; and, if he does not comply with such requisition within a reasonable time after he has received it, he shall be deemed to have elected to confirm the will.

1058. In case of disability, the election shall be postponed until the disability ceases, or until the election is made by some competent authority.

§8. The Joint Will

1059. Two people jointly make a Will that in case of death of any one, the property and assets shall be owned by the other. It is also clarified in the Will that if second person also dies, then how the property and assets would be dealt. It also stipulates what will happen with the assets when the second person dies. This type of Will is essentially a contract between the two makers and requires the consent of both for it to be revoked. On the plus side, a joint Will is designed to prevent the surviving person, usually the spouse, from changing his mind about the disposition of the property after the first person dies. For example, if you were worried that your wife would remarry after your death and might rewrite her Will to leave everything to her new stepchild, the joint Will might make sense. But, on the negative side, joint Wills can tie up property for years until the second person dies, and the survivor is unable to revise the Will to reflect changed circumstances. During those years, the survivor's situation might change so much that a new Will would be appropriate, but the deceased person cannot approve a new Will. The survivor is either stuck with the Will as written, or else will have to go through all kinds of legal hoops to try to invalidate the original contract. For example, suppose your husband dies first, and your daughter later marries a millionaire and does not need your money. Unfortunately, all of the property that came to you through the joint Will will have to be passed on as the Will dictates and you have no choice in the matter.

1060. Under Succession Act, 1925 section 106 if a legacy is given to two persons jointly, and one of them dies before the testator, the other legatee takes the whole. Illustration: The legacy is simply to A and B. A dies before the testator. B takes the legacy.

§9. Bequests

1061. The Bequests in Pakistan are regulated under Chapter-VI of the Succession Act, 1925. The bequest means receiving of property through will. Under the Succession Act, 1925 if a will purports to make two bequests to the same person, and a question arises whether the testator intended to make the second bequest instead of or in addition to the first; if there is nothing in the will to show what he intended, the following rules shall have effect in, determining the construction to be put upon the will: (a) If the same specific thing is bequeathed twice to the same legatee in the same will or in the will and again in the codicil, he is entitled to receive that specific thing only. (b) Where one and the same will or one and the same codicil purports to make, in two places, a bequest to the same person of the same quantity or amount of anything, he shall be entitled to one such legacy only. (c) If two legacies of unequal amount are given to the same person in the same will, or in the same codicil, the legatee is entitled to both. (d) If two legacies, whether equal or unequal in amount, are given to the same legatee, one by a will and the other by a codicil, or each by a different codicil, the legatee is entitled to both legacies. Explanation: In clauses (a) to (d) of this section, the word 'will' does not include a codicil. Illustrations: (i) A, having ten shares, and no more, in this Imperial Bank of

India, made his will, which contain near its commencement the word 'I bequeath my ten shares in the Imperial Bank of India to B'. After other bequests, the will concludes with the words 'and I bequeath my ten shares in the Imperial Bank of India to B'. B is entitled simply to receive A's ten shares in the Imperial Bank of India. (ii) A, having one diamond ring, which was given to him by B, bequeaths to C the diamond ring which was given by B. A afterwards made a codicil to his will, and thereby, after giving other legacies, he bequeathed to C the diamond ring which was given to him by B. C can claim nothing except the diamond ring which was given to A by B. (iii) A, by his will, bequeaths to B the sum of PKR 5,000 and afterwards in the same will repeats the bequest in the same words. B is entitled to one legacy of PKR 5,090 only. (iv) A by, his will bequeaths to B the sum of PKR 5,000 and afterwards in the same will bequeaths to B the sum of PKR 6,000. B is entitled to receive PKR 11,000. (v) A, by his will, bequeaths to B PKR 5,000 and by a codicil to the will he bequeaths to him PKR 5,000. B is entitled to receive PKR 10,000. (vi) A, by one codicil to his will, bequeaths to B PKR 5,000 and by another codicil bequeaths to him PKR 6,000. B is entitled to receive PKR 11,000. (vii) A, by his will, bequeaths 'PKR 500 to B because she was my nurse', and in another part of the will bequeaths PKR 500 to B 'because she went to England with my children'. B is entitled to receive, PKR 1,000, (viii) A, by his will, bequeaths to B the sum of PKR 5,000 and also, in another part of the will, an annuity of PKR 400. B is entitled to both legacies. (ix) A, by his will, bequeaths to B the sum of PKR 5,000 and also bequeaths to him the sum of PKR 5,000 if he shall attain the age of 18. B is, entitled absolutely to one sum of PKR 5,000, and takes a contingent interest in another sum of PKR 5,000.

1062. A residuary legatee may be constituted by any words that show an intention on the part of testator that the person designated shall take the surplus or residue of his property. Illustrations: (i) A makes her will, consisting of several testamentary papers, in one of which are contained the following words: 'I think there will be something left, after all funeral expenses, etc., to give to B, now at school, towards equipping him to any profession he may hereafter be appointed to.' B is constituted residuary legatee. (ii) A makes his will, with the following passage at the end of it: - 'l believe there will be found sufficient in my bankers hands to defray and discharge my debts, which I hereby desire B to do and keep the residue for her own use and pleasure'. E is constituted of the residuary legates, (iii) A bequeaths all his property to B, except certain stocks and funds which he bequeaths to C. B is the residuary legatee.

1063. Under a residuary bequest, the legatee is entitled to all property belonging to the testator at the time of his, death, of which he has not made any other testamentary disposition which is capable of taking effect. Illustration: A, by his will bequeaths certain legacies, of which one is void under section 118, and another lapses by the death of the legatee. He bequeaths the residue of his property to B. After the date of his will, A purchases a zamindari, which belongs to him at the time of his death. B is entitled to the two legacies and the zamindari as part of the residue.

1064. If a legacy is given in general terms, without specifying the time when it is to be paid, the legatee has a vested interest in it from the day of the death of the testator, and, if he dies without having received it, it shall pass to his representatives. If the legatee does not survive the testator, the legacy cannot take effect, but shall lapse and form part of the residue of the testators property, unless it appears by the will that the testator intended that it should go to some other person. In order to entitle the representatives of the legatee to receive the legacy, it must be proved that he survived the testator. Illustrations: (i) The testator bequeaths to B 'PKR 500 which B owes me'. B dies before the testator; the legacy lapses. (ii) A bequest is made to A and his children. A dies before the testator, or happens to be dead when the will is made. The legacy to A and his children lapses. (iii) A legacy is given to A, and, in case of his dying before the testator, to B. A dies before the testator. The legacy goes to B. (iv) A sum of money is bequeathed to A for life, and after his death to B. A dies in the lifetime of the testator; B survives the testator. The request to B takes effect. (v) A sum of money is bequeathed to A on his completing his 18th year, and in case he should die before he completes his 18th year, to B. A completes his 18th year, and dies in the lifetime of the testator. The legacy to A lapses, and the bequest to B does not take effect. (vi) The testator and the legatee perished in the same ship-wreck. There is no evidence to show who died first; the legacy lapses.

1065. If a legacy is given to two persons jointly, and one of them dies before the testator, the other legatee takes the whole. Illustration: The legacy is simply to A and B. A dies before the testator. B takes the legacy. If a legacy is given to legatees in words which show that the testator intended to give them distinct shares of it, then, if any legatee dies before the testator, so much of the legacy as was intended for him shall fall into the residue of the testators property. Illustration: A sum of money is bequeathed to A, B and C, to be equally divided among them. A dies before the testator. B and C will only take so much as they would have had if A had survived the testator. Where a share which lapses is a part of the general residue bequeathed by the will, that share shall go as undisposed of. Illustration: The testator bequeaths the residue of his estate to A, B and C, to be equally divided between them. A dies before the testator. His one-third of the residue goes as undisposed of.

1066. If a bequest has been made to any child or other lineal descendant of the testator, and the legatee dies in the lifetime of the testator, but any lineal descendant of his survives the testator, the bequest shall not lapse, but shall take effect as if the death of the legatee had happened immediately after the death of the testator, unless a contrary intention appears by the will. Illustration: A makes his will, by which he bequeaths a sum of money to his son, B, for his own absolute use and benefit. B dies before A, leaving a son, C, who survives A, and having made his will whereby he bequeaths all his property to his widow, D, The money goes to D.

1067. If a bequest is made to one person for the benefit of another, the legacy does not lapse by the death, in the testators lifetime, of the person to whom the bequest is made.

1068. If a bequest is made simply to a described class of persons, the thing bequeathed shall go only to such as are alive at the testators death. Exception: If property is bequeathed to a class of persons described as standing in a particular degree of kindred to a specified individual, but their possession of it is deferred until a time later than the death of the testator by reason of a prior bequest or otherwise, the property shall at that time go to such of them as are then alive, and to the representatives of any of them who have died since the death of the testator. Illustrations: (i) A bequeaths PKR 1,000 to 'the children of B' without saying when it is to be distributed among them. B had died previous to the date of the will, leaving three children, C, D and E. E died after the date of the will, but before the death of A. C and D survive A. The legacy will belong to C and D, to the exclusion of the representatives of E. (ii) A lease for years of a house was bequeathed to A for his life, and after his decease to the children of B. At the death of the testator, B had two children living, C and D, and he never had any other child. Afterwards, during the lifetime of A, C died, leaving P, his executor. D has survived A. D and E arc jointly entitled to so much of the lease-hold term as remains expired. (iii) A sum of money was bequeathed to A for her life, and after her decease, to the children of B. At the death of the testator, B had two children, living, C and D, and, after that event, two children, E and F, were born to B. C and E died in the lifetime of A, C having made a will, E having made no will. A has died, leaving D and F surviving her. The legacy is to be divided into four equal parts, one of which is to be paid to the executor of C, one to D, one to the administrator of E and one to P. (iv) A bequeaths one-third of his lands to B for his life, and after his decease to the sisters of B. At the death of the testator, B had two sisters living, C and D, and after that event another sister E was born. C died during the life of B, D and E have survived B. One-third of A's lands belong to D, E and the representatives of C, in equal shares. (v) A bequeaths PKR 1,000 to B for life and after his death equally among the children of C. Up to the death of B, C had not had any child. The bequest after the death of B is void. (vi) A bequeaths PKR 1,000 to 'all the children born or to be born' of B to be divided among them at the death of C. At the death of the testator, B has two children living, D and E. After the death of the testator, but in the lifetime of C, two other children, F and G, are born to B. After the death of C, another child is born to B. The legacy belongs to D, E, F and G, to the exclusion of the after-born child of B. (vii) A bequeaths a fund to the children of B, to be divided among them when the eldest shall attain majority. At the testators death, B had one child living, named C. He afterwards had two other children, named D and E. E died, but C and D were living when C attained majority. The final belongs to C, D and the representatives of E, to the exclusion of any child who may be born to B after C's attaining majority.

1069. Under sections 167~170 of the Succession Act, 1925 payment of liabilities in respect of the bequest has been covered. Where property specifically bequeathed is subject at the death of the testator to any pledge, lien or encumbrance created by the testator himself or by any person under whom he claims, then, unless a contrary intention appears by the will, the legatee, if he accepts the bequest, shall accept it subject to such pledge or incumbrance, and shall as between himself and the testators estate be liable to make good the amount of such pledge or incumbrance. A contrary intention shall not be inferred from any direction which the will may contain for the payment of the testators debts generally. Explanation: A periodical payment in the nature of land-revenue or in the nature of rent is not such an incumbrance. Illustrations: (i) A bequeaths to B the diamond ring given to him by C. At A's death, the ring is held in pawn by D, to whom it has been pledged by A. It is the duty of A's executors, if the state of the testators assets will allow them, to allow B to redeem the ring. (ii) A bequeaths to B a zamindari which at A's death is subject to a mortgage for PKR 10,000; and the whole of the principal sum, together with interest to the amount of PKR 1,000, is due at A's death. B, if he accepts the bequest, accepts it subject to this charge, and is liable, as between himself and A's estate, to pay the sum of PKR 11,000 thus due.

1070. Where anything is to be done to complete the testators title to the thing bequeathed, it is to be done at the cost of the testators estate. Illustrations: (i) A, having contracted in general terms for the purchase of a piece of land at a certain price, bequeaths to B, and dies before he has paid the purchase-money. The purchase-money must be made good out of A's assets. (ii) A, having contracted for the purchase of a piece of land for a certain sum of money, one-half of which is to be paid down and the other half secured by mortgage of the land, bequeaths it to B, and dies before he has paid or secured any part of the purchase-money. One-half of the purchase-money must be paid out of A's assets.

1071. Where there is a bequest of any interest in immoveable property in respect of which payment in the nature of land-revenue or in the nature of rent has to be made periodically, the estate of the testator shall (as between such estate and the legatee) make good such payments or a proportion of them, as the case may be, up to the day of his death. Illustration: A bequeaths to B a house, in respect of which PKR 365 are payable annually by way of rent. A pays his rent at the usual time, and dies twenty-five days after. A's estate will make good PKR 25 in respect of the rent.

1072. In the absence of any direction in the will, where there is a specific bequest of stock in a joint stock company, if any call or other payment is due from the testator at the time of his death in respect of the stock, such call or payment shall, as between the testators estate and the legatee, be borne by the estate; but, if any call or other payment becomes due in respect of such stock after the testators death, the same shall, as between the testators estate and the legatee, be borne by the legatee, if he accepts the bequest. Illustrations: (i) A bequeaths to B his shares in a certain railway. At A's death, there was due from him the sum of PKR 100 in respect of each share, being the amount of a call which had been duly made, and the sum of live rupees in respect of each share, being the amount of interest which had accrued due in respect of the call. These payments must be borne by A's estate. (ii) A has agreed to take fifty shares in an intended joint stock company, and has contracted to pay up PKR 100 in respect of each share, which sum must be paid before his title to the shares can be completed. A bequeaths these shares to B. The estate of A must make good the payments which were necessary to complete A's title. (iii) A bequeaths to B his shares in a certain railway. B accepts the legacy. After A's death, a call is made in respect of the shares. B must pay the call. (iv) A bequeaths to B his shares in a joint stock company. B accepts the bequest. Afterwards the affairs of the company are wound up, and each shareholder is called upon for contribution. The amount of the contribution must be borne by the legatee. (v) A is the owner of ten shares in a railway company. At a meeting held during his lifetime a call is made of PKR 50 per share, payable by three instalments. A bequeaths his shares to B, and dies between the day fixed for the payment of the first and the day fixed for the payment of the second instalment, and without having paid the first instalment. A's estate must pay the first instalment and B, if he accepts the legacy, must pay the remaining instalments.

1073. Under the Succession Act, 1925, section 171, if there is a bequest of something described in general terms, the executor must purchase for the legatee what may reasonably be considered to answer the description. Illustrations: (i) A bequeaths to B a pair of carriage-horses or a diamond ring. The executor must provide the legatee with such articles if the state of the assets will allow it. (ii) A bequeaths to B 'my pair of carriage-horses'. A had no carriage-horses at the time of his death. The legacy fails.

1074. Under the Succession Act, 1925 (section 172) where the interest or produce of a fund is bequeathed to any person, and the will affords no indication of an intention that the enjoyment of the bequest should be of limited duration, the principal, as well as the interest, shall belong to the legatee. Illustrations: (i) A bequeaths to B the interest of his 5% promissory notes of the Federal Government. There is no other clause in the will affecting those securities. B is entitled to A's 5% promissory notes of the Federal Government. (ii) A bequeaths the interest of his 5½% promissory notes of the Federal Government to B for his life, and after his death to C. B is entitled to the interest of the notes during his life, and C is entitled to the notes upon B's death. (iii) A bequeaths to B the rents of his lands at X. B, is entitled to the lands.

1075. The Succession Act, 1925 (sections 173~176) describes about bequests annuities. It is stated that where an annuity is created by will, the legatee is entitled to receive it for his life only, unless a contrary intention appears by the will, notwithstanding that the annuity is directed to be paid out of the property generally, or that a sum of money is bequeathed to be invested in the purchase of it. Illustrations: (i) A bequeaths to B PKR 500 a year. B is entitled during his life to receive the annual sum of PKR 500. (ii) A bequeaths to B the sum of PKR 500 monthly. B is entitled during his life to receive the sum of PKR 500 every month. (iii)) A bequeaths an annuity of PKR 500 to B for life, and on B's death to C. B is entitled to an annuity of PKR 500 during his life. C, if he survives B, is entitled to an annuity of PKR 500 from B's death until his own death.

1076. Where the will directs that an annuity shall be provided for any person out of the proceeds of property, or out of property generally, or where money is bequeathed to be invested in the purchase of any annuity for any person, on the testators death, the legacy vests in interest in the legatee, and he is entitled at his option to have an annuity purchased for him or to receive the money appropriated for that purpose by the will. Illustrations: (i) A by his will directs that his executors shall, out of his property, purchase an annuity of PKR 1,000 for B. B is entitled at his option to have an annuity of PKR 1,000 for his life purchased for him or to receive such a sum as will be sufficient for the purchase of such an annuity. (ii) A bequeaths a fund to B for his life, and directs that after B's death, it shall be laid out in the purchase of an annuity for C. B and C survive the testator. C dies in B's lifetime. On B's death, the fund belongs to the representative of C.

1077. Where an annuity is bequeathed, but the assets of the testator are not sufficient to pay all the legacies given by the will, the annuity shall abate in the same proportion as the other pecuniary legacies given by the will.

1078. Where there is a gift of an annuity and a residuary gift, the whole of the annuity is to be satisfied before any part of the residue is paid to the residuary legatee, and, if necessary, the capital of the testators estate shall be applied for that purpose.

1079. Under sections 177~179 of the Succession Act, 1925 where a debtor bequeaths a legacy to his creditor, and it does not appear from the will that the legacy is meant as a satisfaction of the debt, the creditor shall be entitled to the legacy, as well as to the amount of the debt.

1080. Where a parent, who is under obligation by contract to provide a portion for a child, fails to do so, and afterwards bequeaths a legacy to the child, and does not intimate by his will that the legacy is meant as a satisfaction of the portion, the child shall be entitled to receive the legacy, as well as the portion. Illustration: A, by articles entered into in contemplation of his marriage with B, covenanted that he would pay to each of the daughters of the intended marriage a portion of PKR 20,000 on her marriage. This covenant having been broken, A bequeaths PKR 20,000 to each of the married daughters of himself and B. The legatee are entitled to the benefit of this bequest in addition to their portions.

1081. No bequest shall be wholly or partially a deemed by a subsequent provision made by settlement or otherwise for the legatee. Illustrations: (i) A bequeaths PKR 20,000 to his son B. He afterwards gives to B the sum of PKR 20,000. The legacy is not thereby a deemed. (ii) A bequeaths PKR 40,000 to B, his orphan niece whom he had brought up from her infancy. Afterwards, on the occasion of B's marriage, A settles upon her the sum of PKR 30,000. The legacy is not thereby diminished.

§10. Void Bequests

1082. Under the sections 112~118 of the Succession Act, 1925 identifies the bequests which are void under the law. It is stated that if a bequest is made to a person by a particular description, and there is no person in existence at the testators death who answers the description, the bequest is void. Exception: If property is bequeathed to a person described as standing in a particular degree of kindred to a specified individual, but his possession of it is deferred until a time later than the death of the testator, by reason of a prior bequest or otherwise; and if a person answering the description is alive at the death of the testator, or comes into existence between that event and such later time, the property shall, at such later time, go to that person, or, if he is dead, to his representatives. Illustrations: (i) A bequeaths PKR 1,000 to the eldest son of B. At the death of the testator, B has no son. The bequest is void. (ii) A bequeaths PKR 1,000 to B for life, and after his death to the eldest son of C. At the death of the testator, C had no son. Afterwards, during the life of B, a son is born to C. Upon B's death, the legacy goes to C's son. (iii) A bequeaths PKR 1,000 to B for life, and after his death to the eldest son of C. At the death of the testator, C had no son. Afterwards during the life of B, a son, named D, is born to C. D dies, then B dies. The legacy goes to the representative of D. (iv) A bequeaths his estate of Green Acre to B for life, and at his decease, to the eldest son of C. Up to the death of B, C has had no son. The bequest to C's eldest son is void. (v) A bequeaths PKR 1,000 to the eldest son of C, to be paid to him after the death of B. At the death of the testator, C has no son, but a son is afterwards born to him during the life of B and is alive at B's death. C's son is entitled to the PKR 1,000.

1083. Similarly if a bequest is made to a person not in existence at the time of the testators death, subject to a prior bequest contained in the will, the later bequest shall be void, unless it comprises the whole of the remaining interest of the testator in the thing bequeathed. Illustrations: (i) Property is bequeathed to A for his life, and after his death to his eldest son for life, and after the death of the latter to his eldest son. At the time of the testators death, A has no son. Here the bequest to A's eldest son is a bequest to a person not in existence at the testators death. It is not a bequest of the whole interest that remains to the testator. The bequest to A's eldest son for his life is void. (ii) A fund is bequeathed to A for his life, and after his death to his daughters. A survives the testator. A has daughters some of whom were not in existence at the testator's death. The bequest to A's daughters comprises the whole interest that remains to the testator in the thing bequeathed. The bequest to A's daughters is valid. (iii) A fund is bequeathed to A for his life, and after his death to his daughters, with a direction that, if any of them marries under the age of 18, her portion shall be settled so that it may belong to herself for life and may be divisible among her children after her death. A has no daughters living at the time of the testators death, but has daughters born afterwards who survive him. Here the direction for a settlement has the effect in the case of each daughter who marries under 18 of substituting for the absolute bequest to her merely for her life; that is to say, a bequest to person not in existence at the time of the testators death of something which is less than the whole interest that remains to the testator in the thing bequeathed. The direction to settle the fund is void. (iv) A bequeaths a sum of money to B for life, and directs that upon the death of B the fund shall be settled upon his daughters, so that the portion of each daughter may belong to herself for life, and may be divided among her children after her death. B has no daughter living at the time of the testators death. In this case the only bequest to the daughters of B is contained in the direction to settle the fund, and this direction amounts to a bequest to person not yet born, of a life-interest in the fund, that is to say, of something which is less than the whole interest that remains to the testator in the thing bequeathed. The direction to settle the fund upon the daughters of B is void.

1084. However, no bequest is valid whereby the vesting of the thing bequeathed may be deleted beyond the lifetime of one or more persons living at the testators death and the minority of some person who shall be in existence at the expiration of that period, and to whom, if he attains full age, the thing bequeathed is to belong. Illustrations: (i) A fund is bequeathed to A for his life and after his death to B for his life; and after B's death to such of the sons of B as shall first attain the age of 25. A and B survive the testator. Here the son of B who shall first attain the age of 25 may be a son born after the death of the testator; such son may not attain 25 until more than 18 years have elapsed from the death of the longer liver of A and B; and the vesting of the fund may thus be delayed beyond the lifetime of A and B and the minority of the sons of B. The bequest after B's death is void. (ii) A fund is bequeathed to A for his life, and after his death to B for the life, and after B's death to such of B's sons as shall first attain the age of 25. B dies in the lifetime of the testator, leaving one or more sons. In this case the sons of B are persons living at the time of the testators decease, and the time when either of them will attain 25 necessarily falls within his own lifetime. The bequest is valid. (iii) A fund is bequeathed to A for his life, and after his death to B for his life, with a direction that after B's death it shall be divided amongst such of B's children as shall attain the age of 18, but that, if no child of B shall attain that age, the fund shall go to C. Here the time for the division of the fund must arrive at the latest at the expiration of 18 years from the death of B, a person living at the testators decease. All the bequests are valid. (iv) A fund is bequeathed to trustees for the benefit of the testators daughters, with a direction that, if any of them marry under age, her share of the fund shall be settled so as to devolve after her death upon such of her children as shall attain the age of 18. Any daughter of the testator to whom the direction applies must be in existence at his decease, and any portion of the fund which may eventually be settled as directed must vest not later than 18 years from the death of the daughters whose share it was. All these provisions are valid.

1085. If a bequest is made to a class of persons with regard to some of whom it is inoperative by reason of the provisions of section 113, or section 114, such bequest shall be void in regard to those persons only and not in regard to the whole class. Illustrations: (i) A fund is bequeathed to A for life, and after his death to all his children who shall attain the age of 25. A survives the testator, and has some children living at the testators death. Each child of A's living at the testators death must attain the age of 25 (if at all) within the limits allowed for a bequest. But A may have children after the testators decease, some of whom may not attain the age of 25 until more than 18 years have elapsed after the decease of A. The bequest to A's children, therefore, is inoperative as to any child born after the testators death and in regard to those who do not attain the age of 25 within 18 years after A's death, but is operative in regard to the other children of A. (ii) A fund is bequeathed to A for his life, and after his death to B, C, D and all other children of A who shall attain the age of 25. B, C, D arc children of A living at the testators decease. In all other respects the case is the same as that supposed in illustration (i). Although the mention of B, C and D does not prevent the bequest from being regarded as a bequest to a class, it is not wholly void. It is operative as regards any of the children B, C or D, who attains the age of 25 within 18 years after A's death.

1086. If any bequest in favour of a person or of a class of persons is void in regard to such person or the whole of such class, any bequest contained in the same will and intended to take effect after or upon failure of such prior bequest is also void. Illustrations: (i) A fund bequeathed to A for his life, and after his death to such of his sons as shall first attain the age of 25, for his life, and after the decease of such son to B. A and B survive the testator. The bequest to B is intended to take effect after the bequest to such of the sons of A as shall first attain the age of 25, which bequest is void under section 114. The bequest to B is void. (ii) A fund is bequeathed to A for his life, and after his death to such of his sons as shall first attain the age of 25, and, if no son of A shall attain that age, to B. A and B survive the testator. The bequest to B is intended to take effect upon failure of the bequest to such of A's sons as shall first attain the age of 25, which bequest is void under section 114. The bequest to B is void.

1087. If the terms of a will direct that the income arising from any property shall be accumulated either wholly or in part during any period longer than a period of eighteen years from the death of the testator, such direction shall, save as hereinafter provided, be void to the extent to which the period during which the accumulation is directed exceeds the aforesaid period, and at the end of such period of eighteen years the property and the income thereof shall be disposed of as if the period during which the accumulation has been directed to be made had elapsed. However this section shall not affect any direction for accumulation for the purpose of (i) the payment of the debts of the testator or any other person taking any interest under the will, or (ii) the provision of portions for children or remoter issue of the testator or of any other person taking any interest under the will, or (iii) the preservation or maintenance of any property bequeathed; and such direction may be made accordingly.

1088. No man having a nephew or niece or any nearer relative shall have power to bequeath any property to religious or charitable uses, except by a will executed not less than twelve months before his death, and deposited within six months from its execution in some place provided by law for the safe custody of the wills of living persons. Illustrations: A having a nephew makes a bequest by a will not execute and deposited as required: for the relief of poor people; for the maintenance of sick soldiers; for the erection or support of a hospital; for the education and preferment of orphans; for the support of scholars; for the erection or support of a school; for the building and repairs of a bridge; for the making of roads; for the erection or support of a church; for the repairs of a church; for the benefit of ministers of religion; and for the formation or support of a public garden. All these bequests are void.

1089. Where by the terms of a bequest the legatee is not entitled to immediate possession of the thing bequeathed, a right to receive it at the proper time shall, unless a contrary intention appear by the will, become vested in the legatee on the testators death, and shall pass to the legatees representatives if he dies before that time and without having received the legacy, and in such cases the legacy is from the testators death said to be vested in interest. Explanation: An intention that a legacy to any person shall not become vested in interest in him is not to be inferred merely from a provision whereby the payment or possession of the thing bequeathed is postponed, or whereby a prior interest therein is bequeathed to some other person, or whereby the income arising from the fund bequeathed is directed to be accumulated until the time of payment arrives, or from a provision that, if a particular event shall happen, the legacy shall go over to another person. Illustrations: (i) A bequeaths to B PKR 100, to be paid to him at the death of C. On A's death, the legacy becomes vested in interest in B, and if he dies before C, his representatives are entitled to the legacy. (ii) A bequeaths to B PKR 100, to be paid to him upon his attaining the age of 18. On A's death, the legacy becomes vested in interest in B. (iii) A fund is bequeathed to A for life, and after his death to B. On the testators death, the legacy to B becomes vested in interest in B. (iv) A fund is bequeathed to A until B attains the age of 18 and then to B. The legacy to B is vested in interest from the testators death. (v) A bequeaths the whole of his property to B upon trust to pay certain debts out of the income, and then to make over the fund to C. At A's death, the gift to C becomes vested in interest in him. (vi) A fund is bequeathed to A, B and C in equal shares to be paid to them on their attaining the age of 18, respectively, with a proviso that, if all of them die under the age of 18, the legacy shall devolve upon D. On the death of the testator, the shares vested in interest in A, B and C, subject to be divested in case A, B and C shall all die under 18, and, upon the death of any of them (except the last survivor) under the age of 18, his vested interest passes, so subject, to his representatives.

1090. A legacy bequeathed in case a specified uncertain event shall happen does not vest until that event happens. A legacy bequeathed in case a specified uncertain event shall not happen does not vest until the happening of that event becomes impossible. In either case, until the condition has been fulfilled, the interest of the legatee is called contingent. Exception: Where a fund is bequeathed to any person upon his attaining a particular age, and the will also gives to him absolutely the income to arise from the fund before he reaches that age, or directs the income, or so much of it as may be necessary, to be applied for his benefit, the bequest of the fund is not contingent, Illustrations: (i) A legacy is bequeathed to D in case A, B and C shall all die under the age of 18. D has a contingent interest in the legacy until A, B and C all die under 18, or one of them attains that age. (ii) A sum of money is bequeathed to A 'in case he shall attain the age of 18', or 'when he shall attain the age of 18'. A's interest in the legacy is contingent until the condition is fulfilled by his attaining that age. (iii) An estate is bequeathed to A for life, and after his death to B if B shall then be living; but if B shall not be then living to C. A, B and C survive the testator. B and C each take a contingent interest in the estate until the event which is to vest it in one or in the other has happened. (iv) An estate is bequeathed as in the case last supposed. B dies in the lifetime of A and C. Upon the death of B, C acquires a vested right to obtain possession of the estate upon A's death. (v) A legacy is bequeathed to A when she shall attain the age of 18, or shall marry under that age with the consent of B, with a proviso that, if she neither attains 18 nor marries under that age with B's consent, the legacy shall go to C. A and C each take a contingent interest in the legacy. A attains the age of 18. A becomes absolutely entitled to the legacy although she may have married under 18 without the consent of B. (vi) An estate is bequeathed to A until he shall marry and after that event B. B's interest in the bequest is contingent until the condition is fulfilled by A's marrying. (vii) An estate is bequeathed to A until he shall take advantage of any law for the relief of insolvent debtors, and after that event to B. B's interest in the bequest is contingent until A takes advantage of such a law. (viii) An estate is bequeathed to A if he shall pay PKR 500 to B. A's interest in the bequest is contingent until he has paid PKR 500 to B. (ix) A leaves his farm of Sultanpur Khurd to B, if B shall convey his own farm of Sultanpur Buzurg to C. B's interest in the bequest is contingent until he has conveyed the latter farm to C. (x) A fund is bequeathed to A if B shall not marry C within five years after the testators death; A's interest in the legacy is contingent until the condition is fulfilled by the expiration of the five years without B's having married C, or by the occurrence within that period of an event which makes the fulfilment of the condition impossible. (xi) A fund is bequeathed to A if B shall not make any provision for him by will. The legacy is contingent until B's death. (xii) A bequeaths to B PKR 500 a year upon his attaining the age of 18, and directs that the interest, or a competent part thereof, shall be applied for his benefit until he reaches that age. The legacy is vested. (xiii) A bequeaths to B PKR 500 when he shall attain the age of 18, and directs that a certain sum, out of another fund, shall be applied for his maintenance until he arrives at that age. The legacy is contingent.

1091. Where a bequest is made only to such members of a class as shall have attained a particular age, a person who has not attained that age cannot have a vested interest in the legacy. Illustration: A fund is bequeathed to such of the children of A as shall attain the age of 18, with a direction that, while any child of A shall be under the age of 18 the income of the share, to which it may be presumed he will be eventually entitled, shall be applied for his maintenance and education. No child of A who is under the age of 18 has a vested interest in the bequest.

1092. If a bequest imposes an obligation on the legatee, he can take nothing by it unless he accepts it fully. Illustration: A, having shares in (X), a prosperous joint stock company and also shares in (Y), a joint stock company in difficulties, in respect of which shares heavy calls are expected to be made, bequeaths to B all his shares in joint stock companies; B refuses to accept the shares in (Y). He forfeits the shares in (X).

1093. If a will contains two separate and independent bequests to the same person, the legatee is at liberty to accept one of them and refuse the other, although the former may be beneficial and the latter onerous. Illustration: A, having a lease for a term of years of a house at a rent which he and his representatives are bound to pay during the term, and which is higher than the house can be let for, bequeaths to B the case and a sum of money. B refuses to accept the lease. He will not by this refusal forfeit the money.

1094. Where a legacy is given if a specified uncertain event shall happen and no time is mentioned in the will for the occurrence of that event, the legacy cannot take effect, unless such event happens before the period when the fund bequeathed is payable or distributable. Illustrations: (i) A legacy is bequeathed to A, and, in case of his death, to B. If A survives the testator, the legacy to B does not take effect. (ii) A legacy is bequeathed to A, and, in case of his death without children, to B. If A survives the testator or dies in his lifetime leaving a child, the legacy to B does not take effect. (iii) A legacy is bequeathed to A when and if he attains the age of 18, and, in case of his death, to B. A attains the age of 18. The legacy to B does not take effect. (iv) A legacy is bequeathed to A for life, and, after his death to B, and, 'in case of B's death without children', to C. The words 'in case of B's death without children' are to be understood as meaning 'in case B dies without children during the lifetime of A'. (v) A legacy is bequeathed to A for life, and, after his death to B, and, 'in case of B. death', to C. The words 'in case of B's death' are to be considered as meaning 'in case B dies in the lifetime of A'.

1095. Where a bequest is made to such of certain persons as shall be surviving at some period, but the exact period is not specified, the legacy shall go to such of them as are alive at the time of payment or distribution, unless a contrary intention appears by the will. Illustrations: (i) Property is bequeathed to A and B to be equally divided between them, or to the survivor of them. If both A and B survive the testator, the legacy is equally divided between them. If A dies before the testator, and B survives the testator, it goes to B. (ii) Property is bequeathed to A for life, and, after his death, to B and C, to be equally divided between them, or to the survivor of them. B dies during the life of A; C survives A. At A's death the legacy goes to C. (iii) Property is bequeathed to A for life, and after his death to B and C, or the survivor, with a direction that, if B should not survive the testator, his children are to stand in his place. C dies during the life of the testator; B survives the testator, but dies in the life time of A. The legacy goes to the representative of B. (iv) Property is bequeathed to A for life, and, after his death, to B and C, with a direction that, in case either of them dies in the lifetime of A, the whole-shall go to the survivor. B dies in the lifetime of A. Afterwards C dies in the lifetime of A. The legacy goes to the representative of C.

1096. A bequest upon an impossible condition is void. Illustrations: (i) An estate is bequeathed to A on condition that he shall walk 100 miles in an hour. The bequest is void. (ii) A bequeaths PKR 500 to B on condition that he shall marry A's daughter. A's daughter was dead at the date of the will. The bequest is void. A bequest upon a condition, the fulfilment of which would be contrary to law or to morality, is void. Illustrations: (i) A bequeaths PKR 500 to B on condition that he shall murder C. The bequest is void. (ii) A bequeaths PKR 5,000 to his niece if she will desert her husband. The bequest is void.

1097. Where a will imposes a condition to be fulfilled before the legatee can take a vested interest in the tiling bequeathed, the condition shall be considered to have been fulfilled if it has been substantially complied with. Illustrations: (i) A legacy is bequeathed to A on condition that he shall marry with the consent of B, C,

D and E. A marries with the written consent of B, C is present at the marriage. D sends a present to A previous to the marriage. E has been personally informed by A of his intentions, and has made no objection. A has fulfilled the condition. (ii) A legacy is bequeathed to A on condition that he shall marry with the consent of B, C and D. D dies. A marries with the consent of B and C. A has fulfilled the condition. (iii) A legacy is bequeathed to A on condition that he shall marry with the consent of B, C and D. A marries in the lifetime of B, C and D, with the consent of B and C only. A has not fulfilled the condition. (iv) A legacy is bequeathed to A on condition that he shall marry with the consent of B, C and D. A obtains the unconditional assent of B, C and D to his marriage with E. Afterwards B, C and D capriciously retract their consent. A marries E. A has fulfilled the condition. (v) A legacy is bequeathed to A on condition that he shall marry with the consent of B, C and D. A marries without the consent of B, C and D but obtains their consent after the marriage. A has not fulfilled the condition. (vi) A makes his will whereby he bequeaths a sum of money to B if B shall marry with the consent of A's executors. B marries during the lifetime of A, and A afterwards expresses his approbation of the marriage. A dies. The bequest to B takes effect. (vii) A legacy is bequeathed to A if he executes a certain document within a time specified in the will. The document is executed by A within a reasonable time, but not within the time specified in the will. A has not performed the condition, and is not entitled to receive the legacy.

1098. If there is a bequest to one person and a bequest of the same thing to another, if the prior bequest shall fail, the second bequest shall take effect upon the failure of the prior bequest although the failure may not have occurred in the manner contemplated by the testator. Illustrations: (i) A bequeaths a sum of money to his own children surviving him, and, they all die under 18, to B. A dies without having sever had a child. The bequest to B takes effect. (ii) A bequeaths a sum of money to B, on condition that he shall execute a certain document within three months after A's death, and, if he should neglect to do so, to C. B dies in the testators lifetime. The bequest to C takes effect.

1099. If the will shows an intention that the second bequest shall take effect only in the event of the first bequest failing in a particular manner, the second bequest shall not take effect, unless the prior bequest fails in that particular manner. Illustration: A makes a bequest to his wife, but in case she should die in his lifetime, bequeaths to B that which he had bequeathed to her. A and his wife perish together, under circumstances which make it impossible to prove that she died before him; the bequest to B does not take effect.

1100. A bequest may be made to any person with the condition super added that, in case a specified uncertain event shall happen, the thing bequeathed shall go to another person, or that in case a specified uncertain event shall not happen, the thing bequeathed shall go over to another person. In each case the ulterior bequest is subject to the rules contained. Illustrations: (i) A sum of money is bequeathed to A, to be paid to him at the age of 18, and if he shall die before he attains that age, to B. A takes a vested interest in the legacy subject to be divested and to go to B in case

A dies under 18. (ii) An estate is bequeathed to A with a proviso that if A shall dispute the competency of the testator to make a will, the estate shall go to B. A disputes the competency of the testator to make a will. The estate goes to B. (iii) A sum of money is bequeathed to A for life, and, after his death, to B; but if B shall then be dead, leaving a son, such son is to stand in the place of B. B takes a vested interest in the legacy, subject to be divested if he dies leaving a son in A's lifetime. (iv) A sum of money is bequeathed to A and B, and if either should die during the life of C, then to the survivor living at the death of C. A and B die before C. The gift over cannot take effect, but the representative of A takes one-half of the money, and the representative of B takes the other half. (v) A bequeaths to B the interest of a fund for life, and directs the fund to be divided at her death equally among her three children, or such of them as shall be living at her death. All the children of B die in B's lifetime. The bequest over cannot take effect, but the interests of the children pass to their representatives.

1101. An ulterior bequest of the kind contemplated cannot take effect, unless the condition is strictly fulfilled. Illustrations: (i) A legacy is bequeathed to A, with a proviso that, if he marries without the consent of B, C and D, the legacy shall go to E. D dies. Even if A marries without the consent of B and C, the gift to E does not take effect. (ii) A legacy is bequeathed to A, with a proviso that, if he marries without the consent of B, the legacy shall go to C. A marries with the consent of B. He afterwards becomes a widower and marries again without the consent of B. The bequest to C does not take effect. (iii) A legacy is bequeathed to A, to be paid at 18; or marriage, with a proviso that, if A dies under 18 or marries without the consent of B, the legacy shall go to C. A marries under 18, without the consent of B. The bequest to C takes effect.

1102. If the ulterior bequest be not valid, the original bequest is not affected by it. Illustrations: (i) An estate is bequeathed to A for his life with condition super added that, if he shall not on a given day walk 100 miles in an hour, the estate shall go to B. The condition being void, A retains his estate as if no condition had been inserted in the will. (ii) An estate is bequeathed to A for her life and, if she does not desert her husband, to D. A is entitled to the estate during her life as if no condition had been inserted in the will. (iii) An estate is bequeathed to A for life, and, if he marries, to the eldest son of B for life. B, at the date of the testators death had not had a son. The bequest over is void under section 105, and A is entitled to the estate during his life.

1103. A bequest may be made with the condition super added that it shall cease to have effect in case a specified uncertain event shall happen, or in case a specified uncertain event shall not happen. Illustrations: (i) An estate is bequeathed to A for his life, with a proviso that, in case he shall cut down a certain wood, the bequest shall cease to have any effect. A cuts down the wood. He loses his life interest in the estate. (ii) An estate is bequeathed to A, provided that, if he marries under the age of 25 without the consent of the executors named in the will, the estate shall cease to belong to him. A marries under 25 without the consent of the executors. The estate ceases to belong to him. (iii) An estate is bequeathed to A, provided that, if he shall not go to England within three years after the testators death, his interest in the estate shall cease. A does not go to England within the time prescribed. His interest in the estate ceases. (iv) An estate is bequeathed to A, with a proviso that, if she becomes a nun, she shall cease to have any interest in the estate. A becomes a nun. She loses her interest under the will. (v) A fund is bequeathed to A for life, and, after his death, to B, if B shall be then living, with a proviso that, if B shall become a nun, the bequest to her shall cease to have any effect. B becomes a nun in the life time of A. She thereby loses her contingent interest in the fund.

1104. In order for a condition that a bequest shall cease to have effect may be valid, it is necessary that the event to which it relates be one which could legally constitute the condition of a bequest.

1105. Where a bequest is made with a condition superadded that, unless the legatee shall perform a certain act, the subject matter of the bequest shall go to another person, or the bequest shall cease to have effect but no time is specified for the performance of the act; if the legatee takes any step which renders impossible or indefinitely postpones the performance of the act required, the legacy shall go as if the legatee had died without performing such act. Illustrations: (i) A bequest is made to A, with a proviso that, unless he enters the Army, the legacy shall go over to B. A takes Holy Orders, and thereby renders it impossible that he should fulfil the condition. B is entitled to receive the legacy. (ii) A bequest is made to A, with a proviso that it shall cease to have any effect if he does not marry B's daughter. A marries a stranger and thereby indefinitely postpones the fulfilment of the conditions. The bequest ceases to have effect.

1106. Where the will requires an act to be performed by the legatee within a specified time, either as a condition to be fulfilled before the legacy is enjoyed, or as a condition upon the non-fulfilment of which the subject-matter of the bequest is to go over to another person or the bequest is to cease to have effect, the act must be performed within the time specified, unless the performance of it be prevented by fraud, in which case such further time shall be allowed as shall be requisite to make up for the delay caused by such fraud.

§11. Legacies

1107. The Succession Act, 1925, sections 142~149 (Chapter XIV) deals with the specific legacies. If a testator bequeaths to any person a specified part of his property, which is distinguished from all other parts of his property, the legacy is said to be specific. Illustrations: (i) A bequeaths to B 'the diamond ring presented to me by C': 'my gold chain': 'a certain bale of wool': 'a certain piece of cloth': 'all my household goods which shall be in or about my dwelling-house in M Street, in Karachi, at time of my death': 'the sum of PKR 1,000 in a certain chest': 'the debt which B owes me': 'all my bills, bonds and securities belonging to me lying in my lodgings in Karachi': 'all my furniture in my house in Karachi': 'all my goods on board a certain ship now lying in the river Indus': 'PKR 2,000 which I have in the hands of C': 'the money due to me on the bond of D': 'my mortgage on the Rahimyarkhan factory': 'one-half of the money owing to me on my mortgage of Rahimyarkhan factory': 'PKR 1,000, being part of a debt due to me from C': 'my capital stock of PKR 1,000 in East India Stock': 'my promissory notes of the Federal Government for PKR 10,000 in their 4% loan': 'all such sums of money as my executors may, after my death, receive in respect of the debt due to me from the insolvent firm of D and Company': 'all the wine which I may have in my cellar at the time of my death': 'such of my horses as B may select': 'all my shares in the National Bank of Pakistan': 'all my shares in the National Bank of Pakistan which I may possess at the time of my death': 'all the money which I have in the 5½% loan of the federal Government': 'all the Government securities I shall be entitled to at the time of my decease'. Each of these legacies is specific. (ii) A, having Government promissory notes for PKR 10,000, bequeaths to his executors 'Government promissory notes for PKR 10,000 in trust to sell' for the benefit of B. The legacy is specific. (iii) A, having property at Peshawar, and also in other places, bequeaths to B all his property at Peshawar. The legacy is specific. (iv) A bequeaths to B his house in Karachi: his zamindari of Rahimyarkhan: his Talaq of Nawabshah: his lease of the indigo-factory of Salkya: an annuity of PKR 500 out of the rents of his zamindari of W. A directs his zamindari of X to be sold, and the proceeds to be invested for the benefit of B. Each of these bequests is specific. (v) A by his will charges his zamindari of Y with an annuity of PKR 1,000 to C during his life, and subject to this charge he bequeaths the zamindari to D. Each of these bequests is specific. (vi) A bequeaths a sum of money – to buy a house in Karachi for B: to buy an estate in Zila Peshawar for B: to buy a diamond ring for B: to buy a horse for B: to be invested in shares in the National Bank of Pakistan for B: to be invested in Government securities for B. 'A bequeaths to B a diamond ring: a horse': 'PKR 10,000 worth of Government securities': an 'annuity of PKR 500': 'PKR 2,000 to be paid in cash': 'so much money as will produce PKR 5,000 4% Government securities'. These bequests are not specific. (vii) A, having property in England and property in Pakistan, bequeaths a legacy to B, and directs that it shall be paid out of the property which he may leave in Pakistan. He also bequeaths a legacy to C, and directs that it shall be paid out of property which he may leave in England. No one of these legacies is specific.

1108. If a certain sum is bequeathed, the legacy is not specific merely because the stock, funds or securities in which it is invested are described in the will. Illustration: A bequeaths to B 'PKR 10,000 of my funded property': 'PKR 10,000 of my property now invested in shares of the National Bank of Pakistan': 'PKR 10,000, at present secured by mortgage of Rahimyarkhan factory'. No one of these legacies is specific.

1109. If a bequest is made in general terms of a certain amount of any kind of stock, the legacy is not specific merely because the testator was at the date of his will, possessed of stock of the specified kind, to an equal or greater amount than the amount bequeathed. Illustration: A bequeaths to B PKR 5,000, 4% Government securities. A had at the date of the will 5% Government securities for PKR 5,000. The legacy is not specific.

1110. A money legacy is not specific merely because the will directs its payment to be postponed until some part of the property of the testator has been reduced to a certain form, or remitted to a certain place. Illustration: A bequeaths to B PKR 10,000 and directs that this legacy shall be paid as soon as A's property in India shall be realized in England. The legacy is not specific.

1111. If a will contains a bequest of the residue of the testators property alongwith an enumeration of some items of property not previously bequeathed, the articles enumerated shall not be deemed to be specifically bequeathed.

1112. Where property is specifically bequeathed to two or more persons in succession, it shall be retained in the form in which the testator left it, although it may be of such a nature that its value is continually decreasing. Illustrations: (i) A, having lease of a house for a term of years, fifteen of which were unexpired at the time of his death, has bequeathed the lease to B for his life, and after B's death to C. B is to enjoy the property as A left it, although, if B lives for fifteen years. C can take nothing under the bequest. (ii) A, having an annuity during the life of B, bequeaths it to C, for his life, and, after C's death, to D. C is to enjoy the annuity as A left it, although, if B dies before D, D can take nothing under the bequest.

1113. If property comprised in a bequest to two or more persons in succession is not specifically bequeathed, it shall, in the absence of any direction to the contrary, be sold, and the proceeds of the sale shall be invested in such securities as the High Court may by any general rule authorize or direct, and the fund thus constituted shall be enjoyed by the successive legatees according to the terms of the will. Illustration: A, having a lease for a term of years, bequeaths ail his property to B for life, and, after B's death, to C. The lease must be sold, the proceeds invested as stated in this Motion and the annual income arising from the fund is to be paid to B for life. At B's death the capital of the fund is to be paid to C. If there is a deficiency of assets to pay legacies, a specific legacy is not liable to abate with the general legacies.

1114. The Succession Act, 1925 (sections 150 and 151) deals with demonstrative legacy. Where a testator bequeaths a certain sum of money, or a certain quantity of any other commodity, and refers to a particular fund or stock so as to constitute the same the primary fund or stock out of which payment is to be made, the legacy is said to be demonstrative. Explanation: The distinction between a specific legacy and a demonstrative legacy consists in this, that where specified property is given to the legatee, the legacy is specific; where the legacy is directed to be paid out of specified property, it is demonstrative. Illustrations: (i) A bequeaths to B PKR 1,000, being part of a debt due to him from W. He also bequeaths to C PKR 1,000 to be paid out of the debt due to him from W. The legacy to B is specific, the legacy to C is demonstrative. (ii) A bequeaths to B 'ten bushels of the corn which shall grow in my field of Green Acre': '80 chests of the indigo which shall be made at my factory of Rahimyarkhan': 'PKR 10,000 out of my 5% promissory notes of the Federal Government': 'an annuity of PKR 500' 'from my funded property': 'PKR 1,000 out of the sum of PKR 2,000 due to me by C': an annuity, and directs it to be paid 'out of the rents arising from my Taluqa of Nawabshah'. (iii) A bequeaths to B: 'PKR 10,000 out of my estate at Nawabshah', or charges it on his estate at Nawabshah: 'PKR 10,000, being my share of the capital embarked in a certain business', Each of these bequests is demonstrative.

1115. Where a portion of a fund is specifically bequeathed and a legacy is directed to be paid out of the same fund, the portion specifically bequeathed shall first be paid to the legatee and the demonstrative legacy shall be paid out of the residue of the fund and, so far as the residue shall be deficient, out of the general assets of the testator. Illustration: A bequeaths to B PKR 1,000, being part of a debt due to him from W. He also bequeaths to C PKR 1,000 to be paid out of the debt due to him from W. The debt due to A from W is only PKR 1,500 of these PKR 1,500, PKR 1,000 belong to B, and PKR 500 are to be paid to C. C is also to receive PKR 500 out of the general assets of the testator.

1116. The sections 152~166 of the Succession Act, 1925 deals with the redemption of legacies. If anything which has been specifically bequeathed does not belong to the testator at the time of his death, or has been converted into property of a different kind, the legacy is a deemed: that is, it cannot take effect, by reason of the subject-matter having been withdrawn from the operation of the will. Illustrations: (i) 'A bequeaths to B – the diamond ring presented to me by C': 'my gold chain': 'a certain bale of wool': 'a certain piece of cloth': 'all my household goods which shall be in or about my dwelling-house in M Street in Sahiwal, at the time of my death': A in his lifetime, – sells or gives away the ring: converts the chain into a cup: converts the wool into cloth: makes the cloth into a garment: takes another house into which he removes all his goods.

Each of these legacies is a deemed. (ii) A bequeaths to B – 'the sum of PKR 1,000 in a certain chest': 'all the horses in my stable'. At the death of A, no money is found in the chest, and no horses in the stable. The legacies are a deemed. (iii) A bequeaths to B certain bales of goods. A takes the goods with him on a voyage. The ship and goods are lost at sea, and A is drowned. The legacy is a deemed.

1117. A demonstrative legacy is not a deemed by reason that the property on which it is charged by the will does not exist at the time of the death of the testator, or has been converted into property of a different kind, but it shall in such case be paid out of the general assets of the testator.

1118. Where the thing specifically bequeathed is the right to receive something of value from a third party, and the testator himself receives it, the bequest is a deemed. Illustrations: (i) A bequeaths to B 'the debt which C owes me'; 'PKR 2,000 which I have in the hands of D': 'the money due to me on the bond of E': 'my mortgage on the Rahimyarkhan factory'. All these debts arc extinguished in A's lifetime, some with and some without his consent. All the legacies are a deemed. (ii) A bequeaths to B his interest in certain policies of life assurance. A in his lifetime receives the amount of the policies. The legacy is a deemed.

1119. The receipt by the testator of a part of an entire thing specifically bequeathed shall operate as a redemption of the legacy to the extent of the sum so received. Illustration: A bequeaths to B 'the debt due to me by C'. The debt amounts to PKR 10,000. C pays to A PKR 5,000 the one-half of the debt. The legacy is revoked by redemption, so far as regards the PKR 5,000 received by A.

1120. If a portion of an entire fund or stock is specifically bequeathed, the receipt by the testator of a portion of the fund or stock shall operate as a redemption only to the extent of the amount so received; and the residue of the fund or stock shall be applicable to the discharge of the specific legacy. Illustration: A bequeaths to B one-half of the sum of PKR 10,000 due to him from W. A in his lifetime receives PKR 6,000, part of the PKR 10,000. The PKR 4,000 which are due from W to A at the time of his death belong to B under the specific bequest.

1121. Where a portion of a fund is specifically bequeathed to one legatee, and a legacy charged on the same fund is bequeathed to another legatee, then, if the testator receives a portion of that fund, and the remainder of the fund is insufficient to pay both the specific and the demonstrative legacy, the specific legacy shall be paid first, and the residue (if any) of the fund shall be applied so far as it will extend in payment of the demonstrative legacy, and the rest of the demonstrative legacy shall be paid out of the general assets of the testator. Illustration: A bequeaths to B PKR 1,000, part of the debt of PKR 2,000 due to him from W. He also bequeaths to C PKR 1,000 to be paid out of the debt due to him from W. A afterwards receives PKR 500, part of that debt, and dies leaving only PKR 1,500 due to him from W. Of these PKR 1,500, PKR 1,000 belong to B, and PKR 500 are to be paid to C. C is also to receive PKR 500 out of the general assets of the testator.

1122. Where stock which has been specifically bequeathed does not exist at the testator's death, the legacy is a deemed. Illustration: A bequeaths to B 'my capital stock of 1,000 in East India Stock': 'my promissory notes of the Federal Government for PKR 10,000 in their 4% loan'. A sells the stock and the notes. The legacy is a deemed.

1123. Where stock which has been specifically bequeathed exists only in part at the testator's death, the legacy is a deemed so far as regards that part of the stock – which has ceased to exist. Illustration: A bequeaths to B his PKR 10,000 in the 5½% loan of the Federal Government, A sells one-half of his PKR 10,000 in the loan in question. One-half of the legacy is a deemed.

1124. A specific bequest of goods under a description connecting them with a certain place is not a deemed by reason that they have been removed from such place from any temporary cause, or by fraud, or without the knowledge or sanction of the testator. Illustrations: (i) A bequeaths to B 'all my household goods which shall be in or about my dwelling-house in Faisalabad at the time of my death'. The goods are removed from the house to save them from fire. A dies before they are brought back. (ii) A bequeaths to B 'all my household goods which shall be in or about my dwelling-house in Faisalabad at the time of my death'. During A's absence upon a journey, the whole of title goods are removed from the house. A dies without having sanctioned their removal. Neither of these legacies is a deemed.

1125. The removal of the thing bequeathed from the place in which it is stated in the will to be situated does not constitute redemption, where the place is only referred to in order to complete the description of what the testator meant to bequeath. Illustrations: (i) A bequeaths to B 'all the bills, bonds and other securities for money belonging to me now lying in my lodgings in Karachi'. At the time of his death, these effects had been removed from his lodgings in Karachi. (ii) A bequeaths to B all his furniture then in his house in Karachi. The testator has a house at Karachi and another at Quetta, in which he lives alternately, being possessed of one set of furniture only which he removes with himself to each house. At the time of his death, the furniture is in the house at Quetta. (iii) A bequeaths to B all his goods on board a certain ship then lying in the river Indus. The goods are removed by A's directions to a warehouse, in which they remain at the time of A's death. No one of these legacies is revoked by redemption.

1126. Where the thing bequeathed is not the right to receive something of value from a third person, but the money or other commodity which may be received from the third person by the testator himself or by his representatives, the receipt of such sum of money or other commodity by the testator shall not constitute an redemption; but if he mixes it up with the general mass of his property, the legacy is a deemed. Illustration: A bequeaths to B whatever sum may be received from his claim on C. A receives the whole of his claim on C, and sets it apart from the general mass of his property. The legacy is not a deemed.

1127. Where a thing specifically bequeathed undergoes a change between the date of the will and the testators death, and the change takes place by operation of law, or in the course of execution of the provisions of any legal instrument under which the thing bequeathed was held, the legacy is not a deemed by reason of such change. Illustrations: (i) A bequeaths to B 'all the money which I have in the 5½% loan' of the 'Federal Government'. The securities for the 5½% loan are converted during A's lifetime into 5% stock. (ii) A bequeaths to B the sum of 2,000 invested in Consoles in the names of trustees for A. The sum of 2,000 is transferred by the trustees into A's own name. (iii) A bequeaths to B the sum of PKR 10,000 in promissory notes of the Federal Government which he has power under his marriage settlement to dispose of by will. Afterwards, in A's lifetime, the fund is converted into Consoles by virtue of an authority contained in the settlement. No one of these legacies has been a deemed.

1128. Where a thing specifically bequeathed undergoes a change between the date of the will and the testators death, and the change takes place without the knowledge or sanction of the testator, the legacy is not a deemed. Illustrations: A bequeaths to B 'all my 3% Consoles'. The Consoles arc, without A's knowledge, sold by his agent, and the proceeds converted into East India Stock. This legacy is not a deemed.

1129. Where stock which has been specifically bequeathed is lent to a third party on condition that it shall be replaced, and it is replaced accordingly, the legacy is not a deemed. Where stock specifically bequeathed is sold, and an equal quantity of the same stock is afterwards purchased and belongs to the testator at his death, the legacy is not a deemed.

1130. Under sections 332~337 of the Succession Act, 1925, the assent of the executor or administrator is necessary to complete a legatees title to his legacy. Illustrations: (i) A by his will bequeaths to B his Government paper which is in deposit with the National Bank of Pakistan. The Bank has no authority to deliver the securities, nor B a right to take possession of them, without the assent of the executor. (ii) A by his will has bequeathed to C his house in Quetta in the tenancy of B. C is not entitled to receive the rents without the assent of the executor or administrator.

1131. The assent of the executor or administrator to a specific bequest shall be sufficient to divest his interest as executor or administrator therein, and to transfer the subject of the bequest of the legatee, unless the nature or the circumstances of the property require that it shall be transferred in a particular way. This assent may be verbal, and it may be either express or implied from the conduct of the executor or administrator. Illustrations: (i) A horse is bequeathed. The executor requests the legatee to dispose of it, or a third party proposes to purchase the horse from the executor, and he directs him to apply to the legatee. Assent to the legacy is implied. (ii) The interest of a fund is directed by the will to be applied for the maintenance of the legatee during his minority. The executor commences so to apply it. This is an assent to the whole of the bequest. (iii) A bequest is made of a fund to A and after him to B. The executor pays the interest of the fund to A. This is an implied assent to the bequest to B. (iv) Executors die after paying all the debts of the testator, but before satisfaction of specific legacies. Assent to the legacies may be presumed. (v) A person to whom a specific article has been bequeathed takes possession of it and retains it without any objection on the part of the executor. His assent may be presumed.

1132. The assent of an executor or administrator to a legacy may be conditional, and if the condition is one which he has a right to enforce, and it is not performed, there is no assent. Illustrations: (i) A bequeaths to B his lands of Sultanpur, which at the date of the will, and at the death of A, were subject to a mortgage for PKR 10,000. The executor assents to the bequest, on condition that B shall within a limited time pay the amount due on the mortgage at the testators death. The amount is not paid. There is no assent. (ii) The executor assents to a bequest on condition that the legatee shall pay him a sum of money. The payment is not made. The assent is nevertheless valid.

1133. When the executor or administrator is a legatee, his assent to his own legacy is necessary to complete his title to it, in the same way as it is required when the bequest is to another person, and his assent may, in like manner, be expressed or implied. Assent shall be implied if in his manner of administering the property lie does any act which is referable to his character of legatee and is not referable to his character of executor or administrator. Illustration: An executor takes, the rent of a house or the interest of Government securities bequeathed to him, and applies it to his own use. This is assent.

1134. The assent of the executor or administrator to a legacy gives effect to it from the death of the testator. Illustrations: (i) A legatee sells his legacy before it is assented to by the executor. The executor's subsequent assent operates for the benefit of the purchaser and completes his title to the legacy. (ii) A bequeaths PKR 1,000 to B with interest from his death. The executor does not assent to his legacy until the expiration of a year from A's death. B is entitled to interest from the death of A.

1135. An executor or administrator is not bound to pay or deliver any legacy until the expiration of one year from the testator's death. Illustration: A by his will directs his legacies to be paid within six months after his death. The executor is not bound to pay them before the expiration of a year.

1136. The Succession Act, 1925 (sections 349~355) provide detail of legacies. The legatee of a specific legacy is entitled to the clear produce thereof, if any, from the testator's death. Exception: A specific bequest, contingent in its term; does not comprise the produce of the legacy between the death of the testator and the vesting of the legacy. The clear produce of it forms part of the residue of the testator's estate. Illustrations: (i) A bequeaths his flock of sheep to B. Between the death of A and delivery by his executor, the sheep are shorn or some of the ewes produce lambs. The wool and lambs are the property of B. (ii) A bequeaths his Government securities to B, but postpones the delivery of them till the death of C. The interest which falls due between the death of A and the death of C belongs to B, and must, unless he is a minor, be paid to him as it is received. (iii) The testator bequeaths all his 4% Government promissory notes to A when he shall complete the age of 18. A, if he completes that age, is entitled to receive the notes, but the interest which accrues in respect of them between the testator's death and A's completing 18, form part of the residue.

1137. The legatee under a general residuary bequest is entitled to the produce of the residuary fund from the testator's death. Exception: A general residuary bequest contingent in its terms does not comprise the income which may accrue upon the fund bequeathed between the death of the testator and the vesting of the legacy. Such income gees as un-disposed of. Illustrations: (i) The testator bequeaths the residue of his property to A, a minor, to be paid to him when he shall complete the age of 18. The income from the testators death belongs to A. (ii) The testator bequeaths the residue of his property to A when he shall complete the age of 18. A, if he completes that age, is entitled to receive the residue. The income which has accrued in respect of it since the testators death goes as un-disposed of.

1138. Where no time has been fixed for the payment of a general legacy, interest begins to run from expiration of one year from the testator's death. Exception: (1) Where the legacy is bequeathed in satisfaction of a debt, interest runs from the death of the testator. (2) Where the testator was a parent or a more remote ancestor of the legatee, or has put himself in the place of a parent of the legatee, the legacy shall bear interest from the death of the testator. (3) Where a sum is bequeathed to a minor with a direction to pay for his maintenance out of it, interest is payable from the death of the testator.

1139. Where a time has been fixed for the payment of a general legacy, interest begins to run from the time so fixed. The interest upon such time forms part of the residue of the testator's estate. Exception: Where the testator was parent or a work remote ancestor of the legatee, or has put himself in the place of a parent of the legatee and the legatee is a minor, the legacy shall bear interest from the death of the testator, unless a specific sum is given by the will for maintenance, or unless the will contains a direction to the contrary.

1140. The rate of interest shall be 4% per annum in all cases except when the testator was a Hindu, Muslim, Buddhist, Sikh or Jaina or an exempted person, in which case it shall be 6% per annum. No interest is payable on the arrears of an annuity within the first year from the death of the testator, although a period earlier than the expiration of that year may have been fixed by the will for making the first payment of the annuity.

1141. Where a sum of money is directed to be invested to produce an annuity, interest is payable on it from the death of the testator.

1142. Sections 356~367 of the Succession Act, 1925 deals with the refunding of legacies. It is provided that when an executor or administrator has paid a legacy under the order of a Court, he is entitled to call upon the legatee to refund in the event of the assets proving insufficient to pay all the legacies.

1143. When an executor or administrator has voluntarily paid a legacy, he cannot call upon a legatee to refund in the event of the assets proving insufficient to pay all the legacies.

1144. When the time prescribed by the will for the performance of a condition has elapsed, without the condition having been performed, and the executor or administrator has thereupon, without fraud, distributed the assets; in such case, if further time has been allowed under section 137 for the performance of the condition, and the condition has been performed accordingly, the legacy cannot be claimed from the executor or administrator, but those to whom he has paid it are liable to refund the amount.

1145. When the executor or administrator has paid away the assets in legacies, and he is afterwards obliged to discharge a debt of which he had no previous notice, he is entitled to call upon each legatee to refund in proportion.

1146. Where an executor or administrator has given such notices as the High Court may, by any general rule, prescribe or, if no such rule has been made, as the

High Court would give in an administration suit, for creditors and others to send it to him their claims against the estate of the deceased, he shall, at the expiration of the time therein named for sending in claims, be at liberty to distribute the assets, or any part thereof, in discharge of such lawful claims as he knows of, and shall not be liable for the assets so distributed to any person of whose claim he shall not have had notice at the time of such distribution: Provided that nothing herein contained shall prejudice the right of any creditor or claimant to follow the assets, or any part thereof, in the hands of the persons who may have received the same respectively.

1147. A creditor who has not received payment of his debt may call upon a legatee who has received payment of his legacy to refund, whether the assets of the testators estate were or were not sufficient at the time of his death to pay both debts and legacies; and whether the payment of the legacy by the executor or administrator was voluntary or not.

1148. If the assets were sufficient to satisfy all the legacies at the time of the testator's death, a legatee who has not received payment of his legacy, or he has been compelled to refund under section 361, cannot oblige one who has received payment in full to refund, whether the legacy were paid to him with or without suit, although the assets have subsequently become deficient by the wasting of the executor.

1149. If the assets were not sufficient to satisfy all the legacies at the time of the testators death, a legatee who has not received payment of his legacy must, before he can call on a satisfied legatee to refund, first proceed against the executor or administrator if he is solvent; but if the executor or administrator is insolvent or not liable to pay, the unsatisfied legatee can oblige each satisfied legatee to refund in proportion.

1150. The refunding of one legatee to another shall not exceed the sum by which the satisfied legacy ought to have been reduced if the estate had been properly administered. Illustration: A has bequeathed PKR 240 to B, PKR 480 to C, and PKR 720 to D. The assets are only PKR 1,200 and, if properly administered, would give PKR 200 to B, PKR 400 to C, and PKR 600 to D. C and D have been paid their legacies in full, leaving nothing to B. B can oblige C to refund PKR 80, and D to refund PKR 120. The refunding shall in all cases be without interest.

1151. The surplus or residue of the deceased's property, after payment of debts and legacies, shall be paid to the residuary legatee when any has been appointed by the will. Where a person not having his domicile in Pakistan has died leaving assets both in Pakistan and in the country in which he had his domicile at the time of his death, and there has been a grant or probate or letters of administration in Pakistan with respect to the assets there and a grant of administration in the country of domicile with respect to the assets in that country, the executor or administrator, as the case may be, in Pakistan, after having given such notices as are mentioned in section 360, and after having discharged, at the expiration of the time therein named, such lawful claims as he knows of, may, instead of himself distributing any surplus or residue of the deceased's property to persons residing out of Pakistan who are entitled thereto, transfer, with the consent of the executor or administrator, as the case may be, in the country of domicile, the surplus or residue to him for distribution to those persons.

1152. Sections 341~348 details with the investment of funds to provide for legacies. It is stated that where a legacy, not being a specific legacy, is given for life, the sum bequeathed shall at the end of the year be invested in such securities as the High Court may by any general rule authorize or direct, and the proceeds thereof shall be paid to the legatee as the same Investment of sum bequeathed, where legacy, not specific given for life shall accrue due.

1153. Where a general legacy is given to be paid at a future time, the executor or administrator shall invest a sum sufficient to meet it in securities of the kind mentioned in section 341. The intermediate interest shall form part of the residue of the testator's estate.

1154. Where an annuity is given and no fund is charged with its payment or appropriated by the will to answer it, a Government annuity of the specified amount shall be purchased, or, if no such annuity can be obtained, then a sum sufficient to produce the annuity shall be invested for that purpose in securities of the kind mentioned in section 341.

1155. Where a bequest is contingent, the executor or administrator is not bound to invest the amount of the legacy, but may transfer the whole residue of the estate to the residuary legatee, if any, on his giving sufficient security for the payment of the legacy if it shall become due.

1156. Where the testator has bequeathed the residue of his estate to a person for life without, any direction to invest in any particular securities so much thereof as is not at the time of the testator's decease invested in securities of the kind mentioned in section 341 shall be converted into money and invested in such securities. This section shall not apply if the deceased was a Hindu, Muslim, Buddhist, Sikh or Jaina or an exempted person.

1157. Where the testator has bequeathed the residue of his estate to a person for life with a direction that it shall be invested in certain specified securities, so much of the estate as is not at that time of his death invested in securities of the specified kind shall be converted into money and invested in such securities.

1158. Such conversion and investment as are contemplated by sections 345 and 346 shall be made at such times and in such manner as the executor or administrator thinks fit: and, until such conversion and investment are completed, the person who would be for the time being entitled to the income of the fund when so invested shall receive interest at the rate of 4% per annum upon the market value (10 be computed as at the date of the testator's death) of such part of the fund as has not been so invested: Provided that the rate of interest prior to completion of investment shall be 6% per annum when the testator was a Hindu, Muslim, Buddhist, Sikh or Jaina or an exempted person.

1159. (1) Where, by the terms of a bequest, the legatee is entitled to the immediate payment or possession of the money or thing bequeathed, but is a minor, and there is no direction in the will to pay it to any person on his behalf, the executor or administrator shall pay or deliver the same into the Court of the District Judge, by whom or by whose District Delegate the probate was, or letters of administration with the will annexed were, granted, to the account of the legatee, unless the legatee is a ward of the Court of Wards. (2) If the legatee is a ward of the Court of Wards, the legacy shall be paid to the Court of Wards to his account. (3) Such payment into the Court of the District Judge, or to the Court of Wards, as the case may be, shall be a sufficient discharge for the money so paid. (4) Money when paid in under this section shall be invested in the purchase of Government securities, which, with the interest thereon, shall be transferred or paid to the person entitled thereto or otherwise applied for his benefit, as the Judge or the Court of Wards, as the case may be may direct.

§12. Grants

1160. The sections 237~260 of the Succession Act, 1925 deals about the limited grants. Under section 237 when a will has been lost or mislaid since the testators death, or has been destroyed by wrong or accident and not by any act of the testator, and a copy or the draft of the will has been preserved, probate may be granted of such copy or draft, limited until the original or a properly authenticated copy of it is produced.

1161. Under section 238 when a will has been lost or destroyed and no copy has been made nor the draft preserved, probate may be granted of its contents if they can be established by evidence.

1162. When the will is in the possession of a person residing out of the Province in which application for probate is made, who has refused or neglected to deliver it up, but a copy has been transmitted to the executor, and it is necessary for the interests of the estate that probate should be granted without waiting for the arrival of the original, probate may be granted of the copy so transmitted, limited until the will or an authenticated copy of it is produced.

1163. Where no will of the deceased is forthcoming, but there is reason to believe that there is a will in existence, letters of administration may be granted, limited until the will or an authenticated copy of it is produced.

1164. When any executor is absent from the Province in which application is made, and there is no executor within the Province willing to act, letters of administration, with the will annexed, may be granted to the attorney or agent of the absent executor for the use and benefit of his principal, limited until he shall obtain probe or letters of administration granted to himself.

1165. When any person to whom, if present, letters of administration, with the will annexed, might be granted, is absent from the Province, letters of administration, with the will annexed, may be granted to his attorney or agent, limited as mentioned in section 241.

1166. When a person entitled to administration in case of intestacy is absent from the Province, and no person equally entitled is willing to act, letters of administration may be granted to the attorney or agent of the absent person, limited as mentioned in section 241.

1167. When a minor is sole executor or sole residuary legatee, letters of administration, with the will annexed, may be granted to the legal guardian of such minor or to such other person as the Court may think fit until the minor has attained his majority at which period, and not before, probate of the will shall be granted to him.

1168. When there are two or more minor executors and no executor who has attained majority, or two or more residuary legatees and no residuary legatee who has attained majority, the grant shall be limited until one of them shall have attained his majority.

1169. If a sole executor or a sole universal or residuary of legatee, or a person who would be solely entitled to the estate of the intestate according to the rule for the distribution of intestates estates applicable in the case of the deceased, is a minor or lunatic, letters of administration, with or without the will annexed, as the case may be, shall be granted to the person to whom the care of his estate has been committed by competent authority, or, if there is no such person, to such other person as the Court may think fit to appoint, for the use and benefit of the minor or lunatic until he attains majority or becomes of sound mind, as the case may be.

1170. Pending any suit touching the validity of the will of a deceased person or for obtaining or revoking any probate or any grant of letters of administration, the Court may appoint an administrator of the estate of such deceased person, who shall have all the rights and powers of a general administrator, other than the right of distributing such estate, and every such administrator shall be subject to the immediate control of the Court and shall act under its direction.

1171. If an executor is appointed for any limited purpose specified in the will, the probate shall be limited to that purpose, and if he should appoint an attorney or agent to take administration on his behalf, the letters of administration, with the will annexed, shall be limited accordingly.

1172. If an executor appointed generally gives an authority to an attorney or agent to prove a will on his behalf, and the authority is limited to a particular purpose, the letters of administration, with the will annexed, shall be limited accordingly.

1173. Where a person dies, leaving property of which he was the sole or surviving trustee, or in which he had no beneficial interest on his own account, and leaves no general representative, or one who is unable or unwilling to act as such, letters of administration, limited to such property, may be granted to the beneficiary, or to some other person on his behalf.

1174. When it is necessary that the representative of a person deceased be made a party to a pending suit, and the executor or person entitled to administration is unable or unwilling to act, letters of administration may be granted to the nominee of a party in such suit, limited for the purpose of representing the deceased in the said suit, or in any other cause or suit which may be commenced in the same or in any other Court between the parties, or any other parties, touching the matters at issue in the said cause or suit, and until a final decree shall be made therein and carried into complete execution.

1175. If, at the expiration of twelve months from the date of any probate or letters of administration, the executor or administrator to whom the same has been granted is absent from the Province within which the Court which has granted the probate or letters of administration exercises jurisdiction, the Court may grant, to any person whom it may think fit, letters of administration limited to the purpose of becoming and being made a party to a suit to be brought against the executor or administrator, and carrying the decree which may be made therein into effect.

1176. In any case in which it appears necessary for preserving the property of a deceased person, the Court within whose jurisdiction any of the property is situate may grant to any person, whom such Court may think fit, letters of administration limited to the collection and preservation of the property of the deceased and to the giving of discharges for debts due to his estate, subject to the directions of the Court.

1177. When a person has died intestate, or leaving a will of which there is no executor willing and competent to act or where the executor is, at the time of the death of such person, resident out of the Province, and it appears to the Court to be necessary or convenient to appoint some person to administer the estate or any part thereof, other than the person who, in ordinary circumstances, would be entitled to a grant of administration, the Court may, in its discretion, having regard to consanguinity, amount of interest, the safety of the estate and probability that it will be properly administered, appoint such person as it thinks fit to be administrator. In every such case, letters of administration may be limited or not as the Court thinks fit.

1178. Whenever the nature of the case requires that an exception be made, probate of a will, or letters of administration with the will annexed, shall be granted subject to such exception. Whenever the nature of the case requires that an exception be made, letters of administration shall be granted subject to such exception.

1179. Whenever a grant with exception of probate, or of letters of administration with or without the will annexed, has been made, the person entitled to probate or administration of the remainder of the deceased's estate may take a grant of probate or letters of administration, as the case may be, of the rest of the deceased's estate.

1180. If an executor to whom probate has been granted has died, leaving a part of the testator's estate un-administered, a new representative may be appointed for the purpose of administering such part of the estate.

1181. In granting letters of administration of an estate not fully administered, the Court shall be guided by the same rules as apply to original grants, and shall grant Setters of administration to those persons only to whom original grants might have been made.

1182. When a limited grant has expired by efflux of time, or the happening of the event or contingency on which it was limited, and there is still some part of the deceased's estate un-administered, letters of administration shall be granted to those persons to whom original grants might have been made.

1183. The sections 261~263 of the Succession Act, 1925 deals with the alteration and revocation of Grants. Under section 261 if errors in names and descriptions, or in setting forth the time and place of the deceased's death, or the purpose in a limited grant, may be rectified by the Court, the grant of probate or letters of administration may be altered and amended accordingly.

1184. If, after the grant of letters of administration with the will annexed, a codicil is discovered, it may be added to the grant on due proof and identification, and the grant may be altered and amended accordingly.

1185. The grant of probate or letters of administration may be revoked or annulled for just cause. Explanation: Just cause shall be deemed to exist where (a) the proceedings to obtain the grant were defective in substance; or (b) the grant was obtained fraudulently by making a false suggestion, or by concealing from the Court something material to the care; or (c) the grant was obtained by means of an untrue allegation, of a fact essential in point of law to justify the grant, though such allegation was made in ignorance or inadvertently; or (d) the grant has become useless and inoperative through circumstances; or (e) the person to whom the grant was made has wilfully and without reasonable cause omitted to exhibit an inventory or account in accordance with the provisions of Chapter VII of the Succession Act, 1925, or has exhibited under that Chapter an inventory or account which is untrue in a material respect. Illustrations: (i) The Court by which the grant was made had no jurisdiction. (ii) The grant was made without citing parties who ought to have been cited. (iii) The will of which probate was obtained was forged or revoked.

(iv) A obtained letters of administration to the estate of B, as his widow, but it has since transpired that she was never married to him. (v) A has taken administration to the (intestate) of B as if he had died intestate, but a will has since been discovered. (vi) Since probate was granted, a later will has been discovered. (vii) Since probate was granted, a codicil has been discovered which revokes or adds to the appointment of executors under the will. (viii) The person to whom probate was, or letters of administration were, granted has subsequently become of unsound mind.

§13. Protection of Property of Deceased

1186. Sections 192~210 of the Succession Act, 1925 protects the property of deceased. If any person dies leaving property, moveable or immoveable, any person claiming a right by succession thereto or to any portion thereof, may make application to the District Judge of the district where any part of the property is found or situate for relief, either after actual possession has been taken by another person, or when forcible means of seizing possession are apprehended.

1187. Any agent, relative or near friend, or the Court of Wards in cases within their cognizance, may, in the event of any minor, or any disqualified or absent person being entitled by succession to such property as aforesaid, make the like application for relief.

1188. The District Judge to whom such application is made shall, in the first place, examine the applicant on oath, and may make such further inquiry, if any, as he thinks necessary as to whether there is sufficient ground for believing that the party in possession or taking forcible means for seizing possession has no lawful title, and that the applicant, or the person on whose behalf he applies, is really entitled and is likely to be materially prejudiced if left to the ordinary remedy of a suit, and that the application is made bona fide.

1189. If the District Judge is satisfied that there is sufficient ground for believing as aforesaid but not otherwise, he shall summon the party complained of, and give notice of vacant or disturbed possession by publication, and, after the expiration of a reasonable time, shall determine summarily the right to possession (subject to a suit as hereinafter provided) and shall deliver possession accordingly: Provided that the judge shall have the power to appoint an officer who shall take an inventory of effects, and seal or otherwise secure the same, upon being applied to for the purpose, Without delay, whether he shall have concluded the inquiry necessary for summoning the party complained of or not.

1190. If it further appears upon such inquiry as aforesaid that danger is to be apprehended of the misappropriation or waste of the property before the summary proceeding can be determined, and that the delay in obtaining security from the party in possession or the insufficiency thereof is likely to expose the party out of possession to considerable risk, provided he is the lawful owner, the District Judge may appoint one or more curators whose authority shall continue according to the terms of his or their respective appointments, and in no case beyond the determination of the summary proceeding and the confirmation or delivery of possession in consequence thereof: Provided that, in the case of land, the Judge may delegate to the Collector, or to any officer subordinate to the Collector, the power of a curator: Provided, further, that every appointment of a curator in respect of any property shall be duly published.

1191. The District Judge may authorize the curator to take possession of the property either generally, or until security is given by the party in possession, or until inventories of the property have been made, or for any other purpose necessary for securing the property from misappropriation or waste by the party in possession: Provided that it shall be in the discretion of the Judge to allow the party in possession to continue in such possession on giving security or not, and any continuance in possession shall be subject to such orders as the Judge may issue touching inventories, or the securing of deeds or other effects.

1192. Where a certificate has been granted under Part X or under the Succession Certificate Act, 1889, or a grant of probate or letters of administration has been made, a curator appointed shall not exercise any authority lawfully belonging to the holder of the certificate or to the executor or administrator.

1193. All persons who have paid debts or rents to a curator authorized by a Court to receive them shall be indemnified, and the curator shall be responsible for the payment thereof to the person who has obtained the certificate probate or letters of administration, as the case may be.

1194. The District Judge shall take from the curator security for the faithful discharge of his trust, and for rendering satisfactory accounts of the same as hereinafter provided, and may authorize him to receive out of the property such remuneration, in no case exceeding 5% on the moveable property and on the annual profits of the immoveable property, as the District Judge thinks reasonable.

1195. All surplus money realized by the curator shall be paid into Court, and invested in public securities for the benefit of the persons entitled thereto upon adjudication of the summary proceeding.

1196. Security shall be required from the curator with all reasonable dispatch, and, where it is practicable, shall be taken generally to answer all cases for which the person may be afterwards appointed curator; but no delay in the taking of security shall prevent the Judge from immediately investing the curator with the powers of his office.

1197. Where the estate of the deceased person consists to wholly or in part of land paying revenue to Government, in all matters regarding the propriety of summoning the party in possession, of appointing a curator, or of nominating individuals to that appointment, the District Judge shall demand a report from the Collector, and the Collector shall thereupon furnish the same: Provided that in cases of urgency the Judge may proceed, in the first instance, without such report.

1198. The Judge shall not be obliged to act in conformity with any such report, but, in case of his acting otherwise than according to such report, he shall immediately forward a statement of his reasons to the High Court, and the High Court, if it is dissatisfied with such reasons, shall direct the Judge to proceed conformably to the report of the Collector.

1199. The curator shall be subject to all orders of the District Judge regarding the institution or the defence of suits, and all suits may be instituted or defended in the name of the curator on behalf of the estate: Provided that an express authority shall be requisite in the order of the curators appointment or the collection of debts or rents; but such express authority shall enable the curator to give a full acquittance for any sums of money received by virtue thereof.

1200. Pending the custody of the property by the curator, The District Judge may make such allowances to parties having a prima facie right thereto as upon a summary investigation of the rights and circumstances of the parties interested he considers necessary, and may, at his discretion, take security for the repayment thereof with interest, in the event of the party being found, upon the adjudication of the summary proceeding, not to be entitled thereto.

1201. The curator shall file monthly accounts in abstract, and shall, on the expiry of each period of three months, if his administration lasts so long, and, upon giving up the possession of the property, file a detailed account of his administration to the satisfaction of the District Judge.

1202. The accounts of the curator shall be open to the inspection of all parties interested; and it shall be competent for any such interested party to appoint a separate person to keep a duplicate account of all receipts and payments by the curator.

1203. If it is found that the accounts of the curator are in arrear, or that they are erroneous or incomplete, or if the curator does not produce them whenever he is ordered to do so by the District Judge, he shall be punishable with fine not exceeding PKR 1,000 for every such default.

1204. If the Judge of any district has appointed a curator, in respect of the whole of the property of a deceased person, such appointment shall preclude the Judge of any other district within the same Province from appointing any other curator, but the appointment of a curator in respect of a portion of the property of the deceased shall not preclude the appointment within the same Province of another creator in respect of the residue or any portion thereof: Provided that no Judge shall appoint a curator or entertain a summary proceeding in respect of property which is the subject of a summary proceeding previously instituted under Part-VII of the Succession Act, 1925 before another Judge; Provided, further, that if two or more curators are appointed by different Judges for several parts of an estate, the High Court may make such order as it thinks fit for the appointment of one curator of the whole property.

1205. An application under Part-VII of the Succession Act, 1925 to the District Judge must be made within six months of the death of the proprietor whose property is claimed by right in succession.

1206. However, nothing is deemed to authorize the contravention of any public act of settlement or of any legal directions given by a deceased proprietor of any property for the possession of his property after his decease in the event of minority or otherwise, and, in every such case, as soon as the Judge having jurisdiction over the property of a deceased person is satisfied of the existence of such directions, he shall give effect thereto.

1207. Nothing shall be deemed to authorize any disturbance of the possession of a Court of Wards of any property; and in case minor, or other disqualified person whose property is subject to the Court of Wards, is the party on whose behalf application is made under Part-VII of the Succession Act, 1925, the District Judge, if he determines to summon the party in possession and to appoint a curator, shall invest the Court of Wards with the curatorship of the estate pending the proceeding without taking security as aforesaid: and if the minor or other disqualified person, upon the adjudication of the summary proceeding, appears to be entitled to the property, possession shall be delivered to the Court of Wards.

1208. There shall be no impediment to the bringing of a suit either by the party whose application may have been rejected before or after the summoning of the party in possession, or by the party who may have been evicted from the possession under Part-VII of the Succession Act, 1925.

1209. The decision of a District Judge in a summary proceeding shall have no other effect than that of settling the actual possession; but for this purpose it shall be final, and shall not be subject to any appeal or review.

1210. The Provincial Government appoints public curators for any district or number of districts; and the District Judge having jurisdiction shall nominate such public curators in all cases where the choice of a curator is left discretionary with him.

1211. The Succession Act, 1925 (sections 211~216) deals with the representative title to property of deceased on succession. The executor or administrator, as the case may be, of a deceased person is his legal representative for all purposes, and all the property of the deceased person vests in him as such.

1212. When the deceased was a Hindu, Muslim, Buddhist, Sikh Jaina, or Parsi, an exempted person, nothing herein contained shall vest in an executor or administrator any property of the deceased person which would otherwise have passed by survivorship to some other person.

1213. No right to any part of the property of a person who has died intestate can be established in any Court of Justice, unless letters of administration have first been granted by a Court of competent jurisdiction. However, this shall not apply in the case of the intestacy of a Hindu, Muslim, Buddhist, Sikh, Jaina, Parsi or Pakistan Christian.

1214. No right as executor or legatee can be established in any Court of Justice, unless a Court of competent jurisdiction in Pakistan has granted probate of the will under which the right is clamed, or has granted letters of administration with the will or with a copy of an authenticated copy of the will annexed.

1215. However, it shall not apply in the case of wills made by Muslims and Parsis, and shall only apply in the case of wills made by any Hindu Buddhist, Sikh or Jaina; such wills are of the classes specified in clauses (a) and (b) of section 57.

1216. No Court (a) passes a decree against a debtor of a deceased person for payment of his debt to a person claiming on succession to be entitled to the effects of the deceased in person or to any part thereof, or (b) proceed, upon an application of a person claiming to be so entitled, to execute against such a debtor a decree or order for the payment of his debt, except on the production, by the person so claiming, of: (i) a probate or letters of administration evidencing the grant to him of administration to the estate of the deceased; or (ii) a certificate granted under section 31 or section 32 of the Administrator Generals Act, 1913, and having the debt mentioned therein; or (iii) a succession certificate granted under Part X and having the debt specified therein; or (iv) a certificate granted under the Succession Certificate Act, 1989; or (v) a certificate granted under Sind Regulation No. VIII of 1827 and, if granted after the first day of May 1889, having the debt specified therein. The word 'debt' includes any debt except rent, revenue or profits payable in respect of land used for agricultural purposes.

1217. A grant of probate or letters of administration in respect of an estate shall be deemed to supersede any certificate previously granted under Part X or under the Succession Certificate Act, 1889 or Sind Regulation No. VIII of 1827, in respect of any debt or securities included in the estate. When at the time of the grant of the probate or letters any suit or other proceeding instituted by the holder of any such certificate regarding any such debt or security is pending, the person to whom the grant is made shall, on applying to the Court in which the suit or proceeding is pending, be entitled to take the place of the holder of the certificate in the suit or proceeding: Provided that, when any certificate is superseded, all payments made to the holder of such certificate in ignorance of such supersession shall be held good against claims under the probate or letters of administration.

1218. After any grant of probate or letters of administration, no other than the person to whom the same may have been granted shall have power to sue or prosecute any suit, or otherwise act as representative of the deceased, throughout the Province in which the same may have been granted, until such probate or letters of administration has or have been recalled or revoked.

1219. The sections 218~236 of the Succession Act, 1925 deals regarding grant of probate and letters of administration. If the deceased has died intestate and was a Hindu, Muslim, Buddhist, Sikh or Jaina or an exempted person, administration of his estate may be granted to any person who, according to the rules for the distribution of the estate applicable in the case of such deceased, would be entitled to the whole or any part of such deceased's estate. When several such persons apply for such administration, it shall be in the discretion of the Court to grant it to any one or more of them. When no such person applies, it may be granted to a creditor of the deceased.

1220. If the deceased has died intestate and was not a person belonging to any of the classes referred to in section 218, those who are connected with him, either by marriage or by consanguinity, are entitled to obtain letters of administration of his estate and effects in the order and according to the rules hereinafter stated, namely: (a) If the deceased has, left a widow, administration shall be granted to the widow, unless the Court sees cause to exclude her, either on the ground of some personal disqualification, or because she has no interest in the estate of the deceased. Illustrations: (i) The widow is a lunatic or has committed adultery or has been barred by her marriage settlement of all interest in her husband estate. There is cause for excluding her from the administration. (ii) The widow has married again since the decease of her husband. This is not good cause for her exclusion. (b) If the Judge thinks proper, he may associate any person or persons with the widow in the administration who would be entitled solely to the administration if there were no widow. (c) If there is no widow, or if the Court sees cause to exclude the widow, it shall commit the administration to the person or persons who would be beneficially entitled to the estate according to the rules for the distribution of an intestates estate: Provided that, when the mother of the deceased is one of the class of persons so entitled, she shall be solely entitled to administration. (d) Those who stand in equal degree of kindred to the deceased are equally entitled to administration. (e) The husband surviving his wife has the same right of administration of her estate as the widow has in respect of the estate of her husband. (f) When there is no person connected with the deceased by marriage or consanguinity who is entitled to letters of administration and willing to act, they may be granted to a creditor. (g) Where the deceased has left property in Pakistan letters of administration shall be granted according to the foregoing rules, notwithstanding that he had his domicile in a country in which the law relating to testate and intestate succession differs from the law of Pakistan.

1221. Letters of administration entitle the administrator to all rights belonging to the intestate as effectually as if the administration had been granted at the moment after his death. Letters of administration do not render valid any intermediate acts of the administrator tending to the diminution or damage of the intestates estate.

1222. Probate is granted only to an executor appointed by the will. The appointment may be expressed or by necessary implication. Illustrations: (i) A, wills that C, be his executor if B will not. B is appointed executor by implication. (ii) A gives a legacy to B and several legacies to the other persons, among the rest to his daughter-in-law C, and adds 'but should the within-named C be not living I do constitute and appoint B my whole and sole executrix', C is appointed executrix by implication. (iii) A appoints several persons executors of his will and codicils and his nephew residuary legatee, and in another codicil are these words, 'I appoint my nephew my residuary legatee, to discharge all lawful demands against my will and codicils signed of different dates.' The nephew is appointed an executor by implication.

1223. Probate cannot be granted to any person who is a minor or is of unsound mind nor to any association of individuals unless it is a company which satisfies the conditions prescribed by rules to be made by the Provincial Government in this behalf.

1224. When several executors are appointed, probate may be granted to them all simultaneously or at different times. Illustration: A is an executor of B's will by express appointment and C an executor of it by implication. Probate may be granted to A and C at the same time or to A first and then to C, or to C first and then to A.

1225. If a codicil is discovered after the grant of probate, a separate probate of that codicil may be granted to the executor, if it in no way repeals the appointment of executors made by the will. If different executors are appointed by the codicil, the probate of the will shall be revoked, and a new probate granted of the will and the codicil together.

1226. When probate has been granted to several executors, and one of them dies, the entire representation of the testator accrues to the surviving executor or executors. Probate of a will when granted establishes the will from the death of the testator, and renders valid all intermediate acts of the executor as such.

1227. When a will has been proved and deposited in a Court of competent jurisdiction situated beyond the limits of the Province, whether within or beyond the limits of Pakistan and a properly authenticated copy of the will is produced, letters of administration may be granted with a copy of such copy annexed.

1228. When a person appointed an executor has not renounced the executorship, letters of administration shall not be granted to any other person until a citation has been issued, calling upon the executor to accept or renounce his executorship: Provided that, when one or more of several executors have proved a will, the Court may, on the death of the survivor of those who have proved, grant letters of administration without citing those who have not proved.

1229. The renunciation may be made orally in the presence of the Judge, or by a writing signed by the person renouncing, and when made shall preclude him from ever thereafter applying for probate of the will appointing him executor.

1230. If an executor renounces, or fails to accept an executor-ship within the time limited for the acceptance or refusal thereof, the will may be proved and letters of administration, with a copy of the will annexed, may be granted to the person who would be entitled to administration in case of intestacy.

1231. When (a) the deceased has made a will, but has not appointed an executor, or (b) the deceased has appointed an executor who is legally incapable or refuses to act, or who has died before the testator or before he has proved the will, or (c) the executor dies after having proved the will, but before he has administered all the estate of the deceased, an universal or a residuary legatee may be admitted to prove the will, and letters of administration with the will annexed may be granted to him of the whole estate, or of so much thereof as may be un-administered.

1232. When a residuary legatee who has a beneficial interest survives the testator, but dies before the estate has been fully administered, his representative has the same right to administration with the will annexed as such residuary legatee.

1233. When there is no executor and no residuary legatee or representative of a residuary legatee, or he declines or is incapable to act, or cannot be found, the person or persons who would be entitled to the administration of the estate of the deceased if he had died intestate, or any other legatee having a beneficial interest, or a creditor, may be admitted to prove the will, and letters of administration may be granted to him or them accordingly.

1234. Letters of administration with the will annexed shall not be granted to any legatee other than an universal or residuary legatee, until a citation has been issued and published in the manner hereinafter mentioned, calling on the next-of-kin to accept or refuse letters of administration.

1235. Letters of administration cannot be granted to any person who is a minor or is of unsound mind, nor to any association of individuals unless it is a company which satisfies the conditions prescribed by rules to be made by the Provincial Government in this behalf.

§14. GIFTS IN CONTEMPLATION OF DEATH

1236. Under section 191 of the Succession Act, 1925 a man may dispose, by gift made in contemplation of death, of any moveable property which he could dispose of by will. A gift said to be made in contemplation of death where a man, who is ill and expects to die shortly of his illness, delivers to another the possession of any moveable property to keep as a gift in case the donor shall die of that illness. Such a gift may be resumed by the giver and shall not take effect if he recovers from the illness during which it was made; nor if he survives the person to whom it was made. Illustrations: A, being ill, and in expectation of death, delivers to B, to be retained by him in case of A's death: a watch; a bond granted by C to A; a bank-note; a promissory note of the Federal Government endorsed in blank; a bill of exchange endorsed in blank; and certain mortgage-deeds. A dies of the illness during which he delivered these articles. B is entitled to: the watch; the debt secured by C's bond; the bank-note; the promissory note of the Federal Government; the bill of exchange; and the money secured by the mortgage-deeds.

1237. A, being ill, and in expectation of death, delivers to B the key of a trunk or the key of a warehouse in which goods of bulk belonging to A are deposited, with the intention of giving him the control over the contents of the trunk, or over the deposited goods, and desires him to keep them in case of A's death. A dies of the illness during which he delivered these articles. B is entitled to the trunk and its contents or to A's goods of bulk in the warehouse.

1238. A, being ill, and in expectation of death, puts aside certain articles in separate parcels and marks upon the parcels respectively the names of B and C. The parcels are not delivered during the life of A. A dies of the illness during which he set aside the parcels. B and C are not entitled to the contents of the parcel.

§15. Administrators or Executors

1239. The Succession Act, 1925 (sections 305 ~ 315) stipulates the powers of an executor or administrator. An executor or administrator has the same power to sue in respect of all causes of action that survive the deceased, and may exercise the same power for the recovery of debts as the deceased had when living.

1240. All demands whatsoever and all rights to prosecute or defend any action or special proceeding existing in favour of or against a person at the time of his decease, survive to and against his executors or administrator; except causes of action for defamation, assault, as deemed in the Pakistan Penal Code, or other personal injuries not causing the death of the party; and except also cases where, after the death of the party, the relief sought could not be enjoyed or granting it would be nugatory. Illustrations: (i) A collision takes place on a railway in consequence of some neglect or default of an official, and a passenger is severely hurt, but not so as to cause death. He afterwards dies without having brought any action. The cause of action does not survive. (ii) A sues for divorce. A dies. The cause of action does not survive to his representative.

1241. An executor or administrator has power to dispose of the property of the deceased, vested in him under section 211, either wholly or in part, in such manner as he may think fit. Illustrations: (i) The deceased has made a specific bequest of part of his property. The executor, not having assented to the bequest, sells the subject of it. The sale is valid. (ii) The executor in the exercise of his discretion mortgages a part of the immoveable estate of the deceased. The mortgage is valid. If the deceased was a Hindu, Muslim, Buddhist, Sikh or Jaina or an exempted person, shall be subject to the following restrictions and conditions, namely: (i) The power of an executor to dispose of immoveable property so vested in him is subject to any restriction which may be imposed in this behalf by the will appointing him, unless probate has been granted to him and the Court which granted the probate permits him by an order in writing, notwithstanding the restriction, to dispose of any immoveable property specified in the order in a manner permitted by the order. (ii) An administrator may not, without the previous permission of the Court by which the letters of administration were granted, (a) mortgage charge or transfer by sale, gift, exchange or otherwise any immoveable property for the time being vested in him under section 211, or (b) lease any such property for a term exceeding five years. (iii) A disposal of property by an executor or administrator in contravention of clause (i) or clause (ii), as the case may be, is voidable at the instance of any other person interested in the property.

1242. An executor or administrator may, in addition to, and not in derogation of, any other powers of expenditure lawfully exercisable by him, incur expenditure: (a) on such acts as may be necessary for the proper care or management of any property belonging to any estate administered by him; and (b) with the sanction of the High Court, on such religious, charitable and other objects, and on such improvements, as may be reasonable and proper in the case of such property.

1243. An executor or administrator shall not be entitled to receive or retain any commission or agency charges at a higher rate than that for the time being fixed in respect of the Administrator General by or under the Administrator Generals Act 1913.

1244. If any executor or administrator purchases, either directly or indirectly, any part of the property of the deceased, the sale is voidable at the instance of any other person interested in the property sold.

1245. When there are several executors or administrators, the powers of all may, in the absence of any direction to the contrary, be exercised by any one of them who has proved the will or taken out administration. Illustrations: (i) One of several executors has power to release a debt due to the deceased. (ii) One has power to surrender a lease. (iii) One has power to sell the property of the deceased whether moveable or immoveable. (iv) One has power to assent to a legacy. (v) One has power to endorse a promissory note payable to the deceased. (vi) The will appoints A, B, C and D to be executors, and directs that two of them shall be a quorum. No act can be done by a single executor.

1246. Upon the death of one or more of several executors or administrators, in the absence of any direction to the contrary in the will or grant of letters of administration, all the powers of the office become vested in the survivors or survivor.

1247. The administrator of effects un-administered has, with respect to such effects, the same power as the original executor or administrator. An administrator during minority has all the powers of an ordinary administrator. When a grant of probate or letters of administration has been made to a married woman, she has all the powers of an ordinary executor or administrator.

1248. It is the duty of an executor to provide funds for the performance of the necessary funeral ceremonies of the deceased in manner suitable to his condition, if he has left property sufficient for the purpose.

1249. An executor or administrator shall, within six months from the grant of probate or letters of administration, or within such further time as the Court which granted the probate or letters may appoint, exhibit in that Court an inventory containing a full and true estimate of all the property in possession, and all the credits, and also all the debts owing by any person to which the executor or administrator is entitled in that character; and shall in like manner, within one year from the grant or within such further time as the said Court may appoint exhibit an account of the estate, showing the assets which have come to his hands and the manner in which they have been applied or disposed of. The High Court may prescribe the form in which an inventory or account is to be exhibited. If an executor administration being required by the Court to exhibit an inventory or account, intentionally omits to comply with the requisition, he shall be deemed to have committed, an offence under section 176 of the Pakistan Penal Code. The exhibition of an intentionally false inventory or account shall be deemed to be an offence under section 193 of that Code.

1250. In all cases where a grant has been made of probate or letters of administration intended to have effect throughout Pakistan, the executor or administrator shall include in the inventory of the effects of the deceased all his moveable and immoveable property situate in Pakistan, and the value of such property situated in each Province shall be separately stated in such inventory, and the probate or letters of administration shall be chargeable with a fee corresponding to the entire amount or value of the property affected thereby wheresoever's situate within Pakistan.

1251. The executor or administrator shall collect, with reasonable diligence, the property of the deceased and the debts that were due to him at the tune of his death. Funeral expenses to a reasonable amount, according to the degree and quality of the deceased, and death-bed charges, including fees for medical attendance, and board and lodging for one month previous to his death, shall be paid before all debts.

1252. The expenses of obtaining probate or letters of administration, including the costs incurred for or in respect of any judicial proceedings that may be necessary for administering the estate, shall be paid next after the funeral expenses and death-bed charges.

1253. Wages due for services rendered to the deceased within three months next preceding his death by any labourer, artisan or domestic servant shall next be paid, and then the other debts of the deceased according to their respective priorities (if any). Save as aforesaid, no creditor shall have a right of priority over another but the executor or administrator shall pay all such debts as he knows of, including his own, equally and ratably as far as the assets of the deceased will extend.

1254. If the domicile of the deceased was not in Pakistan, the application of his moveable property to the payment of his debts is to be regulated by the law of Pakistan. No creditor who has received payment of a part of his debt shall be entitled to share in the proceeds of the immoveable estate of the deceased unless he brings such payment into account for the benefit of the other creditors. This section shall not apply where the deceased was a Hindu, Muslim, Buddhist, Sikh or Jaina or an exempted person. Illustration: A dies, having his domicile in a country where instruments under seal have priority over instruments not under seal leaving moveable property to the value of PKR 5,000, and immoveable property to the value of PKR 10,000, debts on instruments under seal to the amount of PKR 10,000, and debts on instruments not under seal to the same amount. The creditors holding instruments under seal receive half of their debts out of the proceeds of the moveable estate. The proceeds of the immoveable estate are to be applied in payment of the debts on instruments not under seal until one-half such debts has been discharged. This will leave PKR 5,000 which are to be distributed ratably amongst all the creditors without distinction, in proportion to the amount which may remain due to them.

1255. Debts of every description must be paid before any legacy. If the estate of the deceased is subject to any contingent liabilities, an executor or administrator is not bound to pay any legacy without a sufficient indemnity to meet the liabilities whenever they may become due.

1256. If the assets, after payment of debts, necessary expenses and specific legacies, are not sufficient to pay all the general legacies in full, the latter shall abate or be diminished in equal proportions, and, in the absence of any direction to the contrary in the will, the executor has no right to pay one legatee in preference to another, or to retain any money on account of a legacy to himself or to any person for whom he is a trustee.

1257. Where there is a specific legacy, and the assets are sufficient for the payment of debts and necessary expenses, the thing specified must be delivered to the legatee without any abatement.

1258. Where there is a demonstrative legacy, and the assets are sufficient for the payment of debts and necessary expenses, the legatee has a preferential claim for payment of his legacy out of the fund from which the legacy is directed to be paid until such fund is exhausted and if, after the fund is exhausted, part of the legacy still remains unpaid, he is entitled to rank for the remainder against the general assets as for a legacy of the amount of such unpaid remainder.

1259. If the assets are not sufficient to answer the debts and the specific legacies, an abatement shall be made from the latter ratably in proportion to their respective amounts. Illustration: A has bequeathed to B a diamond ring valued at PKR 500, and to C & horse, valued at PKR 1,000. It is found necessary to sell all the effects of the testator; and his assets, after payment of debts, are only PKR 1,000. Of this sum PKR 333-5-4 are to be paid to B, and PKR 666-10-8 to C.

1260. For the purpose of abatement, a legacy for life, a sum appropriated by the will to produce an annuity, and the value of an annuity when no sum has been appropriated to produce it, shall be treated as general legacies.

1261. The Succession Act, 1925, sections 303 and 304 provide details about executors own wrong. A person who intermeddles with the estate of the deceased, or does any other act which belongs to the office of executor while there is no rightful executor or administrator in existence thereby makes himself an executor of his own wrong. Exceptions: (I) Intermeddling with the goods of the deceased for the purpose of preserving them or providing for his funeral or for the immediate necessities of his family or property, does not make an executor of his own wrong. Dealing in the ordinary course of business with goods of the deceased received from another does not make an executor of his own wrong. Illustrations: (i) A uses or gives away or sells some of the goods of the deceased, or takes them to satisfy his own debt or legacy or receives payment of the debts of the deceased. He is an executor of his own wrong. (ii) A, having been appointed agent by the deceased in his lifetime to collect his debts and sell his goods, continues to do so after he has become aware of his death. He is an executor of his own wrong in respect of acts done after he has become aware of the death of the deceased. (iii) A sues as executor of the deceased, not being such. He is an executor of his own wrong.

1262. When a person has so acted as to become an executor of his own wrong, he is answerable to the rightful executor or administrator, or to any creditor or legatee of the deceased, to the extent of the asset which may have come to his hands after deducting payments made to the rightful executor or administrator, and payments made in due course of administration.

1263. Under sections 368 and 369 of the Succession Act, 1925 when an executor or administrator misapplies the estate of the deceased, or subjects it to loss or damage, he is liable to make good the loss or damage so occasioned. Illustrations: (i) The executor pays out of the estate an unfounded claim. He is liable to make good the loss. (ii) The deceased had a valuable lease renewable by notice which the executor neglects to give at the proper time. The executor is liable to make good the loss. (iii) The deceased had a lease of less value than the rent payable for it, but terminable on notice at a particular time. The executor neglects to give the notice. He is liable to make good the loss.

1264. When an executor or administrator occasions a loss to the estate by neglecting to get in any part of the property of the deceased, he is liable to make good the amount. Illustrations: (i) The executor absolutely releases a debt due to the deceased from a solvent person, or compounds with a debtor who is able to pay in full. The executor is liable to make good the amount. (ii) The executor neglects to sue for a debt till the debtor is able to plead that the claim is barred by limitation, and the debt is thereby lost to the estate. The executor is liable to make good the amount.

1265. The Chapter IV, sections 264~302 of the Succession Act, 1925 deal with the practices in granting and revoking probates and letters of Administration. The District Judge shall have jurisdiction in granting and revoking probates and letters of administration in all cases within his district. Except in cases to which section 57 applies, no Court shall, where the deceased is a Hindu, Muslim, Buddhist, Sikh or Jaina or an exempted person, receive applications for probate or letters of administration until the Provincial Government has, by a notification in the Official Gazette, authorized it so to do.

1266. The High Court may appoint such judicial officers within any district as it thinks fit to act for the District Judge as Delegates to grant probate and letters of administration in non-contentious cases, within such local limits as it may prescribe: Provided that, in the case of High Courts not established by Royal Charter, such appointment shall not be without the previous sanction of the Provincial Government. Persons so appointed shall be called 'District Delegates'.

1267. The District Judge shall have the like powers and authority in relation to the granting of probate and letters of administration, and all matters connected therewith, as are by law vested in him in relation to any civil suit or proceeding pending in his Court.

1268. The District Judge may order any person to produce and bring into Court any paper or writing, being or purporting to be testamentary, which may be shown to be in the possession or under the control of such person. If it is not shown that any such paper or writing is in the possession or under the control of such person, but there is reason to believe that he has the knowledge of any such paper or writing, the Court may direct such person to attend for the purpose of being examined respecting the same. Such person shall be bound to answer truly such questions as may be put to him by the Court, and, if so ordered, to produce and bring in such paper or writing, and shall be subject to the like punishment under the Pakistan Penal Code, in case of default in not attending or in not answering such questions or not bringing in such paper or writing, as he would have been subject to in case he had been a party to a suit and had made such default. The costs of the proceeding shall be in the discretion of the Judge.

1269. The proceedings of the Court of the District Judge in relation to the granting of probate and letters of administration shall, save as hereinafter otherwise provided, be regulated, so far as the circumstances of the case permit, by the Code of Civil Procedure, 1908.

1270. Until probate is granted of the will of a deceased person, or an administrator of his estate is constituted, the District Judge, within whose jurisdiction any part of the property of the deceased person is situate, is authorized and required to interfere for the protection of such property at the instance of any person cleaning to be interested therein, and in all other cases where the judge considers that the property incurs any risk of loss or damage; and for that purpose, if he thinks fit, to appoint an officer to take and keep possession of the property. This section shall not apply when the deceased is a Hindu, Muslim, Buddhist, Sikh or Jaina or an exempted person, nor shall it apply to any part of the property of a Pakistan Christian who has died intestate.

1271. Probate of the will or letters of administration to the estate of a deceased person may be granted by a District Judge under the seal of his Court, if it appears by a petition, verified as hereinafter provided, of the person applying for the same that the testator or intestate, as the case may be, at the time of his decease had a fixed place of abode, or any property, moveable or immoveable, within the jurisdiction of the Judge.

1272. When the application is made to the Judge of a district in which the deceased had no fixed abode at the time of his death, it shall be in the discretion of the Judge to refuse the application, if in his judgment it could be disposed of more justly or conveniently in another district, or, where the application is for letters of administration, to grant them absolutely, or limited to the property within his own jurisdiction.

1273. Probate and letters of administration may, upon application for that purpose to any District Delegate, be granted by him in any case in which there is no contention, if it appears by petition, verified as hereinafter provided, that the testator or intestate, as the case may be, at the time of his death had a fixed place of abode within the jurisdiction of such Delegate.

1274. Probate or letters of administration shall have effect over all the property and estate, moveable or immoveable, of the deceased, throughout the Province in which the same is or are granted, and shall be conclusive as to the representative title against all debtors of the deceased, and all persons holding property which belongs to him, and shall afford full indemnity to all debtors, paying their debts and all persons delivering up such property to the person to whom such probate or letters of administration have been granted: Provided that probates and letters of administration granted (a) by a High Court, or (b) by a District Judge, where the deceased at the time of his death had a fixed place of abode situate within the jurisdiction of such Judge, and such Judge certifies that the value of the property and estate affected beyond the limits of the Province does not exceed PKR 10,000, shall, unless otherwise directed by the grant, have like effect brought-out Pakistan. The said proviso shall also apply in Pakistan after the separation of Pakistan from India to probates and letters of administration granted before the date of the separation, or on or after that date in proceedings pending at that date in any of the territories which on that date were comprised in India.

1275. Where probate or letters of administration has or have been granted by a High Court or District Judge with the effect referred to in the proviso to section 273, the High Court or District Judge shall send a certificate thereof to the following Courts, namely: (a) when the grant has been made by a High Court, to each of the other High Courts; (b) when the grant has been made by a District Judge, to the High Court to which such District Judge is subordinate and to each of the other High Courts. Every certificate referred above shall be made as nearly as circumstances admit in the form set forth in Schedule IV of the Succession Act, 1925, and such certificate shall be filed by the High Court receiving the same. Where any portion of the assets has been stated by the petitioner, as hereinafter provided in sections 276 and 278, to be situated within the jurisdiction of a District Judge in another Province, the Court required to send the certificate referred above to such District Judge, and such copy shall be filed by the District Judge receiving the same.

1276. The application for probate or letters of administration, if made and verified in the manner hereinafter provided, shall be conclusive for the purpose of authorizing the grant of probate or administration; and no such grant shall be impeached by reason only that the testator or intestate had no fixed place of abode or no property within the district at the time of his death, unless by a proceeding to revoke the grant if obtained by a fraud upon the Court.

1277. Application for probate or for letters of administration, with the will annexed, shall be made by a petition distinctly written in English or in the language in ordinary use in proceedings before the Court in which the application is made, with the will or, in the cases mentioned in sections 237, 238, and 239, a copy, draft, or statement of the contents thereof, annexed, and stating (a) the time of the testators death, (b) that the writing annexed is his last will and testament, (c) that it was duly executed, (d) the amount of assets which are likely to come to the petitioners hands, and (e) when the application is for probate, that the petitioner is the executor named in the will. In addition to these particulars, the petition shall further state, (a) when the application is to the District Judge, that the deceased at the time of his death had a fixed place of abode, or had some property, situate within the jurisdiction of the Judge; and (b) when the application is to a District Delegate, that the deceased at the time of his death had a fixed place of abode within the jurisdiction of such Delegate. Where the application is to the District Judge and any portion of the assets likely to come to the petitioners hands is situate in another Province the petition shall further state the amount of such assets in each Province and the District Judges within whose jurisdiction such assets are situate.

1278. In cases wherein the will, copy or draft, is written in any language other than English or than that in ordinary use in proceedings before the Court, there shall be a translation thereof annexed to the petition by a translator of the Court, if the language be one for which a translator is appointed; or, if the will, copy or draft, is in any other language, then by any person competent to translate the same, in which case such translation shall be verified by that person in the following manner, namely: 'I (A.B.) do declare that I read and perfectly understand the language and character of the original, and that the above is a true and accurate translation thereof.'

1279. Application for letters of administration shall be made by petition distinctly written as aforesaid and stating: (a) the time and place of the deceased's death; (b) the family or other relatives of the deceased, and their respective residences; (c) the right in which the petitioner claims; (d) the amount of assets which are likely to come to the petitioners hands; (e) when the application is to the District Judge, that the deceased at the time of his death had a fixed place of abode, or had some property, situate within the jurisdiction of the Judge; and (f) when the application is to a District Delegate, that the deceased at the time of his death had a fixed place of abode within the jurisdiction of such Delegate. Where the application is to the District Judge and any portion of the assets likely to come to the petitioners hands is situate in another Province, the petition shall further state the amount of such assets in each Province and the District Judges within whose jurisdiction such assets are situate.

1280. Every person applying to any of the Courts mentioned in the proviso to section 273 for probate of a will or letters of administration of an estate intended to have effect throughout Pakistan, shall state in his petition, in addition to the matters respectively required by section 276 and section 278, that to the best of his belief no application has been made to any other Court for a probate of the same will or for letters of administration of the same estate, intended to have such effect as last aforesaid, or, where any such application has been made, the Court to which it was made, the person or persons by whom it was made and the proceedings (if any) had thereon. The Court to which any such application is made under the proviso to section 273 may, if it thinks fit, reject the same.

1281. The petition for probate or letters of administration shall in all cases be subscribed by the petitioner and his pleader, if any, and shall be verified by the petitioner in the following manner, namely: 'I (A.B.), the petitioner in the above petition, declare that what is stated therein is true to the best of my information and belief'.

1282. Where the application is for probate, the petition shall also be verified by at least one of the witnesses to the will (when procurable) in the manner or to the effect following, namely:

> I (C.D), one of the witnesses to the last will and testament of the testator mentioned in the above petition, declare that I was present and saw the said testator affix his signature (or mark) thereto (or that the said testator acknowledged the writing annexed to the above petition to be his last will and testament in my presence).

1283. If any petition or declaration which is hereby required to be verified contains any averment which the person making the verification knows or believes to be false, such person shall be deemed to have committed an offence under section 193 of the Pakistan Penal Code.

1284. In all cases the District Judge or District Delegate may, if he thinks proper: (a) examine the petitioner in person, upon oath; (b) require further evidence of the due execution of the will or the right of the petitioner to the letters of administration, as the case may be; (c) issue citations calling upon all persons claiming to have any interest in the estate of the deceased to come and see the proceedings before the grant of probate or letters of administration. The citation shall be fixed up in some conspicuous part of the court-house, and also in the office of the Collector of the district and otherwise published or made known in such manner as the Judge or District Delegate issuing the same may direct. Where any portion of the assets has been stated by the petitioner to be situate within the jurisdiction of a District Judge in another Province, the District Judge issuing the same shall cause a copy of the citation to be sent to such other District Judge, who shall publish the same in the same manner as if it were a citation issued by himself, and shall certify such publication to the District Judge who issued the citation.

1285. Caveats against the grant of probate or administration may be lodged with the District Judge or a District Delegate. Immediately on any caveat being lodged with any District Delegate, he shall send copy thereof to the District Judge. Immediately on a caveat being entered with the District Judge, a copy thereof shall be given to the District Delegate, if any, within whose jurisdiction it is alleged the deceased had a fixed place of abode at the time of his death, and to any other Judge or District Delegate to whom it may appear to the District Judge expedient to transmit the same. The caveat shall be made as nearly as circumstances admit in the form set forth in Schedule V.

1286. No proceeding shall be taken on a petition for probate or letters of administration after a caveat against the grant, thereof has been entered with the Judge or District Delegate to whom the application has been made or notice has been given of its entry with some other Delegate, until after such notice to the person by whom the same has been entered as the Court may think reasonable.

1287. A District Delegate shall not grant probate or letters of administration in any case in which there is contention as to the grant, or in which it otherwise appears to him that probate or letters of administration ought not to be granted in his Court. Explanation: 'Contention' means the appearance of any one in person, or by his recognized agent, or by a pleader duly appointed to act on his behalf, to oppose the proceeding.

1288. In every case in which there is no contention, but it appears to the District Delegate doubtful whether the probate or letters of administration should or should not be granted, or when any question arises in relation to the grant, or application for the grant, of any probate or letters of administration, the District Delegate may, if he thinks proper, transmit a statement of the matter in question to the District Judge, who may direct the District Delegate to proceed in the matter of the application, according to such instructions as the Judge may seem necessary, or may forbid any farther proceeding by the District Delegate in relation to the matter of such application, leaving the party applying for the grant in question to make application to the Judge.

1289. In every case in which there is contention, or the District Delegate is of opinion that the probate or letters of administration should be refused in his Court, the petition, with any documents which may have been filed therewith, shall be returned to the person by whom the application was made, in order that the same may be presented to the District Judge, unless the District Delegate thinks it necessary, for the purposes of justice, to impound the same, which he is hereby authorized to do; and, in that case, the same shall be sent by him to the District Judge.

1290. When it appears to the District Judge or District Delegate that probate of a will should be granted, he shall grant the same under the seal of his Court in the form set forth in Schedule VI.

1291. When it appears to the District Judge or District Delegate that letters of administration to the estate of a person deceased, with or without a copy of the will annexed, should be granted, he shall grant the same under the seal of his Court in the form set forth in Schedule VII.

1292. Every person to whom any grant of letters of administration, other than a grant under section 241, is committed, shall give a bond to the District Judge with one or more surety or sureties, engaging for the due collection, getting in, and administering the estate of the deceased, which bond shall be in such form as the Judge may, by general or special order, direct. When the deceased was a Hindu, Muslim, Buddhist, Sikh or Jaina or an exempted person (a) the exception made in respect of a grant under section 241 shall not operate; (b) the District Judge may demand a like bond from any person to whom probate is granted.

1293. The Court may, on application made by petition and on being satisfied that the engagement of any such bond has not been kept, and upon such terms as to security, or providing that the money received be paid into Court, or otherwise, as the Court may think fit, assign the same to some person, his executors or administrators, who shall thereupon be entitled to sue on the said bond in his or their own name or names as if the same had been originally given to him or them instead of the Judge of the Court, and shall be entitled to recover thereon, as trustees for all person interested, the full amount recoverable in respect of any breach thereof.

1294. No probate of a will shall be granted until after the expiration of seven clear days, and no letters of administration shall be granted until after the expiration of fourteen clear days from the day of the testator or intestates death.

1295. Every District Judge, or District Delegate, shall file and preserve all original wills, of which probate or letters of administration with the will annexed may be granted by him, among the records of his Court, until some public registry for wills is established. The Provincial Government shall make regulations for the preservation and inspection of the wills so filed.

1296. In any case, before the District Judge in which there is contention, the proceedings shall take, as nearly as may be, the form of a regular suit, according to the provisions of the Code of Civil Procedure, 1908 in which the petitioner for probate or letters of administration, as the case may be, shall be the plaintiff, and the person who has appeared to oppose the grant shall be the defendant.

1297. When a grant of probate or letters of administration is revoked or annulled under this Act, the person to whom the grant was made shall forthwith deliver up the probate or letters to the Court which made the grant. If such person wilfully and without reasonable cause omits so to deliver up the probate or letters, he shall be punishable with fine which may extend to PKR 1,000, or with imprisonment for a term which may extend to three months, or with both.

1298. When a grant of probate or letters of administration is revoked, all payments bona fide made to any executor or administrator under such grant before the revocation thereof shall, notwithstanding such revocation, be a legal discharge to the person making the same; and the executor or administrator who has acted under any such revoked grant may retain and reimburse himself in respect of any payments made by him which the person to whom probate or letters of administration may afterwards be granted might have lawfully made.

1299. Notwithstanding anything hereinbefore contained it shall, where the deceased was a Muslim, Buddhist or exempted person, or a Hindu, Sikh or Jaina to whom section 57 does not apply, be in the discretion of the Court to make an order refusing, for reasons to be recorded by it in writing, to grant any application for letters of administration made under this Act.

1300. Every order made by a District Judge by virtue of the powers hereby conferred upon him shall be subject to appeal to the High Court in accordance with the provisions of the Code of Civil Procedure, 1908, applicable to appeals. The High Court shall have concurrent jurisdiction with the District Judge in the exercise of all the powers hereby conferred upon the District Judge. Except in cases to which section 57 applies, no High Court, in exercise of the concurrent jurisdiction hereby conferred over any local area shall, where the deceased is a Hindu, Muslim, Buddhist, Sikh or Jaina or an exempted person, receive applications for probate or letters of administration until the Provincial Government has, by a notification in the Official Gazette, authorized it to do so.

1301. The High Court may on application made to it suspend remove or discharge any private executor or administrator and provide for the succession of another person to the office of any such executor or administrator who may cease to hold office and the vesting in such successor of any property belonging to the estate.

1302. Where probate or letters of administration in respect of any estate has or have been granted under this Act, the High Court may on application made to it, give to the executor or administrator any general or special directions in regard to the estate or in regard to the administration thereof.

§16. Succession Certificates

1303. The Succession Act, 1925, sections 370~390 (Chapter-X) deals with the Succession Certificate. The District Judge within whose jurisdiction the deceased ordinarily resided at the time of his death, or, if at that time he had no fixed place of residence, the District Judge, within whose jurisdiction any part of the property of the deceased may be found, may grant a succession certificate.

1304. Application for such a certificate is made to the District Judge by a petition signed and verified by or on behalf of the applicant in the manner prescribed by the Code of Civil Procedure, 1908, for the signing and verification of a plaint by or on behalf of a plaintiff, and setting forth the following particulars, namely: (a) the time of the death of the deceased; (b) the ordinary residence of the deceased at the time of his death and, if such residence was not within the local limits of the jurisdiction of the Judge to whom the application is made, then the property of the deceased within those limits; (c) the family or other near relatives of the deceased and their respective residences; (d) the right in which the petitioner claims; (e) the absence of any impediment under section 370 or under any other provision of the Succession Act, 1925 or any other enactment, to the grant of the certificate or to the validity thereof if it were granted; and (f) the debts and securities in respect of which the certificate is applied for. If the petition contains any averment which the person verifying it knows or believes to be false, or does not believe to be true, that person shall be deemed to have committed an offence under section 198 of the Pakistan Penal Code. Application for such a certificate may be made in respect of any debt or debts due to the deceased creditor or in respect of portions thereof.

1305. If the District Judge is satisfied that there is ground for entertaining the application, he shall fix a day for the hearing thereof and cause notice of the application and of the day fixed for the hearing (a) to be served on any person to whom, in the opinion of the Judge, special notice of the application should be given; and (b) to be posted on some conspicuous part of the court-house and published in such other manner, if any, as the Judge, subject to any rules made by the High Court in this behalf, thinks fit, and upon the day fixed, or as soon thereafter as may be practicable, shall proceed to decide in a summary manner the right to the certificate. When the Judge decides the right thereto to belong to the applicant, the Judge shall make an order for the grant of the certificate to him. If the Judge cannot decide the right to the certificate without determining questions of law or fact which seem to be too intricate and difficult for determination in a summary proceeding, he may nevertheless grant a certificate to the applicant if he appears to be the person having prima facie the best title thereto. When there are more applicants than one for a certificate, and it appears to the Judge that more than one of such applicants are interested in the estate of the deceased, the Judge may, in deciding to whom the certificate is to be granted, have regard to the extent of interest and the fitness in other respects of the applicants.

1306. When the District Judge grants a certificate, he specifies the debts and securities set forth in the application for the certificate, and may thereby empower the person to whom the certificate is granted (a) to receive interest or dividends on, or (b) to negotiate or transfer, or (c) both to receive interest or dividends on, and to negotiate or transfer, the securities or any of them.

1307. The District Judge shall in any case in which he proposes to proceed under section 373, and may, in any other case, require, as a condition precedent to the granting of certificate, that the person to whom he proposes to make the grant shall give to the Judge a bond with one or more surety or sureties, or other sufficient security, for rendering an account of debts and securities received by him and for indemnity of persons who may be entitled to the whole or any part of those debts and securities. The Judge may, on application made by petition and on cause shown to his satisfaction and upon such terms as to security or providing that the money received be paid into Court, or otherwise, as he thinks fit, assign the bond or other security to some proper person, and that person shall thereupon be entitled to sue thereon in his own name as if it had been originally given to him instead of to the Judge of the Court, and to recover, as trustee for all persons interested, such amount as may be recoverable thereunder.

1308. A District Judge may, on the application of the holder of a certificate, extend the certificate to any debt or security not originally specified therein, and every such extension shall have the same effect as if the debt or security, or which the certificate is extended had been originally specified therein. Upon the extension of a certificate, powers with respect to the receiving of interest or dividends on, or the negotiation or transfer of, any security to which the certificate has been extended may be conferred, and a bond or further bond or other security for the purposes mentioned in section 375 may be required, in the same manner as upon the original grant of a certificate.

1309. The Succession Certificate is granted, and extensions of certificates are made as per form set forth in Schedule-VIII of the Succession Act, 1925.

1310. If the District Judge has not conferred on the holder of a certificate any power with respect to a security specified in the certificate, or has only empowered him to receive interest or dividends on, or to negotiate or transfer, the security, the Judge may, on application made by petition and on cause shown to his satisfaction, amend the certificate by conferring any of the powers mentioned in section 374 or by substituting any one for any other of those powers.

1311. Every application for a succession certificate or for the extension of a certificate is accompanied by a deposit of a sum equal to the fee payable under the Court fees Act, 1870, in respect of the certificate or extension applied for. If the application is allowed, the sum deposited by the applicant shall be expended, under the direction of the Judge, in the purchase of the stamp to be used for denoting the fee payable as aforesaid. Any sum received and not expended shall be refunded to the person who deposited it.

1312. The Succession Certificates have effect throughout Pakistan. It also applies in Pakistan after the separation of Pakistan from India to certificates granted before the date of the separation, or on or after that date in proceedings pending at that date in any of the territories which on that date were comprised in India.

1313. The certificate of the District Judge shall, with respect to the debts and securities specified therein, be conclusive as against the persons owing such debts or liable on such securities, and shall, notwithstanding any contravention of section 370, or other defect, afford full indemnity to all such persons as regards all payments made, or dealings had, in good faith in respect of such debts or securities to or with the person to whom the certificate was granted.

1314. If a Succession Certificate is granted, to a resident within a Foreign State by the Pakistan representative accredited to the State, or where a certificate so granted has been extended in such form by such representative, the certificate shall, when stamped in accordance with the provisions of the Court Fees Act, 1870.

1315. A Succession Certificate can be revoked for any of the following causes, namely: (a) that the proceedings to obtain the certificate were defective in substance; (b) that the certificate was obtained fraudulently by the making of a false suggestion, or by the concealment from the Court of something material to the case; (c) that the certificate was obtained by means of an untrue allegation of a fact essential in point of law to justify the grant thereof, though such allegation was made in ignorance or inadvertently; (d) that the certificate has become useless and inoperative through circumstances; (e) that a decree or order made by a competent Court in a suit or other proceeding with respect to effects comprising debts or securities specified in the certificate renders it proper that the certificate should be revoked.

1316. An appeal shall lie to the High Court from an order of a District Judge granting, refusing or revoking a certificate and the High Court may, if it thinks fit, by its order on the appeal, declare the person to whom the certificate should be granted, and direct the District Judge, on application being made therefore, to grant it accordingly, in supersession of the certificate, if any, already granted. An appeal must be preferred within the time allowed for an appeal under the Code of Civil Procedure, 1908.

1317. Subject to the other conditions of the Succession Act, 1925, a certificate granted thereunder in respect of any of the effects of a deceased person shall be invalid if there has been a previous grant of such a certificate or of probate or letters of administration in respect of the estate of the deceased person and if such previous grant is in force.

1318. If a Succession Certificate has been superseded or is invalid by reason of the certificate having been revoked under section 383, or by reason of the grant of a certificate to a person named in an appellate order under section 384, or by reason of a certificate having been previously granted, or for any other cause, all payments made, or dealings had, as regards debts and securities specified in the superseded or invalid certificate to or with the holder of that certificate in ignorance of its supersession or invalidity, shall be held good against claims under any other certificate.

§17. CASE LAWS

1319. PHC (2010 CLC 610) Suit for declaration, injunction and possession. Inheritance. Plaintiffs had sought declaration, injunction and possession of land transferred through inheritance mutation to defendants who were the children of predeceased son of original owner of the suit-land. Trial Court vide its judgment and decree non-suited the plaintiffs under section 4 of Muslim Family Laws Ordinance, 1961, holding that children of the deceased son of original owner were entitled to the share equivalent to the one which their father would have received, if alive, at the time of opening of succession. Appeal filed against judgment and decree of the Trial Court, was also dismissed by the Appellate Court. Validity: Counsel for the plaintiffs could not point out and illegality in the impugned judgments and decrees of the two courts below, which could not be interfered with, in circumstances [section 4. Specific Relief Act (I of 1877), sections 8, 42 & 54].

1320. (LHC – 2009 CLC 1273) Succession. Plaintiffs, in the present case, were the widow and children of deceased who had predeceased his father. Succession opened on 28 January 1972 on the death of father of the predeceased son and in terms of section 4, Muslim Family Laws Ordinance, 1961, the children of the said predeceased son were entitled to receive the share of their father in the estate of father of predeceased son. Share of predeceased son in the estate of his father will devolve only on his children and not the widow in terms of section 4, Muslim Family Laws Ordinance, 1961. Contention that in view of the judgment of FSC declaring section 4, Muslim Family Laws Ordinance, 1961 to be repugnant to the Injunctions of Islam and as such the very preliminary decree be declared to be void, was repelled, as an appeal against the said judgment of Federal Shariat Court was pending before the Shariat Appellate Bench of the Supreme Court; under Article 203D(2) of the Constitution, FSC while declaring any provision of law to be repugnant to the Injunctions of Islam had to specify a date on which the judgment was to take effect; such a date specified by FSC in the judgment was 31 March 2000; in the present case, the preliminary decree was passed by the Trial Court on 14 April 1990 and finally approved by High Court on 7 November 1994; final decree thus, was passed before target date fixed by FSC and under proviso to Article 203D(2) of the Constitution the decision of Federal Shariat Court shall not be deemed to take effect wherein an appeal had been preferred to the Supreme Court before the decision of the said appeal. Order accordingly. [section 4. Constitution of Pakistan (1973), Article 203D(2)].

1321. SHC (2008 YLR 1256) Issuance of Letter of Administration and grant of succession certificate. Objection to. Deceased was issueless and petitioners who being brothers and sisters were legal heirs of deceased, had claimed that deceased was married to respondent/objector in whose name deceased had purchased apartment in question and that thereafter she had gifted said apartment to the deceased. Petitioners had claimed that as deceased had divorced respondent/objector in his lifetime, letter of administration of property of deceased could be issued in favour of petitioners as deceased had died issueless. Respondent had claimed that intimation notice of her divorce having not been given to Chairman Arbitration Council, under section 7 of Muslim Family Laws Ordinance, 1961, she was not divorcee in the eyes of law as divorce had not become effective. Respondent had further contended that she had spent more than 40 years with the deceased as his wife, and that deceased had pronounced divorce due to his old-age being issueless and under the influence of the petitioners and divorce was never acted upon by him. Matter being contentious one, under section 295 of Succession Act, 1925, same could only be adjudicated upon by converting petition into civil suit. Petition was converted into civil suit accordingly [sections 273, 278 & 295].

1322. PHC (2007 CLC 1787) Succession. Inheritance mutation, in respect of landed property of deceased owner was sanctioned in favour of his two sons and two daughters/petitioners. Respondents who were sons of predeceased daughter of deceased original owner and were deprived of inheritance of deceased, instituted a declaratory suit challenging the validity, of said mutation and claimed, one-seventh share in the said property. Suit was contested by the petitioners on the ground that mother of respondents having died prior to the death of her father/original owner, respondents being her legal heirs were not entitled to any share out of estate of the deceased owner. Trial Court decreed the suit in favour of respondents/legal heirs of deceased daughter of original owner, and appeal against judgment of the Trial Court had also been dismissed by the Appellate Court. Counsel for the petitioners had contended that section 4 of Muslim Family Laws Ordinance, 1961 under, which respondents that is, legal heirs of deceased daughters of original owner had claimed share in the property of deceased original owner, having been declared violative of Injunctions of Islam by the Federal Shariat Courts, respondents could not inherit any share out of disputed property; and that the Courts below had wrongly and illegally declared them entitled to inheritance of deceased. Validity: Contention was repelled, because since appeal against the judgment of the Shariat Court was pending adjudication in the Supreme Court, in view of Article 203D of the Constitution, decision of Federal Shariat Court would stand suspended till disposal of appeal by the Supreme Court. Even otherwise verdict given by Federal Shariat Court was not applicable to the case because provisions of section 4 of Muslim Family Laws Ordinance, 1961, had been held repugnant to injunction of Islam subsequent to opening of succession in respect of the property of the deceased. Respondents being legal heirs of deceased were entitled to get their due share out of property of deceased original owner. Concurrent findings of the Courts below not suffering from any illegality or irregularity, would not call for interference by the High Court in revision [section 4 of Muslim Family Laws Ordinance, 1961].

Selected Bibliography

Mulla Principles of Mahomedan Law by M. Hidayatullah (seventeenth Edition 1972) published by Bombay N.M. Tripathi Private Ltd.

Family Laws in Pakistan by Mr M. Farani, of Lincoln's Inn (Edition 2009) published by Nadeem Law Book House, Lahore.

Manual of Succession Laws by Tariq Shamim (Edition 2010) published by Nadeem Law Book House, Lahore.

D.F. Mulla's Principles of Muhammadan Law by Al-Qanoon Publishers Lahore.

D.F. Mulla's Prinicples of Muhammadan Law by Afsari Printers, Lahore.

Mulla's Principles of Mohammedan Law by M. Hidayatullah and Arshad Hidayatullah – Pakistan Civil & Criminal Law Publication, Law Publishers & Booksellers, Lahore (Edition 2007).

Dr Nishi Purohit – The Principles of Mohammedan Law by Eastern Law Book House, Lahore.

Mr Anees Jillani paper on 'Law of Guardianship in Pakistan'.

Dr M. U. S. Jang, Dissertation on the Development of Muslim Law in British India.

Dr Sherif Mohammed Article on 'On Marriage in Islam'.

Website <www.wikipedia.org>.

Website <www.islamweb.net>.

Website Ministry of Information and Broadcasting, Pakistan <www.pak.gov.pk>.

Website Government of Punjab <www.punjab.gov.pk>.

Website Sustainable Development Policy Institute <www.sdpi.org>.

Index

The numbers here refer to paragraph numbers

Index

www.ingramcontent.com/pod-product-compliance
Lightning Source LLC
Chambersburg PA
CBHW071425230926
51846CB00001B/124
9789041146397